PENGUIN BOOKS

THE BEST AMERICAN SHORT STORIES 1980

Stanley Elkin's most recent novel is *The Living End*. He teaches at Washington University in St. Louis.

Shannon Ravenel, a former fiction editor for a major publisher, has been annual editor of *The Best American Short Stories* since 1977. She, too, lives in St. Louis.

The Best AMERICAN SHORT STORIES 1980

Selected from
U.S. and Canadian Magazines
by Stanley Elkin
with Shannon Ravenel

With an Introduction by Stanley Elkin

INCLUDING THE YEARBOOK OF THE
AMERICAN SHORT STORY

PENGUIN BOOKS

Penguin Books Ltd, Harmondsworth,
Middlesex, England
Penguin Books, 625 Madison Avenue,
New York, New York 10022, U.S.A.
Penguin Books Australia Ltd, Ringwood,
Victoria, Australia
Penguin Books Canada Limited, 2801 John Street,
Markham, Ontario, Canada L3R 1B4
Penguin Books (N.Z.) Ltd, 182–190 Wairau Road,
Auckland 10, New Zealand

First published in the United States of America by
Houghton Mifflin Company 1980
Published in Penguin Books 1981

Printed in the United States of America by
Offset Paperback Mfrs., Inc., Dallas, Pennsylvania
Set in Baskerville

Contents

Introduction

MOST FELLOWS, they put together a collection like this, they go all humble on you. Or they break out in qualification as in rash. They're all over themselves with conditions, strings, all the head's fine print, all the heart's crossed fingers. Or they're quibbled as an Oscar winner. (Do I fetch it myself or send the surrogate? Am I in Paris on a gig? Is it Tuesday, my night for the sweat bath, my day at the races? Or am I actually disruptive? What *is* the mode for eleventh-hour reservation, qualm, the brain's butterflies?)

Or they'll tell you how hard they worked to reach a decision. The pains they took, all invigilate, watchdog scrupulosity and fastidiousness. With pointers accusing the relief map, the sifted minefields, the sluiced ores. ("Here the mind went ginger. Here judgment went two rounds with will.")

Not me. I *have* no qualifications.

And my decisions were a breeze, easy as falling off a log.

Because these are, quite simply, the very best short stories published in American magazines in 1979, and they declared themselves to whatever sense I have of the wonderful as succinctly as so many logos.

Because we're talking about taste, the buds of judgment. And of *course* there's an accounting for taste. This is an attempt to account for mine.

Only the flat-out hero — I mean the medalist, the beribboned, the campaigner; I mean the champ, the Heisman winner, the MVP — is valued for his deeds. The rest of us are esteemed, or not, for our opinions, judgment calls, the soul's favorite tunes. Even men of the world wheel and deal in mood, the artifact of temperament. We tend to take people at their word, extend credence like credit, and lead an *ipse dixit* sort of life. (We cash their checks. The woman in the coffee shop accepts on faith that we are guests and rarely asks to see the room key. Tape recordings are inadmissible but an eye-witness will do you in. Some fuddled soul can't tell you three things that are wrong with this picture, but if she picks you out of the line-up you're done for. Any lawyer will tell you: one implication is worth two inferences. See? I made that last bit up, but you'd already cashed my check. For all you know I might not be regis-tered in this hotel and may just have charged breakfast to some other guy's room.)

Walter Cronkite says that after yesterday's Florida primary Reagan is the frontrunner, and so, in fact, he seems to be. Repub-licans are steamed. The budget is unbalanced. Chase Manhattan's best customers can get better terms from a loan shark by the docks than they can from the prime. America is everywhere on the defensive. Afghanistan. Colombia. The Mideast. The hostages have been in Iran 130 days and the commission has come back without even seeing them. Mary, called "Mary," in her guerrilla's *chador,* is making monkeys out of us paper tigers. What this country needs, it is claimed, is a return to sound fiscal principles, to princi-ple itself. A beefed-up military. A trimmed-down bureaucracy. A conservative Republican frontrunner. But what did Mr. Reagan ever actually *do* that was conservative? When he was governor of California? What did he actually *do?* The point is, I think, that conservatism is only another opinion, only, that is, a kind of taste, as liberalism is, or fascism too. And, like all taste, it proceeds from a view in equilibrium, the prerogative of an essential disengage-ment — a question of druthers, of all else being equal.

Taste is the luxury of abeyant claims and occurs, like Words-worth's poetry, in a kind of tranquillity, a repose of soul, when the mind (or not even the mind), like a pointer on a Ouija board, lurches simplistic alternative. It is an ideal, the choice we make when we have no choice, what we might look like when no one is looking, what we might look like invisible.

Taste is, finally, a series of first impressions, lodestar aesthetics that last a lifetime. A man's character is his taste, and he is as much a victim of it as the pictures, foods, music, films, books, furnishings, and clothes he chooses are the subjects of his necessity. It, taste, may even be one of the famous drives, like sex or appetite. And it has always a quality of aspiration, its eye on the next step up forever. My mother-in-law would be incapable of furnishing a living room without slipcovers, and, for her, the development of clear plastic was a technological breakthrough, a hinge event in science, up there with washable mahjong tiles. Because we're talking, in my mother-in-law's case, about cleanliness, lifelong shmutz-dread, that first impression she must have taken as a little girl in Russia of actual biological *traif*, fear of the Gentile, some sense of caste deeper than a Hindu's, a notion, finally, of *order*. Which is all that taste ever is. (I, who, like you, feel I have perfect taste, am no better. It ain't the Gentile I fear, it's everybody, everything. The germs on pennies, people coughing, the shit on dogshit.) Not the niceties and not notions gleaned from study, education, the great books. (The idea of an educated taste is absurd. You might as well speak of educating your need for shelter.) Taste can't, I think, be heightened, sharpened. It comes with the territory, is fixed as birthmark. Indeed, it *is* birthmark, what the gypsy wishes for us in the crib, the customized, bespoke astrology of the self.

Here is a little of what the gypsy whispered to me:

Delicatessen and the midnight nosh. Lox, whitefish, sturgeon, rye. Scrambled eggs and onions, corn bread, butter. Cel-Ray tonic, Philadelphia cream cheese. Milk, chopped liver, corned beef, rolls. Cheesecake, coffee, cole slaw, fruit. (Because taste is also nostalgia, see? It's love, staying up late, some stroked sense of privilege. It's being where the adults are, boon and holiday and overhearing shoptalk. It's unearned and not to be counted on and never to be expected. It strikes like emergency, but emergency in reverse. Someone has free passes, somebody has samples. *It's sentimental.*) And to this day a freezer case in a deli stops my heart. Not just the speckled food, the flecked pastrami like a meat confetti, the bins of bagel and the sesame lint, but the little engine itself, like a Scotch-tape dispenser, which pokes out your number, bespeaking order, crowds, prosperity.

The Brooklyn neighborhood where my mother's folks lived, the Bronx one where my dad's did. I was raised in Chicago, we moved from New York when I was three years old. When we went back east in the summer it was to a bungalow in New Jersey. Since the time I lived in those neighborhoods, I've spent maybe five months of my life in them. But taste is nostalgia, first impressions struck like a coin, and no *tabula* is ever not *rasa,* and we're all cases of arrested development with arrest records long as your life. So a sweet tooth for cities, for some hustle-bustle un-Nature, though I live in a house across from a park, in a suburb sedate as Connecticut.

The first grown-up books I ever read were Marion Hargrove's *See Here, Private Hargrove!,* Elmer Rice's plays in Pocketbook — *Street Scene* is the one I recall best — Kaufman's and Hart's in Modern Library, and Whit Burnett's *This Is My Best,* quite possibly the finest anthology ever published. (Or quite possibly not, but only the first one I read.)

The films — we're getting on now; I'm no longer in the crib but am still impressionable; maybe I'm twenty; what the hell, it's *all* crib — of Robert Mitchum. (Since this is an attempt to clarify my taste, there, right there, may be the paradigm for it. I have no patience with detective stories but will line up around the block to watch Robert Mitchum play Philip Marlowe. Mitchum in a trench coat is what men *ought* to look like. There should be his rumpled statues in our parks.)

But, in truth, my taste has less to do with aromas and neighborhoods and Modern Library editions and the projected vision — that's just the sweet side of nature, my suckered ethnics recollected in tranquillity — than it does with that bungalow in Jersey, my dual sense of myself as a kid midwesterner come east in summer and a would-be New Yorker laid over in Chicago the rest of the year. (I can't help it if it's silly. All pasts are silly.) My pals in New Jersey were from New York. They lived, they said, in the city. Their fathers were sign painters for Schulte's Cigar Stores. They were cab drivers, elevator starters, or, orthodox Jews, they simplified their names and opened furniture stores in Boonton, New Jersey, miles from the *minyan.* They were cutters in the garment trade. They sold Ship 'n Shore blouses out of suitcases. And they seemed — and their kids, my pals, too — to me real, much realer than myself, than my father who made more money, who wore custom suits and traveled great distances in airplanes, who played gin for money he would not accept when he won but insisted on paying if he lost, who kept a room in a good Manhattan hotel the entire summer and came to camp — we called it "camp" — only on weekends. Who had orchestra seats he bought from the scalpers. Who picked up checks all around and took it badly when others didn't.

Who was, at last, a snob with a heart of gold who had no patience with the dross tickers (my father had several heart attacks between his first one and the one that finally killed him seven years later in low season in the good hotel) he suspected in others. He was this geologist of the heart, my dad, no alchemist but the true forty-niner, a panner of other people's instincts, an assay artist. "Four flusher," he'd say of this one or that, and never make his case, withholding details. So I looked for myself, New Jersey this side show, midsummer night's dream. And came away with my taste for worried men. (Mitchum a variation on a theme, bulk a signal of grace, like fat men dancing.)

What's wanted then, unless voice or invention override, is this quality of nice guys in trouble, troubled. (I didn't know this about myself, I wouldn't have suspected it from my own work, but then that's taste for you — the left hand that doesn't know what the right hand is doing. It's an emotional no-man's-land of neutralized pressure, the head and heart weightless and the soul in free fall, the will not so much sidetracked as simply not at issue, on holiday, gone fishing, if you will.) There is a distance between one's slumbrous, unsuspected tastes and one's expectations for oneself. It's the difference between saying "I know what I like" and "I know what I like to do." Something a little hypocritical at either end of things, the receiving and the working. Taste is circumstantial, there's something windfall and passive about it. It smacks of the high summer hammock condition, and we take our pleasures stretched out, our hands behind our heads. (While there isn't a story in this collection I wouldn't have wanted to write, there are several I would have wanted to write differently. And would've wound up perhaps with stories I wouldn't necessarily have wanted to read.) This accounts for the allowances nearly all of us make, for your serious friend who devours mystery stories, for "Auld Lang Syne" and the Bert Parks fuss and the Super Bowl — all those stock gems of pop culture like some rhinestoned Las Vegas of the gut, our Whitman's Sampler appetite. There is, that is, something peculiarly indulgent about our real tastes. Which is why our real tastes are so often, if we have any stake at all in the intellectual or artistic life, our best-kept secrets, right up there with our sexual fantasies and that yen for the salami sandwich at the gourmet dinner. Sometimes this becomes a guarded theme in some of our most demanding literature. All Aunt Rosa's demon lover, Thomas Sutpen, in *Absalom, Absalom!*, ever wanted was a son, to be a family man is all. — Rosebud, Rosebud!

What is wanted then is sadness. (We're talking literature, not life. We're talking Kenny Rogers's chipped and country voice, not music.) This, it seems to me, is the absolute, ideal humor for respectable men. Sadness, mind you, not grief. Or grief under control, made courteous, deferential, the keening and lamentation practically inaudible, indistinguishable but unextinguished in the generalized white noise of the world. A sadness like a mourner's button on an M.C.'s lapel. There for the weight, the sharp ballast it lends to tumult. Sadness like an intelligent conviction, like a badge of bearing — a short cut, you see, a short cut and a convenience. (So many of the characters in these stories are widowered — it's a man's world — so many are divorced.) Sadness like documents, the heart's papers, what these characters show us or what we find on them at the borders to prove they're serious.

And if the sadness is suddenly mitigated, or even retracted, so much the better. If it is mitigated by some unscrupulous vision — I mean when the *deus* in the *deus ex machina* is actually God, or when the character, acting on his own, sublimely lets go, or when the sadness is not repudiated at all but actively embraced in some higher emotional game of razzle-dazzle performance and shell-game dexterity — so much the better yet. (If the story can only hang on till the ending . . . Endings tend to be wonderful . . .) Isn't reprieve literature's last act anyway? Isn't it some notion of acquittal or deliverance that off and on vouches for our condition and cosigns our lives? (It's precisely the off-and-on nature of our visions that *makes* them unscrupulous, but now we're talking life, not literature.)

Anyway, most of the stories in this collection (though not consciously picked for these qualities, which I discovered afterwards, and this introduction a sort of apologia for criteria I had not realized were even operating) aim, consciously or not, for just this sort of justification of the character's life. They conclude with an overview, however partial, and some suggestive illusion of the vision's continuing momentum. Perhaps it's a concession to realism that causes several of the writers to have their characters lie down, literally or figuratively, on deathbeds. (Bellow has a character in *The Adventures of Augie March* wonder, How do you keep the feelings up? Well one way is to make the protagonist terminal, fore-shortening the time he has to sustain them.) It's what Frederick Busch does in "Long Calls" and what Singer does in "The Safe Deposit" and what Gordon Weaver does in "Hog's Heart." But, in a way, it's what most of them do. There is usually something sum-mary and terribly final about the concluding rhetoric — the ring-ing long-range long view of language. Consider this piece of business from the end of John Updike's story, "Gesturing":

> *The motion was eager, shy, exquisite, diffident, trusting: He saw all its meanings and knew that she would never stop gesturing within him, never; though a decree come between them, even death, her gestures would endure, cut into glass.*

Or Donald Barthelme's "The Emerald," at the point where Moll's strange offspring asks its mother what happens next:

> *We resume the scrabble for existence, said Moll. We resume the scrab-ble for existence, in the sweet of the here and now.*

Mavis Gallant's "The Remission":

> *Escorting lame Mrs. Massie to a sofa, Mr. Cranefield said they might as well look on the bright side. (He was still speaking about the second half of the 1950s.) Wilkinson, sitting down because he felt sick, and thinking the remark was intended for him, assured Mr. Cranefield, truth-fully, that he had never looked anywhere else. It then happened that every person in the room, at the same moment, spoke and thought of something other than Alec. This lapse, this inattention, lasting no longer than was needed to say "No, thank you" or "Oh, really?" or "Yes, I see," was enough to create the dark gap marking the end of Alec's span. He ceased to be, and it made absolutely no difference after that whether or not he was forgotten.*

The same author's wonderful "Speck's Idea":

> *Because this one I am keeping, Speck decided; this one will be signed: "By Sandor Speck." He smiled at the bright wet streets of Paris as he and Cruche, together, triumphantly crossed the Alps.*

As Schiff, in Busch's "Long Calls," on the sidewalk lies dying:

> *Schiff heard himself snorting, half-naked on the sidewalk. He touched at his burns. The klaxons were close. Now he had to call his wife back, now, he had to. He had to tell her he knew what to do — save things, place long calls — in emergencies at least.*

Isaac Bashevis Singer concludes "The Safe Deposit":

> *Although he was aching, he felt a rest he had never known before — the sublime enjoyment of fearing nothing, having no wish, no worry, no resentment . . .*

And Gordon Weaver writes, "Dying, Hog looks into the glare of the sun, finds his death is not pain or sweetness but totality and transcendence." Hog goes "into such light as makes light and darkness one."

One or two more and I'll explain what I'm trying to mean.

Grace Paley's "Friends" ends when the narrator tells us, "He was right to call my attention to its suffering and danger. He was right to harass my responsible nature. But I was right to invent for my friends and our children a report on these private deaths and the condition of our lifelong attachments."

The old activists in John Sayles's story, "At the Anarchists' Convention," team up at one last barricade:

> *And when the manager returns with his two befuddled street cops to find us standing together, arms linked, the lame held up out of their wheelchairs, the deaf joining from memory as Bud Odum leads us in "We Shall Not Be Moved," my hand in Sophie's, sweaty-palmed at her touch like the old days, I look at him in his brown blazer and think Brickman, I think, my God if Brickman was here we'd show this bastard the Wrath of the People!*

Well maybe just two more.

Barry Targan's English professor in his story "The Rags of Time," having escaped with his tenure intact after a reckless fling with a beautiful undergraduate, calms down in his office:

> *When she was gone he sat quite still and let the first terror she had brought in with her subside. He let fade the jagged collage of public*

accusation and denial that had first sprung through him, the tumult of fear that he would lose . . . what? Everything? But what could that mean? No. The loss he had sustained would be a small one, something he would hardly notice in his life as it had been and would be lived hereafter. There would be no more chances.

At last he was empty.

And, finally, T. Gertler's "In Case of Survival":

Helplessness settled on Harold with the steam from reheated potatoes. He opened his eyes and breathed in homely odors. The kitchen offered itself to him: burners, counter, sink, dishwasher, refrigerator, table, chairs, all vibrating against yellow-and-white-and-silver-foil wallpaper. The salt and pepper shakers danced on the tile shelf above the sink. His wife, in a blue kimono, presented him with a bowl of chopped vegetables. He sighed. Questions of guilt and innocence fell away; he contemplated instead his endless and enduring helplessness. The knowledge of it soothed him as the kitchen dipped, shuddered, grew still.

(Some of the best stories are not exampled here, not because they don't fit my category but because they don't save their rhetoric, as some of those quoted do, till last.)

I've used eleven stories. In three of them — Weaver's, Singer's, and Gertler's — visions quite literally occur. In Updike's ("He saw all its meanings . . ."), and in "Speck's Idea" ("He smiled at the bright wet streets of Paris as he and Cruche, together, triumphantly crossed the Alps"), and in Busch's ("Schiff heard himself snorting, half-naked on the sidewalk. He touched at his burns . . . Now he had to call his wife . . . He had to tell her how he knew what to do . . ."), and in Targan's (the character knows everything that will happen to him and everything that won't for all the rest of his life) something very like a vision takes over. In an eighth story, Mavis Gallant's "The Remission," the language of magic ("It then happened that every person in the room, at the same moment . . .") controls what the characters *fail* to think and say, liberating them from their connection to Alec for all time. In Sayles's piece, the narrator's emotion is running so high as he thinks of the dead Brickman that his age practically drops away from him and it is "like the old days." A tenth story, "The Emerald," is itself a vision.

In all instances (those quoted as well as those that have not even been mentioned) we are dealing, at the end, with a kind of rhetorical sacrament. We are dealing with *solace,* the *idea* of solace, art's and language's consolation prize. The notion that the character needs bucking up. And the writer begins to play for keeps, laying on a from-now-on syntax that suggests, and powerfully too, that the conditions that obtain will somehow manage to sustain themselves forever. It's something a bit beyond the conventional notion of epiphany, inasmuch as epiphany is usually some sudden, fell-swoop blast of insight. This is epiphany that sticks to the ribs. "He saw all its meanings and knew that she would never stop gesturing within him, never"; the emerald is told twice — just as the word *never* is repeated in Updike's sentence and *helplessness* in the passage from Gertler — that what is resumed is "the scrabble for existence." Alec, in magical language already quoted, quite suddenly ceases to be, chased by Mavis Gallant's incantation, and the characters are not only consoled for their loss but freed. "Because this one I am keeping," Speck thinks, "this one will be signed." (Again the repetition.) So, through repetition, magic, visions, inversion ("He let fade the jagged collage . . ."; "Dying, Hog looks . . ."; "Because this one I am keeping . . ."), or series ("This lapse, this inattention, lasting no longer than was needed to say 'No, thank you' or 'Oh, really?' or 'Yes, I see' "; "He was right to call my attention to its suffering and danger. He was right to harass my responsible nature. But I was right to . . ."; "The motion was eager, shy, exquisite, diffident, trusting") the rhetoric lifts subtly away from the story, its attention no longer really focused on the character's problems so much as it is on a kind of conversion, on bottom lines from the heart. There is a solace in finality and a grace in resignation no matter *what* one is resigned to — death, helplessness, the end of chance, resignation itself. But life's tallest order is to keep the feelings up, to make two dollars' worth of euphoria go the distance. And life can't do that. So fiction does. And there, right there, is the real — I want to say "only" — morality of fiction.

Not much, is it? It's all there is.

Taste is a gift of condition. In my own instance it is for the disheveled, what the cat dragged in, the rumpled in spirit, the soiled of heart. It is for Lily and Peter in James Robison's story, "Home," and Delia, their thirteen-year-old daughter who doesn't listen to them; for Lucas, the mourning biology professor of Robert Henderson's "Into the Wind." For senile Dr. Cahn, with his crippled vocabulary, in Richard Stern's "Dr. Cahn's Visit"; for Luther Glick in David Evanier's "The One-Star Jew"; and for the married man in Curt Johnson's "Lemon Tree," who dates a room clerk in Cleveland. It is for Elizabeth Hardwick's Dr. Z in "The Faithful," always true to everyone in his fashion. And for Markowitz, everybody's mark in Norman Waksler's "Markowitz and the Gypsies," a story structured like a joke and written in the idiom of one. I can't help it, these are my people. I too wish this taste of mine were not so one-sided. I wish it were for Henry James types, impeccable at tea, whose crumpets don't crumb, nobles of the middle class who know their way around a foreign language and can parse the value of another human just by the way his pocket handkerchief is folded; but that, Officer Krupke, wasn't the hand I was dealt. So I take my taste — which is always lazy, which ever, like physical law, seeks least resistances — and convert it to a kind of affection, to rooter interest (and it isn't even, all of it anyway, self-pity; my own pocket handkerchief waves like a little trapezoid above the breast pocket of my Harris tweed), to some low-down snatch of the sentimental (or what would *be* sentimental if the writers weren't so skillful) till all losses are reconciled, till, that is, they're underwritten by their authors with the beautiful cool comfort of a language that makes it all better, the soiled history, the rotten luck. My job in all this, as I say, is simply to lie back and enjoy myself, my sympathy floating the surface of these lives like fat in soup. I know what the characters can't, what probably even the writers don't believe — that it won't work, that it can't last, that inversion and magic and series and transcendence and saying something twice aren't enough, that in real life they would have to print a retraction. But I'm easy. I love my remote virtue. I'm moved by my morality. *I enjoy my heart.*

Yet some of the best stories in this collection don't do that.

Peter Taylor's long story, "The Old Forest," must surely be a masterpiece, but in a way it's almost sociology, and a sociology that isn't even operative anymore — the stiff, cold codes of a Memphis of the mind. Never mind, that's all art, you see, and has nothing to do with my taste or anyone else's either.

And if I read Leon Rooke's story, "Mama Tuddi Done Over," correctly, it's about a woman my sentimentality couldn't touch.

And, finally, two stories are included here because, quite simply, they are so beautifully written — Larry Heinemann's "The First Clean Fact" and William Gass's "The Old Folks."

Some note should, I suppose, be made of the fact that Mavis Gallant is represented by two stories in this collection. That also was a decision easily arrived at. What was tougher was the problem of whether to include a third, "The Burgundy Weekend." We decided not to because we — Shannon Ravenel and myself — figured it might be construed as showing off.

About Shannon Ravenel. Anyone who has been keeping up with this annual for the last couple of years must surely know by now that Shannon does all the work. She reads *everything*. Fifteen hundred stories for this year's collection alone. And that's at the inside. (The guest editor is only required to read 125 or so.) I know that I've seen everything I should have seen, that very little, if anything, has fallen through the cracks. One has pals. One is under obligations. One asks, "What about So-and-so?" One says, "I don't see Whoosis." "So-and-so was a disappointment this year," says Shannon. "Whoosis is in a slump." "Please show one," one says. "Sure, buddy, it's your funeral," Shannon says. And goes to her files. Which are exhaustive. And hauls out So-and-so, and hands one Whoosis. But she's right. She lives, breathes, and eats short stories, and I am privileged to have worked with her.

STANLEY ELKIN

The Best
AMERICAN
SHORT
STORIES
1980

DONALD BARTHELME

The Emerald

(FROM ESQUIRE)

HEY BUDDY what's your name?

My name is Tope. What's your name?

My name is Sallywag. You after the emerald?

Yeah I'm after the emerald you after the emerald too?

I am. What are you going to do with it if you get it?

Cut it up into little emeralds. What are you going to do with it?

I was thinking of solid emerald armchairs. For the rich.

That's an idea. What's your name, you?

Wide Boy.

You after the emerald?

Sure as shootin'.

How you going to get in?

Blast.

That's going to make a lot of noise isn't it?

You think it's a bad idea?

Well . . . What's your name, you there?

Taptoe.

You after the emerald?

Right as rain. What's more, I got a plan.

Can we see it?

No it's my plan I can't be showing it to every —

Okay okay. What's that guy's name behind you?

My name is Sometimes.

You here about the emerald, Sometimes?

I surely am.

Have you got an approach?

Tunneling. I've took some test borings. Looks like a stone cinch. *If* this is the right place.

You think this may not be the right place?

The last three places haven't been the right place.

You tryin' to bring me down?

Why would I want to do that? What's that guy's name, the one with the shades?

My name is Brother. Who are all these people?

Businessmen. What do you think of the general situation, Brother?

I think it's crowded. This is my pal, Wednesday.

What say, Wednesday. After the emerald, I presume?

Thought we'd have a go.

Two heads better than one, that the idea?

Yep.

What are you going to do with the emerald, if you get it?

Facet. Facet and facet and facet.

Moll talking to a member of the news media.

Tell me, as a member of the news media, what do you do?

Well we sort of figure out what the news is, then we go out and talk to people, the news makers, those who have made the news —

These having been identified by certain people very high up in your organization.

The editors. The editors are the ones who say this is news, this is not news, maybe this is news, damned if I know whether this is news or not —

And then you go out and talk to people and they tell you everything.

They tell you a surprising number of things, if you are a member of the news media. Even if they have something to hide, questionable behavior or one thing and another, or having killed their wife, that sort of thing, still they tell you the most amazing things. Generally.

About themselves. The newsworthy.

Yes. Then we have our experts in the various fields. They are experts in who is a smart cookie and who is a dumb cookie. They write pieces saying which kind of cookie these various cookies are, so that the reader can make informed choices. About things.

Fascinating work I should think.

Your basic glamour job.

I suppose you would have to be very well educated to get that kind of job.

Extremely well educated. Typing, everything.

Admirable.

Yes. Well, back to the pregnancy. You say it was a seven-year pregnancy.

Yes. When the agency was made clear to me —

The agency was, you contend, extraterrestrial.

It's a fact. Some people can't handle it.

The father was —

He sat in that chair you're sitting in. The red chair. Naked and wearing a morion.

That's all?

Yes he sat naked in the chair wearing only a morion, and engaged me in conversation.

The burden of which was —

Passion.

What was your reaction?

I was surprised. My reaction was surprise.

Did you declare your unworthiness?

Several times. He was unmoved.

Well I don't know, all this sounds a little unreal, like I mean unreal, if you know what I mean.

Oui, je sais.

What role were you playing?

Well obviously I was playing myself. Mad Moll.

What's a morion?

Steel helmet with a crest.

You considered his offer.

More in the nature of a command.

Then, the impregnation. He approached your white or pink as yet undistended belly with his hideously engorged member —

It was more fun than that.

I find it hard to believe, if you'll forgive me, that you, although quite beautiful in your own way, quite lush of figure and fair of face, still the beard on your chin and that black mark like a furry caterpillar crawling in the middle of your forehead —

It's only a small beard after all.

That's true.

And he seemed to like the black mark on my forehead. He caressed it.

So you did in fact enjoy the . . . event. You understand I
wouldn't ask these questions, some of which I admit verge on the
personal, were I not a duly credentialed member of the press.
Custodian as it were of the public's right to know. Everything.
Every last little slippy-dippy thing.

Well okay yes I guess that's true strictly speaking. I suppose
that's true. Strictly speaking. I could I suppose tell you to buzz off
but I respect the public's right to know. I think. An informed
public is, I suppose, one of the basic bulwarks of —

Yes I agree but of course I would wouldn't I, being I mean in
my professional capacity my professional role —

Yes I see what you mean.

But of course I exist aside from that role, as a person I mean, as
a woman like you —

You're not like me.

Well no in the sense that I'm not a witch.

You must forgive me if I insist on this point. You're not like
me.

Well, yes, I don't disagree, I'm not arguing, I have not after all
produced after a pregnancy of seven years a gigantic emerald
weighing seven thousand and thirty-five carats — can I, could I, by
the way, see the emerald?

No not right now it's sleeping.

The emerald is sleeping?

Yes it's sleeping right now. It sleeps.

It sleeps?

Yes didn't you hear me it's sleeping right now it sleeps just like
any other —

What do you mean the emerald is sleeping?

Just what I said. It's asleep.

Do you talk to it?

Of course, sure I talk to it, it's mine, I mean I *gave birth* to it, I
cuddle it and polish it and talk to it, what's so strange about that?

Does it talk to you?

Well I mean it's only one month old. How could it talk?

Hello?

Yes?

Is this Mad Moll?

Yes this is Mad Moll who are you?

You the one who advertised for somebody to stand outside the door and knock down anybody tries to come in?

Yes that's me are you applying for the position?

Yes I think so what does it pay?

Two hundred a week and found.

Well that sounds pretty good but tell me lady who is it I have to knock down for example?

Various parties. Some of them not yet known to me. I mean I have an inkling but no more than that. Are you big?

Six eight.

How many pounds?

Two forty-nine.

IQ?

One forty-six.

What's your best move?

I got a pretty good shove. A not-bad bust in the mouth. I can trip. I can fall on 'em. I can gouge. I have a good sense of where the ears are. I know thumbs and kneecaps.

Where did you get your training?

Just around. High school, mostly.

What's your name?

Soapbox.

That's not a very tough name if you'll forgive me.

You want me to change it? I've been called different things in different places.

No I don't want you to change it. It's all right. It'll do.

Okay do you want to see me or do I have the job?

You sound okay to me Soapbox. You can start tomorrow.

What time?

Dawn?

Understand, ye sons of the wise, what this exceedingly precious Stone crieth out to you! Seven years, close to tears. Slept for the first two, dreaming under four blankets, black, blue, brown, brown. Slept and pissed, when I wasn't dreaming I was pissing, I was a fountain. After the first year I knew something irregular was in progress, but not what. I thought, moonstrous! Salivated like a mad dog, four quarts or more a day, when I wasn't pissing I was spitting. Chawed moose steak, moose steak and morels, and fluttered with new men — the butcher, baker, candlestick maker, especially the butcher, one Shatterhand, he was neat. Gobbled a lot of iron, liver, and rust from the bottoms of boats, I had serial nosebleeds every day of the seventeenth trimester. Mood swings of course, heigh-de-ho, instances of false labor in years six and seven, palpating the abdominal wall I felt edges and thought, edges? Then on a cold February night the denouement, at six sixty-six in the evening, or a bit past seven, they sent a Miss Leek to do the delivery, one of us but not the famous one, she gave me scopolamine and a little swan-sweat, that helped, she turned not a hair when the emerald presented itself but placed it in my arms with a kiss or two and a pat or two and drove away, in a coach pulled by a golden pig.

Vandermaster has the Foot.
  Yes.
  The Foot is very threatening to you.
  Indeed.
  He is a mage and goes around accompanied by a black bloodhound.
  Yes. Tarbut. Said to have been raised on human milk.
  Could you give me a little more about the Foot. Who owns it?
  Monks. Some monks in a monastery in Merano or outside of Merano. That's in Italy. It's their Foot.
  How did Vandermaster get it?
  Stole it.
  Do you by any chance know what order that is?
  Let me see if I can remember — Carthusian.
  Can you spell that for me?
  C-a-r-t-h-u-s-i-a-n. I think.
  Thank you. How did Vandermaster get into the monastery?
  They hold retreats, you know, for pious laymen or people who just want to come to the monastery and think about their sins or be edified, for a week or a few days . . .
  Can you describe the Foot? Physically?
  The Foot proper is encased in silver. It's about the size of a foot, maybe slightly larger. It's cut off just above the ankle. The toe part is rather flat, it's as if people in those days had very flat toes. The whole is quite graceful. The Foot proper sits on top of this rather elaborate base, three levels, gold, little claw feet . . .
  And you are convinced that this, uh, reliquary contains the true Foot of Mary Magdalene.

Mary Magdalene's Foot. Yes.

He's threatening you with it.

It has a history of being used against witches, throughout history, to kill them or mar them —

He wants the emerald.

My emerald. Yes.

You won't reveal its parentage. Who the father was.

Oh well hell. Yes. It was the man in the moon. Deus Lunus.

The man in the moon ha-ha.

No I mean it, it was the man in the moon. Deus Lunus as he's called, the moon god. Deus Lunus. Him.

You mean you want me to believe —

Look woman I don't give dandelions what you believe you asked me who the father was. I told you. I don't give a zipper whether you believe me or don't believe me.

You're actually asking me to —

Sat in that chair that chair right there. The red chair.

Oh for heaven's sake all right that's it I'm going to blow this pop stand I know I'm just a dumb ignorant media person but if you think for one minute that . . . I respect your uh conviction but this has got to be a delusionary belief. The man in the moon. A delusionary belief.

Well I agree it sounds funny but there it is. Where else would I get an emerald that big, seven thousand and thirty-five carats? A poor woman like me?

Maybe it's not a real emerald?

If it's not a real emerald why is Vandermaster after me?

You goin' to the hog wrassle?

No I'm after the emerald.

What's your name?

My name is Cold Cuts. What's that machine?

That's an emerald cutter.

How's it work?

Laser beam. You after the emerald too?

Yes I am.

What's your name?

My name is Pro Tem.

That a dowsing rod you got there?

No it's a giant wishbone.

Looks like a dowsing rod.

Well it dowses like a dowsing rod but you also get the wish.
Oh. What's his name?
His name is Plug.
Can't he speak for himself?
He's deaf and dumb.
After the emerald?
Yes. He has special skills.
What are they?
He knows how to diddle certain systems.
Playing it close to the vest is that it?
That's it.
Who's that guy there?
I don't know, all I know about him is he's from Antwerp.
The Emerald Exchange?
That's what I think.
What are all those little envelopes he's holding?
Sealed bids?

Look here, Soapbox, look here.
What's your name, man?
My name is Dietrich von Dietersdorf.
I don't believe it.
You don't believe my name is my name?
Pretty fancy name for such a pissant-looking fellow as you.
I will not be balked. Look here.
What you got?
Silver thalers, my friend, thalers big as onion rings.
That's money, right?
Right.
What do I have to do?
Fall asleep.
Fall asleep at my post here in front of the door?
Right. Will you do it?
I could. But should I?
Where does this "should" come from?
My mind. I have a mind, stewing and sizzling.
Well deal with it, man, deal with it. Will you do it?
Will I? Will I? Will I? *I don't know!*

Where is my daddy? asked the emerald. My da?
Moll dropped a glass, which shattered.

Your father.

Yes, said the emerald, amn't I supposed to have one?

He's not here.

Noticed that, said the emerald.

I'm never sure what you know and what you don't know.

I ask in true perplexity.

He was Deus Lunus. The moon god. Sometimes thought of as the man in the moon.

Bosh! said the emerald. I don't believe it.

Do you believe I'm your mother?

I do.

Do you believe you're an emerald?

I am an emerald.

Used to be, said Moll, women wouldn't drink from a glass into which the moon had shone. For fear of getting knocked up.

Surely this is superstition?

Hoo, hoo, said Moll. I like superstition.

I thought the moon was female.

Don't be culture-bound. It's been female in some cultures at some times, and in others, not.

What did it feel like? The experience.

Not a proper subject for discussion with a child.

The emerald sulking. Green looks here and there.

Well it wasn't the worst. Wasn't the worst. I had an orgasm that lasted for three hours. I judge that not the worst.

What's an orgasm?

Feeling that shoots through one's electrical system giving you little jolts, *spam spam*, many little jolts, *spam spam spam spam* . . .

Teach me something. Teach me something, mother of mine, about this gray world of yours.

What have I to teach? The odd pitiful spell. Most of them won't even put a shine on a pair of shoes.

Teach me one.

"To achieve your heart's desire, burn in water, wash in fire."

What does that do?

French fries. Anything you want French fried.

That's all?

Well.

I have buggered up your tranquillity.

No no no no no.

I'm valuable, said the emerald. I am a thing of value. Over and above my personhood, if I may use the term.

You are a thing of value. A value extrinsic to what I value.

How much?

Equivalent I would say to a third of a sea.

Is that much?

Not inconsiderable.

People want to cut me up and put little chips of me into rings and bangles.

Yes. I'm sorry to say.

Vandermaster is not of this ilk.

Vandermaster is an ilk unto himself.

The more threatening for so being.

Yes.

What are you going to do?

Make me some money. Whatever else is afoot, this delight is constant.

Now the Molljourney the Molltrip into the ferocious Out with a wire shopping cart what's that sucker there doing? tips his hat bends his middle shuffles his feet why he's doing courtly not seen courtly for many a month he does a quite decent courtly I'll smile, briefly, out of my way there citizen sirens shrieking on this swarm summer's day here an idiot there an idiot that one's eying me eyed me on the corner and eyed me round the corner as the Mad Moll song has it and that one standing with his cheek crushed against the warehouse wall and that one browsing in a trash basket and that one picking that one's pocket and that one with the gotch eye and his hands on his I'll twoad 'ee bastard I'll —

Hey there woman come and stand beside me.

Buzz off buster I'm on the King's business and have no time to trifle.

You don't even want to stop a moment and look at this thing I have here?

What sort of thing is it?

Oh it's a rare thing, a beautiful thing, a jim-dandy of a thing, a thing any woman would give her eyeteeth to look upon.

Well yes okay but what is it?

Well I can't tell you. I have to show you. Come and stand over here in the entrance to this dark alley.

Naw man I'm not gonna go into an alley with you what do you think I am a nitwit?

I think you're a beautiful woman even if you do have that bit of beard there on your chin like a piece of burnt toast or something, most becoming. And that mark like a dead insect on your forehead gives you a certain —

Cut the crap daddy and show me what you got. Standing right here. Else I'm on my way.

No it's too rich and strange for the full light of day we have to have some shadow, it's too —

If this turns out to be an ordinary —

No no no nothing like that. You mean you think I might be a what-do-you-call-'em, one of those guys who —

Your discourse sir strongly suggests it.

And your name?

Moll. Mad Moll. Sometimes Moll the Poor Girl.

Beautiful name. Your mother's name or the name of some favorite auntie?

Moll totals him with a bang in the balls.

Jesus Christ these creeps what can you do?

She stops at a store and buys a can of gem polish.

Polish my emerald so bloody bright it will bloody blind you.

Sitting on the street with a basket of dirty faces for sale. The dirty faces are all colors, white black yellow tan rosy-red.

Buy a dirty face! Slap it on your wife! Buy a dirty face! Complicate your life!

But no one buys.

A boy appears pushing a busted bicycle.

He lady what are those things there they look like faces.

That's what they are, faces.

Lady, Halloween is not until —

Okay kid move along you don't want to buy a face move along.

But those are actual faces lady Christ I mean they're *actual faces* —

Fourteen ninety-five kid you got any money on you?

I don't even want to *touch* one, look like they came off dead people.

Would you feel better if I said they were plastic?

Well I hope to God they're not —

Okay they're plastic. What's the matter with your bike?

Chain's shot.

Give it here.

The boy hands over the bicycle chain.

Moll puts the broken ends in her mouth and chews for a moment.

Okay here you go.

The boy takes it in his hands and yanks on it. It's fixed.

Shit how'd you do that, lady?

Moll spits and wipes her mouth on her sleeve.

Run along now kid beat it I'm tired of you.

Are you magic, lady?

Not enough.

Moll at home playing her oboe.

I love the oboe. The sound of the oboe.

The noble, noble oboe!

Of course it's not to every taste. Not everyone swings with the oboe.

Whoops! Goddamn oboe let me take that again.

Not perhaps the premier instrument of the present age. What would that be? The bullhorn, no doubt.

Why did he interfere with me? Why?

Maybe has to do with the loneliness of the gods. Oh thou great one whom I adore beyond measure, oh thou bastard and fatherer of bastards —

Tucked-away gods whom nobody speaks to anymore. Once so lively.

Polish my emerald so bloody bright it will bloody blind you.

Good God what's that?

Vandermaster used the Foot!

Oh my God look at that hole!

It's awful and tremendous!

What in the name of God?

Vandermaster used the Foot!

The Foot did that? I don't believe it!

You don't believe it? What's your name?

My name is Coddle. I don't believe the Foot could have done that. I one hundred percent don't believe it.

Well it's right there in front of your eyes. Do you think Moll and the emerald are safe?

The house seems structurally sound. Smoke-blackened, but sound.

What happened to Soapbox?

You mean Soapbox who was standing in front of the house poised to bop any mother's son who —

Good Lord Soapbox is nowhere to be seen!

He's not in the hole!

Let me see there. What's your name?

My name is Mixer. No, he's not in the hole. Not a shred of him in the hole.

Good, true Soapbox!

You think Moll is still inside? How do we know this is the right place after all?

Heard it on the radio. What's your name by the way?

My name is Ho Ho. Look at the ground smoking!

The whole thing is tremendous, demonstrating the awful power of the Foot!

I am shaking with awe right now! Poor Soapbox!

Noble, noble Soapbox!

Mr. Vandermaster.

Madam.

You may be seated.

I thank you.

The red chair.

Thank you very much.

May I offer you some refreshment?

Yes I will have a splash of something thank you.

It's scotch I believe.

Yes scotch.

And I will join you I think, as the week has been a most fatiguing one.

Care and cleaning I take it.

Yes, care and cleaning and in addition there was a media person here.

How tiresome.

Yes it was tiresome in the extreme her persistence in her peculiar vocation is quite remarkable.

Wanted to know about the emerald I expect.

She was most curious about the emerald.

Disbelieving.

Yes disbelieving but perhaps that is an attribute of the profession?

So they say. Did she see it?

No it was sleeping and I did not wish to —

Of course. How did this person discover that you had as it were made yourself an object of interest to the larger public?

Indiscretion on the part of the midwitch I suppose, some people cannot maintain even minimal discretion.

Yes that's the damned thing about some people. Their discretion is out to lunch.

Blabbing things about would be an example.

Popping off to all and sundry about matters.

Ah well.

Ah well. Could we, do you think, proceed?

If we must.

I have the Foot.

Right.

You have the emerald.

Correct.

The Foot has certain properties of special interest to witches.

So I have been told.

There is a distaste, a bad taste in the brain, when one is forced to put the boots to someone.

Must be terrible for you, terrible. Where is my man Soapbox by the way?

That thug you had in front of the door?

Yes, Soapbox.

He is probably reintegrating himself with the basic matter of the universe, right now. Fascinating experience I should think.

Good to know.

I intend only the best for the emerald, however.

What is the best?

There are as you are aware others not so scrupulous in the field. Chiselers, in every sense.

And you? What do you intend for it?

I have been thinking of emerald dust. Emerald dust with soda, emerald dust with tomato juice, emerald dust with a dash of bitters, emerald dust with Ovaltine.

I beg your pardon?

I want to live twice.

Twice?

In addition to my present life, I wish another, future life.

A second life. Incremental to the one you are presently enjoying.
As a boy, I was very poor. Poor as pine.
And you have discovered a formula.
Yes.
Plucked from the arcanum.
Yes. Requires a certain amount of emerald. Powdered emerald.
Ugh!
Carat's weight a day for seven thousand thirty-five days.
Coincidence.
Not at all. Only *this* emerald will do. A moon's emerald born of human witch.
No.
I have been thinking about bouillon. Emerald dust and bouillon with a little Tabasco.
No.
No?
No.
My mother is eighty-one, said Vandermaster. I went to my mother and said, Mother, I want to be in love.
And she replied?
She said, me too.

Lily the media person standing in the hall.
I came back to see if you were ready to confess. The hoax.
It's talking now. It talks.
It what?
Lovely complete sentences. Maxims and truisms.
I don't want to hear this. I absolutely —
Look kid this is going to cost you. Sixty dollars.
Sixty dollars for what?
For the interview.
That's checkbook journalism!
Sho' nuff.
It's against the highest traditions of the profession!
You get paid, your boss gets paid, the stockholders get their whack, why not us members of the raw material? Why shouldn't the raw material get paid?
It talks?
Most assuredly it talks.
Will you take a check?

If I must.

You're really a witch.

How many times do I have to tell you?

You do tricks or anything?

Consulting, you might say.

You have clients? People who come to see you regularly on a regular basis?

People with problems, yes.

What kind of problems, for instance?

Some of them very simple, really, things that just need a specific, bit of womandrake for example —

What's womandrake?

Black bryony. Called the herb of beaten wives. Takes away black-and-blue marks.

You get beaten wives?

Stick a little of that number into the old man's pork and beans, he retches. For seven days and seven nights. It near to kills him.

I have a problem.

What's the problem?

The editor, or editor-king, as he's called around the shop.

What about him?

He takes my stuff and throws it on the floor. When he doesn't like it.

On the floor?

I know it's nothing to you but it *hurts me.* I cry. I know I shouldn't cry but I cry. When I see my stuff on the floor. Pages and pages of it, so carefully typed, *every word spelled right* —

Don't you kids have a union?

Yes but he won't speak to it.

That's this man Lather, right?

Mr. Lather. Editor-imperator.

Okay I'll look into it that'll be another sixty you want to pay now or you want to be billed?

I'll give you another check. *Can* Vandermaster live twice?

There are two theories, the General Theory and the Special Theory. I take it he is relying on the latter. Requires ingestion of a certain amount of emerald. Powdered emerald.

Can you defend yourself?

I have a few things in mind. A few little things.

Can I see the emerald now?

You may. Come this way.

Thank you. Thank you at last. My that's impressive what's that?

That's the thumb of a thief. Enlarged thirty times. Bronze. I use it in my work.

Impressive if one believed in that sort of thing ha-ha I don't mean to —

What care I? What care I? In here. Little emerald, this is Lily. Lily, this is the emerald.

Enchanté, said the emerald. What a pretty young woman you are!

This emerald is young, said Lily. Young, but good. I do not believe what I am seeing with my very eyes!

But perhaps that is a sepsis of the profession? said the emerald.

Vandermaster wants to live twice!

Oh, most foul, most foul!

He was very poor, as a boy! Poor as pine!

Hideous presumption! Cheeky hubris!

He wants to be in love! In love! Presumably with another person!

Unthinkable insouciance!

We'll have his buttons for dinner!

We'll clean the gutters with his hair!

What's your name, buddy?

My name is Tree and I'm smokin' mad!

My name is Bump and I'm just about ready to bust!

I think we should break out the naked-bladed pikes!

I think we should lay hand to torches and tar!

To live again! From the beginning! *Ab ovo!* This concept riles the very marrow of our minds!

We'll flake the white meat from his bones!

And that goes for his damned dog, too!

Hello is this Mad Moll?

Yes who is this?

My name is Lather.

The editor?

Editor-king, actually.

Yes Mr. Lather what is the name of your publication I don't know that Lily ever —

World. I put it together. When *World* is various and beautiful, it's

because I am various and beautiful. When *World* is sad and dreary,
it's because I am sad and dreary. When *World* is not thy friend, it's
because *I* am not thy friend. And if I am not thy friend, baby —

I get the drift.

Listen, Moll, I am not satisfied with what Lily's been giving me.
She's not giving me potato chips. I have decided that I am going to
handle this story personally, from now on.

She's been insufficiently insightful and comprehensive?

Gore, that's what we need, actual or psychological gore, and this
twitter she's been filing — anyhow, I have sent her to Detroit.

Not Detroit!

She's going to be second night-relief paper clipper in the Detroit
bureau. She's standing here right now with her bags packed and
ashes in her hair and her ticket in her mouth.

Why in her mouth?

Because she needs her hands to rend her garments with.

All right Mr. Lather send her back around. There is new bad
news. Bad, bad, new bad news.

That's wonderful!

Moll hangs up the phone and weeps every tear she's capable of
weeping, one, two, three.

Takes up a lump of clay, beats it flat with a Bible.

Let me see what do I have here?

I have Ya Ya Oil, that might do it.

I have Anger Oil, Lost & Away Oil, Confusion Oil, Weed of
Misfortune, and War Water.

I have graveyard chips, salt, and coriander — enough coriander
to freight a ship. Tasty coriander. Magical, magical coriander!

I'll eye-bite the son of a bitch. Have him in worm's hall by
teatime.

Understand, ye sons of the wise, what this exceedingly precious
Stone crieth out to you!

I'll fold that sucker's tent for him. If my stuff works. One never
knows for sure, dammit. And where is Papa?

Throw in a little dwale now, a little orris . . .

Moll shapes the clay into the figure of a man.

So mote it be!

What happened was that they backed a big van up to the back
door.

Yes.

There were four of them or eight of them.

Yes.

It was two in the morning or three in the morning or four in the morning — I'm not sure.

Yes.

They were great big hairy men with cudgels and ropes and pads like movers have and a dolly and come-alongs made of barbed wire — that's a loop of barbed wire big enough to slip over somebody's head, with a handle —

Yes.

They wrapped the emerald in the pads and placed it on the dolly and tied ropes around it and got it down the stairs through the door and into the van.

Did they use the Foot?

No they didn't use the Foot they had four witches with them.

Which witches?

The witches Aldrin, Endrin, Lindane, and Dieldrin. Bad-ass witches.

You knew them.

Only by repute. And Vandermaster was standing there with clouds of 1, 1, 2, 2-tetrachloroethylene seething from his nostrils.

That's toxic.

Extremely. I was staggering around bumping into things, tried to hold on to the walls but the walls fell away from me and I fell after them trying to hold on.

These other witches, they do anything to you?

Kicked me in the ribs when I was on the floor. With their pointed shoes. I woke up emeraldless.

Right. Well I guess we'd better get the vast resources of our organization behind this. *World.* From sea to shining sea to shining sea. I'll alert all the bureaus in every direction.

What good will that do?

It will harry them. When a free press is on the case, you can't get away with anything really terrible.

But look at this.

What is it?

A solid silver louse. They left it.

What's it mean?

Means that the devil himself has taken an interest.

A free press, madam, is not afraid of the devil himself.

*

Who cares what's in a witch's head? Pretty pins for sticking pish-toshio redthread for sewing names to shrouds gallant clankers I'll twoad 'ee and the gollywobbles to give away and the trinkum-trankums to give away with a generous hand pricksticks for the eye damned if I do and damned if I don't what's that upon her fore-head? said my father it's a mark said my mother black mark like a furry caterpillar I'll scrub it away with the Ajax and what's that upon her chin? said my father it's a bit of a beard said my mother I'll pluck it away with the tweezers and what's that upon her mouth? said my father it must be a smirk said my mother I'll wipe it away with the heel of my hand she's got hair down there already said my father is that natural? I'll shave it said my mother no one will ever know and those said my father pointing *those?* Just what they look like said my mother I'll make a bandeau with this nice clean dish towel she'll be flat as a jack of diamonds in no time and where's the belly button? said my father flipping me about I don't see one anywhere must be coming along later said my mother I'll just pencil one in here with the Magic Marker this child is a bit of a mutt said my father recall to me if you will the circumstances of her conception it was a dark and stormy night said my mother . . . But who cares what's in a witch's head caskets of cankers shelves of twoads for twoading paxwax scalpel polish people with scares stick-ing to their faces memories of God who held me up and sustained me until I fell from His hands into the world . . .

Twice? Twice? Twice? Twice?

Hey Moll.
    Who's that?
    It's me.
    Me who?
    Soapbox.
    Soapbox!
    I got it!
    Got what?
    The Foot! I got it right here!
    I thought you were blown up!
    Naw I pretended to be bought so I was out of the way. Went with them back to their headquarters, or den. Then when they put the Foot back in the refrigerator I grabbed it and beat it back here.

They kept it in the refrigerator?

It needs a constant temperature or else it gets restless. It's hot tempered. They said.

It's elegant. Weighs a ton though.

Be careful you might —

Soapbox, I am not totally without — it's warm to the hand.

Yes it is warm I noticed that, look what else I got.

What are those?

Thalers. Thalers big as onion rings. Forty-two grand worth.

What are you going to do with them?

Conglomerate!

It is wrong to want to live twice, said the emerald. If I may venture an opinion.

I was very poor, as a boy, said Vandermaster. Nothing to eat but gruel. It was gruel, gruel, gruel. I was fifteen before I ever saw an onion.

These matters are matters upon which I hesitate to pronounce, being a new thing in the world, said the emerald. A latecomer to the welter. But it seems to me that, having weltered, the wish to *re*welter might be thought greedy.

Gruel today, gruel yesterday, gruel tomorrow. Sometimes gruel substitutes. I burn to recoup.

Something was said I believe about love.

The ghostfish of love has eluded me these forty-five years.

That Lily person is a pleasant person I think. And pretty too. Very pretty. Good-looking.

Yes she is.

I particularly like the way she is dedicated. She's extremely dedicated. Very dedicated. To her work.

Yes I do not disagree. Admirable. A free press is, I believe, an essential component of —

She is true-blue. Probably it would be great fun to talk to her and get to know her and kiss her and sleep with her and everything of that nature.

What are you suggesting?

Well, there's then, said the emerald, that is to say, your splendid second life.

Yes?

And then there's now. Now is sooner than then.

You have a wonderfully clear head, said Vandermaster, for a rock.

Okay, said Lily, I want you to tap once for yes and twice for no. Do you understand that?
   Tap.
   You are the true Foot of Mary Magdalene?
   Tap.
   Vandermaster stole you from a monastery in Italy?
   Tap.
   A Carthusian monastery in Merano or outside Merano?
   Tap.
   Are you uncomfortable in that reliquary?
   Tap tap.
   Have you killed any witches lately? In the last year or so?
   Tap tap.
   Are you morally neutral or do you have opinions?
   Tap.
   You have opinions?
   Tap.
   In the conflict we are now witnessing between Moll and Vandermaster, which of the parties seems to you to have right and justice on her side?
   Tap tap tap tap.
   That mean Moll? One tap for each letter?
   Tap.
   Is it warm in there?
   Tap.
   Too warm?
   Tap tap.
   So you have been, in a sense, an unwilling partner in Vandermaster's machinations.
   Tap.
   And you would not be averse probably to using your considerable powers on Moll's behalf.
   Tap.
   Do you know where Vandermaster is right now?
   Tap tap.
   Have you any idea what his next move will be?
   Tap tap.

What is your opinion of the women's movement?

Tap tap tap tap tap tap tap tap tap tap tap tap tap tap.

I'm sorry I didn't get that. Do you have a favorite color what do you think of cosmetic surgery should children be allowed to watch television after ten P.M. how do you feel about aging is nuclear energy in your opinion a viable alternative to fossil fuels how do you deal with stress are you afraid to fly and do you have a chili recipe you'd care to share with the folks?

Tap tap.

The first interview in the world with the true Foot of Mary Magdalene and no chili recipe!

Mrs. Vandermaster.

Yes.

Please be seated.

Thank you.

The red chair.

You're most kind.

Can I get you something, some iced tea or a little hit of Sanka?

A Ghost Dance is what I wouldn't mind if you can do it.

What's a Ghost Dance?

That's one part vodka to one part tequila with half an onion. Half a regular onion.

Wow wow wow wow wow.

Well when you're eighty-one, you know, there's not so much. Couple of Ghost Dances, I begin to take an interest.

I believe I can accommodate you.

Couple of Ghost Dances, I begin to look up and take notice.

Mrs. Vandermaster, you are aware are you not that your vile son has, with the aid of various parties, abducted my child? My own true emerald?

I mighta heard about it.

Well have you or haven't you?

'Course I don't pay much attention to that boy myself. He's bent.

Bent?

Him and his dog. He goes off in a corner and talks to the dog. Looking over his shoulder to see if I'm listening. As if I'd care.

The dog doesn't —

Just listens. *Intently.*

That's Tarbut.

Now I don't mind somebody who just addresses an occasional remark to the dog, like "Attaboy, dog," or something like that, or "Get the ball, dog," or something like that, but he *confides in* the dog. Bent.

You know what Vandermaster's profession is.

Yes, he's a mage. Think that's a little bent.

Is there anything you can do, or would do, to help me get my child back? My sweet emerald?

Well I don't have that much say-so.

You don't.

I don't know too much about what-all he's up to. He comes and goes.

I see.

The thing is, he's bent.

You told me.

Wants to live twice.

I know.

I think it's a sin and a shame.

You do.

And your poor little child.

Yes.

A damned scandal.

Yes.

I'd witch his eyes out if I were you.

The thought's appealing.

His eyes like onions . . .

A black bloodhound who looks as if he might have been fed on human milk. Bloodhounding down the center of the street, nose to the ground.

You think this will work?

Soapbox, do you have a better idea?

Where did you find him?

I found him on the doorstep. Sitting there. In the moonlight.

In the moonlight?

Aureoled all around with moonglow.

You think that's significant?

Well I don't think it's happenstance.

What's his name?

Tarbut.

There's something I have to tell you.

What?

I went to the refrigerator for a beer?

Yes?

The Foot's walked.

Dead! Kicked in the heart by the Foot!

That's incredible!

Deep footprint right over the breastbone!

That's ghastly and awful!

After Lily turned him down he went after the emerald with a sledge!

Was the emerald hurt?

Chipped! The Foot got there in the nick!

And Moll?

She's gluing the chips back with grume!

What's grume?

Clotted blood!

And was the corpse claimed?

Three devils showed up! Lily's interviewing them right now!

A free press is not afraid of a thousand devils!

There are only three!

What do they look like?

Like Lather, the editor!

And the Foot?

Soapbox is taking it back to Italy! He's starting a security-guard business! Hired Sallywag, Wide Boy, Taptoe, and Sometimes!

What's your name by the way?

My name is Knucks. What's your name?

I'm Pebble. And the dog?

The dog's going to work for Soapbox too!

Curious, the dog showing up on Moll's doorstep that way!

Deus Lunus works in mysterious ways!

Deus Lunus never lets down a pal!

Well how 'bout a drink!

Don't mind if I do! What'll we drink to?

We'll drink to living once!

Hurrah for the here and now!

Tell me, said the emerald, what are diamonds like?

I know little of diamonds, said Moll.

Is a diamond better than an emerald?

Apples and oranges I would say.

Would you have *preferred* a diamond?

Nope.

Diamond-hard, said the emerald, that's an expression I've encountered.

Diamonds are a little ordinary. Decent, yes. Quiet, yes. But *gray*. Give me step-cut zircons, square-cut spodumenes, jasper, sardonyx, bloodstones, Baltic amber, cursed opals, peridots of your own hue, the padparadscha sapphire, yellow chrysoberyls, the shifty tourmaline, cabochons . . . But best of all, an emerald.

But what is the *meaning* of the emerald? asked Lily. I mean overall? If you can say.

I have some notions, said Moll. You may credit them or not.

Try me.

It means, one, that the gods are not yet done with us.

Gods not yet done with us.

The gods are still trafficking with us and making interventions of this kind and that kind and are not dormant or dead as has often been proclaimed by dummies.

Still trafficking. Not dead.

Just as in former times a demon might enter a nun on a piece of lettuce she was eating so even in these times a simple Mailgram might be the thin edge of the wedge.

Thin edge of the wedge.

Two, the world may congratulate itself that desire can still be raised in the dulled hearts of the citizens by the rumor of an emerald.

Desire or cupidity?

I do not distinguish qualitatively among the desires, we have referees for that, but he who covets not at all is a lump and I do not wish to have him to dinner.

Positive attitude toward desire.

Yes. Three, I do not know what this Stone portends, whether it portends for the better or portends for the worse or merely portends a bubbling of the in-between but you are in any case rescued from the sickliness of same and a small offering in the hat on the hall table would not be ill regarded.

And what now? said the emerald. What now, beautiful mother?

We resume the scrabble for existence, said Moll. We resume the scrabble for existence, in the sweet of the here and now.

FREDERICK BUSCH

Long Calls

(FROM THE NORTH AMERICAN REVIEW)

WHEN SCHIFF received the assignment and had to leave town, he telephoned some people to say good-bye. They said the same. The last call was to his former wife. He said good-bye to Noah, his son, who was six. Noah put Schiff's former wife back on, but they had used their farewells up, and there was nothing to do but what they did: talked low, then disconnected.

He flew from New York to Chicago, from Chicago to a college town where a bookstore called Greenspan's didn't pay its bills. On behalf of the Brothers Vogel, the law firm that employed his former wife, Schiff was to administer the inventory and mount a kind of watch while the bankruptcy suit began. He had done worse.

His motel room was a motel room. On the damage-proof surface of the bedside table was a small keyboard that turned the TV on and off. And there were his canvas suitcases, and his old BOAC flight bag containing books and cassettes and his little recorder. And, standing exhausted at the bathroom mirror, tall and wet-eyed, bald and bearded, was Schiff: former father, former husband, former older brother, once more told to be in charge.

From the motel by rented car, through the grid of streets that surrounded the school, to Greenspan's, a sea of printed paper with a four-walled desk that was an island in the center of the store. On the island, behind the cash register, a terribly pale man with red eyelids, yellow-white hair, a joint in his mouth. From speakers on the walls, Kiki Dee crying her love for music, the bass reverberating through the spines of the books.

A short fat boy in farmer's overalls and lumber jacket carried a book to the desk. His face was red, and he snorted a laugh as he handed money to the stoned man. The albino said, "Hey, let's see, what's it say — five? *Five*? Yeah, but the book only says two. Right? That say two? You giving me five, right? So — what, you want me to make you change. Right?"

Stacks, along the floor near the walls, of old quarterlies. Unlabeled shelves along the walls, going from A in fiction to R, then lapsing into philosophy. Around the corner, on the far wall, two rows of books about women.

A sly smile moved across the albino's face and he waggled his white eyebrows. "Okay," he said, "okay. I'll make — I'll make you change into a Big *Mac!*" He giggled and the fat boy pushed the five-dollar bill across the counter. The albino said, "You really want me to do it, right? Aw-*right*. Here we *go*."

A young man browsing beyond the island. Boxes of bright periodicals with naked women on the covers. A wall of books called *She Did It for Everyone* and *Bondage Boy*. In an alcove opposite the desk, film and theater books, a wall of poetry, books about homosexual love. The music changing to Sly, and a song about the danger of love and amphetamines. Schiff wiped his hands against his clothes: the dust on the wood of the store, on its books, in its air, the smell of very old salad dressing and slowly leaking natural gas.

The albino leaned over the cash register. He pushed a button with one finger, then looked at the book, at the money, at the fat blushing boy, and then pushed another button. He sat back, shifted on his stool, nodded, leaned to the register again, said, "Now we do a ze-ro. *Choong*." He pushed another key, nodded, and leaned in. "Now we do a tax thing — *choong*." He leaned back, licked his lips, and said, "Now we push this big mother over *here*," and he pushed. The bell rang, the drawer slid out, and white cards in the register window stood up to say $14.05 TX. Schiff turned back to the books.

From a gray and brown curtain in the farthest end of the alcove came a tall man with long curling uncombed black hair who wore dungarees and a work shirt and boots that banged on the floor. A filtered cigarette in the corner of his mouth made him squint and tear from the right eye. He walked to the cash-register island and made change, slapped it wordlessly onto the table beside the paperback book. Turning from the fat boy he said to the albino in a deep voice, "You gotta build my confidence, you know? You're not making me confident you can handle the job. Understand?"

The fat boy left with his book, the music changed again, someone whose voice Schiff couldn't recognize told him to seek comfort in a woman who could hold her whiskey and care for his need. The albino climbed down through a small door in the back of the island and walked past Schiff through the curtain, and the man with the cigarette in his mouth seated himself behind the cash register. Schiff walked over to the island and stood before him as the man smoked, squinting and watering from his right eye and reading a Des Moines paper.

"Excuse me?" Schiff said.

The man looked up, squinted at Schiff with a lizard's ungenerous eye. He waited.

Schiff said, "I'm from Vogel? In New York?"

The man looked at Schiff; one eye squinted, the other eye blinked. His mouth made no expression, simply held the cigarette in place. Then emotion grew around the long beaked nose, the high cheekbones, long jaw: a forced belligerent calm. Schiff was someone's enemy again.

The man said nothing, stepped through the back of the island, and walked in heavy boots through the curtain. A few minutes later he was back with a short, stocky man dressed in brown corduroy trousers and brown buckskin shirt whose hair was almost the color of his outfit and was artfully whorled over his head to hide the baldness. The short man squinted, but with no cigarette in his mouth, and Schiff thought at first that he smiled. He didn't. He said, loudly, against the music, "You the bankruptcy guy from New York? You here to fuck us over and sell us out?"

Schiff said, "I'm the bankruptcy guy. Hey — it's a job. All right?"

The short one said, "Eichmann said that too, Mr. Bankruptcy. Everybody who killed the Jews said that. You're just obeying your orders, right?"

The tall one nodded and spat his cigarette butt onto the floor and let the filter burn there. Schiff stepped on it. "Sure," the tall one said. "Hey: Fuck you. How's that?"

The short one said, "You want to burn these books or what? You want us to make a bonfire and burn the books for you? You know how long we been serving the people in this community who love *books*?"

Schiff said, "I'm sorry I stepped on your cigarette. I thought you were finished with it."

The short one said, "That was his cigarette. *I'm* talking to you. *I'm* the one, Mr. Bankruptcy. I think I hate you, you know that?"

"Listen," Schiff said, 'I'll come back tomorrow and maybe you can show me the accounts and I can start the inventory. I can check the receipts tomorrow."

"You gonna check our receipts?" the tall one said. "That's nice." His voice was deep and getting louder with rage. "You gonna give us an allowance every Friday?"

Schiff put his hands in his pockets. He moved his foot away from the cigarette butt. "Which one of you is Mr. Greenspan?" he asked them.

The short one said, "We're both Mr. Greenspan. Tough luck, huh? You gotta do us *both.*"

"I don't want to do anyone," Schiff said. "I'm making money so I can pay my child-support, and I'm sorry about your store. You deserve your store. It even *looks* like you. But I'm coming back tomorrow. I'll be here. I'll be wearing my storm-trooper boots."

Schiff made his exit by walking into an iron revolving rack of paperback books. He rebounded, went out into the crowded dusk of a university town. After some errant turns, he got back to the Treetop Motel — not a tree in sight, only a bright shopping mall across a four-lane arterial highway — and, after stopping at the chicken restaurant next door, he went into his room and gnawed at wings and watched a program about radiation leaks.

Later, he filled the tub and carried in the Panasonic, put a cassette on — Schubert's *Moments Musicaux* — and slid in, wincing, under the hot water, lay still. He drew his knees up because the tub was too small and then he stretched his legs out, his feet on the wall straddling the faucets. He lay like that, uncomfortably, and then closed his eyes anyway and let the music do what it did for him — allowed him to leak away.

The next morning the short one, still in buckskins, was sitting in the little island at Greenspan's. He ate pound cake set out on waxed paper in slices like playing cards. He wrinkled his forehead as Schiff came in, then nodded, sipped coffee from a carton, pointed to the cake. Schiff shook his head and stood before the man, waiting to see what, as occupying fascist force, Schiff could expect in the way of resistance. The music wasn't on, and that made it easier. Then the short one made it easier still. He said, "You Jewish?"

"Why?"

"You know, like the joke — you *look* Jewish."

"Okay."

"You're a Jew, right?"

"Yeah. Right. So what?"

"So I said some things about Jews and Germans yesterday. Very far out of line, all right? Easy-mouth. Everybody calls everybody a Nazi if they don't like them, right? And if they feel a little paranoid, they call themselves Jews. Right?"

Schiff nodded.

"It so happens," the man said, "that the Greenspan boys ain't Jews. We're German Lutherans, right? And you're a Jew, right? So you come in here to do what you're supposed to do — I *hate* this, I want you to know I *hate* all this — and the German calls himself a Jew and he calls the Jew a Nazi, which is, uhm" — he put the yellow cake in his mouth and chewed it into a paste which flecked his tongue as he spoke again — "anyway, *that* ain't fair. So listen. Listen: We got a lawyer here, and he's gonna try and shove this involuntary bankruptcy up this New York lawyer's nose — what's his name?"

"Vogel. The Brothers Vogel."

"They Germans or Jews?"

"Both, I think."

"Yeah? That's far out. So listen, I think maybe we'll win, but what the hell. We split for the coast, we get some warm weather and some sun, right? We change the name to something very mellow, like Joe and Gordy Sweetstuff — you like that? We open a new line of credit, which is too easy to do, and meantime you do us a free inventory."

His face looked the same as it had the day before, when he'd squinted against no smoke and hated Schiff for a Jew-killer. Schiff nodded at the man and said it was his pleasure.

"I don't know what the hell we can *do* with an inventory," the man said. "We got a mess here. When you get done, we'll have a mess except with numbers attached to it. You know? Now listen: Go ahead. Just don't talk to my brother too much. Joseph? Joe, he's got a hair up his ass about you. He's not a polite guy. No, you're gonna find out he's a hot-shit *person.* I mean, that aspect's cool. But his manners really suck. It's a defense mechanism." Greenspan smiled and his eyes crinkled again. Schiff held his hand out between them, as a barrier, and Greenspan reached out of his island and put a cold dry little hand in Schiff's and squeezed back.

That was his first day on the job. Gordy, the shorter brother, gave him a clipboard and a sheet of legal paper and a brown bag filled with invoices dating back several months. Schiff borrowed a felt-tip pen from him and began to compare inventory to actual stock. He soon gave up, since it was clear that the invoices were incomplete. He called New York, collect, asked a junior partner at the Brothers Vogel — she was Schiff's wife — to send their records of billings to Greenspan's, and then Schiff started to count stock listing by category — fiction, poetry, philosophy, and so on — because it was easy to do. He listed within those categories by author or editor alphabetically. Eudora Welty was on the third shelf from the bottom near the door at the front of the store — two Modern Library *Selected Stories*. Next to them was one copy of a Signet Katherine Anne Porter *Collected Stories*. He found out, after ten minutes of asking questions, then searching on his own, that they were together because Katherine Anne Porter had written the introduction to the Welty *Selected Stories*. An hour later Schiff found Welty's *The Robber Bridegroom* next to the pornographic paperbacks on an unstained wooden shelf on the front of which, in pencil, was printed MARRIAGE. Gordy was able to tell him where it was when Schiff asked for more Welty, because, Gordy said, he knew the shop's geography by heart. Schiff decided he'd find Welty's *Losing Battles* in the section on war; but when Schiff could not find such a section, Gordy proudly told him that he and Joe didn't believe in war.

Schiff worked, and Gordy turned the radio up louder. Having decided to do the alphabet at random, Schiff was at the Zs when Joe came in, about 11:45. Joe Greenspan wore the same clothes and wore his cigarette the same way, and instead of talking to his brother or to Schiff, he stood at the door and stared at Schiff as he worked. Schiff waited for the man to speak. He didn't. He stared at Schiff and rubbed his flat belly and slowly pushed his palm through the air, in Schiff's direction and down, dismissing him from the earth. Then Joe walked through to the back room, came out with a khaki book bag, and left. Gordy Greenspan smiled what might have been his smile. Schiff listened to Judy Collins sing a song about cooking with honey.

After lunch the albino kid, not stoned, came in, and Gordy left, saying he might not come back for the weekend, and if Joe didn't return the albino was to lock up.

Schiff said, "Gordy, I think I'm supposed to have a key."

Gordy smiled his possible smile and bounced on the balls of his little feet. "You're a pistol," he said. He smiled more broadly and wiped his mouth as if he still were eating. "Okay. In the back, back there. One of you guys lock up if we're gone till Monday. I don't care if you close it early, late, whatever. Everybody take care of everything, right?"

And after Gordy Greenspan had left and the albino had settled down — the register drawer open so he didn't have to solve the mysteries of the keyboard to make change — the sour spice smell of marijuana now settling onto the dust and the hard surface of the music, Schiff went into the alcove and through the curtain into the back room.

There was an aluminum folding cot on one wall, and photographs were pasted everywhere — every poet he'd heard of, and some fiction writers, and people who had written about the release of psychic energy and sexual tension. The wall at the back was taken up by a soot-streaked stove and a small refrigerator. Here the smell of gas was violent and threatening. A large carton on the floor in front of the cot held foreign magazines that specialized in vulvas, and on top of the magazines was a length of chain to which were attached several keys. One had a piece of tape on it labeled STORE, and Schiff removed it and went back into the shop to tell the albino he was leaving.

After lunch in a bar crowded with students, Schiff grew tired of thinking he was old, so he went back to the car and drove to the motel. He watched two giants punch themselves into exhaustion. He watched a program about nature. He watched news: Rath's reported hogs up, and beans appeared to be holding their own. First Avenue in Cedar Rapids was closed by an explosive fire. The President was confident. Schiff went out for hamburgers. He returned to watch a film about American Indian potters and then a longer film about John Wayne's triumph over other American Indians. News came on at ten o'clock in the Midwest, while the people Schiff knew in New York still were waiting for it, or were listening to blues piano at the Cookery, or were in a bedroom being useful to one another.

He went to bed after putting a cassette of Boccherini on the machine. It began with the Quintet No. 2 in C Major for guitar and strings, and Schiff fell into it and through it at once, floated into Gordy Greenspan, his brother, the dust in the store, and the crazy listings. Schiff thought of how, when he was married, he would hide within the cycles of their days, silently washing dishes, or coming back from a free-lance assignment, or bathing their child, or sitting with an article in the *Times* on the Giants' need for linemen. He would not speak and still would not, and soon he would smell shampoo and hear the sounds of cloth against her skin, which meant that the day was over again. And still he would speak in the coldest language only, the vocabulary of crossed legs or of scratchings at the neck. Or the sigh of wind inside the body that arrives outside as if from a great distance. And then the baby would murmur in its room, an innocent sound without meaning or need, and Schiff would be up from the chair and chattering — *found* — and would be surprised that no one in that apartment wanted his company, or wished to praise his attentions to the very young. He slept alone, such nights.

The tape recorder clicked to a halt, and he reached in darkness to turn the cassette onto its other side for the Quintet in E. The music marched and he went with it, past his wife and son, thinking of his brother, and here he goes, a guerrilla stealing into his brother's room more than thirty years ago. He slides the door of his closet back on its silent track, stands among the innocent smells of small shirts and trousers, closes himself in, and waits. Here comes his brother, seven years younger than Schiff, underweight, serious, awed by his older brother's height and heft, bewildered by his lack of love or comprehension of a little brother's needs. Schiff waits until it is absolutely time. He slowly slides the door wide and makes no sound. He waits. The little brother's body moves beneath the secret of Schiff's presence. Still silent, his face drawn tight to hide his teeth, a gangster's mask, Schiff is waiting until the little brother finally *knows* he's there. He turns to see the stranger's face on the edge of his life, and he weeps. Schiff smiles with his mouth open wide.

We hope you have enjoyed this recording, said no one in an official voice, *which has been programmed to reduce program interruption for your continuous listening pleasure.* Then there was silence as the empty length of tape, left for his continuous listening pleasure, moved on, then halted with a click. Schiff was sitting in bed and feeling his chest pound, was wiping at his mouth, making himself understand that there was too little tape left for more music.

On Sunday he went in for a while and worked at Greenspan's, enjoying the job. He was through M and almost finished with L. He did another couple of titles and then, carrying the clipboard with him, turning off the few lights he'd been using, he went into the dark cold gassy back room. It was like being underground, surrounded by stone and pools of black icy water. Lichen on the walls. Tiny white things moving slowly under rocks. He turned on a desk lamp attached to a metal cabinet above the stove. Lay on the cot in intense light. Let his legs go limp. Carried a wad of glossy magazines onto his chest and read them. Looked at thighs and crotches and great soft breasts with irritated nipples. And soon he was massaging his groin. And soon his fly was open. And soon, slowly, with lazy pleasure and no mind, he was holding and stroking and rasping himself. And soon, before a two-page photo of a fat girl sucking her own glistening finger as her membranes gleamed at him, Schiff released his sperm in gusts across his knees to the floor and the tops of his shoes. He slowly, sweatily wiped himself, and then his shoes, with a soiled blanket. He waited in half sleep until he was soft. He went back to the motel and watched Julius Erving fly through the Chicago Bulls like a giant brown bird, again and again, to *slam* the ball through the hoop in vengeance for unnamed offenses.

On Monday Schiff worked. The usual flow of customers and the usual music. Gordy stayed away and Joe sat at the island, drinking coffee and smoking cigarettes which he held in his mouth except when he drank. He looked at Schiff with scorn, and Schiff tried not to look back. After lunch, when the albino hadn't come in, Joe returned from the back room, smelling of canned ravioli, and stood at Schiff's side, too close, while Schiff worked. He said, "Hey. Hey. Shithead, hey. You know what we're tryin' to *do* in here?"

Schiff didn't turn around. He said, "No."

Joe said, "Yeah. That don't surprise me, you know that?"

Schiff said, "Right. Right, Joe."

"You're *humoring* me? Hey! *You're* humoring *me?*"

Schiff clipped the sheets tighter into the clipboard and put the pen in his pocket and said, "Bye, Joe. Have a nice night."

"That might've been your last chance, stupid."

But Schiff went past him and out.

That night, in the motel room and in darkness, a thousand miles from home but really farther, thinking of the people he had told good-bye, Schiff heard Joe at the door. He slapped it, then thumped hard, calling, "Hey! Hey, Bankruptcy! You wanna smoke some dope? You wanna make peace?"

Schiff turned on the TV set but kept the sound off.

Joe called, "Yeah, okay. But I think this was the last chance, you know?"

Schiff watched a rerun of *Star Trek* in the darkness and silence, and after a while Joe went away. He continued to watch the space ship's crewmen disappear from the craft into tingling dotted lines, then reappear, filling their outlines again, in a barren world where there were awful creatures who meant the crewmen no good.

He was awakened again, he didn't know how much later, but he had seen American bombers and rippling flags on three channels before he'd fallen asleep. He seized the phone, a ripe new layer of sweat over his body — shins even, and even the insides of his forearms — and he tried to sound calm, as if he were being graded for courage. He accepted the long-distance call, acknowledging who he was and then saying hello to his former wife.

He asked if Noah was all right. She assured him Noah was fine. She asked after his inventory work. He said fine. But then they got to business because she wanted to. He didn't care yet; he still savored Noah's safety. She had gone to check his mail, she said. He said nothing. She had thought that burglars shouldn't have clues — uncollected mail was a clue for crooks, she told him, in her business tones — and there was the Dartmouth alumni magazine. Reading it to see if his name was mentioned, she had found no catalogue of his recent minor accomplishments. But she had seen his brother's name listed. With appropriate sorrow expressed by the class of '64. He was *dead,* she told Schiff. The line was silent for seconds. Then: Why hadn't Schiff *told* her? Had he known? Was it true? What could he *do?*

Schiff said that they had grown so estranged, his brother *would,* Schiff thought, neglect to tell him of his death.

She didn't think Schiff was funny. She wanted to know how Schiff felt.

Schiff didn't know. Then he did: "I feel like an orphan," he said. "Cheated. The bastard."

He thanked her and told her he would be in touch.

Sure, she said, wouldn't he just.

"Noah's all right?" he asked again.

She said, "He doesn't know."

"It wouldn't make any difference, I guess. I'll call you."

She said, "You won't call me back. You never call me back. You don't know *how* to call me back."

Then hung up. He sat on the bed, then went to his flight bag for his notebook of names and addresses. He set out the clipboard of inventoried titles, flipped back pages of the long legal pad until he had a clean sheet ready and the clipboard set by the phone. He dialed for an outside line, reached an operator, and started to call across the country, to verify his brother's dying.

First his brother's number in San Diego. No answer.

Then the San Diego night supervisor. Confirmation that the number worked. Schiff asked how long it would take to disconnect a dead man's phone. The operator said probably a month or three weeks after the last bill was due.

Then Schiff's local operator said, "Are you all right, honey?" When he told her why he wasn't, she said, "Make sure you're sitting down. Are you sitting down?"

Schiff's operator called the central police station in San Diego. Giving his brother's address, she learned which local station might have responded if Schiff's brother had fallen over from a charge of drugs too bright and hard for his body, or had been stabbed on the sidewalk near his loft. She worked through exchanges and raised a sergeant near his brother's address. Schiff told the sergeant how he'd learned of his brother's death, and when he thought it might have taken place. Schiff told the sergeant he was guessing. The sergeant sighed into the phone. Schiff gave him the name and address and the sergeant went away to check, returned with no information, told Schiff he would send a car to the loft, instructed him to call back in half an hour. Meanwhile, the sergeant said, did Schiff want to make more calls? Schiff did, and the sergeant gave him the name of the hospital into whose emergency room his brother might have been brought. "If he was mugged, you know, or DOA," the sergeant said.

Schiff said, "That means dead on arrival?"

So his operator, still on the line, obtained and called the number for Metropolitan Hospital's emergency room. Schiff spoke to a nurse who gave him over to an orderly, who, with great calmness and almost tender care, went back through records, finding no reference to Schiff's brother. Schiff thought of himself in the closet in his brother's room, sliding the door back slowly, no expression on his face.

"But that doesn't mean he didn't die," the orderly said. "It just means he didn't die *here*. He might have died on the street and been brought into the medical examiner's office DOA."

"That means dead on arrival," Schiff said. "Am I right?"

The orderly gave Schiff the medical examiner's number — the operator cut in to say, "I have that, sir" — and they went again through the dancing high-sung notes of the long-distance wire.

A man in the medical examiner's office was bored by Schiff's story, though not cruel — he was only conducting his business. He went back through records, further back, then said Schiff's name aloud and spelled it to Schiff. Schiff said, "Yes." The man spelled it again. Schiff said, "Yes."

Then the man said, "No, this one's too young. Your brother's thirty-two? No. This one's twenty-eight."

"It's pretty close, though," Schiff said.

"Your brother a Negro?"

He wouldn't tell me if he was.

Or: Not the last time I looked, but that was so long ago.

Or: Quite possibly, by now.

Schiff said, "No, I have a Caucasian brother."

"You're clear as far as I can see. This guy was black."

"Thank you," Schiff said.

"Thank *him*," the man said.

Schiff thought of his wife on the floor of their living room — his former wife — with Noah leaning against her drawn-up knees, her hand on his hair and the back of his neck, reading him the story, again, of Arthur Cluck, and of how Arthur Cluck disappeared from his loving mother hen, and how Ralph the Owl, barnyard detective, found Arthur Cluck and brought him home. Schiff's wife's low voice, telling about losses.

His operator asked if he was all right, and Schiff told her he was, then gave her numbers: the art school where his brother had taught — still taught? once taught? — part-time; the name of his brother's chairman; the number of a woman whom his brother had claimed once to love. Schiff's toes felt cold on the motel carpet, and clamping the phone to his shoulder with his head, he wrapped a blanket around his body. He felt tender toward himself.

The chairman did not answer. The woman wasn't home and the man who answered didn't know when she would be; the man said he didn't care. The operator said this was important. The man said he still didn't care. The watchman at the art school said no one was there and Schiff should *know* that no one was there.

So Schiff thanked the operator, told her how fine she'd been, told her of his gratitude — his voice began to wobble, then — and said he'd try the numbers later on. He hung up.

He wanted food. He had to have food, so he dressed and went down the corridor to the vending machines. With all his change he bought four Mars bars, went back to sit on the bed, dropping wrappers on the carpet, filling himself with sweetness. He lay on the bed, turned on the remote-control switch, worked through the channels, found glaring whiteness and the high hum of empty air, turned the set off, closed his eyes. He didn't sleep, but lay there, and lay there, and then he rolled and sat up, planted his feet on the carpet again. He said to the room, "My brother's dead. My brother is dead. My brother is dead."

He answered: "You should have thought of that before." But he didn't understand what he meant. He picked up the phone and dialed the number in San Diego at four in the morning and listened to the telephone ring.

Nothing. Schiff hung up. The phone rang, and Schiff ripped it from the cradle: "Hello? *Hello?*"

"This is the operator, honey. Can I get any more numbers for you? Did you find anything out?"

Schiff said, "Oh. Oh. You're wonderful, you know that?" He was crying, but he tried to sound businesslike, and said, "Thank you, no thank you, it'll be fine, thank you very much, thank you."

And then the phone did not ring, and he watched it, and then dialed to San Diego again, and listened to it ring for no one in California, and then he hung up to wait.

He rewound the Boccherini, and let it play.

He dialed the number in San Diego.

His brother answered at once: "Yeah?"

"Hey," Schiff said, tightening his throat and eyes. "Hey, it's me."

There was a new silence — the music of estrangement — and then his brother said, "Hey, hey, man. What's up?" What's up: What is the business we have to transact.

"I heard you were dead," Schiff said.

"Who told you that? Are they right?" Schiff's brother giggled, then was silent, then barked a laugh, and said "Oh, wow. Oh, *wow.* What a mess. What a —"

"Me?" Schiff said, with the innocence of begged love.

"I was getting those, you know, alumni letters? You know: We need a hundred million dollars by next week, so please send all your money? I got so goddamn tired of getting all that junk —"

"*You* did it??"

"What?"

"No, tell me, you go ahead."

"I wrote them this letter from my widow, see? I told them I died — my husband, who was me. I told them it really got me upset — the widow — to keep getting these letters to him. *Me.* Him. You know?"

Schiff tried to whistle and couldn't. "Got it. Right. Right. Listen — I made about fifty dollars' worth of calls. I believed it. See, I thought you were *dead.* I called the cops near you, and — Jesus! I forgot to call the cops back!"

"Maybe you didn't miss me as much as you thought."

"No," Schiff said, "I was calling hospitals and emergency rooms and the medical examiner to find out if you got DOA'd, that's dead on arrival. I called your chairman. I called all your friends I ever heard of."

"You really tracked me down, huh?"

Schiff's brother's voice sounded to Schiff like Schiff's.

His brother said, "Well, you know what to do in emergencies at least, don't you?"

"Yeah, I guess I'm good at that."

They let the line stay silent for a long time.

"I hope you see the humor in all this," his brother said.

"Well."

"It sounds like you're having a hard time seeing the humor in all this."

Schiff held onto the receiver with both hands and heard their silence.

"Well," Schiff said, his voice pitching. "Well, maybe I will. Maybe next week or something. I believed it."

Their silence again, and then, as if he'd suddenly got very busy,

Schiff's brother said, "Well, I tell you what. Why don't you drop me a postcard or something when you see how all this is kind of funny. All right? How's that?"

Schiff stood up, and all his words for anger and apology came to the back of his teeth and died there. He swallowed them. He said, "All right. All right. All right. I'm glad you're alive." He waited to say something better for himself, and maybe even for his brother, but his brother disconnected and Schiff put his phone down too.

The Boccherini went on for a little while, and then the room was still. Schiff sat on the bed, cross-legged, cold. He picked up the telephone and dialed his wife's number, but hung up. He walked around the room, lay down in bed, and slept.

He woke, went back to sleep, woke an hour later in light and told himself what had happened. He drove downtown to work.

Melissa Manchester sang "Midnight Blue." Joe sat in the island, his cigarette in place, his hands in his lap, and anger, as ever, on his face. The smell of gas was harsher this morning, and there seemed to be more magazines piled in the dirty-books section, and a box of what looked like old bedclothes. Schiff thought of his recently invested sperm. Gordy came from the back room, crinkled his face in what might have been a smile, and said, "Okay."

Joe nodded back. Gordy went out of the store and Joe beckoned Schiff to the island. Schiff went, carrying the clipboard. "I came to see you, Bankruptcy."

"I heard you, Joe. I was trying to stay alone last night. And some things came up. Maybe I would have called you, but some things came up."

"I knew you were there." He squinted through his smoke. Schiff wiped at his face because the gas smell was heavier. "That was it, pal, last night. You wouldn't've called me."

Schiff said, "No." He turned around and went to the section of poetry books in the alcove near the curtain. The gas was dense there and Schiff turned to tell him, but Joe was gone. Schiff went back to the island and saw that the store was empty. The sign that hung in the glass door said OPEN. But that was the side facing Schiff. He went to the alcove and through the curtain and smelled the gas leaking into the store from the stove. He heard it hiss from all four open unlit burners, and from the oven, a great black mouth that gaped at his own.

He shut the burners off and went back to the far side of the shop where dirty smoke made Schiff sneeze in shrieks. The rags that Joe had lit before leaving had caught onto some silky sex magazines, and Schiff saw the filter of Joe's cigarette nested in burning pages. He kicked the box along the floor before it could light a shelf of books and, as the Greenspans had planned, build up heat enough to ignite the leaking gas and blow the books away, their debts away, and their bankruptcy caretaker away too.

The flames and black smoke jumped back at him as Schiff shoved the box with his feet. He couldn't see through the smoke, so he had to dance around the burning box and then back behind it once he'd set his course. He unlocked the front door and, holding it open, kicked the box as far into the street as he could. A woman walking past with her child screamed and pulled the child out of the way. A man in a peacoat walked over to inspect the flames.

"Hey!" Schiff shouted. "Hey! *Call* someone!"

He was dizzy with smoke or excitement, and his legs tingled. He went back to the other burning magazines and kicked them away from the wall, then danced on them — nipples and pubic mounds, rounded offering mouths — until his heavy feet had put the fires out. And then, gagging, moving his legs with difficulty, Schiff ran into the back room and put the clipboard under his arm, grabbed his parka, and went coughing into the street.

Schiff heard sirens, his skin simmered with excitement. He went to his knees, an altar boy. He felt a hard push or punch at his back, and he went all the way down. While he still was trying to ask who had attacked him, and why, there were hands on him, pulling at his legs, his belt, hands holding him and tearing his trousers away. The man in the peacoat held Schiff's trousers up for Schiff to see — they were charred below the knees and on one thigh an oval hole burned steadily at the edges, growing wider as Schiff watched.

He let his head drop back. Someone's hand cushioned it. He moaned. He let the clipboard fall away. Schiff discovered that he wept. He laughed and then he started weeping again, daintily touching his injured thighs. Above him, the man who had torn off his trousers flinched from Schiff's eyes.

Schiff said, "I have to make a call."

The man said, "*What?*"

"It *hurts!* I have to make a call."

"Wait a second, will you? Will you wait? First get fixed up. *Then* you make your call, for chrissakes. Don't be a nuisance right away. Lie down and wait, for chrissakes."

Schiff said, "No —"

The man turned away.

Schiff heard himself snorting, half-naked on the sidewalk. He touched at his burns. The klaxons were close. Now he had to call his wife back, now, he had to. He had to tell her how he knew what to do — save things, place long calls — in emergencies at least.

DAVID EVANIER

The One-Star Jew

(FROM THE PARIS REVIEW)

STIFF AS A RAMROD, a straight arrow, six foot three, his face a starched white, Isaac Zavelson stands in the elevator beside some of the other employees of Jews for Israel, waiting for it to move. Entering the building, he has saluted the American flag and the Israeli flag. In his hand he is holding an envelope addressed Hon. Richard Nixon, San Clemente, Calif. Inside the envelope is a birthday card. Zavelson heads the Ethnics division of the organization. He is sixty-one. Under him are shorter men than he, more indecisive men, who shuffle when they walk, who do not speak English as well as Yiddish, who like to remain on the sidelines. Zavelson drives them hard — a ten-hour day, and weekends — except Ruthie. Zavelson takes long lunch hours with Ruthie at her apartment; they return to the office beaming, and, forgetting, immediately send down for lunch. Ruthie did not climb the ladder to get her position and salary, or wait ten years as the others did in the department. In order to move her up more quickly, Zavelson became impatient with one of his men, Mendel Berger. Zavelson took away his desk, his Israeli flag, and made Mendel sit on a chair by himself in the corner waiting for assignments. Mendel packed his things and left one day. Ruthie was given his job.

A man enters the elevator and moves into the corner as much as possible: a thin man in his mid-fifties, with a beard and a mustache, his gray hair forming a ponytail in the back, held together by a rubber band. He wears a sports jacket from Klein's, has a red handkerchief in his back pants pocket, and carries a dungaree bag over his shoulder, his initials sewn on the bag in suede: L.G. for Luther Glick. He has a paperback in his hand — Zavelson peers sharply at the title: *The Way and the Light* by Krishna Ramanujam. Luther is just returning from a month's vacation.

"How are you, Luther?" Zavelson says.

"Tip top."

"Luther!" barks Zavelson. "So when will you read a Jewish book for a change, a novelty?"

Luther Glick pauses. "I'm not a six-star Jew like you, Isaac."

Zavelson laughs his polite laugh. "I am a full-fledged, proud Jew, Luther. I have nothing to be ashamed of."

"You know, Isaac," Luther begins, "there are other things, other states of consciousness in this world besides —"

But the elevator has opened again, and Zavelson has marched out, leaving Luther with his unfinished sentence. Luther shakes his head and joins the line into the office.

Luther is a member of the three-man publicity crew, or, as he calls himself, a "minion" of Jews for Israel. He walks slowly this morning, his first day back at work, for Luther is tired. He is not a well man. He has had four heart attacks. And he spent six hours the previous night kneeling on the wooden floor of a church attic in Westchester with six others (all of whom happen to have been Jewish) who are interested in a new Buddhist sect in the neighborhood. Luther is not a member, but, with the new "cosmic consciousness" he discovered five years ago, he is searching.

II

Jews for Israel (or JFI) is not a place for listeners. Almost everyone there has finished with listening. So Luther is not surprised by Zavelson's behavior. I am not used to it, as I have only been with the publicity staff for six months and am, by twenty years, the youngest member of the organization. Our department occupies a corner of the office — a glass alcove for our head, Stephen Greenberg, and two desks on the outside for myself and Luther. Luther sits behind me. He greets me, our obese secretary Bea, whom he calls Queenie, and our second secretary Jill. Luther waters his plants, lights his pipe, thumbs through his copy of *Ms.*, and unfolds today's *New York Times*. He settles back.

III

Luther has spent his month's vacation in the New England area. First he traveled to Vermont with his wife for the trial of one of my predecessors in this job, the man who sat at my desk ten years ago: Rom Schwartz. Rom, a poet, teacher, and the son of a world-famous Jewish scholar, was on trial for murdering his wife with a pickax. The two children testified against him. He was found guilty. Luther tells me that he went up to Rom while the trial was still going on, held out his hand and said, " 'Rom — Glick, Luther Glick, from JFI. You may not remember me. I was a colleague. Rom, if you want somebody to just lend an ear, someone to talk to, I'll be glad to come back and see you tonight.' He looked at me, and he had a glazed air, as if he was far away, and suddenly he smiled — just for a moment — Rom's old smile — a light of rec-ognition — I think — of who I was, and then that look of despair came back, and he said, 'I'm just so —' and he couldn't say any more — he choked — and walked away with his lawyers." Luther did not stay for the remainder of the trial, but has brought back the newspaper clippings from the Vermont newspaper about the trial, which he shows to me, Stephen Greenberg, and our two secretaries.

(Rom, who was sentenced to thirty years, has changed his mailing address in the Poet's Yearbook from his Vermont home to the jail in which he is staying.)

Stephen Greenberg, a short man also in his mid-fifties, with a round cherubic face, is seated listening to Luther, his short hands folded in his lap, his feet not touching the floor, shaking his head. When he is not at JFI, Stephen is a scholar and historian, the author of more than twenty books. One book he has been working on for years is a biography of Rom's father, who bequeathed him his private papers when he died.

As to the second half of the trip — which he had taken alone, without his wife — Luther is less communicative. Luther had been carrying on an intense correspondence with Molly Bethune, the Maine author of the best seller about living the simple country life, in tune with the lakes, the forest, and the birds. Before the book became widely known, Luther had been delighted with it and had mailed Molly Bethune a cassette in which he talked about himself, his life, his new consciousness, and her book. She had been taken with it, and in turn mailed Luther a cassette.

Luther had been very excited by this contact with an author whose book began to move up the best-seller lists, and whose picture on the jacket was of an attractive woman in her thirties. He had told us that he had planned to travel in the vicinity of Maine — "Molly's territory," he had said with a possessive, intimate smile — but he would not elaborate. He had let it hang. Now we both ask him about Maine.

"I was there," he says, and doesn't seem to want to go on. Then he says, "I didn't see Molly."

"Not only didn't he see her," says Stephen to me in his glass cubicle as soon as Luther has gone out to lunch, "he told me he didn't even call her. Luther probably didn't tell you this, David, but —" Stephen begins, crossing his legs. Stephen is a gossip, but the most unmalicious one I have ever met. He really cares about Luther.

"— This is really quite moving. After Luther and Molly Bethune exchanged a few more cassettes, one day last fall she writes him that she is coming to New York. She gives him the name of the hotel, she gives him her room number, and she tells him the *time* she will be there. Luther was so excited. He talked about it for weeks. He had two of her books but he had a hell of a time tracking down the third — a poetry book. The crisis became finding that third early book — he had a search service looking for it. Finally he had all three books. Then the time came. He was in quite a state. He put on a modern suit and tie.

"Well, he didn't see Molly. He took her three books and rode the subway to her publishing house. He walked in the door and stood before the receptionist, who didn't know him from Adam. 'Look,' he said, 'my name is Glick. I have here all three of Molly Bethune's books. She knows who I am. Would you ask her to autograph them for me?' The receptionist shrugged and said that she would try. Luther returned in a few days to pick up the books. They were autographed."

IV

I remember one of the first things Luther said to me. It was on the third morning of my first week at the office. He was sniffling. "You know," he said, "sometimes I'm crazy — foolish, just like my wife says. I sleep in the nude. There was a storm last night. I woke up, went down to the kitchen, and then I just walked out into my back yard. I just walked on the grass, the water pouring down on me, looking up at the sky."

V

Since he returned from his vacation, Luther has spent several nights with another sect, a Nichiren Buddhist group. They hold their services in the home of a woman he knows. "Last night they set up the new altar," he tells me. "The leader, a black man, kept making it parallel, and then he started the service. He stopped it again. 'It's too low,' he said. He's six foot four, by the way. So all of his little flunkies started lifting it.

"This leader," Luther continues, "is thin as a pencil, all teeth. When he smiles, you see teeth. He stopped the services again in the middle, annoyed, and turned to the woman who donates her house for the evening: 'When we chant,' he says, 'the leader should be predominantly heard. If others chant louder than the leader, the leader is not heard and cannot lead.' She smiled and shook her head, thanking the leader for the whipping, and said she would be quieter. The Nichiren Buddhists stress positive benefits. This same woman testified to the positive effects of chanting: in order to get compensation from her medical insurance, she had to produce evidence of medical bills of several years ago. A letter had arrived that day from her doctor, with a large contemporary bill, which he had dated, by mistake, several years back. So she submitted the doctor's mistakenly dated bill. She didn't question the honesty of what she was doing . . .

"The chanting," Luther concludes, "sounds like a railing buzz. It's hard to take at first."

VI

I am replacing Melvin Bronstein, who sat at this desk for ten years. Rom Schwartz was here earlier, and it is Mel who most people at JFI talk about. "A saint," they all say, looking at me as if it would be impossible for me to be as good, as useful as Mel was to them. Mel died three months before I arrived.

There are pictures on the wall of the three of them: Stephen, Luther, and Mel. Luther's and Stephen's memories are of their long association with Mel, sharing his tribulations. They talk about how Mel could never turn away from anyone, could never say no;

of his alcoholism, of how his wife helped to destroy him: his wife with her three-inch high heels that drilled holes into the floor of his car, and who did not come to Mel's funeral because she wanted to see California. They talk about the huge hotel bills his wife racked up on credit cards while Mel was in the hospital because she said she could not bear to be at home alone. The finance companies still call the office and are upset to hear they have lost Mel. "Kind, wonderful Mel," the people in the office all say. They shake their heads. "He was too good for this world."

Except Luther. "I never liked him," says Luther. "He should have been a whore. He could never say no. He had no backbone." Luther thinks about that for a moment and adds, "That's true of Stephen as well.

"Mel used to say to me, looking away, not facing me, never facing me, when he sat at your desk, 'You know, Luther, I wasn't always like this. There are certain things that do something to people.' Well, he was trying to tell me — trying to hint that once there was a stronger, angrier Melvin: a dynamo. But I didn't believe that for one minute."

They both talk about the extra little jobs Mel took on at the office. He drew signs.

"Signs?" I say.

"Sure," Luther explains. "Like Quiet Please, No Smoking, Admission Two Dollars, This Way Out, and so forth. Whenever the secretaries needed a sign for one of our dinners or rallies, they would come to Melvin. He printed very well. Watch out, David. They'll be asking you."

"We'll never forget his last party," Stephen says. "We just arrived, me and Luther, and we were standing in his living room. We smelled smoke. 'Mel, there's a fire!' we said.

"Mel looked at us and beamed his beatific smile, and said, 'No, no, it's nothing. Nothing is wrong. Everything's fine. My daughter had a little problem earlier but it was resolved.'

"We had to take his word. But the smell got worse and worse, and the smoke was filling the living room. Finally we said, 'Mel, you better do something.' He insisted nothing was wrong, but Luther and I opened the door to the next room.

"What we saw was amazing. The entire room was burnt to a crisp. There was water and debris everywhere. Everything was black and charred. Water buckets stood in a row. The remaining pieces of wood were crackling. The walls were charred. The smoke was heavy. Mel's daughter had set fire to her room an hour before the party."

They both shake their heads. "Where is the daughter now?" I ask.

"In a mental institution."

I look at Mel's face in the pictures. He has a blank, brown corduroy look. He smiles. I look for traces of him in the desk. There are none.

I ponder the fate of my predecessors at this desk.

VII

I look behind me. Luther is doing twenty-five pushups on the floor. He touches his toes twenty-five times. He prepares his lunch. It is bright on his desk: carrots, celery, tomatoes, chicken, okra, an orange, and a quart of skimmed milk. He talks about his new consciousness.

"Nowhere is it written that I have to be numero uno. That's the most important thing I've learned, David. I know where it came from originally. I was a skinny malink of a kid . . . my brother, though, was a husky busker. And my grandfather was a butcher. That's how it started.

"When I went back to Toronto after some years, there was no excitement on my grandfather's part about my arrival . . . nothing. Then my brother came down the street. My grandfather dashed across the street to him. He brought him into the kitchen. He plunked black bread on the table, sour cream, sat my brother down and said 'Eat!' I noticed the difference.

"I used to be so influenced by what other people thought . . . and that was *so wrong*. Competition is nonsense. Nature did not decree that it be this way.

"I began reading books about different religions. I realized, and formulated for myself, that there are just two things, David, that we need: peace and purpose. Peace and purpose. I found that I disagreed with not one thing about Islam, one thing about Buddhism (can't remember which), and many things about Judaism.

"Have you heard of an author who signs his name, 'The Gentleman with a Duster?'"

I said that I hadn't.

"I've been looking for his novel for ten years. I read it as an impressionable youth, but it would have more meaning for me today: *Julius Levine*. It was about a young man who searches out an erudite uncle to teach him about Judaism. But the uncle talks about the East — he isn't hung up on Judaism. He knows all the religions have wisdom.

"People around here aren't tuned in to this wavelength. Being a truth seeker isn't an easy thing.

"You know, David, recently I had an experience. Alvin was someone I knew thirty-five years ago. I used to sneer at him. He was an astrology expert, a truth seeker even then. He has become a big business success. On an impulse, I took a journey to see him.

"I traveled far. When I arrived, I went up to his offices. When I saw him in the hall I said, 'Hello, Alvin,' and Alvin threw his arms around me, flashing his smile. I was conscious of his admiration.

"I sez to him, I sez, 'I recognize that lovely smile, Alvin — your father had it when he greeted strangers. But you don't know me. Glick. Luther Glick.'

"He closed his eyes, opened them, recognized me, and threw his arms about me.

"He took me into his private office. He sat down behind his desk, and I sat facing him. 'I have a series of questions for you, Alvin.'

" 'Shoot,' he sez. 'Anything you want to know.'

" 'Alvin, when did your daydreams stop . . . ?'

"He paused; then he said, 'I don't remember.'

"Then I asked, 'What do you say when people scorn you for your seances, for your ideas, when they laugh at you? How can you stand it?'

"And Alvin smiled broadly, paused for a long time, and said, 'Nothing. *I know what I know.*' "

Luther smiled at me, repeating the phrase, shaking his head in admiration.

VIII

Luther has many scrapbooks in the office. He saves clippings about events, books, but mainly about people he admires. He has two Norman Mailer scrapbooks: Mailer stabbing his wife, Mailer running for Mayor of New York and answering a reporter's question about what he will do, if he is elected, to clear up the snow: "I will piss on it."

Luther is reading the *Rolling Stone* interview with Mailer. "Jesus!" he keeps exclaiming. Then he says, "Listen to this. The man's insight is amazing. Charles Manson chose horseshit — not dogshit or human shit — because his girls came from upper-class homes where they had been around horses all their lives. He had them roll in horseshit. It was much less objectionable and more familiar." Luther looks up, giving me that same admiring smile, inviting me to share his admiration with him.

I look up. Stephen is running back and forth with assignments from the director. I have come to realize that he does most of the work. As our secretary Bea says, "Luther panics if he has more than one piece of paper on his desk at one time. Also if he is called into the director's office."

Stephen's face is chalk white from running. "Stephen really knocks himself out, doesn't he?" I say to Luther.

Luther raises his head from the *Rolling Stone*. "Yes. That comes from a sense of responsibility."

IX

Luther takes his job seriously — a possible source of contention between us. "Our standards are not one whit lower than the competition — unless there is a weakening at this desk." He snaps at Jill: "I countermanded my comma after Fink." Or at Bea, who is talking to her husband on the phone: "Hang up. We have priorities. When I open my lips, let no dog bark." Stephen reminds me, "The job is his whole life."

X

The most unpopular person in the office, lately Luther has gotten worse. I feel him storming behind me at his desk, his back rigid, his breath war clouds, his fingers tapping. We are talking about China, a country he approves of, especially since Luther firmly believes in the theory of the survival of the fittest. I really don't give a damn about the politics of China, but I do say, "Well, but of course, China is a totalitarian country." On my way out the door at lunchtime, a voice reaches me across the entire length of the floor-through office. "BEFORE YOU GO OUT INTO THE WORLD TO TELL THEM, DAVID, I AM NOT TOTALITAR-IAN!" Luther's voice carries above the talk of fifty secretaries, the clatter of their typewriters, and the conversations of over one hundred JFI fund raisers. My hand is on the doorknob. "DAVID! DO YOU HEAR ME!"

I walk slowly back to our desks.

"Tell who, Luther?"

"TOTALITARIAN! TOTALITARIAN! YOU SAID I WAS TOTALITARIAN!"

"I didn't mean you —"

"IN YOUR QUIET WAY, DAVID, YOU REALLY TWIST THE KNIFE."

I try to mollify Luther. I reassure him that I will not talk to anyone about our conversation.

XI

That afternoon, Luther says that he has had a long-standing argument with his wife. She has opened an antique store in Westchester and has wanted Luther to work there on weekends. Thinking of his heart condition, I say,

"When would you rest?"

"During the week at the office, according to her."

He says that immediately after his third heart attack, he continued to work in the garden he loved. He felt like collapsing. His wife and four daughters told him not to do the gardening, but they left it for him.

"They didn't know how I felt . . . it was overwhelming . . . the pain . . . sometimes I thought I would collapse in the compost heap . . . that I would die there . . . but I never told my wife. I was afraid to lose her love . . . her support would continue, but it wouldn't be the same . . . and I gradually got better. I suppose I remember as a boy my father breaking his back in the machine shop with a heart condition. I know how I felt toward him . . . and toward my mother, who was sick too. I hated their illness. It was a drag, going on and on. And I thought my wife would feel that way toward me."

Luther stays late tonight. He talks about his correspondence with Buddies of the Earth recommending Molly Bethune's book to

them, we talk about an article concerning an artist who shoots
bullets as his art form (Luther asks my opinion of that), and then
he suddenly says, straining forward, "You see, my wife left me last
night."

Part Two

I

"Hare Krishna, Hare Krishna, Hare Rama, Hare Rama, Hare
Krishna, Hare Hare, Hare Rama, Hare Krishna."

Luther is chanting behind me. In the last weeks since his wife's
departure, he has moved more closely toward mysticism and Eastern religion. Luther chants the words from a file card he holds
before him. The book on his empty desk is the *I Ching*.

Before going home this evening, Luther is in an animated mood.
He gives me and Bea an example of ESP. He shows us his raincoat
with a button missing.

"I was walking along at lunch thinking I needed a button . . .
then suddenly . . . there on the ground . . ." Luther scoops out a
blue button from his pocket and places it against the brown buttons
on his raincoat, and says, "Exactly!"

We look at the button. "But it's a different color," we both say.

"It certainly isn't," Luther says, hurt. "It's as close as you could
come to finding an exact duplicate —"

"But —" Bea and I say.

"And it's the same size!"

Luther says angrily, "You hard-nosed rationalists!" Stalking out,
he calls out his last words to us: "You people don't know how much
a button costs nowadays . . ."

Luther has been dating the woman who has the Buddhist group
at her house. She wants Luther to join her circle. She is looking for
recruits.

She calls him at the office and asks him how his Buddhism is
coming. "You're the master," he tells her over the phone. "There's
so much for me to learn — technique, background, rhythm."

He tells me he has had a conversation with her the night before
in which he said, "I want to see you and you to see me as more
than a member of this group." She replied to him, "I thought you
thought that."

She went on to tell Luther that her sex life during the last year with two black men "has been more completely satisfying than ever before."

"She attributes this to the benefits of chanting," Luther comments, "but I don't know — I think she's trying to tell me something."

He says the song that keeps running through his mind is Ray Charles singing "I Can't Stop Loving You."

He reminisces with me about his boyhood, his father, his years in Hollywood, and his wife.

Luther takes out a roll of quarters. "Like my father," he says. "I like to have a lot of change in my pocket, for the sound of having money." He jingles the quarters, and smiles.

"One time, just one time, my father told me about sex. He was standing by the window, and he said 'Come here. Look down there.' I looked down — one flight. We lived one flight above the street. 'You see him?' my father asked me. I saw a kid from the neighborhood: sagging mouth, popping eyes, a lopsided walk. My father said, 'That's what comes from self-abuse. That's all I want to say.' And my father walked away.

"My father wasn't a violent man. One time I played hooky from school. I remember coming home and an aunt was waiting for me on the corner. She was a mean one; she told me I was going to get it when my father got home. My mother said the same thing. So it built up, and when my father arrived, he saw what was going on. He looked grim. For the first time I saw him reach to his belt and slowly take it off, fingering it. Then he waved me into the next room. When we were alone, he said, 'I have a story to tell you. There was a rowboat out on the sea in a storm. You don't throw away the oars when you're out there.' Then my father hit the bed with his belt three times so they would hear." Luther laughed gently.

"My father invented words without knowing it. Like in his candy store. He'd say 'I have to relemplish my stock.' Or, if I came home late, he'd ask, 'Where have you been pulverooting all night?' "

II

"I was always a questioner. Even as a young man I made waves. I always had to know how things worked, and why. And I was always getting myself into trouble — I was full of piss and vinegar. I worked in Hollywood for a while, at Paramount. There were two categories: extras and wavers. All the wavers were allowed to do in a scene was wave. I was a waver. The extras belonged to a union, they got paid more and didn't even fraternize with the wavers. They shunned us.

"As a truth seeker even then, I got into hot water. The director was giving instructions, see, and he's telling us we should react to a home run in the baseball game with enthusiasm: the extras should cheer, and the wavers should wave. It didn't make sense to me as I understood the script up to that point. I didn't understand what he was getting at. Then he said were there any questions. No one had ever asked questions — it was just a formality. I raised my hand and said, 'Yes. I have a question. Isn't it true that in this scene if we applaud this play —'

"I heard murmurs, and then boos and hisses from the extras. There were catcalls. I heard them calling out, *'What gaff! And he's only a waver!'* "

III

On the lunch hour, Stephen says to me, "When his wife walked out on Luther, I wasn't at all surprised. You may not know this, David, but Luther hasn't slept with his wife in five years. He moved out of their bedroom into his own room after his last heart attack. I asked him if he thought the lack of a sexual relationship had affected their marriage. Luther said he had thought of this and he had asked his wife. He said she said no. I also asked him if his daughters and friends were surprised at his wife's leaving. He said no, no one was surprised except himself."

IV

Luther tells me that since his wife has left him he has a funny feeling of weakness in his chest. "I've tried to remember what it was," he says, "and now I do. When I was a boy, looking for a job, out on my own, leaving my mother, I had that feeling."

I asked Luther if the separation isn't a challenge to live a freer life. "No," he replies. "I'm not a WASP . . . I don't want to prove myself . . ."

V

Luther has begun to collect green bottles. He has a shelf of them in his bedroom window. In the morning when he wakes, the bare branches of the trees and the copper of the sun are reflected through them.

VI

Mornings are Luther's best times. He comes in, announcing that his "evacuation and digestion" are both excellent. He shows me the copper bracelet he wears to cure his arthritis. "The body needs certain minerals," he explains.

On his walk from the garage to the office he frequently sees people who interest him. "I don't want to come into work. I see people I just like, something about their looks and their gait . . . I want to spend the day with them . . . a feeling of freedom. But you can't hold on to it . . . by the afternoon you're back in your suit . . .

"I saw a girl . . . very pretty . . . lollygagging down the street . . . I wanted to talk to her. But I had the wrong uniform on. She was wearing jeans. She would have turned off the minute she saw me . . .

"I hear a guy behind me as I'm walking say, 'I'm getting tired of looking like everybody else.' I turn and I see a guy with a beard, unshaved hair all over his face, torn jeans and sneakers, and he's seated in a hallway talking to three other guys who are dressed exactly the same way." Luther laughs and shakes his head.

VII

He is waiting to see if his wife is serious about the separation. She is living in a single room in the home of friends near her store.

"I've been leaving hard-boiled eggs in the refrigerator. I had one left over, and so in order to know it was the oldest, I drew a cartoon on it. Then, knowing my wife comes by while I'm gone during the day, I drew a little balloon on it with the words, 'Hello, Nosey.' A week went by. I checked the eggs every day and nothing had happened. Then, last night, there it was. She had written — not on the same egg but on another — 'Very funny.' Which is her way of saying something to me. She doesn't take a joke well. But it was okay — it was her way of talking the same language."

VIII

Being single again, he has to learn to cook. He puts two saccharine tablets in his soup by mistake.

Jill explains to him: "If you have three apples and four men, you make applesauce . . ."

"There's a lot more freewheeling in this cooking business than I thought," Luther comments. "I thought it was scientific."

He gets information from all the secretaries about cooking, on the difference between a roaster, broiler, and pullet. He has a 2½-pound roast beef and wants to know at what heat he should cook it and for how long.

IX

Things are disappearing from Luther's house. His wife is removing them. He finds the bone-china cups and saucers that were wedding presents gone. He can't bring himself to object to his wife.

One day the reading lamp over his bed is missing.

He gets up in the morning and goes into the hallway to knot his tie before the mirror. The mirror is gone.

X

His wife notices the effect of the sun on the stained-glass lamp in the living room. She is visiting him one evening. She praises the effect. Luther is pleased, as he has placed it there. But then his wife says, "I think I'll take that with me."

Luther's house is burgled. He returns home to find the TV set gone. The hi-fi is neatly stacked on the floor, unplugged, ready to go. He must have interrupted the burglars. Now he is afraid they will come back when he is gone, since there is no one at the house.

XI

Being alone, Luther now rises at six A.M. and listens to a radio program every morning in which blind people talk about their lives.

The word gets around that Luther is single again.

Ann Stark, a woman in the office, is about sixty. She has a beaked nose, a homely face, a dowdy figure, and she carries two shopping bags.

She approaches Luther, and stops several feet from his desk. From that distance she says "I love you," and walks quickly away.

She does the same thing the next morning.

When she meets Luther at the door, or by the elevator, she whispers, "I love you."

"My speed," Luther comments.

He goes to a singles night at the insistence of a friend. "Not being a gay blade, I was reluctant. But I went. There was a fat woman at the door and a sign that said Admission, $3.50. She asked my name and wrote it down, and, unsmiling, slapped a sticker on my shoulder with my name on it, and pointed the way. I walked into this cold, dank stone church cellar. There I was. People were standing around. I did see one attractive woman and thought to myself, this is wrong of me, chauvinistic. I'm thinking only of her physical appearance, not her mind. I stood around. No one approached me. They had coffee and doughnuts. I decided I would sit down in a corner and let them come to me. No one did. Although I noticed the attractive one's eyes moved toward me a dozen times, or at least I thought so.

"I've often wondered why attractive people so studiously avoid other attractive people. On a train, if I see a pretty woman, and there's an empty seat beside her, I'll never sit there. And if a pretty woman walks into the train, and I'm sitting alone, she'll never sit down beside me . . . Anyway, I'm sitting alone and a woman wearing a black beret comes through the door. She looks like Nancy Walker, worse, and, just as I thought, she made a beeline right for me. Why do these types always find me? She said she found these singles nights 'valuable, very valuable experiences' " — Luther laughed — "talked away like that with complete ease and assurance. Then they got us together in groups, and the leader says, 'I'm not your leader. Don't look upon me as a leader. I'm just here to get things moving. This is not group therapy. This is not psychoanalysis. This is just a rap session . . .' Then he said the topic was: Would I marry myself? And he went around the circle asking. They all said yes. I said no, I wouldn't. After I said no, some of the others also said no. So there we were, paying $3.50 to talk to other people.

"I feel . . . it's like being back where you started, when I was a young man. I know why I married my wife: she fed me, clothed me, took care of me . . . she was my blanket against the world."

XII

Luther looks thinner and more haggard. One morning he tells me that his wife has returned from a trip to Michigan. When he saw her, he proposed that they get together again. "She said no, she couldn't . . . that I was overpowering. She said that she was afraid of me."

XIII

The town in which Luther lives has a large Chassidic Jewish community. "When I walk into town I see all these arcane Jewish types . . . with their black hats and suits and long black beards . . . there's not much possibility of finding a friend."

XIV

Luther fingers the things on his desk — a dried meat bone, a Buddha made from crushed concrete — and says, "There was an old man who used to visit our family when I was a kid. His name was Harry Bard. He was a distant relative. He came by for handouts: old clothes, food, whatever my mother gave him. He had an apologetic, smiling, impotent air. I felt sorry for him." Luther paused. "Now I feel like that old man — Harry Bard."

XV

In a few days, he says, "Something happened last night that tells me it's *fini* with my wife . . . my youngest daughter had called and asked if anything was new. I said no, and hung up. I looked around, and there was . . . I collect bottles. Green ones, turquoise, I put them in little displays . . . and I have begun to collect blue ones. I had put a little collection of blue bottles in my bedroom; including a blue vase, a small one that my wife liked. It had been in her bedroom, and I took it and put it in mine with the others. It had an association, this vase, for us, a memory of an evening, nothing sentimental, nevertheless it meant something. I know it did, because she never sold it, although she sold many things from the house in her shop. The house is piled with junk, and she would just take something and sell it. But not this. But apparently yesterday, during the day when I wasn't home, she came in and took it.

"It means either of two things, and they both mean the end. One, that she just wanted to take it to the shop and sell it for materialistic reasons, even though she saw that I had placed it in my collection. The fact that she didn't feel anything about it, or consider my feelings in the matter. Or, two, that the vase does have meaning to her. She's fond of it, and wants to have it beside her. In which case she's really decided it's over between us, and wants to have things near her that she likes. That she's really moving out for good."

XVI

Peter Black sits talking to me at my desk. He is considered a JFI eccentric — a man in his late sixties with frightened eyes and a scatterbrained way of talking. Luther often gives him a long blank stare and begins reading the newspaper when Peter is talking to him. Peter laughs a lot and boasts that he has never been sick a day in his life. He was a poet in Russia; he knew Mayakovsky and Andreyev and Gorky; he takes out of his pockets crumbling yellowed pages of pamphlets published fifty years ago, of Russian poetry and short stories. "The Jews are an enigma!" he says one day, his fingers pointing at me. Pleased with the phrase, he repeats it: "an enigma, yes, what they have accomplished"; his eyes have lit to the phrase, and he walks away, his shuffling walk, mumbling and smiling to himself. He likes our department best of all; he lights on us and says, his eyes twinkling, "I sense a creative force here. Yes, a creative power. Am I right?"

One afternoon we are chatting and I say, "Do you have any brothers and sisters?"

"Yes," Peter answers, "I had a brother — a doctor. He's gone. He was in Buchenwald; they burned him at Auschwitz." I see the tears falling from his eyes; he shakes them away. He chokes on the words. "Excuse me. I am not crying"; and he hurries away.

In a few minutes I look for him, but he is not at his desk. My phone rings. It is Peter. "Someone came over to me and asked me why I was crying. They saw me at your desk, and they said I was crying. It's ridiculous. I wasn't crying —"

"But you shouldn't be ashamed —"

"I'm sorry. I shouldn't talk about these things. I don't know what came over me. But I wasn't crying. I explained that to this person, so it's all right now."

XVII

Now that Luther's wife seems to have walked out permanently, there are no major changes in Luther's daily routine.

He spends the evening watching TV, "talking back to the box" when he gets angry at what he is watching. His daughters do not call him. He says about children, "My experience has always been that kids are cannibals and killers." When a child comes into the office, Stephen's face brightens and he goes over to it. Luther calls out sarcastically across the office, "Pet her, Stephen. Go ahead and pet the little killer." He recalls saying good-bye to his uncle and getting caught on a train when it lurched away — "with three stinking kids waiting in the car for me knowing nothing."

He grows reflective about his life, thinking back to when he was single and running a pottery shop in Santa Monica with his uncle. It was his wife who insisted that they move back East.

"I was a good Jewish husband. I only did things she liked. I never went hiking because my wife Lil didn't like it. I was wrong . . . it demolishes you.

"Judy, my youngest daughter, leaves the curtains wide open at night. She likes to be shocked awake by the dawn. The way I was raised, you lower the curtains. When you piss, you piss on the rim. You don't hit the water and make noise.

"We make the small decisions, David. The big decisions are made for us. We drift in a half-lotus position, in complete unawareness. I used to have this little imp telling me how to think, how to dress, how to behave properly. He's still talking to me all the time. Now I tell the little imp to just fuck off."

XVIII

"I know I'm not supposed to say this around here, but it's the Jews who have destroyed this country."

"The Jews?"

"Hear me out. I was . . . slightly gifted as a young man. I published some poems." Luther swallows a handful of raisins and offers the box to me.

"The Jews, with their brazen arrogance, ran Hollywood. Harry Cohn, Louis B. Mayer. Every week I went to the movies and they filled us with all those romantic notions, those impossible illusions of heroism and success. They didn't prepare us for life — they left us completely unprepared to cope with life as it really is. I blame the Jews, for they destroyed my creativity. And don't think I'm the only one, David. The Jews around here don't admit these things."

XIX

Luther was agitated all day yesterday, bristling at all of us. I learn why. He asked his wife to buy a kosher chicken for him. She did, and cooked it for him. He invited her over to eat it with him. They ate the chicken together. Afterwards, Luther turned on the television set and settled down to watch all his favorite Channel 13 programs. About ten o'clock his wife said she thought she might as well leave.

Luther mulls this over today. "I realize now she must have expected that we would talk . . . about something important."

XX

Luther is haunted by his conviction that he should have been a writer.

"But you published poems when you were in your twenties. What happened then?"

Luther thinks a moment.

"My wife was . . . counterproductive. She loved everything I wrote. Then I saw that when she had the babies, she gave them just as effusive attention as she did my writing . . ." He shakes his head.

The last time he took a creative-writing class, his teacher had encouraged him. This meant a great deal to him, and he had begun writing seriously. Then he had his fourth heart attack and stopped writing.

Now Luther is taking a new writing class at the local library. He is trying to regain what he feels he has lost.

"A woman read a sex poem about her husband's cock, using the

metaphor of a whale. Jesus Christ. Then a girl read some poems.
A businessman, a member of the class, called out after she read:
'Terrific! *Terrific!* I wish more people could hear that! Let's hire a
bigger hall!' "

XXI

Luther hands me a poem he has written for the class:

> *Fear has shells*
> *People wear them*
> *willy-nilly*
> *   like shirts and ties*
> *and wide lapels . . .*

In the poem he says that his wife's desertion has made him feel
like "discarded junk."

XXII

Luther is the chief fire warden of our floor. There is a fire drill on
Thursday, and Stephen, who is at home ill, does not attend. "Don't
forget to mark Stephen absent," he tells Bea.

"But he's sick, Luther," she says.

"You're argumentative! Mark him down. Come on, Bea! I also
have a memo for you on fire exits. The situation is egregious."

After twenty-three years, Stephen and Luther have a complicated relationship. Stephen's father was a renowned Hebrew
scholar, whose only shortcoming was his inability to criticize people.

Stephen likes everything Jewish; also Tony Bennett, Ray
Charles, Iris Murdoch, Howard Cosell, Anita O'Day, Ruby Dee,
Frederick Manfred, Judy Collins, Margaret Drabble, Anaïs Nin,
James Hanley, Helen Humes, Laurie Lee, Erica Jong, V. S. Pritch-
ett, Jane Fonda, and John Jacob Niles. He is a compulsive talker
and a careful listener. If he does not read an entire book every
day, he feels he is losing ground. He is interested in butterflies,
ants, and cats. He loves London; Edinburgh; Jerusalem; food; box-
ing; photography; baseball; literature above all. The author of
twenty books, he understands Luther well. He does not agree with

his wife Susan, who says, "There's a summer fool and a winter fool. The summer fool doesn't dress up and hide what he is. With the winter fool it takes longer to get past the beard, the mustache . . . Luther is a winter fool."

He brings little treats for Luther every day: an article, a book of interest to Luther. He worries about him, and it pains him to see Luther retreat more and more into his mysticism books. While Luther is quick to say to me, "Stephen has a hell of a lot more blemishes and hangups than you know," Stephen is always looking for Luther's good points. "Luther tells a story well, he's intelligent . . ." He pauses and thinks.

At points of tension, Luther says to Stephen, "Hold me up. I'm crumbling." Luther comes in to work an hour after Stephen and leaves work an hour before Stephen does. While he is in the office, he does a fraction of what Stephen does.

Stephen reads every newspaper, every literary magazine, most popular magazines — he bounces around Brentano's every lunch hour. Stephen is highly regarded for his scholarship and good nature at JFI. But by carving out a creative life of his own, working nights and weekends, he has paid a terrible price. In his mid-fifties, he is deathly sick. Even to walk in the New York air — he who loves life beyond anyone I have ever known — leaves him gasping for breath.

Stephen and Luther both read the *Times* in the morning. Stephen reads it at breakfast, and Luther reads it during work. Stephen calls out over the glass to Luther what the front page of the *Times* says. Although he already knows, Luther welcomes the chance to air his views.

Stephen gets to the obituary page ahead of Luther and sometimes calls out the important names.

"Don't be a killjoy, Stephen," says Luther.

Luther and I both look up from what we are doing. Stephen is talking to a woman fund raiser. He is jabbing at the pages of the *Times* with a finger, turning them rapidly and shouting, "He's Jewish! He's Jewish! He's Jewish! She's Jewish! She's Jewish! He's Jewish! He's Jewish! She's Jewish! He's Jewish!"

The woman is nodding her head.

Luther tries to find holes in Stephen's relationship to his wife. Susan is considerably taller and much stouter than Stephen; Luther calls her "The Cossack."

"She smokes cigars. You should hear Stephen. He doesn't realize how revealing his comments are. When she bites the tip of the cigar and spits it out, Stephen says, 'She has teeth like an elephant!' When her foot was hurt and she laid it across a chair, Stephen said, 'Her foot is like a rhino!'

"The guy is terrified of his wife," Luther says, smiling. "You know, David, I have a gimlet perception of these things. It's fascinating to watch the mechanism that's at work. People simply don't recognize themselves. It's a biochemical process."

Luther sits in Stephen's cubicle talking to him. Through the glass he had heard Stephen summarize an article by Daniel Patrick Moynihan. "JUSTIFY THAT FOR ME, STEPHEN!" he had shouted across the glass, jumping up and running into the cubicle. "YOU'RE NOT GOING TO GET AWAY WITH THAT FLIM-FLAM WITH ME."

Luther sits on the edge of his chair, his thin, taut body squinched up, his sneakers clenched, questioning Stephen in a fury. "Moynihan is a fool! They stopped Kennedy — why can't they stop him?"

Stephen patiently explains, and summarizes the article.

"YOU'RE WAFFLING —"

Luther has bought a six-pound pillow. It arrives in the office and he shows it to all of us.

Stephen looks at it and says, "I have a twelve-pound pillow — as big as him." He points at the tallest and heftiest man in the office.

Luther zips across the office, shouting at people at random, furiously: "Do you believe him? Do you believe that? He always has to top me! If I've read one book, he's read ten!"

Stephen, with his patience and understanding, usually wins. But there is one area where Luther has the upper hand.

Stephen has a penchant for reason, calm, and order. He is put off by scatological talk, raunchy sex, deviant behavior.

Luther begins, "Did you see the film *The Last Detail,* Stephen?"

"I saw it. I have no interest in that —"

Luther pounces. This is his best moment. "Are you paying attention, David? What do you mean, Stephen, *it doesn't interest you?*"

"Sailor talk, salty language, brothels — it doesn't interest me."

"Just because it doesn't happen to interest *you* — does that mean it's not good?"

"Of course not. I'm just saying there are many other things that interest me more —"

"We don't *care* if it interests you or not, friend; it interests other people. Did it ever occur to you that what you are really saying is that it *threatens* you?"

"Possibly; I think not —"

"BUT HOW CAN YOU SAY IT DOESN'T INTEREST YOU? It's a fact, a reality." Luther's eyes keep darting to me for approval. "You're a college man, David. I hope you're listening to this."

XXIII

On New Year's Eve, Luther prepares to go home alone.

"Ever thine . . . forever thine . . . that keeps running through my mind . . . where do I remember that from?" Luther muses. "Oh yes. This winter day reminded me . . . a picture on the piano of herself that my mother inscribed to my father . . . it was in winter she gave it to him . . . 'Ever thine . . .' We laughed at the Victorian sentimentality."

He talks at random. He recalls being eighteen and a friendship with another fellow. On New Year's Eve they would go from table to table, talking to people. "What courage I had then!"

He says to me, "You haven't hit this season yet . . . I look at the books on my shelves and it makes me sick. I should throw them out. I built the library for my family . . . but they don't read. Not one of them is a natural reader. My first greatest pleasure was to read . . . I should unload. How can I take off to Pago Pago if I feel like it?"

Luther tucks his scarf in his coat, and takes his umbrella. At my desk, on his way out, he suddenly begins reciting:

> *When I was one-and-twenty*
> *I heard a wise man say,*
> *"Give crowns and pounds and guineas*
> *But not your heart away;*
>
> *Give pearls away and rubies*
> *But keep your fancy free."*
> *But I was one-and-twenty,*
> *No use to talk to me . . .*

He trails off and does not finish. "Good night, David," he says. "Have a happy."

Part Three

I

Ben Knapp, a fund raiser, dies suddenly at the bottom of the stairs of the subway station at Times Square. "Imagine, dainty Ben — so clean and proper, to go like that!" Luther comments.

Pressure at the office is building. It is a busy month. Stephen is running back and forth. By noon his face is chalk white; then it turns beet red. He is gasping for breath. "He is going to have another heart attack," I tell my wife.

Luther is more crotchety every day. The three of us visit a bookstore. All the books are marked one dollar. Luther, on the watch for a bargain, finds a dirty copy that is not marked. He takes the book to the clerk. "How much is that?" The clerk looks it over and says, "It's not marked, but all the books are one dollar."

"That's not what I'm asking you!" Luther shouts. "How much is this book?"

There is a Chinese fellow in line behind him. He tries to explain to Luther that all the books are the same price. Luther turns and shouts at him: "I'm not talking to you!"

Standing in line at the bank, Luther's eye is caught by the sight of a pretty girl. As he waits for his money, he follows the girl with his eyes. As he leaves the bank, he sees that the clerk, "a young fibbity-gibbett," has given him $100 less than his check. Luther complains to the head of the bank. At the end of the day the loss is verified, and he receives his money.

He has written Molly Bethune several times, and after a long silence he receives a letter from her. Shattered, Luther hands me the letter. Addressing Luther as "Sweet Sir," she says that she cannot write him anymore: "I can only answer the first-time people . . . Here's a weird deal: you can write me — and I promise to read your letters — and more than once . . ."

He asks me what I think of the letter. I hem and haw — he interrupts me to say, "Let's be frank. I just didn't have enough to engage her . . . I didn't have enough brain for her to pick . . ."

Luther's oldest daughter visits him at the office for the first time in months. All of his daughters live in Manhattan, but he rarely sees them. "How are your sisters?" he asks her.

It is almost time for Stephen's vacation. I hope he will make it.

Suddenly his mother-in-law dies. The person who takes it the hardest is Stephen's millionaire brother-in-law, Harry.

Harry weeps and talks on the phone to Stephen for hours. The tears run down Stephen's cheeks. Stephen, who was heartsick for years after the death of his own father, identifies with Harry's feelings about the loss of his mother. Stephen's wife Susan tries to remain strong for Stephen's sake, but Harry is inconsolable. He calls Stephen at the office during the day; he comes over to Stephen's house at midnight and weeps. Harry needs a minyan (ten people) for the nightly service of prayer at the synagogue in memory of his mother. When the minyan lacks one, he calls Stephen to drop everything and come across town to the synagogue. Stephen comes.

"Listen," Luther says, "the man allows himself to be taken advantage of. That's the way he is."

"He's sympathetic —" I begin.

"He's a marshmallow," says Luther.

Two weeks pass. Stephen's vacation finally arrives. Stephen is happy on the last day of work; just before he leaves he sings a song that he has heard sung by John Jacob Niles — "Matty Groves," an Elizabethan folk song. I ask him about it, and he tells me all the lyrics, their derivation, and the history of the record.

He begins to sing it again as he scoots out the door.

II

Stephen has a heart attack that night.

We wait for the news. Within two days we know that Stephen will survive. Luther calls him and wants to know when he will be back at the office, whether he will be out longer than the two-week vacation. He does not receive a firm answer to his question. Luther keeps asking Stephen to speak louder over the phone.

Within a week I visit Stephen on a Sunday at the hospital. He is plugged into several machines; a jumping light records his heartbeats. A tube is stuck up his nose and held to his cheeks with adhesive tape.

Stephen is propped up, trying to make me feel at ease, trying to do all the talking and to comfort me, but his voice is a whisper. He has already read Sunday's *Times Book Review* section ahead of me. He summarizes Irving Howe's review of a new book by Lucy

Davidowicz, *The War Against the Jews 1933–1945,* giving me the high points of the review. Then he analyzes Howe's opinions.

Stephen's son, David Ben-Gurion Greenberg, comes in. Five years younger than I, David Ben-Gurion is a playwright. He is dressed in a dungaree outfit. His hair and beard are in meticulous disarray. David Ben-Gurion is as guarded as Stephen is open, and maybe, I think, he has good reason to be. Stephen's face glows at the sight of his son; it says, this is everything in the world I need.

Stephen says in a whisper, gently, "You look like a hobo."

David Ben-Gurion winces. "Why are you giving me grief about my appearance?"

"What?" Stephen says, amazed.

David Ben-Gurion squirms at having to repeat it, but he does.

Stephen's wife, who has been hovering over him, walks us out. "He worries about Luther — that Luther's whole life is his job, and that without Stephen, Luther would have to retire — he worries about you, David, but you have a life outside JFI — he worries about Bea and Jill —"

I tell her yes, he must quit, the job is killing him. I see him, and I know. I tell Luther the next morning that I have seen Stephen. I say, "He was reading —"

"Never mind all that. All I want to know is when he'll be back at his desk."

III

The secretaries want to collect money for a gift for Stephen. Luther forbids them.

"Forbids?" I say to Bea. "How can he forbid you?"

"Luther says that it's too early to get a gift, and he won't allow it. He really just doesn't want to have to give a dollar —"

"Well, I insist that you do collect for Stephen."

The collection goes on. Luther is on the defensive. "It so happens that the last time Stephen was in the hospital, I asked him if he wanted a present. He said no."

Luther watches ruefully as the money is collected.

Abe Stern, a staff member, comes over to us and expresses shock at Stephen's illness. After he leaves, Luther comments, "He's shocked? What do I care if he's shocked? These immature fifty-year-olds looking for self-congratulation!"

IV

It is uncertain when, and if, Stephen will be able to return to work. After four weeks Luther is climbing the wall, and so am I. He has to come in early in the morning and leave late. He has to report to the director and do most of Stephen's chores. He is very tense, and snaps at all of us. Without Stephen's blanket of good will that kept things smooth, I find myself more and more impatient with Luther's irascibility. If my eyes turn while he is talking, he shouts, "DAVID! DAVID! YOU'RE NOT LOOKING AT ME!" He is visibly hurt that I do not watch the TV programs he is so fond of — Stephen always made the effort of watching them so that Luther could discuss them with him. He begins to talk about a program, then checks himself and trails off, muttering, "Oh, you don't watch TV . . ."

I do not accept Luther's games the way Stephen does.

Luther says that he saw a TV show about cripples.

"How was it?" I ask.

"How was what?" Luther snaps with a straight face. "What are you talking about?"

Later, trying to keep things going for his sake, I make a comment. "Some people feel squeamish about those programs."

"Who does? The people on the program? You, David? People watching the program? Get to the point!"

I finally burst out: "Who do you think, Luther? You know damn well who I'm talking about."

Luther retreats, but he is boiling. The secretaries watch and listen.

V

Each day gets worse. Near the end of one afternoon, I see Luther sitting at Stephen's desk wearing a black skull cap. His head and shoulders are swaying and ducking forward in a parody of Jewish orthodox prayer — "dovenning." He has a crowd around him laughing. "Maybe this way I'll get a little respect!" he shouts.

VI

Murray Farber has popping frightened eyes, a freckled face, a look of perpetual pain. He is one of us — a former member of our staff — now working for the national office of JFI on the floor above us. Ever since I came to JFI, we go through the same routine every week.

He comes over to me and says: "You know Hy Bookspan?"

"Yes —"

"What a hostile guy! His wife too. Such hostile vibrations. Ah, the hell with him."

"He never seemed that way to —"

"I don't know the man!" shouts Murray, throwing up his hands, stuttering, waving me off, backing up, shaking his head in denial. "I don't know him at all." Then he puts his hands in his pockets, approaches me again, and asks,

"You know Esther Kravitz?"

"A little."

"Such a name-dropper. No sense of style, class, intelligence — no d-d-dignity. Ah, the hell with her."

"Really? I thought —"

"I don't know her!" shouts Murray. "I saw her in a crowd! Yeah, I don't know her at all!"

He is filled with disgust with his present job and associates. He has said to me of Luther: "Poor guy. And so pretentious." Murray is a veteran of the radical movement and Jewish causes. He is also a former newspaperman, writer, and radio commentator for the Yiddish station, WEVD. "Sure, I reviewed books and did interviews on WEVD. So did Melvin, and other people around here. So what? It all adds up to nothing."

When we are walking on the street, Murray suddenly stops me, grabs my arm, and shouts, his finger pointing, "There goes Abie the Ape! There he goes. Look over there, David." Later he tells me that Abie is an old anarchist, and that he hadn't seen him in fifteen years. "Ah, what's the point . . ." he trails off.

VII

The news comes to us on one of the yellow pieces of paper that daily announce deaths of JFI staff members and their families.

Murray Farber's father has died. The funeral is scheduled for that day.

"I'm not going," Luther announces. "We do these things — these so-called good deeds — just to make others think well of us and to make ourselves feel good. Therefore they aren't really worth doing. Especially in Murray's case, since his opinion of me wouldn't change anyway. I know he doesn't like me."

As the day goes on, only I and one other person on the staff, a secretary, plan to go to the funeral. Usually a dozen or more people will go. But Murray doesn't carry clout at JFI.

The tension between Luther and myself keeps building. I write a press release that doesn't follow our usual format. I don't use any of Luther's phrases, which invariably describe our guests of honor as "pillars of strength," "towers of light," "true champions of Israel," and "sources of inspiration to many." Luther grabs my release off the desk and screams, "You could get fired for a release like this! The date and address must be in the first line! I never saw anything like this in my life!"

"Luther, there's no need to get upset —"

"YOU MAKE ME FEEL FREAKISH! . . . WHEN *I'M* THE ONE WHO'S BEEN FIGHTING FOR INDIVIDUALITY ALL MY LIFE . . ."

Later he says, "There are certain things we must do, certain patterns we must follow . . . this is not a creative-writing class, David."

Luther hears Bea talking about the restaurant on the corner changing ownership and asks: "Who runs it now?"

"The waitress is the same," Bea answers.

"That has nothing to do with the ethnic cuisine!" Luther shouts.

I feel myself bristling. Luther is talking about the national JFI convention that is coming up.

"Where is it being held?" I ask, knowing as I say it I have made a mistake.

"YOU DON'T KNOW? YOU'VE BEEN HERE ALL THIS TIME AND YOU DON'T KNOW?"

"Miami?" I say, but it's too late.

"I MEAN DO YOU KNOW THAT YOU'RE WORKING HERE DAVID? I THINK IT'S ABOUT TIME THAT YOU WOKE UP TO YOUR RESPONSIBILITIES. I KNOW YOU DON'T LIKE TO HEAR THESE THINGS, DAVID, THEY IRRITATE YOU, BUT YOU'RE A MEMBER OF A TEAM. YOU MAY NOT LIKE

IT, AND I MAY NOT LIKE IT, BUT THAT'S WHAT WE'RE
BEING PAID FOR, THAT'S WHAT IT'S ALL ABOUT —"

"And I think, Luther, that you are a pain in the ass."

There is silence. The secretaries have stopped their work. Luther nods his head, "Okay." He does not look at me for the rest of
the day.

VIII

"All right, I'll go to the funeral," Luther announces.

Three of us sit in the car with Luther. We travel through the
Bronx, through Luther's old neighborhood. He sees landmarks he
remembers — as well as a place he doesn't recall named Glick
House. "Must have been named for me," he jokes.

We do not talk to each other.

Four funerals are being held in four chapels at the funeral home.
The smoothie at the door makes sure we go into the right room.

There is Murray, and, near him, his wife. He says to me, "Who
was it — which playwright — who said 'I lived my whole life in fear
of death, but when it came, I wasn't prepared for it'?"

The rabbi greets Luther and asks him only one question — if
Luther had known Ben Elias. Elias, a well-known figure at JFI, had
committed suicide fifteen years before. He had been discovered
stealing over $100,000 in JFI funds.

Before Luther can answer, the rabbi holds up his hands. "Don't
tell me anything. I liked the man."

I sit beside Murray's wife, who is much taller and more solid-
looking than Murray. She carries a little white paper bag. As the
service is announced, she opens the paper bag and takes out little
rocks and stones — "from the Jordan, the old city of Jerusalem."
They are for Murray's father.

IX

When we are back in the office, Luther continues to avert his eyes
from me.

Just before he leaves, he says to Jill and Bea, not to me:

"My father was in the oxygen tent in the hospital. One night I
said, 'So long, Pop — see you in the morning.'

"My father waved by moving the fingers of his hand.

"I just got in the car and drove home.

"When I got home, my mother said, 'It's over.'"

X

The next day Luther does not look at me. When I come near the office, he tries to go the other way.

By the end of the day, I take a chair and sit down next to his desk.

"Look Luther, what I said — I meant it — for the moment. I felt you were being a pain in the ass. But I wouldn't want you to think I felt that way about you — about our relationship, the things we've talked about. I wanted you to know I didn't mean that."

He shakes his head. "I didn't think you were that kind of a guy."

Our eyes meet.

XI

Things have returned to normal.

Stephen is back at work. He now walks with a cane.

Luther is relieved. Before Stephen returned, he was thinking about what he would do if Stephen could not come back.

He told me of the mysterious ways the bums in Bryant Park were attracted to him, and of his fear that he would wind up like them. He frequently described his encounters with them.

On his lunch hour a big black man came up to him, bouncing a grapefruit in his hand. "Mister," he said to Luther, "this is all I got in the world; could you help me out?" Luther reached into his own pocket and said: "Here." Luther took out an orange and bounced it in his hand. "This is all I got in the world," said Luther. "Could you help me out?" The black man laughed, patted Luther on the back, said "Touché," and walked away.

Another day a black man on a bench with a liquor bottle in a paper bag called out to Luther. Luther went over to him. "May I make so bold . . . you have a face that tells me you're someone with a deep understanding." The man talked to Luther about the white man's arrogance and the submergence of the black man. Luther agreed completely with him and gave him a lecture of his own, saying, "You've stopped a talker, you realize . . ." When Luther finished, the black man, pointing to his bottle, said, "I hope you'll forgive this liquid refreshment . . ." Luther took a little paper bag out of his dungaree bag, took his liquor miniature out of it, tilted it back and said: "I hope you'll forgive mine . . ."

Luther commented about the black man's choosing him to talk-with: "I can understand it. I myself wouldn't stop to talk with one of those dressed-up, flashy guys with their business talk, their clever phrases, their rush to nowhere."

Luther continues to be puzzled by me and tries to figure me out. He tends to idolize all "creative people."

"How do you feel about Jane Fonda?" he asks.

High on boredom and liquor at this job, I reply, "I'd like to slit her throat."

He looks at me. "I thought artists were kind, gentle souls. I thought they had an "Is-ness,' a joie de vivre."

"They're not, Luther. I keep telling you."

"Yes, I see that," he says solemnly, shaking his head.

Now that Stephen is here, Luther settles back. "Really," he says, "if you can maintain a kind of panoramic overview, it's all so amusing."

He talks often now about the women he knew before he got married, and about his shyness. "I never went near another woman when I was married. Except once. In our car pool, I had seen the other guys, when they were sitting beside a young girl in the car. When she slept, they would put their arms around her. Well, one day, see, I was sitting next to this pretty girl. She falls asleep. After thinking about it for maybe ten minutes, I finally let my hand kind of drop on her shoulder — and then I even let my hand cuddle her breast. I don't know what came over me. Finally she stretched, like she was waking up, and moved away. I worried myself sick about it, about her telling my daughters, or my wife, or both. Just one time.

"When I was twenty, I published maybe six poems in the newspaper. I got a letter in a perfumed envelope. From a writer. Her name was Magna Wand. Well, we exchanged a few letters, and then we arranged to meet in a hotel lobby. She would wear a broad-brimmed hat and I would wear a white flower in my lapel. First I saw an eighty-five-year-old woman and I thought I better get out of there. Going through the revolving hotel door to leave, I got stuck; there, on the other side, also stuck, she was. She was about thirty-five. We walked around the city. Finally we went up to her room. She had a big bottle of red wine. I got out of there as fast as I could. Maybe the wine didn't mean anything, but I thought it did.

"And in a similar way, I got together with Lil. You know, I knew

Lil from way back. She was always the prettiest girl in school, and I had a crush on her since I was fifteen. Well, another girl wrote me about my poems in the newspaper. This one lived in New York, but wrote and said she was coming to Toronto. She asked me to rent a room for her." He pauses. "We rendezvoused. Well, she had hair on her chest. I have always been one quick to find an excuse not to fuck a woman. I got out of there and that's how I called Lil for a date and began courting her. I remember telling her, 'Do you know, Lil, I've been wasting my time with a girl with hair on her chest when I could have been with you?' "

XII

Luther came in on a Friday morning with a sunny face. "I planted a social seed today . . . with this woman, Yolanda, who teaches a yoga class. I mentioned bird watching to her . . . and her eyes lit up!"

On Monday morning, he was still excited, but for a different reason. "I went to Yolanda's house yesterday morning. I came into the kitchen. Yolanda wasn't there, and the door was open. There was a woman leaning against the edge of the table in pajamas and kimono . . . she had a luminescence of skin . . . a glow . . . and a tight little smile. It was Yolanda's mother. We went outside and sat on a couch of leaves in a grove. Then some stinking little kids started throwing stones at us, and we had to get up. What knowledge this woman has . . . she lives on a hilltop . . . and I went there later in the day to spend more time with her. She has a bad back. She too believes in Yoga, yet she said it was caused by the will of God!" Luther smiled and shook his head in admiration.

He seems to have adjusted to his new life. He does not really form any serious relationships with women. As he has often said about sex: "That's out of my league." He grows increasingly forgetful and absent-minded. He continues to watch TV, and writes letters of protest — to Barbara Walters: "She has a speech defect that I find offensive in a woman who's a phony"; and to *Time* magazine for their bicentennial issue: "Dear Sirs: I just wasted a dollar. May I proffer the observation that nothing could be more offensive than turning the first page and finding an ad for Marlboro country — not even especially written for this occasion." After dictating the letter to Bea, Luther offers to sell the magazine to her for fifty cents.

The starlings continue to seek protection under the eaves of Luther's house.

Luther has new stories to tell, as relatives and friends briefly cross his life. Aunt Ida and Uncle Igor invite him over for an occasional evening in Manhattan.

"My mother wasn't on a straight line, I know, but Ida takes the cake," he tells us. "Aunt Ida visited the bank last week. She sat down at the bank manager's desk, leaned on her cane, and said, 'I have $25,000 to deposit in your bank. You may think this odd — but this neighborhood has changed so much in recent years, the kind of people who are handling money. You don't *know* what the person who handled the money just before you was doing with himself. Sir, I want clean new bills.' " She writes letters of complaint to the presidents of companies, and the responses, Luther says, come back "with crests on the letterheads." She complains to the president of a tea company that the tea is dyed because it darkens immediately, and to a bank president about the procedure of giving away "cheap merchandise" to lure customers. "Of course," Luther says laughing, "the bank president writes back that he understands Ida's concern — 'but we were the last to succumb — and you wouldn't want us not to be able to compete freely?' "

Luther is still reading his texts on Eastern religion, as well as *The Outsider* by Colin Wilson and Houston Smith's *The Religions of Man*. He goes to the Yoga gatherings, although the younger members "look at me like Methuselah."

He sees Lil occasionally. She asks him: "How can you be so insecure and have such an enormous ego at the same time?"

He recalls his wedding day. He went into the boss's office on a Thursday and asked for the next day off. He said he was shaking. The boss said that in view of the wedding, Luther would be permitted to leave at 4 P.M. on Friday.

"Were you that afraid?" I ask him.

"I was full of fear."

He continues to save his money. At a JFI affair at the Plaza, at the conclusion, on his way out, he reaches over to the hood of the piano, lifts it up, and takes his coat out.

He thinks and rethinks his life. "You know," he says, "I don't just wash my face; I *attack* it. My first heart attack occurred when I was washing; I scrunch up my face and smack it. One day my wife Lil looked at me and said: 'Just what in the world are you doing to yourself?' I've thought this over and analyzed it. It relates to my childhood — I'm acting out the role of myself as a child who hated to be washed by my parents, and the role of my parents who are vigorously washing me."

But more than anything else, Luther thinks about Lil.

Stephen tells me that what hurts Luther most is that Lil doesn't even have a boy friend. "At least that would be a plausible reason for leaving him," Stephen explains. "But to leave him to live in a furnished room all by herself — that to her even such a life is better than living with Luther — that hurts him most of all."

Luther tells me one day, with a look that is full of pain, that his wife, who knew he was dating Yolanda, told him that Yolanda was a "man junkie." He asked her if that was a phrase of the "sisterhood," and his wife said it was. "The implication," he says to me, is that "one, Yolanda is just hung up on men, so that it could be any man she was dating, not just me, and two, that men are a nasty addiction."

XV

Luther wants to find out above all why he did not become a writer.

He remembers the six poems he published when he was twenty or twenty-one, and the circle of young friends who regarded him as a "poet philosopher" who would make his mark in the world.

He recalls the pottery shop he ran with his uncle in California, and that he was happy then.

He draws a blank about what happened then to make him stop writing.

At twenty-one, Luther courted and married Lil. "I didn't want to marry her," Luther says, "but I loved her — I always loved her from the first day I laid eyes on her — and she wouldn't agree to anything but marriage. And she had to have kids.

"And it was Lil who didn't like California and the pottery shop. It wasn't a realistic way to make a living, she thought. Yes, she made me give that up and go back east with her to New York. She insisted I take the job with JFI. She said she was sure I could do it.

"She had that faith in me."

MAVIS GALLANT

The Remission

(FROM THE NEW YORKER)

WHEN IT BECAME CLEAR that Alec Webb was far more ill than anyone had cared to tell him, he tore up his English life and came down to die on the Riviera. The time was early in the reign of the new Elizabeth, and people were still doing this — migrating with no other purpose than the hope of a merciful sky. The alternative (Alec said to his only sister) meant queuing for death on the National Health Service, lying on a regulation mattress and rubber sheet, hearing the breath of other men dying.

Alec — as obituaries would have it later — was husband to Barbara, father to Will, Molly, and James. It did not occur to him or to anyone else that the removal from England was an act of unusual force that could rend and lacerate his children's lives as well as his own. The difference was that their lives were barely aboveground and not yet in flower.

The five Webbs arrived at a property called Lou Mas in the course of a particularly hot September. Mysterious Lou Mas, until now a name on a deed of sale, materialized as a pink house wedged in the side of a hill between a motor road and the sea. Alec identified its style as Edwardian-Riviera. Barbara supposed he must mean the profusion of balconies and parapets, and the slender pillars in the garden holding up nothing. In the new southern light everything looked to her brilliant and moist, like color straight from a paintbox. One of Alec's first gestures was to raise his arm and shield his eyes against this brightness. The journey had exhausted him, she thought. She had received notice in dreams that their change of climates was irreversible; not just Alec but none of them could go back. She did not tell him so, though in better times it might have interested that part of his mind he kept fallow: being entirely rational, he had a prudent respect for second sight.

The children had never been in a house this size. They chased each other and slid along the floors until Alec asked, politely, if they wouldn't mind playing outside, though one of the reasons he had wanted to come here was to be with them for the time remaining. Dispatched to a flagged patio in front of the house, the children looked down on terraces bearing olive trees, then a railway line, then the sea. Among the trees was a cottage standing empty that Barbara had forbidden them to explore. The children were ten, eleven, and twelve, with the girl in the middle. Since they had no school to attend and did not know any of the people living around them, and since their mother was too busy to invent something interesting for them to do, they hung over a stone balustrade waving and calling to trains, hoping to see an answering wave and perhaps a decapitation. They had often been warned about foolish passengers and the worst that could happen. Their mother came out and put her arms around Will, the eldest. She kissed the top of his head. "Do look at that sea," she said. "Aren't we lucky?" They looked, but the vast, flat sea was a line any of them could have drawn on a sheet of paper. It was there, but no more than there; trains were better — so was the ruined cottage. Within a week James had cut his hand on glass breaking into it, but by then Barbara had forgotten her injunction.

The sun Alec had wanted turned out to be without compassion, and he spent most of the day indoors, moving from room to room, searching for some gray, dim English cave in which to take cover. Often he sat without reading, doing nothing, in a room whose one window, none too clean, looked straight into the blank hill behind the house. Seepage and a residue of winter rainstorms had traced calm yellow patterns on its walls. He guessed it had once been assigned to someone's hapless, helpless paid companion, who would have marveled at the thought of its lending shelter to a dying man. In the late afternoon he would return to his bedroom, where, out on the balcony, an angular roof shadow slowly replaced the sun. Barbara unfolded his deck chair on the still-burning tiles. He stretched out, opened a book, found the page he wanted, and at once closed his eyes. Barbara knelt in a corner, in a triangle of light. She had taken her clothes off — all but a sun hat; bougainvillea grew so thick no one could see. She said, "Would you like me to read to you?" No; he did everything alone, or nearly. He was — always — bathed, shaved, combed, and dressed. His children would not remember him unkempt or disheveled, though it might not have mattered to them. He did not smell of sweat or sickness or medicine or fear.

When it began to rain, later in the autumn, the children played indoors. Barbara tried to keep them quiet. There was a French school up in the town, but neither Alec nor Barbara knew much about it; and, besides, there was no use settling them in. He heard the children asking for bicycles so they could ride along the motor road, and he heard Barbara saying no, the road was dangerous. She must have changed her mind, for he next heard them discussing the drawbacks and advantages of French bikes. One of the children — James, it was — asked some question about the cost.

"You're not to mention things like that," said Barbara. "You're not to speak of money."

Alec was leaving no money and three children — four, if you counted his wife. Barbara often said she had no use for money, no head for it. "Thank God I'm Irish," she said. "I haven't got rates of interest on the brain." She read Irishness into her nature as an explanation for it, the way some people attributed their gifts and failings to a sign of the zodiac. Anything natively Irish had dissolved long before, leaving only a family custom of Catholicism and another habit, fervent in Barbara's case, of anticlerical passion. Alec supposed she was getting her own back, for a mysterious reason, on ancestors she would not have recognized in heaven. Her family, the Laceys, had been in Wales for generations. Her brothers considered themselves Welsh.

It was Barbara's three Welsh brothers who had put up the funds for Lou Mas. Houses like this were to be had nearly for the asking then. They stood moldering at the unfashionable end of the coast, damaged sometimes by casual shellfire, difficult to heat, costly to renovate. What the brothers had seen as valuable in Lou Mas was not the villa, which they had no use for, but the undeveloped sea front around it, for which each of them had a different plan. The eldest brother was a partner in a firm of civil engineers; another managed a resort hotel and had vague thoughts about building one of his own. The youngest, Mike, who was Barbara's favorite, had converted from the RAF to commercial flying. Like Alec, he had been a prisoner of war. The two men had that, but nothing else, in common. Mike was the best traveled of the three. He could see, in place of the pink house with its thick walls and high ceilings, one of the frail, domino-shaped blocks that were starting to rise around the Mediterranean basin, creating a vise of white plaster at the rim of the sea.

Because of United Kingdom income-tax laws, which made it awkward for the Laceys to have holdings abroad, Alec and Barbara had been registered as owners of Lou Mas, with Desmond, the engineer, given power of attorney. This was a manageable operation because Alec was entirely honorable, while Barbara did not know a legal document from the ace of diamonds. So when the first scouts came round from the local British colony to find out what the Webbs were like and Barbara told them Lou Mas belonged to her family, she was speaking the truth. Her visitors murmured that they had been very fond of the Vaughan-Thorpes and had been sorry to see them go — a reference to the previous owners, whose grandparents had built Lou Mas. Barbara did not suppose this to be a snub: she simply wondered why it was that a war out of which her brothers had emerged so splendidly should have left Alec, his sister, and the unknown Vaughan-Thorpes worse off than before.

The scouts reported that Mr. Webb was an invalid, that the children were not going to school, that Mrs. Webb must at one time have been pretty, and that she seemed to be spending a good deal of money, either her husband's or her own. When no improvements were seen in the house, the grounds, or the cottage, it began to be taken for granted that she had been squandering, on trifles, rather more than she had.

Her visitors were mistaken: Barbara never spent more than she had, but only the total of all she could see. What she saw now was a lump of money like a great block of marble, from which she could chip as much as she liked. It had come by way of Alec's sister. Alec's obstinate refusal to die on National Health had meant that his death had somehow to be paid for. Principle was a fine thing, one of Barbara's brothers remarked, but it came high. Alec's earning days were done for. He had come from a long line of medium-rank civil servants who had never owned anything except the cottages to which they had eventually retired, and which their heirs inevitably sold. Money earned, such as there was, disappeared in the sands of their male progeny's education. Girls were expected to get married. Alec's sister, now forty-four, had not done so, though she was no poorer or plainer than most. "I am better off like this," she had told Alec, perhaps once too often. She was untrained, unready, unfitted for any life save that of a woman civilian in wartime; peace had no use for her, just as the postwar seemed too fast, too hard, and too crowded to allow for Alec. Her only asset was material: a modest, cautiously invested sum of money settled on her by a godparent, the income from which she tried to add to by sewing. Christening robes had been her special joy, but fewer babies were being baptized with pomp, while nylon was gradually replacing the silks and lawns she worked with such care. Nobody wanted the bother of ironing flounces and tucks in a world without servants.

Barbara called her sister-in-law "the mouse." She had small brown eyes; was vegetarian; prayed every night of her life for Alec and for the parents who had not much loved her. "If they would just listen to me," she was in the habit of saying — about Alec and Barbara, for instance. She never complained about her compressed existence, which seemed to her the only competent one at times; at least it was quiet. When Alec told her that he was about to die, and wanted to emigrate, and had been provided with a house but with nothing to run it on, she immediately offered him half her capital. He accepted in the same flat way he had talked about death — out of his driving need, she supposed, or because he still held the old belief that women never require much. She knew she had made an impulsive gesture, perhaps a disastrous one, but she loved Alec and did not want to add to her own grief. She was assured that anything left at the end would be returned enriched and amplified by some sort of nimble investment, but as Alec and his family intended to live on the capital she did not see how this could be done.

Alec knew that his sister had been sacrificed. It was merely another of the lights going out. Detachment had overtaken him even before the journey south. Mind and body floated on any current that chose to bear them.

For the first time in her life Barbara had enough money and no one to plague her with useless instructions. While Alec slept, or seemed to, she knelt in the last triangle of sun on the balcony reading the spread-out pages of the *Continental Daily Mail*. It had been one thing to have no head for money when there was none to speak of; the present situation called for percipience and wit. Her reading informed her that dollars were still stronger than pounds. (Pounds were the decaying cottage, dollars the Edwardian house.) Alec's background and training made him find the word *dollars* not overnice, perhaps alarming, but Barbara had no class prejudice to hinder her. She had already bought dollars for pounds, at giddy loss, feeling each time that she had put it over on banks and nations, on snobs, on the financial correspondent of the *Mail*, on her own clever brothers. (One of the Webbs' neighbors, a retired Army officer named Major Lamprey, had confided to Alec that he was expecting the Russians to land in the bay below their villas at any time. He intended to die fighting on his doorstep; however, should anything happen to prevent his doing so, he had kept a clutch of dollars tucked in the pocket of an old dressing gown so that he and his mother could buy their way out.)

In Alec's darkened bedroom she combed her hair with his comb. Even if he survived, he would have no foothold on the 1950s. She, Barbara, had been made for her time. This did not mean she wanted to live without him. Writing to one of her brothers, she advised him to open a hotel down here. Servants were cheap — twenty or thirty cents an hour, depending on whether you worked the official or the free-market rate. In this letter her brother heard Barbara's voice, which had stayed high and breathless though she must have been thirty-four. He wondered if this was the sort of prattle poor dying old Alec had to listen to there in the south.

"South" was to Alec a place of the mind. He had not deserted England, as his sad sister thought, but had moved into one of its oldest literary legends, the Mediterranean. His part of this legend was called Rivabella. Actually, "Rivebelle" was written on maps and road signs, for the area belonged to France — at least for the present. It had been tugged between France and Italy so often that it now had a diverse, undefinable character and seemed to be remote from any central authority unless there were elections or wars. At its heart was a town sprawled on the hill behind Lou Mas and above the motor road. Its inhabitants said "Rivabella"; they spoke, among themselves, a Ligurian dialect with some Spanish and Arabic expressions mixed in, though their children went to school and learned French and that they descended from a race with blue eyes. What had remained constant to Rivabella was its poverty, and the groves of ancient olive trees that only the strictest of laws kept the natives from cutting down, and the look and character of the people. Confined by his illness, Alec would never meet more of these than about a dozen; they bore out the expectation set alight by his reading, seeming to him classless and pagan, poetic and wise, imbued with an instinctive understanding of light, darkness, and immortality. Barbara expected them to be cunning and droll, which they were, and to steal from her, which they did, and to love her, which they seemed to. Only the children were made uneasy by these strange new adults, so squat and ill-favored, so quarrelsome and sly, so destructive of nature and pointlessly cruel to animals. But, then, the children had not read much, were unfamiliar with films, and had no legends to guide them.

Barbara climbed up to the town quite often during the first weeks, looking for a doctor for Alec, for a cook and a maid, for someone to give lessons to the children. There was nothing much to see except a baroque church from which everything removable had long since been sold to antiquarians, and a crumbling palace along the very dull main street. In one of the palace rooms, she was given leave to examine some patches of peach-colored smudge she was told were early-Renaissance frescoes. Some guidebooks referred to these, with the result that a number of the new, hard-working breed of postwar traveler panted up a steep road not open to motor traffic only to find that the palace belonged to a cranky French countess who lived alone with her niece and would not let anyone in. (Barbara, interviewing the niece for the post of governess, had been admitted but was kept standing until the countess left the room.) Behind the palace she discovered a town hall with a post office and a school attached, a charming small hospital — where a doctor was obtained for Alec — and a walled graveyard. Only the graveyard was worth exploring; it contained Victorian English poets, who had probably died of tuberculosis in the days when an enervating climate was thought to be good for phthisis, and Russian aristocrats, who had owned some of the English houses, and Garibaldian adventurers, who, like Alec, had never owned a thing. Most of these graves were overgrown and neglected, with the headstones all to one side, and wild grasses grown taller than roses. The more recent dead seemed to be commemorated by marble plaques on a high concrete wall; these she did not examine. What struck her about this place was its splendid view: she could see Lou Mas, and quite far into Italy, and of course over a vast stretch of the sea. How silly of all those rich foreigners to crowd down by the shore, with the crashing noise of the railway. I would have built up here in a minute, she thought.

Alec's new doctor was young and ugly and bit his nails. He spoke good English and knew most of the British colony, to whose colds, allergies, and perpetually upset stomachs he ministered. British ailments were nursery ailments; what his patients really wanted was to be tucked up next to a nursery fire and fed warm bread-and-milk. He had taken her to be something like himself — an accomplice. "My husband is anything but childish," she said gently.

"Rivabella has only two points of cultural interest," he said. "One is the market on the church square. The other is the patron saint, St. Damian. He appears on the church roof, dressed in armor, holding a flaming sword in the air. He does this when someone in Rivabella seems to be in danger." She saw, in the way he looked at her, that she had begun her journey south a wife and mother whose looks were fading, and arrived at a place where her face seemed exotic. Until now she had thought only that a normal English family had taken the train and the caricature of one had descended. It amounted to the same thing — the eye of the beholder.

From his balcony Alec saw the hill as a rough triangle, with a few straggling farms beneath the gray and umber town (all he could discern was its color) and the apex of graveyard. This, in its chalky whiteness, looked like an Andalusian or a North African village washed up on the wrong part of the coast. It was alien to the lush English gardens and the foreign villas, which tended to pinks, and beiges, and to a deep shade known as Egyptian red. Within those houses was a way of being he sensed and understood, for it was a smaller, paler version of colonial life, with chattering foreign servants who might have been budgerigars, and hot puddings consumed under brilliant sunlight. Rules of speech and regulations for conduct were probably observed, as in the last days of the dissolving Empire. Barbara had told him of one: it was bad form to say "Rivebelle" for "Rivabella," for it showed one hadn't known about the place in its rich old days, or even that Queen Victoria had mentioned "*pretty* little Rivabella" to the Crown Princess of Prussia in one of her affectionate letters.

"All snobs," said Barbara. "Thank God I'm Irish," though there was something she did in a way mind: saying "Rivebelle" had been one of her first mistakes. Another had been hiring a staff without taking advice. She was also suspected of paying twice the going rate, which was not so much an economic blunder as a social affront. "All snobs" was not much in the way of ammunition, but, then, none of the other villas could claim a cook, a maid, a laundress, a gardener, and a governess marching down from Rivabella, all of them loyal, devoted, cheerful, hardworking, and kind.

She wrote to her pilot brother, the one she loved, telling him how self-reliant people seemed to be here, what pride they took in their jobs, how their philosophy was completely alien to the modern British idea of strife and grab. "I would love it if you would come and stay for a while. We have more rooms than we know what to do with. You and I could talk." But no one came. None of them wanted to have to watch poor old Alec dying.

The children would recall later on that their cook had worn a straw hat in the kitchen so that steam condensing on the ceiling would not drop on her head, and that she wore the same hat to their father's funeral. Barbara would remind them about the food. She had been barely twenty at the beginning of the war, and there were meals for which she had never stopped feeling hungry. Three times a day, now, she sat down to cream and butter and fresh bread, new-laid eggs, jam you could stand a spoon in: breakfasts out of a storybook from before the war. As she preferred looking at food to eating it, it must have been the idea of her table spread that restored richness to her skin, luster to her hair. She had been all cream and gold once, but war and marriage and Alec's illness and being hard up and some other indefinable disappointment had skimmed and darkened her. And yet she felt shot through with happiness sometimes, or at least by a piercing clue as to what bliss might be. This sensation, which she might have controlled more easily in another climate, became so natural, so insistent, that she feared sometimes that its source might be religious and that she would need to reject — out of principle — the felicity it promised. But no; she was, luckily, too earthbound for such nonsense. She could experience sudden felicity merely seeing her cook arrive with laden baskets, or the gardener crossing the terrace with a crate of flowering plants. (He would bed these out under the olive trees, where they perished rapidly.) Lou Mas at such times seemed to shrink to a toy house she might lift and carry; she would remem-

ber what it had been like when the children were babies still, and
hers alone.

Carrying Alec's breakfast try, she came in wearing the white
dressing gown that had been his sister's parting gift to her. Her
hair, which she now kept thick and loose, was shades lighter than
it had been in England. He seemed barely to see her. But, then,
everything dazzled him now. She buttered toast for him, and
spread it with jam, saying, "Do try it, darling. You will never taste
jam like this again." Of course, it thundered with prophecy. Her
vision blurred — not because of tears, for she did not cry easily. It
was as if a sheet of pure water had come down with an enormous
crashing sound, cutting her off from Alec.

Now that winter was here, he moved with the sun instead of
away from it. Shuffling to the balcony, he leaned on her shoulder.
She covered him with blankets, gave him a book to read, combed
his hair. He had all but stopped speaking, though he made an
effort for strangers. She thought, What would it be like to be shot
dead? Only the lingering question contained in a nightmare could
account for this, but her visionary dreams had left her, probably
because Alec's fate, and so to some measure her own, had been
decided once and for all. Between house and sea the gardener
crouched with a trowel in his hand. His work consisted of
bedding-out, and his imagination stopped at salvia: the ground
beneath the olive trees was dark red with them. She leaned against
the warm parapet and thought of what he might see should he
look up — herself, in white, with her hair blazing in the sun. But
when he lifted his face it was only to wipe sweat from it with the
shirt he had taken off. A dream of loss came back: she had been
ordered to find new names for refugee children whose names had
been forgotten. In real life, she had wanted her children to be
called Giles, Nigel, and Samantha, but Alec had interfered. All
three had been conceived on his wartime leaves, before he was
taken prisoner. The children had her gray eyes, her skin that
freckled, her small bones and delicate features (though Molly
showed signs of belonging to a darker, sturdier race), but none of
them had her richness, her shine. They seemed to her, and perhaps to each other, thin and dry, like Alec.

Everything Mademoiselle said was useless or repetitive. She explained, " 'Lou Mas' means 'the farm,' " which the children knew.
When they looked out the dining-room window, she remarked,

"You can see Italy." She came early in order to share their breakfast; the aunt she lived with, the aunt with the frescoes, kept all the
food in their palace locked up. "What do you take me for?" she
sometimes asked them, tragically, of some small thing, such as their
not paying intense attention. She was not teaching them much —
only some French, and they were picking this up faster now than
she could instruct. Her great-grandfather had been a French vol-
unteer against Garibaldi (an Italian bandit, she explained); her
grandfather was founder of a nationalist movement; her father
had been murdered on the steps of his house at the end of the war.
She was afraid of Freemasons, Socialists, Protestants, and Jews, but
not of drowning or falling from a height or being attacked by a
mad dog. When she discovered that the children had been chris-
tened (Alec having considered baptism a rational start to agnostic
life), she undertook their religious education, which was not at all
what Barbara was paying for.

After lunch, they went upstairs to visit Alec. He lay on his deck
chair, tucked into blankets, as pale as clouds. James suddenly
wailed out, believing he was singing, "We'll ring all the bells and
kill all the Protestants." Silence; then James said, "Are there any
left? Any Protestants?"

"I am left, for one," said his father.

"It's a good thing we came down here, then," said the child
calmly. "They couldn't get at you."

Mademoiselle said, looking terrified, "It refers to old events in
France."

"It wouldn't have mattered." Alec's belief had gone to earth as
soon as he had realized that the men he admired were in doubt.
His conversation, like his reading, was increasingly simple. He was
reading a book about gardening. He held it close to his face. Daylight tired him; it was like an intruder between memory and the
eye. He read, "Nerine. Guernsey Lily. Ord. Amarylidaceae. First
introduced, 1680." Introduced into England, that meant. "Olean-
der, 1596. East Indian Rose Bay, 1770. Tamarind Tree, 1633.
Chrysanthemum, 1764." So England had flowered, become be-
decked, been bedded-out.

The book had been given him by a neighbor. The Webbs not
only had people working for them, and delicious nursery food to
eat, and a garden running down to the sea, but distinguished people living on either side — Mr. Edmund Cranefield of Villa Osiris

to the right, and Mrs. Massie at Casa Scotia on the left. To reach
their houses you had to climb thirty steps to the road, then descend
more stairs on their land. Mr. Cranefield had a lift, which looked
like a large crate stood on its side. Within it was a kitchen chair. He
sat on the chair and was borne up to the road on an electric rail.
No one had ever seen him doing this. When he went to Morocco,
during the worst of the winter, he had the lift disconnected and
covered with rugs, the pond drained and the fish put in tanks, and
his two peacocks, who screamed every dawn as if a fox were at
them, boarded for a high fee with a private zoo. Casa Scotia belonged to Mrs. Massie, who was lame, wore a tweed cape, never
went out without a hat, walked with a stick, and took a good twenty
minutes to climb her steps.

Mr. Cranefield was a novelist, Mrs. Massie the author of a whole
shelf of gardening books. Mr. Cranefield never spoke of his novels
or offered to lend them; he did not even say what their titles were.
"You must tell me every one!" Barbara cried, as if she were about
to rush out and return with a wheelbarrow full of books by Mr.
Cranefield.

He sat upstairs with Alec, and they talked about different things,
quite often about the war. Just as Barbara was beginning to imagine Mr. Cranefield did not like her, he invited her to tea. She
brought Molly along for protection, but soon saw he was not drawn
to women — at least, not in the way she supposed men to be. She
wondered then if she should keep Will and James away from him.
He showed Barbara and Molly the loggia where he worked on
windless mornings; a strong mistral had once blown one hundred
and forty pages across three gardens — some were even found in
a hedge at Casa Scotia. On a table were oval picture frames holding
the likeness of a fair girl and a fair young man. Looking more
closely, Barbara saw they were illustrations cut out of magazines.
Mr. Cranefield said, "They are the pair I write about. I keep them
there so that I never make a mistake."

"Don't they bore you?" said Barbara.

"Look at all they have given me." But the most dispossessed
peasant, the filthiest housemaid, the seediest nailbiting doctor in
Rivabella had what he was pointing out — the view, the sea. Of
course, a wave of the hand cannot take in everything; he probably
had more than this in reserve. He turned to Molly and said kindly,
"When you are a little older you can do some typing for me,"

because it was his experience that girls liked doing that — typing for Mr. Cranefield while waiting for someone to marry. Girls were fond of him: he gave sound advice about love affairs, could read the future in handwriting. Molly knew nothing about him then, but she would recall later on how Mr. Cranefield, who had invented women deep-sea divers, women test pilots, could not imagine — in his innocence, in his manhood — anything more thrilling to offer a girl when he met one than "You can type."

Barbara broke in, laughing: "She is only eleven."

This was true, but it seemed to Molly a terrible thing to say.

Mrs. Massie was not shy about bringing *her* books around. She gave several to Alec, among them *Flora's Gardening Encyclopedia*, seventeenth edition, considered her masterpiece. All her books were signed "Flora," though it was not her name. She said about Mr. Cranefield, "Edmund is a great, pampered child. Spoiled by adoring women all his life. Not by me." She sat straight on the straightest chair, her hands clasped on her stick. "I do my own typing. My own gardening, too," though she did say to James and Will, "You can help in the garden for pocket money, if you like."

In the late spring, the second Elizabeth was crowned. Barbara ordered a television set from a shop in Nice. It was the first the children had seen. Two men carried it with difficulty down the steps from the road, and soon became tired of lifting it from room to room while Barbara decided where she wanted it. She finally chose a room they kept shut usually; it had a raised platform at one end and until the war had been the site of amateur theatricals. The men set the box down on the stage and began fiddling with antennae and power points while the children ran about arranging rows of chairs. One of the men said they might not have a perfect view of the queen the next day, the day of the Coronation, because of Alps standing in the way. The children sat down and stared at the screen. Horizontal lightning streaked across its face. The men described implosion, which had killed any number of persons all over the world. They said that should the socket and plug begin to smoke, Barbara was to make a dash for the meter box and pull out the appropriate fuse.

"The appropriate fuse?" said Barbara. The children minded sometimes about the way she laughed at everything.

When the men had gone, they trooped upstairs to tell Alec about the Alps and implosion. He was resting in preparation for tomorrow's ceremony, which he would attend. It was clear to Molly that her father would not be able to get up and run if there was an accident. Kneeling on the tiles (this was in early June), she pressed her face to his hand. Presently he slipped the hand away to turn a page. He was reading more of the book Mrs. Massie had pounded out on her 1929 Underwood — four carbons, single-spaced, no corrections, every page typed clean: "Brussels sprouts — see Brassica." Brassica must be English, Alec thought. That was why he withdrew his hand — to see about Brassica. What use was his hand to Molly or her anxiety to him now? Why hold her? Why draw her into his pale world? She was a difficult, dull, clumsy child, something of a moper when her brothers teased her but sulky and tough when it came to Barbara. He had watched Barbara, goaded by Molly, lose control of herself and slap the girl's face, and he had heard Molly's pitiful credo: "You can't hurt me. My vaccination hurt worse than that." "Hurt more," Alec in silence had amended. "Hurt me *more* than that."

He found Brassica. It was Borecole, Broccoli, Cabbage, Cauliflower. His eyes slid over the rest of what it was until "Native to Europe — BRITAIN," which Mrs. Massie had typed in capital letters during the war, with a rug around her legs in unheated Casa Scotia, waiting for the Italians or the Germans or the French to take her away to internment in a lorry. He was closer in temper to Mrs. Massie than to anyone else except his sister, though he had given up priorities. His blood was white (that was how he saw it), and his lungs and heart were bleached, too, and starting to disintegrate like snowflakes. He was a pale giant, a drained Gulliver, cast up on the beach, open territory for invaders. (Barbara and Will were sharing a paperback about flying saucers whose occupants had built Stonehenge.) Alec's intrepid immigrants, his microscopic colonial settlers, had taken over. He had been easy to subdue, being courteous by nature, diffident by choice. He had been a civil servant, then a soldier; had expected the best, relied on good behavior; had taken to prison camp thin books about Calabria and Greece; had been evasive, secretive, brave, unscrupulous only sometimes — had been English and middle-class, in short.

That night Alec had what the doctor called "a crisis" and Alec termed "a bad patch." There was no question of his coming down for the Coronation the next day. The children thought of taking the television set up to him, but it was too heavy, and Molly burst into tears thinking of implosion and accidents and Alec trapped. In the end the queen was crowned in the little theater, as Barbara had planned, in the presence of Barbara and the children, Mr. Cranefield and Mrs. Massie, the doctor from Rivabella, Major Lamprey and his old mother, Mrs. Massie's housekeeper, Barbara's cook and two of her grandchildren, and Mademoiselle. One after the other, these people turned their heads to look at Alec, gasping in the doorway, holding on to the frame. His hair was carefully combed and parted low on one side, like Mr. Cranefield's, and he had dressed completely, though he had a scarf around his neck instead of a tie. He was the last, the very last, of a kind. Not British but English. Not Christian so much as Anglican. Not Anglican but giving the benefit of the doubt. His children would never feel what he had felt, suffer what he had suffered, relinquish what he had done without so that this sacrament could take place. The new queen's voice flowed easily over the Alps — thin, bored, ironed flat by the weight of what she had to remember — and came as far as Alec, to whom she owed her crown. He did not think that, precisely, but what had pulled him to his feet, made him stand panting for life in the doorway, would not occur to James or Will or Molly — not then, or ever.

He watched the rest of it from a chair. His breathing bothered the others: it made their own seem too quiet. He ought to have died that night. It would have made a reasonable ending. This was not a question of getting rid of Alec (no one wanted that) but of being able to say later, "He got up and dressed to see the Coronation." However, he went on living.

A nurse came every day, the doctor almost as often. He talked quietly to Barbara in the garden. A remission as long as this was unknown to him; it smacked of miracles. When Barbara would not hear of that, he said that Alec was holding on through will power. But Alec was not holding on. His invaders had pushed him off the beach and into a boat. The stream was white, and the shoreline, too. Everything was white, and he moved peacefully. He had glimpses of his destination — a room where the hems of thin curtains swept back and forth on a bare floor. His vision gave him green bronze doors sometimes; he supposed they were part of the same room.

He could see his children, but only barely. He had guessed what the boys might become — one a rebel, one turned inward. The girl was a question mark. She was stoic and sentimental, indifferent sometimes to pleasure and pain. Whatever she was or could be or might be, he had left her behind. The boys placed a row of bricks down the middle of the room they shared. In the large house they fought for space. They were restless and noisy, untutored and bored. "I'll always have a packet of love from my children," Barbara had said to a man once (not Alec).

At the start of their second winter one of the Laceys came down to investigate. This was Ron, the hotel keeper. He had dark hair and was thin and pale and walked softly. When he understood that what Barbara had written about servants and dollars was true, he asked to see the accounts. There were none. He talked to Barbara without raising his voice; that day she let everyone working for her go, with the exception of the cook, whom Ron had said she was to keep because of Alec. He seemed to feel he was in a position of trust, for he ordered her — there was no other word for it — to place the children at once in the Rivabella town school: Lou Mas was costing the Lacey brothers enough in local taxes — they might as well feel they were getting something back. He called his sister "Bab" and Alec "Al." The children's parents suddenly seemed to them unlike anyone.

When Ron left, Barbara marched the children up to Rivabella and made them look at the church. They had seen it, but she made them look again. She held the mistaken belief that religion was taught in French state schools, and she wanted to arm them. The children knew by now that what their mother called France was not really France down here but a set of rules, a code for doing things, such as how to recite the multiplication table or label a wine. Instead of the northern saints she remembered, with their sorrowful preaching, there was a southern St. Damian holding up a blazing sword. Any number of persons had seen him; Mademoiselle had, more than once.

"I want you to understand what superstition is," said Barbara, in clear, carrying English. "Superstition is what is wrong with Uncle Ron. He believes what he can't see, and what he sees he can't believe in. Now, imagine intelligent people saying they've seen this — this apparition. This St. George, or whatever." The church had two pink towers, one bearing a cross and the other a weather vane.

St. Damian usually hovered between them. "In armor," said Barbara.

To all three children occurred "Why not?" Protect me, prayed the girl. Vanquish, said Will. Lead, ordered the youngest, seeing only himself in command. He looked around the square and said to his mother, "Could we go soon, please? Because people are looking."

That winter Molly grew breasts; she thought them enormous, though each could have been contained easily in a small teacup. Her brothers teased her. She went about with her arms crossed. She was tall for her age, and up in the town there was always some man staring. Elderly neighbors pressed her close. Major Lamprey, calling on Alec, kissed her on the mouth. He smelled of gin and pipe smoke. She scrubbed her teeth for minutes afterward. When she began to menstruate, Barbara said, "Now, Molly, you are to keep away from men," as if she weren't trying to.

The boys took their bicycles and went anywhere they wanted. In the evening they wheeled round and round the church square. Above them were swallows, on the edge of the square were men and boys. Both were starting to speak better French than English, and James spoke dialect better than French. Molly disliked going up to Rivabella, unless she had to. She helped Barbara make the beds and wash the dishes, and she did her homework and then very often went over to talk to Mr. Cranefield. She discovered, by chance, that he had another name — E. C. Arden. As E. C. Arden, he was the author of a series of thumbed, comfortable novels (it was Mrs. Massie who lent Molly these), one of which, called *Belinda at Sea*, was Molly's favorite book of any kind. It was about a girl who joined the crew of a submarine, disguised as a naval rating, and kept her identity a secret all the way to Hong Kong. In the end, she married the submarine commander, who apparently had loved her all along. Molly read *Belinda at Sea* three or four times without even mentioning to Mr. Cranefield that she knew he was E. C. Arden. She thought it was a matter of deep privacy and that it was up to him to speak of it first. She did, however, ask what she thought of the saint on the church roof, using the name Barbara had, which was St. George.

"What?" said Mr. Cranefield. "That Ethiopian?"

The girl looked frightened — not of Ethiopians, certainly, but of confusion as to person, the adult world of muddle. Even Mr. Cranefield was *also* E. C. Arden, creator of Belinda.

Mr. Cranefield explained, kindly, that up at Rivabella they had made a patron saint out of a mixture of St. Damian, who was an intellectual, and St. Michael, who was not, and probably a local pagan deity as well. St. Michael accounted for the sword, the pagan for the fire. Reliable witnesses had seen the result, though none of these witnesses were British. "We aren't awfully good at seeing saints," he said. "Though we do have an eye for ghosts."

Another thing still troubled Molly, but it was not a matter she could mention: she did not know what to do about her bosom — whether to try to hold it up in some way, or, on the contrary, bind it flat. She had been granted, by the mistake of a door's swinging wide, an upsetting glimpse of Mrs. Massie changing out of a bathing suit, and she had been worried about the future shape of her own body ever since. She pored over reproductions of statues and paintings in books belonging to Mr. Cranefield. The Eves and Venuses represented were not reassuring — they often seemed to be made of India rubber. There was no one she could ask. Barbara was too dangerous; the mention of a subject such as this always made her go too far and say things Molly found unpleasant.

She did remark to both Mrs. Massie and Mr. Cranefield that she hated the Rivabella school. She said, "I would give anything to be sent home to England, but I can't leave my father."

After a long conversation with Mrs. Massie, Mr. Cranefield agreed to speak to Alec. Interfering with other people was not his way, but Molly struck him as being pathetic. Something told him that Molly was not useful leverage with either parent and so he mentioned Will first: Will would soon be fourteen, too old for the school at Rivabella. Unless the Webb children were enrolled, and quickly, in good French establishments — say, in lycées at Nice — they would become unfit for anything save menial work in a foreign language they could not speak in an educated way. Of course, the ideal solution would be England, if Alec felt he could manage that.

Alec listened, sitting not quite straight in his chair, wearing a dressing gown, his back to a window. He found all light intolerable now. Several times he lifted his hand as if he were trying to see through it. No one knew why Alec made these odd gestures; some people thought he had gone slightly mad because death was too long in coming. He parted his lips and whispered, "French school . . . If you would look after it," and then, "I would be grateful."

Mr. Cranefield dropped his voice, too, as if the gray of the room called for hush. He asked if Alec had thought of appointing a guardian for them. The hand Alec seemed to want transparent waved back and forth, stiffly, like a shut ivory fan.

All Barbara said to Mr. Cranefield was "Good idea," once he had assured her that French high schools were not priest-ridden.

"It might have occurred to *her* to have done something about it," said Mrs. Massie, when this was repeated.

"Things do occur to Barbara," said Mr. Cranefield. "But she doesn't herself get the drift of them."

The only disturbing part of the new arrangement was that the children had been assigned to separate establishments, whose schedules did not coincide; this meant they would not necessarily travel in the same bus. Molly had shot up as tall as Will now. Her hair was dark and curled all over her head. Her bones and her hands and feet were going to be larger, stronger, than her mother's and brothers'. She looked, already, considerably older than her age. She was obstinately innocent, turning her face away when Barbara, for her own good, tried to tell her something about men.

Barbara imagined her willful, ignorant daughter being enticed, trapped, molested, impregnated, and disgraced. *And* ending up wondering how it happened, Barbara thought. She saw Molly's seducer, brutish and dull. I'd get him by the throat, she said to herself. She imagined the man's strong neck and her own small hands, her brittle bird bones. She said, "You are never, ever to speak to a stranger on the bus. You're not to get in a car with a man — not even if you know him."

"I don't know any man with a car."

"You could be waiting for a bus on a dark afternoon," said Barbara. "A car might pull up. Would you like a lift? No, you must answer. No and no and no. It is different for the boys. There are the two of them. They could put up a fight."

"Nobody bothers boys," said Molly.

Barbara drew breath but for once in her life said nothing.

Alec's remission was no longer just miraculous — it had become unreasonable. Barbara's oldest brother hinted that Alec might be better off in England, cared for on National Health: they were paying unholy taxes for just such a privilege. Barbara replied that Alec had no use for England, where the Labour government had sapped everyone's self-reliance. He believed in having exactly the amount of suffering you could pay for, no less and no more. She knew this theory did not hold water, because the Laceys and Alec's own sister had done the paying. It was too late now; they should have thought a bit sooner; and Alec was too ravaged to make a new move.

The car that, inevitably, pulled up to a bus stop in Nice was driven by a Mr. Wilkinson. He had just taken Major Lamprey and the major's old mother to the airport. He rolled his window down and called to Molly, through pouring rain, "I say, aren't you from Lou Mas?"

If he sounded like a foreigner's Englishman, like a man in a British joke, it was probably because he had said so many British-sounding lines in films set on the Riviera. Eric Wilkinson was the chap with the strong blue eyes and ginger mustache, never younger than thirty-four, never as much as forty, who flashed on for a second, just long enough to show there was an Englishman in the room. He could handle a uniform, a dinner jacket, tails, a monocle, a cigarette holder, a swagger stick, a polo mallet, could open a cigarette case without looking like a gigolo, could say without being an ass about it, "Bless my soul, wasn't that the little Maharani?" or even "Come along, old boy — fair play with Monica, now!" Foreigners meeting him often said, "That is what the British used to be like, when they were still all right, when the Riviera was still fit to live in." But the British who knew him were apt to glaze over: "You mean Wilkinson?" Mrs. Massie and Mr. Cranefield said, "Well, Wilkinson, what are you up to now?" There was no harm to him: his one-line roles did not support him, but he could do anything, even cook. He used his car as a private taxi, driving people to airports, meeting them when they came off cruise ships. He was not a chauffeur, never said "sir," but at the same time kept a certain distance, was not shy about money changing hands — no fake pride, no petit-bourgeois demand for a slipped envelope. Good-natured. Navy blazer. Summer whites in August. Wore a tie that carried a message. What did it stand for? A third-rate school? A disgraced, disbanded regiment? A club raided by the police? No one knew. Perhaps it was the symbol of something new altogether. "Still playing in those films of yours, Wilkinson?" He would flash on and off — British gent at roulette, British Army officer, British diplomat, British political agent, British anything. Spoke his line, fitted his monocle, pressed the catch on his cigarette case. His ease

with other people was genuine, his financial predicament un-
feigned. He had never been married, and had no children that he
knew of.

"By Jove, it's nippy," said Wilkinson, when Molly had settled
beside him, her books on her lap.

What made her do this — accept a lift from a murderer of
schoolgirls? First, she had seen him somewhere safe once — at Mr.
Cranefield's. Also, she was wet through, and chilled to the heart.
Barbara kept refusing or neglecting or forgetting to buy her the
things she needed: a lined raincoat, a jersey the right size. (The
boys were wearing hand-me-down clothes from England, but no
one Barbara knew of seemed to have a daughter.) The sleeves of
her old jacket were so short that she put her hands in her pockets,
so that Mr. Wilkinson would not despise her. He talked to Molly as
he did to everyone, as if they were of an age, informing her that
Major Lamprey and his mother were flying to Malta to look at a
house. A number of people were getting ready to leave the south
of France now; it had become so seedy and expensive, and all the
wrong people were starting to move in.

"What kind of wrong people?" She sat tense beside him until he
said, "Why, like Eric Wilkinson, I should think," and she laughed
when his own laugh said she was meant to. He drove beyond his
destination — a block of flats that he waved at in passing and that
Molly in a confused way supposed he owned. They stopped in the
road behind Lou Mas; she thanked him fervently, and then, struck
with something, sat staring at him: "Mr. Wilkinson," she said.
"Please — I am not allowed to be in cars with men alone. In case
someone happened to see us, would you mind just coming and
meeting my mother? Just so she can see who you are?"

"God bless my soul," said Wilkinson, sincerely.

Once, Alec had believed that Barbara was not frightened by
anything, and that this absence of fear was her principal weakness.
It was true that she had begun drifting out of her old life now, as
calmly as Alec drifted away from life altogether. Her mock phrase
for each additional Lou Mas catastrophe had become "the usual
daily developments." The usual developments over seven rainy
days had been the departure of the cook, who took with her all she
could lay her hands on, and a French social-security fine that had
come down hard on the remains of her marble block of money,
reducing it to pebbles and dust. She had never filled out employer's

forms for the people she had hired, because she had not known
she was supposed to and none of them had suggested it; for a
number of reasons having to do with government offices and tax
files, none of them had wanted even this modest income to be
registered anywhere. As it turned out, the gardener had also been
receiving unemployment benefits, which, unfairly, had increased
the amount of the fine Barbara had to pay. Rivabella turned out to
be just as grim and bossy as England — worse, even, for it kept up
a camouflage of wine and sunshine and olive trees and of amiable
southern idiots who, if sacked, thought nothing of informing on
one.

   She sat at the dining-room table, wearing around her shoulders
a red cardigan Molly had outgrown. On the table were the Sunday
papers Alec's sister continued to send faithfully from England, and
Alec's lunch tray, exactly as she had taken it up to him except that
everything on it was now cold. She glanced up and saw the two of
them enter — one stricken and guilty-looking, the other male, confident, smiling. The recognition that leaped between Barbara and
Wilkinson was the last thing that Wilkinson in his right mind
should have wanted, and absolutely everything Barbara now de-
sired and craved. Neither of them heard Molly saying, "Mummy,
this is Mr. Wilkinson. Mr. Wilkinson wants to tell you how he came
to drive me home."

It happened at last that Alec had to be taken to the Rivabella
hospital, where the local poor went when it was not feasible to let
them die at home. Eric Wilkinson, new family friend, drove his car
as far as it could go along a winding track, after which they placed
Alec on a stretcher; and Wilkinson, Mr. Cranefield, Will, and the
doctor carried him the rest of the way. A soft April rain was falling,
from which they protected Alec as they could. In the rain the
doctor wept unnoticed. The others were silent and absorbed. The
hospital stood near the graveyard — shamefully near, Wilkinson
finally remarked, to Mr. Cranefield. Will could see the cemetery
from his father's new window, though to do so he had to lean out,
as he'd imagined passengers doing and having their heads cut off
in the train game long ago. A concession was made to Alec's status
as owner of a large villa, and he was given a private room. It was
not a real sickroom but the place where the staff went to eat and
drink when they took time off. They cleared away the plates and

empty wine bottles and swept up most of the crumbs and wheeled a bed in.

The building was small for a hospital, large for a house. It had been the winter home of a Moscow family, none of whom had come back after 1917. Alec lay flat and still. Under a drift of soot on the ceiling he could make out a wreath of nasturtiums and a bluebird with a ribbon in its beak.

At the window, Will said to Mr. Cranefield, "We can see Lou Mas from here, and even your peacocks."

Mr. Cranefield fretted. "They shouldn't be in the rain."

Alec's neighbors came to visit. Mrs. Massie, not caring who heard her (one of the children did), said to someone she met on the hospital staircase, "Alec is a gentleman and always will be, but Barbara . . . Barbara." She took a rise of the curved marble stairs at a time. "If the boys were girls they'd be sluts. As it is, they are ruffians. Their old cook saw one of them stoning a cat to death. And now there is Wilkinson. Wilkinson." She moved on alone, repeating his name.

Everyone was saying "Wilkinson" now. Along with "Wilkinson" they said "Barbara." You would think that having been married to one man who was leaving her with nothing, leaving her dependent on family charity, she would have looked around, been more careful, picked a reliable kind of person. "A foreigner, say," said Major Lamprey's mother, who had not cared for Malta. Italians love children, even other people's. She might have chosen — you know — one of the cheerful sort, with a clean shirt and a clean white handkerchief, proprietor of a linen shop. The shop would have kept Barbara out of mischief.

No one could blame Wilkinson, who had his reasons. Also, he had said all those British-sounding lines in films, which in a way made him all right. Barbara had probably said she was Irish once too often. "What can you expect?" said Mrs. Massie. "Think how they were in the war. They keep order when there is someone to bully them. Otherwise . . ." The worst she had to say about Wilkinson was that he was preparing to flash on as the colonel of a regiment in a film about desert warfare; it had been made in the hilly country up behind Monte Carlo.

"Not a grain of sand up there," said Major Lamprey. He said he wondered what foreigners thought they meant by "desert."

"A colonel!" said Mrs. Massie.

"Why not?" said Mr. Cranefield.

"They must think he looks it," said Major Lamprey. "Gets a fiver a day, I'm told, and an extra fiver when he speaks his line. He says, 'Don't underestimate Rommel.' For a fiver I'd say it" — though he would rather have died.

The conversation veered to Wilkinson's favor. Wilkinson was merry; told irresistible stories about directors, unmalicious ones about film stars; repeated comic anecdotes concerning underlings who addressed him as "Guv." "I wonder who they can be," said Mrs. Massie. "It takes a Wilkinson to find them." Mr. Cranefield was more indulgent; he had to be. A sardonic turn of mind would have been resented by E. C. Arden's readers. The blond-headed pair on his desk stood for a world of triumphant love, with which his readers felt easy kinship. The fair couple, though competent in any domain, whether restoring a toppling kingdom or taming a tiger, lived on the same plane as all human creatures except England's enemies. They raised the level of existence — raised it, and flattened it.

Mr. Cranefield — as is often and incorrectly said of children — lived in a world of his own, too, in which he kept everyone's identity clear. He did not confuse St. Damian with an Ethiopian, or Wilkinson with Raffles, or Barbara with a slut. This was partly out of the habit of neatness and partly because he could not make up his mind to live openly in the world he wanted, which was a homosexual one. He said about Wilkinson and Barbara and the blazing scandal at Lou Mas, "I am sure there is no harm in it. Barbara has too much to manage alone, and it is probably better for the children to have a man about the place."

When Wilkinson was not traveling, he stayed at Lou Mas. Until now his base had been a flat he'd shared with a friend who was a lawyer and who was also frequently away. Wilkinson left most of his luggage behind; there was barely enough of his presence to fill a room. For a reason no one understood, Barbara had changed everyone's room around: she and Molly slept where Alec had been, the boys moved to Barbara's room, and Wilkinson was given Molly's bed. It seemed a small bed for so tall a man.

Molly had always slept alone, until now. Some nights, when Wilkinson was sleeping in her old room, she would waken just before dawn and find that her mother had disappeared. Her feeling at the sight of the empty bed was one of panic. She would get up,

too, and go in to Will and shake him, saying, "She's disappeared."

"No, she hasn't. She's with Wilkinson." Nevertheless, he would
rise and stumble, still nearly sleeping, down the passage — Alec's
son, descendant of civil servants, off on a mission.

Barbara slept with her back against Wilkinson's chest. Outside,
Mr. Cranefield's peacocks greeted first light by screaming murder.
Wilkinson never moved. Had he shown he was awake, he might
have felt obliged to say a suitable line — something like "I say, old
chap, you are a bit of a trial, you know."

Will's mother picked up the nightgown and robe that lay white
on the floor, pulled them on, flung her warm hair back, tied her
sash — all without haste. In the passage, the door shut on the quiet
Wilkinson, she said tenderly, "Were you worried?"

"Molly was."

Casual with her sons, she was modest before her daughter.
Changing to a clean nightdress, she said, "Turn the other way."
Turning, Molly saw her mother, white and gold, in the depths of
Alec's mirror. Barbara had her arms raised, revealing the profile
of a breast with at its tip the palest wash of rose, paler than the
palest pink flower. (Like a Fragonard, Barbara had been told, like
a Boucher — not by Alec.) What Molly felt now was immense relief. It was not the fate of every girl to turn into India rubber. But
in no other way did she wish to resemble her mother.

Like the residue left by winter rains, awareness of Barbara and
Wilkinson seeped through the house. There was a damp chill about
it that crept to the bone. One of the children, Will, perceived it as
torment. Because of the mother defiled, the source of all such
knowledge became polluted, probably forever. The boys withdrew
from Barbara, who had let the weather in. James imagined ways of
killing Wilkinson, though he drew the line at killing Barbara. He
did not want her dead, but different. The mother he wanted did
not stand in public squares pointing crazily up to invisible saints,
or begin sleeping in one bed and end up in another.

Barbara felt that they were leaving her; she put the blame on
Molly, who had the makings of a prude, and who, at worst, might
turn out to be something like Alec's sister. Barbara said to Molly,
"I had three children before I was twenty-five, and I was alone,
and there were all the air raids. The life I've tried to give you and
the boys has been so different, so happy, so free." Molly folded her

arms, looked down at her shoes. Her height, her grave expression, her new figure gave her a bogus air of maturity: she was only thirteen, and she felt like a pony flicked by a crop. Barbara tried to draw near: "My closest friend is my own daughter," she wanted to be able to say. "I never do a thing without talking it over with Molly." So she would have said, laughing, her bright head against Molly's darker hair, if only Molly had given half an inch.

"What a cold creature you are," Barbara said sadly. "You live in an ice palace. There is so little happiness in life unless you let it come near. I always at least had an *idea* about being happy." The girl's face stayed shut and locked. All that could cross it now was disappointment.

One night when Molly woke Will, he said, "I don't care where she is." Molly went back to bed. Fetching Barbara had become a habit. She was better off in her room alone.

When they stopped coming to claim her, Barbara felt it as mortification. She gave up on Molly, for the moment, and turned to the boys, sat curled on the foot of their bed, sipping wine, telling stories, offering to share her cigarette, though James was still twelve. James said, "He told us it was dangerous to smoke in bed. People have died that way." "He" meant Alec. Was this all James would remember? That he had been warned about smoking in bed?

James, who was embarrassed by this attempt of hers at making them equals, thought she had an odd smell, like a cat. To Will, at another kind of remove, she stank of folly. They stared at her, as if measuring everything she still had to mean in their lives. This expression she read as she could. Love for Wilkinson had blotted out the last of her dreams and erased her gift of second sight. She said unhappily to Wilkinson, "My children are prigs. But, then, they are only half mine."

Mademoiselle, whom the children now called by her name — Geneviève — still came to Lou Mas. Nobody paid her, but she corrected the children's French, which no longer needed correcting, and tried to help with their homework, which amounted to interference. They had always in some way spared her; only James, her favorite, sometimes said, "No, I'd rather work alone." She knew now that the Webbs were poor, which increased her affection: their descent to low water equaled her own. Sometimes she brought a packet of biscuits for their tea, which was a dull affair now the cook had gone. They ate the biscuits straight from the paper wrapping: nobody wanted to wash an extra plate. Wilkinson, playing at British something, asked about her aunt. He said "Madame la Comtesse." When he had gone, she cautioned the children not to say that but simply "your aunt." But as Geneviève's aunt did not receive foreigners, save for a few such as Mrs. Massie, they had no reason to ask how she was. When Geneviève realized from something said that Wilkinson more or less lived at Lou Mas, she stopped coming to see them. The Webbs had no further connection with Rivabella then except for their link with the hospital, where Alec still lay quietly, still alive.

Barbara went up every day. She asked the doctor, "Shouldn't he be having blood transfusions — something of that kind?" She had never been in a hospital except to be born and to have her children. She was remembering films she had seen — bottles dripping liquids, needles taped to the crook of an arm, nursing sisters wheeling oxygen tanks down white halls.

The doctor reminded her that this was Rivabella — a small town where half the population lived without employment. He had been so sympathetic at first, so slow to present a bill. She could not understand what had changed him; but she was hopeless at reading faces now. She could scarcely read her children's.

She bent down to Alec, so near that her eyes would have seemed enormous had he been paying attention. She told him the name of the scent she was wearing; it reminded her and perhaps Alec, too, of jasmine. Eric had brought it back from a dinner at Monte Carlo, given to promote this very perfume. He was often invited to these things, where he represented the best sort of Britishness. "Eric is being the greatest help," she said to Alec, who might have been listening. She added, for it had to be said sometime, "Eric has very kindly offered to stay at Lou Mas."

Mr. Cranefield and Mrs. Massie continued to plod up the hill, she with increasing difficulty. They brought Alec what they thought he needed. But he had no addictions, no cravings, no use for anything now but his destination. The children were sent up evenings. They never knew what to say or what he could hear. They talked as if they were still eleven or twelve, when Alec had stopped seeing them grow.

To Mr. Cranefield they looked like imitations of English children — loud, humorless, dutiful, clear. "James couldn't come with us tonight," said Molly. "He was quite ill, for some reason. He brought his dinner up." All three spoke the high, thin English of expatriate children who, unknowingly, mimic their mothers. The light bulb, hanging crooked, left Alec's face in shadow. When the children had kissed Alec and departed, Mr. Cranefield could hear them taking the hospital stairs headlong, at a gallop. The children were young and alive, and Alec was forty-something and nearly always sleeping. Unequal chances, Mr. Cranefield thought. They can't really beat their breasts about it. When Mrs. Massie was present, she never failed to say, "Your father is tired," though nobody knew if Alec was tired or not.

The neighbors pitied the children. Meaning only kindness, Mr. Cranefield reminded Molly that one day she would type, Mrs. Massie said something more about helping in the garden. That was how everyone saw them now — grubbing, digging, lending a hand. They had become Wilkinson's secondhand kin but without his panache, his ease in adversity. They were Alec's offspring: stiff. Humiliated, they overheard and garnered for memory: "We've asked Wilkinson to come over and cook up a curry. He's hours in the kitchen, but I must say it's worth every penny." "We might get Wilkinson to drive us to Rome. He doesn't charge all that much, and he's such good company." Always Wilkinson, never Eric, though that was what Barbara had called him from their first meeting. To the children he was, and remained, "Mr. Wilkinson," friend of both parents, occasional guest in the house.

The rains of their third southern spring were still driving hard against the villa when Barbara's engineer brother wrote to say they were letting Lou Mas. Everything dripped wet as she stood near a window, with bougainvillea soaked and wild-looking on one side of the pane and steam forming on the other, to read this letter. The new tenants were a family of planters who had been forced to leave Malaya; it had a connection with political events, but Barbara's life was so full now that she never looked at the papers. They would be coming there in June, which gave Barbara plenty of time to find another home. He — her brother — had thought of giving her the Lou Mas cottage, but he wondered if it would suit her, inasmuch as it lacked electric light, running water, an indoor lavatory, most of its windows, and part of its roof. This was not to say it could not be fixed up for the Webbs in the future, when Lou Mas had started paying for itself. Half the rent obtained would be turned over to Barbara. She would have to look hard, he said, before finding brothers who were so considerate of a married sister. She and the children were not likely to suffer from the change, which might even turn out to their moral advantage. Barbara supposed this meant that Desmond — the richest, the best-educated, the most easily flabbergasted of her brothers — was still mulling over the description of Lou Mas Ron must have taken back.

With Wilkinson helping, the Webbs moved to the far side of the hospital, on a north-facing slope, away from the sea. Here the houses were tall and thin with narrow windows, set in gardens of raked gravel. Their neighbors included the mayor, the more prosperous shopkeepers, and the coach of the local football team. Barbara was enchanted to find industrial activity she had not suspected — a thriving ceramics factory that produced figurines of monks whose heads were mustard pots, dogs holding thermometers in their paws, and the patron saint of Rivabella wearing armor of pink, orange, mauve, or white. These were purchased by tourists who had trudged up to the town in the hope of seeing early-Renaissance frescoes.

Barbara had never missed a day with Alec — not even the day of the move. She held his limp hand and told him stories. When he was not stunned by drugs, or too far lost in his past, he seemed to be listening. Sometimes he pressed her fingers. He seldom spoke more than a word at a time. Barbara described to him the pleasures of moving, and how pretty the houses were on the north side, with their gardens growing gnomes and shells and tinted bottles. Why make fun of such people, she asked his still face. They probably know, by instinct, how to get the best out of life. She meant every word, for she was profoundly in love and knew that Wilkinson would never leave her except for a greater claim. She combed Alec's hair and bathed him; Wilkinson came whenever he could to shave Alec and cut his nails and help Barbara change the bedsheets; for it was not the custom of the hospital staff to do any of this.

Sometimes Alec whispered, "Diana," who might have been either his sister or Mrs. Massie. Barbara tried to remember her old prophetic dreams, from that time when, as compensation for absence of passion, she had been granted second sight. In none had she ever seen herself bending over a dying man, listening to him call her by another woman's name.

They lived, now, in four dark rooms stuffed with furniture, some of it useful. Upstairs resided the widow of the founder of the ceramics factory. She had been bought out at a loss at the end of the war, and disapproved of the new line of production, especially the monks. She never interfered, never asked questions — simply came down once a month to collect her rent, which was required in cash. She did tell the children that she had never seen the inside of an English villa, but did not seem to think her exclusion was a slight; she took her bearings from a very small span of the French middle-class compass.

Barbara and Wilkinson made jokes about the French widow lady, but the children did not. To replace their lopped English roots they had grown the sensitive antennae essential to wanderers. They could have drawn the social staircase of Rivabella on a blackboard, and knew how low a step, now, had been assigned to them. Barbara would not have cared. Wherever she stood now seemed to suit her. On her way home from the hospital she saw two men, foreigners, stop and stare and exchange remarks about her. She could not understand the language they spoke, but she saw they had been struck by her beauty. One of them seemed to be asking the other, "Who can she be?" In their new home she took the only bedroom — an imposing matrimonial chamber. When Wilkinson was in residence he shared it as a matter of course. The boys slept on a pullout sofa in the dining room, and Molly had a couch on a glassed-in verandah. The verandah contained their landlady's rubber plants, which Molly scrupulously tended. The boys had stopped quarreling. Alec's children seemed to have been collected under one roof by chance, like strays, or refugees. Their narrow faces, their gray eyes, their thinness and dryness were similar but not alike; a stranger would not necessarily have known they were of the same father and mother. The boys still wore secondhand clothes sent from England; this was their only connection with English life.

On market days Molly often saw their old housemaid or the laundress. They asked for news of Alec, which made Molly feel cold and shy. She was dressed very like them now, in a cotton frock and rope-soled shoes from a market stall. "Style is all you need to bring it off," Barbara had assured her, but Molly had none — at least not that kind. It was Molly who chose what the family would eat, who looked at prices and kept accounts and counted her change. Barbara was entirely busy with Alec at the hospital, and with Wilkinson at home. With love, she had lost her craving for nursery breakfasts. She sat at table smoking, watching Wilkinson tell stories. When Wilkinson was there, he did much of the cooking. Molly was grateful for that.

The new people at Lou Mas had everyone's favor. If there had been times when the neighbors had wondered how Barbara and Alec could possibly have met, the Malayan planter and his jolly wife were an old novel known by heart. They told about jungle terrorists, and what the British ought to be doing, and they described the owner of Lou Mas — a Welshman who was planning to go into politics. Knowing Barbara to be Irish, no one could place the Welshman. The story started up that Barbara's family were bankrupt and had sold Lou Mas to a Welsh war profiteer.

Mrs. Massie presented the new people with *Flora's Gardening Encyclopedia*. "It is by way of being a classic," she said. "Seventeen editions. I do all my typing myself."

"Ah, well, poor Barbara," everyone said now. What could you expect? Luckily for her, she had Wilkinson. Wilkinson's star was rising. "Don't underestimate Rommel" had been said to some effect — there was a mention in the *Sunday Telegraph*. "Wilkinson goes everywhere. He's invited to everything at Monte Carlo. He must positively live on lobster salad." "Good for old Wilkinson. Why shouldn't he?" Wilkinson had had a bad war, had been a prisoner somewhere.

Who imagined that story, Mr. Cranefield wondered. Some were mixing up Wilkinson with the dying Alec, others seemed to think Alec was already dead. By August it had become established that Wilkinson had been tortured by the Japanese and had spent the years since trying to leave the memory behind. He never mentioned what he'd been through, which was to his credit. Barbara and three kids must have been the last thing he wanted, but that was how it was with Wilkinson — too kind for his own good, all too ready to lend a hand, to solve a problem. Perhaps, rising, he would pull the Webbs with him. Have you seen that girl hanging about in the market? You can't tell her from the butcher's child.

From Alec's bedside Barbara wrote a long letter to her favorite brother, the pilot, Mike. She told about Alec, "sleeping so peacefully as I write," and described the bunch of daisies Molly had put in a jug on the windowsill, and how well Will had done in his finals ("He will be the family intellectual, a second Alec"), and finally she came round to the matter of Wilkinson: "You probably saw the rave notice in the *Telegraph*, but you had no way of knowing of course it was someone I knew. Well, here is the whole story. Please, Mike, do keep it to yourself for the moment, you know how Ron takes things sometimes." Meeting Eric had confirmed her belief that there was something in the universe more reasonable than God — at any rate more logical. Eric had taken a good look at the Lou Mas cottage and thought something might be done with it after all. "You will adore Eric," she promised. "He is marvelous with the children and so kind to Alec," which was true.

"Are you awake, love?" She moistened a piece of cotton with mineral water from a bottle that stood on the floor (Alec had no table) and wet his lips with it, then took his hand, so light it seemed hollow, and held it in her own, telling him quietly about the Lou Mas cottage, where he would occupy a pleasant room overlooking the sea. He flexed his fingers; she bent close: "Yes, dear. What is it, dear?" For the first time since she'd known him he said, "Mother." She waited; but no, that was all. She saw herself on his balcony at Lou Mas in her white dressing gown, her hair in the sun, saw what the gardener would have been struck by if only he had looked up. She said to herself, "I gave Alec three beautiful children. That is what he is thanking me for now."

Her favorite brother had been away from England when her letter came, so that it was late in September when he answered to call her a bitch, a trollop, a crook, and a fool. He was taking up the question of her gigolo boy friend with the others. They had been supporting Alec's family for three years. If she thought they intended to take on her lover (this written above a word scratched out); and here the letter ended. She went white, as her children did, easily. She said to Wilkinson, "Come and talk in the car, where we can be quiet," for they were seldom alone.

She let him finish reading, then said, in a voice that he had never heard before but that did not seem to surprise him, "I grew up blacking my brothers' boots. Alec was the first man who ever held a door open for me."

He said, "Your brothers all did well," without irony, meaning there was that much to admire.

"Oh," she said, "if you are comparing their chances with Alec's, if that's what you mean — the start Alec had. Well, poor Alec. Yes, a better start. I often thought, Well, there it is with him, that's the very trouble — a start too good."

This exchange, this double row of cards face up, seemed all they intended to reveal. They instantly sat differently, she straighter, he more relaxed.

Wilkinson said, "Which one of them actually owns Lou Mas?"

"Equal shares, I think. Though Desmond has power of attorney and makes all the decisions. Alec and I *own* Lou Mas, but only legally. They put it in our name because we were emigrating. It made it easier for them, with all the taxes. We had three years, and not a penny in rent."

Wilkinson said, in a kind of anguish, "Oh, God bless my soul."

It was Wilkinson's English lawyer friend in Monte Carlo who drew up the papers with which Alec signed his share of Lou Mas over to Barbara, and Alec and Barbara revoked her brother's power of attorney. Alec, his obedient hand around a pen and the hand firmly held in Barbara's, may have known what he was doing but not why. The documents were then put in the lawyer's safe to await Alec's death, which occurred not long after.

The doctor, who had sat all night at the bedside, turning Alec's head so that he would not strangle vomiting (for that was not the way he wished him to die), heard him breathing deeply and ever more deeply and then no longer. Alec's eyes were closed, but the doctor pressed the lids with his fingers. Believing in his own and perhaps Alec's damnation, he stood for a long time at the window while the roof and towers of the church became clear and flushed with rose; then the red rim of the sun emerged, and turned yellow, and it was as good as day.

There was only one nurse in the hospital, and a midwife on another floor. Summoning both, he told them to spread a rubber sheet under Alec, and wash him, and put clean linen on the bed.

At that time, in that part of France, scarcely anyone had a telephone. The doctor walked down the slope on the far side of Rivabella and presented himself unshaven to Barbara in her nightdress to say that Alec was dead. She dressed and came at once; there was no one yet in the streets to see her and to ask who she was. Eric followed, bringing the clothes in which Alec would be buried. All he could recall of his prayers, though he would not have said them around Barbara, were the first words of the Collect: "Almighty

God, unto whom all hearts be open, all desires known, and from whom no secrets are hid."

Barbara had a new friend — her French widowed landlady. It was she who arranged to have part of Barbara's wardrobe dyed black within twenty-four hours, who lent her a black hat and gloves and a long crepe veil. Barbara let the veil down over her face. Her friend, whose veil was tied round her hat and floated behind her, took Barbara by the arm, and they walked to the cemetery and stood side by side. The Webbs' former servants were there, and the doctor, and the local British colony. Some of the British thought the other woman in black must be Barbara's Irish mother: only the Irish poor or the Royal Family ever wore mourning of that kind.

The graveyard was so cramped and small, so crowded with dead from the time of Garibaldi and before, that no one else could be buried. The coffins of the recent dead were stored in cells in a thick concrete wall. The cells were then sealed, and a marble plaque affixed in lieu of a tombstone. Alec had to be lifted to shoulder level, which took the strength of several persons — the doctor, Mr. Cranefield, Barbara's brothers, and Alec's young sons. (Wilkinson would have helped, but he had already wrenched his shoulder quite badly carrying the coffin down the hospital steps.) Molly thrust her way into this crowd of male mourners. She said to her mother, "Not you — you never loved him."

God knows who might have heard that, Barbara thought.

Actually, no one had, except for Mrs. Massie. Believing it to be true, she dismissed it from memory. She was composing her own obituary: "Two generations of gardeners owed their . . ." "Two generations of readers owed their gardens . . ."

"Our Father," Alec's sister said, hoping no one would notice and mistake her for a fraud. Nor did she wish to have a scrap of consideration removed from Barbara, whose hour this was. Her own loss was beyond remedy, and so not worth a mention. There was no service — nothing but whispering and silence. To his sister, it was as if Alec had been left, stranded and alone, in a train stalled between stations. She had not seen him since the day he left England, and had refused to look at him dead. Barbara was aware of Diana, the mouse, praying like a sewing machine somewhere behind her. She clutched the arm of the older widow and thought, I know, I know, but she can get a job, can't she? I was working when

I met Alec, wasn't I? But what Diana Webb meant by "work" was the fine stitching her own mother had done to fill time, not for a living. In Diana's hotel room was a box containing the most exquisite and impractical child's bonnet and coat made from some of the white silk Alec had sent her from India, before the war. Perhaps a luxury shop in Monte Carlo or one of Barbara's wealthy neighbors would be interested. Perhaps there was an Anglican clergyman with a prosperous parish. She opened her eyes and saw that absolutely no one in the cemetery looked like Alec — not even his sons.

The two boys seemed strange, even to each other, in their dark, new suits. The word *father* had slipped out of their grasp just now. A marble plaque on which their father's name was misspelled stood propped against the wall. The boys looked at it helplessly.

Is that all? people began wondering. What happens now?

Barbara turned away from the wall and, still holding the arm of her friend, led the mourners out past the gates.

It was I who knew what he wanted, the doctor believed. He told me long before. Asked me to promise, though I refused. I heard his last words. The doctor kept telling himself this. "I heard his last words" — though Alec had not said anything, had merely breathed, then stopped.

"Her father was a late-Victorian poet of some distinction," Mrs. Massie's obituary went on.

Will, who was fifteen, was no longer a child, did not look like Alec, spoke up in that high-pitched English of his: "Death is empty without God." Now, where did that come from? Had he heard it? Read it? Was he performing? No one knew.

As they shuffled out, all made very uncomfortable by Will, Mrs. Massie leaned half on her stick and half on James, observing, "You were such a little boy when I saw you for the first time at Lou Mas." Because his response was silence, she supposed he was waiting to hear more. "You three must stick together now. The Three Musketeers." But they were already apart.

Major Lamprey found himself walking beside the youngest of the Laceys. He told Mike what he told everyone now — why he had not moved to Malta. It was because he did not trust the Maltese. "Not that one can trust anyone here," he said. "Even the mayor belongs to an anarchist movement, I've been told. Whatever happens, I intend to die fighting on my own doorstep."

The party was filing down a steep incline. "You will want to be with your family," Mrs. Massie said, releasing James and leaning half her weight on Mr. Cranefield instead. They picked up with no trouble a conversation dropped the day before. It was about how Mr. Cranefield — rather, his other self, E. C. Arden — was likely to fare in the second half of the 1950s: "It is a question of your not being too modern and yet not slipping back," Mrs. Massie said. "I never have to worry. Gardens don't change."

"I am not worried about new ideas," he said. "Because there are none. But words, now. 'Permissive.' "

"What's that?"

"It was in the *Observer* last Sunday. I suppose it means something. Still. One mustn't. One can't. There are limits."

Barbara met the mayor coming the other way, too late, carrying a wreath with a purple ribbon on which was written, in gold, "From the Municipality — Sincere Respects." Waiting for delivery of the wreath had made him tardy. "For a man who never went out, Alec made quite an impression," Mrs. Massie remarked.

"His funeral was an attraction," said Mr. Cranefield.

"Can one call that a funeral?" She was still thinking about her own.

Mike Lacey caught up to his sister. They had once been very close. As soon as she saw him, she stood motionless, bringing the line behind her to a halt. He said he knew this was not the time or place, but he had to let her know she was not to worry. She would always have a roof over her head. They felt responsible for Alec's children. There were vague plans for fixing up the cottage. They would talk about it later on.

"Ah, Mike," she said. "That is so kind of you." Using both hands, she lifted the veil so that he could see her clear gray eyes.

The procession wound past the hospital and came to the church square. Mr. Cranefield had arranged a small after-funeral party, as a favor to Barbara, who had no real home. Some were coming and some were not; the latter now began to say good-bye. Geneviève, whose face was like a pink sponge because she had been crying so hard, flung herself at James, who let her embrace him. Over his governess's dark shoulder he saw the faces of people who had given him secondhand clothes, thus (he believed) laying waste to his life. He smashed their faces to particles, left the particles dancing in the air like midges until they dissolved without a sound. Wait, he was thinking. Wait, wait.

Mr. Cranefield wondered if Molly was going to become her mother's hostage, her moral bail — if Barbara would hang on to her to show that Alec's progeny approved of her. He remembered Molly's small, anxious face, and how worried she had been about St. George. "You will grow up, you know," he said, which was an odd thing to say, since she was quite tall. They walked down the path Wilkinson had not been able to climb in his car. She stared at him. "I mean, when you grow up you will be free." She shook her head. She knew better than that now, at fourteen.

Mr. Cranefield's attention slipped from Molly to Alec to the funeral, to the extinction of one sort of Englishman and the emergence of another. Most people looked on Wilkinson as a prewar survival, what with his I say's and By Jove's, but he was really an English mutation, a new man, wearing the old protective coloring. Alec would have understood his language, probably, but not the person behind it. A landscape containing two male figures came into high relief in Mr. Cranefield's private image of the world, as if he had been lent trick spectacles. He allowed the vision to fade. Better to stick to the blond pair on his desk; so far they had never let him down. I am not impulsive, or arrogant, he explained to himself. No one would believe the truth about Wilkinson even if he were to describe it. I shall not insist, he decided, or try to have the last word. I am not that kind of fool. He breathed slowly, as one does when mortal danger has been averted.

The mourners attending Mr. Cranefield's party reached the motor road and began to straggle across: it was a point of honor for members of the British colony to pay absolutely no attention to cars. The two widows had fallen back, either so that Barbara could make an entrance or because the older woman believed it would not be dignified for her to exhibit haste. A strong west wind flattened the black dresses against their breasts and lifted their thick veils.

How will he hear me, Molly wondered. You could speak to someone in a normal grave, for earth is porous and seems to be life, of a kind. But how to speak through marble? Even if she were to place her hands flat on the marble slab, it would not absorb a fraction of human warmth. She had to tell him what she had done — how it was she, Molly, who had led the intruder home, let him in, causing Alec, always courteous, to remove himself first to the hospital, then farther on. Disaster, the usual daily development, had to have a beginning. She would go back to the cemetery, alone, and say it, whether or not he could hear. The disaster began with two sentences: "Mummy, this is Mr. Wilkinson. Mr. Wilkinson wants to tell you how he came to drive me home."

Barbara descended the steps to Mr. Cranefield's arm in arm with her new friend, who was for the first time about to see the inside of an English house. "Look at that," said the older widow. One of the peacocks had taken shelter from the wind in Mr. Cranefield's electric lift. A minute earlier Alec's sister had noticed, too, and had thought something that seemed irrefutable: no power on earth would ever induce her to eat a peacock.

Who is to say I never loved Alec, said Barbara, who loved Wilkinson. He was highhanded, yes, laying down the law as long as he was able, but he was always polite. Of course I loved him. I still do. He will have to be buried properly, where we can plant something — white roses. The mayor told me that every once in a while they turn one of the Russians out, to make room. There must be a waiting list. We could put Alec's name on it. Alec gave me three children. Eric gave me Lou Mas.

Entering Mr. Cranefield's, she removed her dark veil and hat and revealed her lovely head, like the sun rising. Because the wind had started blowing leaves and sand, Mr. Cranefield's party had to be moved indoors from the loggia. This change occasioned some confusion, in which Barbara did not take part; neither did Wilkinson, whose wrenched shoulder was making him feel ill. She noticed her children helping, carrying plates of small sandwiches and silver buckets of ice. She approved of this; they were obviously well brought up. The funeral had left Mr. Cranefield's guests feeling hungry and thirsty and rather lonely, anxious to hold on to a glass and to talk to someone. Presently their voices rose, overlapped, and created something like a thick woven fabric of blurred design, which Alec's sister (who was not used to large social gatherings) likened to a flying carpet. It was now, with Molly covertly watching her, that Barbara began in the most natural way in the world to live happily ever after. There was nothing deliberate about this: she was simply borne in a single direction, though she did keep seeing for a time her black glove on her widowed friend's black sleeve.

Escorting lame Mrs. Massie to a sofa, Mr. Cranefield said they might as well look on the bright side. (He was still speaking about the second half of the 1950s.) Wilkinson, sitting down because he felt sick, and thinking the remark was intended for him, assured Mr. Cranefield, truthfully, that he had never looked anywhere else. It then happened that every person in the room, at the same moment, spoke and thought of something other than Alec. This lapse, this inattention, lasting no longer than was needed to say "No, thank you" or "Oh, really?" or "Yes, I see," was enough to create the dark gap marking the end of Alec's span. He ceased to be, and it made absolutely no difference after that whether or not he was forgotten.

MAVIS GALLANT

Speck's Idea

(FROM THE NEW YORKER)

SANDOR SPECK's first art gallery in Paris was on the Right Bank, near the Church of St. Elisabeth, on a street too narrow for cars. When his block was wiped off the map to make way for a five-story garage, Speck crossed the Seine to the shadow of Saint-Julien-le-Pauvre, where he set up shops in a picturesque slum protected by law from demolition. When this gallery was blown up by Basque separatists, who had mistaken it for a travel agency exploiting the beauty of their coast, he collected his insurance money and moved to the Faubourg Saint-Germain.

Here, at terrifying cost, he rented four excellent rooms — two on the loggia level, and a clean dry basement for framing and storage. The entrance, particularly handsome, was on the street side of an eighteenth-century *hôtel particulier* built around an elegant court now let out as a parking concession. The building had long before been cut up into dirty, decaying apartments, whose spiteful, quarrelsome, and avaricious tenants were forgiven every failing by Speck for the sake of being the count of this and the prince of that. Like the flaking shutters, the rotting windowsills, the slops and oil stains in the ruined court, they bore a Proustian seal of distinction, like a warranty, making up for his insanely expensive lease. Though he appreciated style, he craved stability even more. In the Faubourg, he seemed at last likely to find it: not a stone could be removed without the approval of the toughest cultural authorities of the nation. Three Marxist embassies installed in former ducal mansions along the street required the presence of armed policemen the clock around. The only commercial establishments anywhere near Speck's — a restaurant and a bookstore — seemed unlikely targets for firebombs; the first catered to lower-echelon civil servants, the second was painted royal blue, a conservative color he found reassuring. The bookstore's name, Amandine, suggested shelves of calm regional novels and accounts of travel to Imperial Russia signed "A Diplomat." Pasted inside the window, flat on the pane, was an engraving that depicted an old man, bearded and mitred, tearing a small demon limb from limb. The old man looked self-conscious, the imp resigned. He supposed that this image concealed a deep religious meaning, which he did not intend to plumb. If it was holy, it was respectable; as the owner of the gallery across the street, he needed to know nothing more.

Speck was now in the parish of St. Clotilde, near enough to the church for its bells to give him migraine headache. Leaves from the church square blew as far as his door — melancholy reminders of autumn, a season bad for art. (Winter was bad, too, while the first chestnut leaves unfolding heralded the worst season of all. In summer the gallery closed.) In spite of his constant proximity to churches he had remained rational. Generations of highly intellectual Central European agnostics and freethinkers had left in his bones a mistrust of the bogs and quicksands that lie beyond reality perceived. Neither loss nor grief nor guilt nor fear had ever moved him to appeal to the unknown — any unknown, for there were several. Nevertheless, after signing his third lease in seven years, he decided to send Walter, his Swiss assistant, a lapsed Calvinist inching toward Rome, to light a candle at St. Clotilde's. Walter paid for a five-franc taper and set it before St. Joseph, the most reliable intermediary he could find: a wave of postconciliar puritanism seemed to have broken at St. Clotilde's, sweeping away most of the mute and obliging figures to whom desires and gratitude could be expressed. Walter was willing to start again in some livelier church — Notre Dame de Paris, for instance — but Speck thought enough was enough.

On a damp October evening about a year after this, there could be seen in Speck's window a drawing of a woman drying her feet (Speck permanent collection); a poster announcing the current exhibition, "Paris and Its Influence on the Tirana School, 1931–2"; five catalogues displayed attractively; and the original of the picture on the poster — a shameless copy of Foujita's *Mon*

Intérieur reëntitled *Balkan Alarm Clock.* In defiance of a government circular reminding Paris galleries about the energy crisis, Speck had left the lights on. This was partly to give the lie to competitors who might be putting it about that he was having money troubles. He had set the burglar alarm, bolted the security door, and was now cranking down an openwork iron screen whose art nouveau loops and fronds allowed the works inside to be seen but nothing larger than a mouse to get in. The faint, floating sadness he always felt while locking up had to do with the time. In his experience, love affairs and marriages perished between seven and eight o'clock, the hour of rain and no taxis. All over Paris couples must be parting forever, leaving like debris along the curbs the shreds of canceled restaurant dates, useless ballet tickets, hopeless explanations, and scraps of pride; and toward each of these disasters a taxi was pulling in, the only taxi for miles, the light on its roof already dimmed in anticipation to the twin dots that in Paris mean "occupied." But occupied by whom?

"You take it."

"No, you. You're the one in a hurry."

The lover abandoned under a dripping plane tree would feel a damp victory of a kind, awarding himself a first-class trophy for selfless behavior. It would sustain him ten seconds, until the departing one rolled down the taxi window to hurl her last flint: "You Fascist!" Why was this always the final shot, the coup de grâce delivered by women? Speck's wife, Henriette, book critic on an uncompromising political weekly, had said it three times last spring — here, in the street, where Speck stood locking the iron screen into place. He had been uneasily conscious of his well-born neighbors hanging out their windows, not missing a thing. Henriette had then gone away in a cab to join her lover, leaving Speck, the gallery, her job — everything that mattered.

He mourned Henriette; he missed her steadying influence. Her mind was like a one-way thoroughfare, narrow and flat, maintained in repair. As he approached the age of forty he felt that his own intellect needed not just a direction but retaining walls. Unless his thoughts were nailed down by gallery business they tended to glide away to the swamps of imagination, behind which stretched the steamier marshland of metaphysics. Confessing this to Henriette was unlikely to bring her back. There had been something brisk and joyous about her going — her hailing of a taxi as though of a friend, her surprised smile as the third "Fascist!" dissolved in the April night like a double stroke from the belfry of St. Clotilde's. He supposed he would never see her again now, except by accident. Perhaps, long after he had forgotten Henriette, he would overhear someone saying in a restaurant, "Do you see that poor mad intellectual talking to herself in the corner? That is Henriette, Sandor Speck's second wife. Of course, she was very different then; Speck kept her in shape."

While awaiting this sop, which he could hardly call consolation, he had Walter and the gallery. Walter had been with him five years — longer than either of his marriages. They had been years of spiritual second-thinking for Walter and of strain and worry for Speck. Walter in search of the Eternal was like one of those solitary skippers who set out to cross an ocean only to capsize when barely out of port. Speck had been obliged to pluck his assistant out of Unitarian waters and set him on the firm shore of the Trinity. He had towed him to Transubstantiation and back; had charted the shoals and perils of careless prayer. His own aversion to superstitious belief made Speck particularly scrupulous; he would not commit himself on Free Will, for instance, uncertain if it was supposed to be an uphill trudge wearing tight boots or a downhill slide sitting on a tea tray. He would lie awake at night planning Walter's dismissal, only to develop a traumatic chest cold if his assistant seemed restless.

"What will the gallery do without you?" he would ask on the very morning he had been meaning to say, "Walter, sit down, please. I've got something to tell you." Walter would remind him about saints and holy men who had done without everything, while Speck would envision the pure hell of having to train someone new.

On a rainy night such as this, the street resembled a set in a French film designed for export, what with the policemen's white rain capes aesthetically gleaming and the lights of the bookstore, the restaurant, and the gallery reflected, quivering, in European-looking puddles. In reality, Speck thought, there was not even hope for a subplot. Henriette had gone forever. Walter's mission could not be photographed. The owner of the restaurant was in his eighties; the waiters were poised on the brink of retirement. As for the bookseller, M. Alfred Chassepoule, he seemed to spend most of his time wiping blood off the collected speeches of Mussolini, bandaging customers, and sweeping up glass. The fact was that Amandine's had turned out to have a fixed right-wing view-point, which made it subject to attack by commandos wielding iron bars. Speck, who had chosen the street for its upper-class hush, had grown used to the hoarse imprecation of the Left and shriller keening of the Right; he could tell the sob of an ambulance from the wail of a police van. The commerce of art is without bias: when insurance inspectors came round to ask what Speck might have seen, he invariably replied, "Seen where?" to which Walter, unsolicited, would add, "And I am Swiss."

Since Henriette's departure, Speck often ate his meals in the local restaurant, which catered to his frugal tastes, his vegetarian principles, and his desire to be left in peace. On the way, he would pause outside Amandine's, just enough to mark the halt as a comforting bachelor habit. He would glance over the secondhand books, the yellowing pamphlets, and the overpriced cartoons. The tone of the window display seemed old-fashioned rather than dangerous, though he knew that the slogan crowning the arrangement, "Europe for Europeans," echoed from a dark political valley. But even that valley had been full of strife and dissension and muddle, for hadn't the Ur-Fascists, the Italian ones, been in some way against an all-Europe? At least, some of their poets were. But who could take any of that seriously now? Nothing political had ever struck Speck as being above the level of a low-grade comic strip. On the cover of one volume, Uncle Sam shook hands with the Russian Bear over prostrate Europe, depicted as a maiden in a dead faint. A drawing of a spider on a field of banknotes (twelve hundred francs with frame, nine hundred without) jostled the image of a crablike hand clawing away at the map of France. Pasted against the pane, survivor of uncounted assaults, the old man continued to dismember his captive imp. Walter had told Speck he believed the old man to be St. Amand, Apostle of Flanders, Bishop in 430. "Or perhaps," said Walter, after thinking it over, "435." The imp probably stood for Flemish paganism, which the apostle had been hard put to it to overcome.

From the rainy street Speck could see four or five of Amandine's customers — all men; he had never noticed a woman in the place — standing, reading, books held close to their noses. They had the weak eyes, long chins, and sparse, sparrow-colored hair he associated with low governmental salaries. He imagined them living with grim widowed mothers whose company they avoided after work.

He had seen them, or young men like them, staggering out of the
store, cut by flying glass, kicked and beaten as they lay stunned on
the pavement; his anxious imagination had set them on their feet,
booted and belted, the right signal given at last, swarming across to
the gallery, determined to make Speck pay for injuries inflicted on
them by total strangers. He saw his only early Chagall (quite likely
authentic) ripped from its frame; Walter, his poor little spectacles
smeared with blood, lambasted with the complete Charles Maurras,
fourteen volumes, full morocco; Speck himself, his ears offended
by acute right-wing cries of "Down with foreign art!" attempting a
quick counterstroke with *Significant Minor French Realists, Twentieth
Century,* which was thick enough to stun an ox. Stepping back from
the window, Speck saw his own smile reflected. It was pinched and
tight, and he looked a good twenty years older than thirty-nine.

His restaurant, crammed with civil servants at noon, was now
nearly empty. A smell of lunchtime pot roast hung in the air. He
made for his own table, from which he could see the comforting
lights of the gallery. The waiter, who had finally stopped asking
how Henriette was liking Africa, brought his dinner at once, setting
out like little votive offerings the raw-carrot salad, the pot-roast
vegetables without the meat, the quarter ounce of low-fat cheese,
and a small pear. It had long been established that Speck did not
wish to be disturbed by the changing of plates. He extracted a
yellow pad and three pencils from his briefcase and placed them
within the half-circle of dishes. Speck was preparing his May–June
show.

The right show at the right time: it was trickier than getting
married to the right person at any time. For about a year now,
Paris critics had been hinting at something missing from the world
of art. These hints, poignant and patriotic on the Right, neonation-
alist and pugnacious on the Left, wistful but insistent dead Center,
were all in essence saying the same thing: "The time has come."
The time had come; the hour had struck; the moment was ripe for
a revival of reason, sanity, and taste. Surely there was more to art
than this sickness, this transatlantic blight? Fresh winds were
needed to sweep the museums and galleries. Two days ago there
had been a disturbing article in *Le Monde* (front page, lower middle, turn to page 26) by a man who never took up his pen unless
civilization was in danger. Its title, "Redemption Through Art —

Last Hope for the West?" had been followed by other disturbing questions: When would the merchants and dealers, compared rather unfairly to the moneychangers driven from the temple, face up to their share of responsibility as the tattered century declined? Must the flowering gardens of Western European culture wilt and die along with the decadent political systems, the exhausted parliaments, the shambling elections, the tired liberal impulses? What of the man in the street, too modest and confused to mention his cravings? Was he not gasping for one remedy and one only — artistic renovation? And where was this to come from? "In the words of Shakespr," the article concluded, supposedly in English, "That is the qustn."

As it happened, Speck had the answer: say, a French painter, circa 1864–1949, forgotten now except by a handful of devoted connoisseurs. Populist yet refined, local but universal, he would send rays, beacons, into the thickening night of the West, just as Speck's gallery shone bravely into the dark street. Speck picked up a pencil and jotted rapidly: "Born in France, worked in Paris, went his own way, unmindful of fashion, knowing his hour would strike, his vision be vindicated. Catholical, as this retrospective so eloquently . . ." Just how does "catholical" come in, Speck wondered, forking up raw carrots. Because of ubiquity, the ubiquity of genius? No; not genius — leave that for the critics. His sense of harmony, then — his discretion.

Easy, Speck told himself. Easy on the discretion. This isn't interior decoration.

He could see the notices, knew which of the critics would write "At last" and "It has taken Sandor Speck to remind us." Left, Right, and Center would unite on a single theme: how the taste of two full generations had been corrupted by foreign speculation, cosmopolitan decadence, and the cultural imperialism of the Anglo-Saxon hegemony.

"The calm agnostic face," Speck wrote happily, "the quiet Cartesian voice are replaced by the snarl of a nation betrayed (1914), as startling for the viewer as a child's glimpse of a beloved adult in a temper tantrum. The snarl, the grimace vanish (1919) as the serene observer of Universal Will (1929) and of Man's responsibility to himself return. But we are left shaken. We have stopped trusting our feelings. We have been shown not only the smile but the teeth."

Here Speck drew a wavy line and turned to the biography, which was giving him trouble. On a fresh yellow page he tried again:

1938 — Travels to Nice. Sees Mediterranean.
1939 — Abandons pacifist principle. Lies about age. Is mobilized.
1940 — Is mobilized.
1941 —

It was here that Speck bogged down. Should he say, "Joins Resistance"? "Resistance" today meant either a heroic moment sadly undervalued by the young or a minor movement greatly inflated in order to absolve French guilt. Whatever it is, thought Speck, it is not chic. The youngest survivor must be something like seventy-three. They know nothing about art, and never subscribe to anything except monuments. Some people read "Resistance" in a chronology and feel quite frankly exasperated. On the other hand, what about museums, state-subsidized, Resistance-minded on that account? He chewed a boiled leek and suddenly wrote, "1941 — Conversations with Albert Camus." I wonder where all this comes from, Speck said to himself. Inspiration was what he meant.

These notes, typed by Walter, would be turned over to the fashionable historian, the alarming critic, the sound political figure unlikely to be thrown out of office between now and spring, whom Speck would invite to write the catalogue introduction. "Just a few notes," Speck would say tactfully. "Knowing how busy you are." Nothing was as inspiriting to him as the thought of his own words in print on a creamy catalogue page, even over someone else's name.

Speck took out of his briefcase the Directoire snuffbox Henriette had given him about a fortnight before suddenly calling him "Fascist." (Unexpected feminine generosity — first firm sign of adulterous love affair.) It contained three after-dinner tablets — one to keep him alert until bedtime, another to counter the stimulating effect of the first, and a third to neutralize the germ known as Warsaw flu now ravaging Paris, emptying schools and factories and creating delays in the postal service. He sat quietly, digesting, giving the pills a chance to work.

He could see the structure of the show, the sketchbooks and letters in glass cases. It might be worthwhile lacquering the walls black, concentrating strong spots on the correspondence, which straddled half a century, from Degas to Cocteau. The scrawl posted by Drieu la Rochelle just before his suicide would be particularly effective on black. Céline was good; all that crowd was back in vogue now. He might use the early photo of Céline in regimental dress uniform with a splendid helmet. Of course, there would be word from the Left, too, with postcards from Jean Jaurès, Léon Blum, and Paul Éluard, and a jaunty get-well message from Louis Aragon and Elsa. In the first room Speck would hang the stiff, youthful landscapes and the portraits of the family, the artist's first models — his brother wearing a sailor suit, the awkward but touching likeness of his sister (*Germaine-Isabelle at the Window*).

"Yes, yes," Speck would hear in the buzz of voices at the opening. "Even from the beginning you can tell there was *something*." The "something" became bolder, firmer in the second room. See his cities; watch how the streets turn into mazes, nets, prison corridors. Dark palette. Opaqueness, the whole canvas covered, immensities of indigo and black. "Look, 1929; he was doing it before What's-His-Name." Upstairs, form breaking out of shadow: bread, cheese, wine, wheat, ripe apples, grapes.

Hold it, Speck told himself. Hold the ripeness. This isn't social realism.

He gathered up the pencils, the snuffbox, and the pad, and put them back in the briefcase. He placed seventy francs, tip included, in a saucer. Still he sat, his mind moving along to the second loggia room, the end room, the important one. Here on the neutral walls would be the final assurance, the serenity, the satire, the power, and the vision for which, at last, the time had come. For that was the one thing Speck was sure of: the bell had rung, the hour had struck, the moment was at hand.

Whose time? Which hour? Yes — whose, which, what? That was where he was stuck.

The street was now empty except for the policemen in their streaming capes. The bookstore had put up its shutter. Speck observed the walls of the three Marxist embassies. Shutters and curtains that once had shielded the particular privacy of the aristocracy — privacy open to servants but not to the street — now concealed the receptions and merry dinner parties of people's democracies. Sometimes at this hour gleaming motorcars rolled past the mysterious gates, delivering passengers Speck's fancy continued to see as the Duchesse de Guermantes and anyone she did not happen to despise. He knew that the chauffeurs were armed and that half the guests were spies; still, there was nothing to stop a foreign agent from having patrician tastes, or from admiring Speck's window as he drove by.

"This gallery will be an oasis of peace and culture," Walter had predicted as they were hanging the first show, "Little-Known Aspects of Post-Decorator Style." "An oasis of peace and culture in the international desert."

Speck breathed germ-laden night air. Boulevard theaters and music halls were deserted, their managers at home writing letters to the mayor of Paris deploring the decline of popular entertainment and suggesting remedies in the form of large cash subsidies. The sluggish river of autumn life congealed and stagnated around millions of television sets as Parisians swallowed aspirin and drank the boiling-hot scotch believed to be a sovereign defense against Warsaw flu.

A few determined intellectuals slunk, wet, into the Métro, on their way to cultural centers where, in vivid translations from the German, actors would address the occasional surly remark to the audience — that loyal, anxious, humorless audience in its costly fake working-class clothes. Another contingent, dressed in Burberry trenchcoats, had already fought its way into the Geographical Institute, where a lecture with colored slides, "Ramblings in Secret Greenland," would begin, after a delay owing to trouble with the projection machine, at about nine-twenty. The advantage of slides over films was that they were not forever jumping about and confusing one, and the voice describing them belonged to a real speaker. When the lights went up, one could see him, talk to him, challenge him over the thing he had said about shamanism on Disko Island. What had drawn the crowd was not Greenland but the word *secret*. In no other capital city does the population wait more trustfully for the mystery to be solved, the conspiracy to be laid bare, the explanation of every sort of vexation to be supplied: why money slumps, why prices climb, why it rains in August, why children are ungrateful. The answers might easily come from a man with a box of slides.

In each of the city's twenty administrative districts, Communists, distinguished by the cleanliness of their no-iron shirts, the sobriety of their washable neckties, and the modesty of their bearing, moved serenely toward their local cell meetings. I must persuade

Walter to take out membership sometime, Speck thought. It might be useful and interesting for the gallery, and it would take his mind off salvation.

Walter was at this moment in the Church of St. Gervais, across the Seine, where an ecumenical gathering of prayer, music, and debate on Unity of Faith had been marred the week before by ugly scuffling between middle-aged latecomers and young persons in the lotus position, taking up too much room. Walter had turned to his neighbor, a stranger to him, and asked courteously, "Is it a string ensemble tonight, or just the organ?" Mistaken for a traditionalist demanding the Latin Mass, he had been punched in the face and had to be led to a side chapel to mop up his nosebleed. God knows what they might do to him tonight, Speck thought.

As for Speck himself, nine-thirty found him in good company, briskly tying the strings of his Masonic apron. No commitment stronger than prudence kept him from being at St. Gervais, listening for a voice in the night of the soul, or at a Communist Party cell meeting, hoping to acquire a more wholesome slant on art in a doomed society, but he had already decided that only the Infinite could be everywhere at once. The Masonic Grand Architect of the Universe laid down no rules, appointed no prophets, required neither victims nor devotion, and seemed content to exist as a mere possibility. At the lodge Speck rubbed shoulders with men others had to be content to glimpse on television. He stood now no more than three feet away from Kléber Schaumberger, of the Alsatian Protestant banking Schaumbergers; had been greeted by Olivier Ombrine, who designed all the Arabian princesses' wedding gowns; could see, without craning, the plume of white hair belonging to François-Xavier Blum-Bloch-Weiler — former ambassador, historian, member of the French Academy, author of a perennially best-selling book about Vietnam called *When France Was at the Helm.* Speck kept the ambassador's family tree filed in his head. The Blum-Bloch-Weilers, heavy art collectors, produced statesmen, magistrates, anthropologists, and generals, and were on no account to be confused with the Blum-Weiler-Blochs, their penniless and mystical cousins, who produced poets, librarians, and Benedictine monks.

Tonight Speck followed the proceedings mechanically; his mind was set on the yellow pad in his briefcase, now lying on the back seat of his car. Direct address and supplication to the unknown were frowned on here. Order reigned in a complex universe where the Grand Architect, insofar as he existed, was supposed to know what he was doing. However, having nowhere to turn, Speck decided for the first time in his life to brave whatever cosmic derangement might ensue and to unburden himself.

Whoever and whatever you are, said Speck silently, as many had said before him, remember in my favor that I have never bothered you. I never called your attention to the fake Laurencin, the stolen Magritte, the Bonnard the other gallery was supposed to have insured, the Maurice Denis notebook that slipped through my fingers, the Vallotton woodcut that got lost between Paris and Lausanne. All I want . . . But there was no point in his insisting. The Grand Architect, if he was any sort of omnipresence worth considering, knew exactly what Speck needed now: he needed the tiny, enduring wheel set deep in the clanking, churning machinery of the art trade — the artist himself.

Speck came out to the street refreshed and soothed, feeling that he had shed some of his troubles. The rain had stopped. A bright moon hung low. He heard someone saying, ". . . hats." On the glistening pavement a group of men stood listening while Senator Antoine Bellefeuille told a funny story. Facts from the Bellefeuille biography tumbled through Speck's mind: twenty years a deputy from a rich farming district, twice a Cabinet minister, now senator; had married a sugar-beet fortune, which he inherited when his wife died; no children; his mother had left him majority shares in milk chocolate, which he had sold to invest in the first postwar plastics; owned a racing stable in Normandy, a château in Provence, one of the last fine houses in Paris; had taken first-class degrees in law and philosophy; had gone into politics almost as an afterthought.

What had kept the old man from becoming prime minister, even president of the Republic? He had the bearing, the brains, the fortune, and the connections. Too contented, Speck decided, observing his lodge brother by moonlight. But clever, too; he was supposed to have kept copies of files from the time he had been at Justice. He splashed around in the arts, knew the third-generation dealers, the elegant bachelor curators. He went to openings, was not afraid of new movements, but he never bought anything. Speck tried to remember why the wealthy senator who liked art never bought pictures.

"She was stunning," the senator said. "Any man of my generation will tell you that. She came down Boulevard Saint-Michel on her husband's arm. He barely reached her shoulder. She had a smile like a fox's. Straight little animal teeth. Thick red-gold hair. A black hat tilted over one eye. And what a throat. And what hands and arms. A waist no larger than this," said the senator, making a circle with his hands. "As I said, in those days men wore hats. You tipped a bowler by the brim, the other sort you picked up by the crown. I was so dazzled by being near her, by having the famous Lydia Cruche smile at me, I forgot I was wearing a bowler and tried to pick it up by the crown. You can imagine what a fool I looked, and how she laughed."

And of course they laughed, and Speck laughed, too.

"Her husband," said the senator. "Hubert Cruche. A face like a gargoyle. Premature senile dementia. He'd been kicked by Venus at some time or other"— the euphemism for syphilis. "In those days the cure was based on mercury — worse than the disease. He seemed to know me. There was light in his eyes. Oh, not the light of intelligence. It was too late for that, and he'd not had much to begin with. He recognized me for a simple reason. I had already begun to assemble my Cruche collection. I bought everything Hubert Cruche produced for sixteen years — the oils, the gouaches, the pastels, the watercolors, the etchings, the drawings, the woodcuts, the posters, the cartoons, the book illustrations. Everything."

That was it, Speck remembered. That was why the senator who liked art never bought so much as a wash drawing. The house was full of Cruches; there wasn't an inch to spare on the walls.

With a monarch's gesture, the senator dismissed his audience and stepped firmly toward the chauffeur, who stood holding the door of his Citroën. He said, perhaps to himself, perhaps to Speck, thin and attentive in the moonlight, "I suppose I ought to get rid of my Cruches. Who ever thinks about Cruche now?"

"No," said Speck, whom the Grand Architect of the Universe had just rapped over the head. The senator paused — benevolent, stout. "Don't get rid of the Cruches," said Speck. He felt as if he were on a distant shore, calling across deep cultural waters. "Don't sell! Hang on! Cruche is coming back!"

Cruche, Cruche, Hubert Cruche, sang Speck's heart as he drove homeward. Cruche's hour had just struck, along with Sandor

Speck's. At the core of the May–June retrospective would be his lodge brother's key collection: "Our thanks, in particular . . . who not only has loaned his unique and invaluable . . . but who also . . . and who . . ." Recalling the little he knew of Cruche's obscure career, Speck made a few changes in the imaginary catalogue, substituting with some disappointment *The Power Station at Gagny-sur-Orme* for *Misia Sert on Her Houseboat,* and *Peasant Woman Sorting Turnips* for *Serge Lifar as Petrouchka.* He wondered if he could call Cruche heaven-sent. No; he would not put a foot beyond coincidence, just as he had not let Walter dash from saint to saint once he had settled for St. Joseph. And yet a small flickering marsh light danced upon the low-lying metaphysical ground he had done so much to avoid. Not only did Cruche overlap to an astonishing degree the painter in the yellow notebook, but he was exactly the sort of painter that made the Speck gallery chug along. If Speck's personal collection consisted of minor works by celebrated artists, he considered them his collateral for a rainy, bank-loan day. Too canny to try to compete with international heavyweights, unwilling to burden himself with insurance, he had developed as his specialty the flattest, palest, farthest ripples of the late-middle-traditional Paris school. This sensible decision had earned him the admiration given the devoted miniaturist who is no threat to anyone. "Go and see Sandor Speck," the great lions and tigers of the trade would tell clients they had no use for. "Speck's the expert."

Speck was expert on barges, bridges, cafés at twilight, nudes on striped counterpanes, the artist's mantelpiece with mirror, the artist's street, his staircase, his bed made and rumpled, his still life with half-peeled apple, his summer in Mexico, his wife reading a book, his girlfriend naked and dejected on a kitchen chair. He knew that the attraction of customer to picture was always accidental, like love; it was his business to make it overwhelming. Visitors came to the gallery looking for decoration and investment, left it believing Speck had put them on the road to a supreme event. But there was even more to Speck than this, and if he was respected for anything in the trade it was for his knack with artists' widows. Most dealers hated them. They were considered vain, greedy, unrealistic, and tougher than bulldogs. The worst were those whose husbands had somehow managed the rough crossing to recognition only to become washed up at the wrong end of the beach. There the widow waited, guarding the wreckage. Speck's skill in dealing with them came out of a certain sympathy. An artist's widow was bound to be suspicious and adamant. She had survived the discomfort and confusion of her marriage; had lived through the artist's drinking, his avarice, his affairs, his obsession with constipation, his feuds and quarrels, his cowardice with dealers, his hypocrisy with critics, his depressions (which always fell at the most joyous seasons, blighting Christmas and spring); and then — oh, justice! — she had outlasted him.

Transfiguration arrived rapidly. Resurrected for Speck's approval was an ardent lover, a devoted husband who could not work unless his wife was around, preferably in the same room. If she had doubts about a painting, he at once scraped it down. Hers was the only opinion he had ever trusted. His last coherent words before dying had been of praise for his wife's autumnal beauty.

Like a swan in muddy waters, Speck's ancient Bentley cruised the suburbs where his painters had lived their last resentful seasons. He knew by heart the damp villa, the gravel path, the dangling bellpull, the shrubbery containing dead cats and plastic bottles. Indoors the widow sat, her walls plastered with portraits of herself when young. Here she continued the struggle begun in the Master's lifetime — the evicting of the upstairs tenant — her day made lively by the arrival of mail (dusty beige of anonymous threats, grim blue of legal documents), the coming and going of process servers, the outings to lawyers. Into this spongy territory Speck advanced, bringing his tactful presence, his subtle approximation of courtship, his gift for listening. Thin by choice, pale by nature, he suggested maternal need. Socks and cufflinks suggested breeding. The drift of his talk suggested prosperity. He sent his widows flowers, wooed them with food. Although their taste in checks and banknotes ran to the dry and crisp, when it came to eating they craved the sweet, the sticky, the moist. From the finest pastry shops in Paris Speck brought soft macaroons, savarins soaked in rum, brioches stuffed with almond cream, mocha cake so tender it had to be eaten with a spoon. Sugar was poison to Speck. Henriette had once reviewed a book that described how refined sugar taken into one's system turned into a fog of hideous green. Her brief, cool warning, "A Marxist Considers Sweets," unreeled in Speck's mind if he was confronted with a cookie. He usually pretended to eat, reducing a *mille-feuille* to paste, concealing the wreck of an éclair under napkin and fork. He never lost track of his purpose — the prying of paintings out of a dusty studio on terms anesthetizing to the artist's widow and satisfactory to himself.

The senator had mentioned a wife; where there had been wife there was relict. Speck obtained her telephone number by calling a rival gallery and pretending to be looking for someone else. "Cruche's widow can probably tell you," he finally heard. She lived in one of the gritty suburbs east of Paris, on the far side of the Bois de Vincennes — in Speck's view, the wrong direction. The pattern of his life seemed to come unfolded as he dialed. He saw himself stalled in industrial traffic, inhaling pollution, his Bentley pointed toward the seediest mark on the urban compass, with a vanilla cream cake melting beside him on the front seat.

She answered his first ring; his widows never strayed far from the telephone. He introduced himself. Silence. He gave the name of the gallery, mentioned his street, recited the names of painters he showed.

Presently he heard "D'you know any English?"

"Some," said Speck, who was fluent.

"Well, what do you want?"

"First of all," he said, "to meet you."

"What for?"

He cupped his hand round the telephone, as if spies from the embassies down the street were trying to overhear. "I am planning a major Cruche show. A retrospective. That's what I want to talk to you about."

"Not unless I know what you want."

It seemed to Speck that he had already told her. Her voice was languid and nasal and perfectly flat. An index to English dialects surfaced in his mind, yielding nothing useful.

"It will be a strong show," he went on. "The first big Cruche since the nineteen-thirties, I believe."

"What's that got to do with me?"

He wondered if the senator had forgotten something essential — that Lydia Cruche had poisoned her husband, for instance. He said, "You probably own quite a lot of his work."

"None of it's for sale."

This, at last, was familiar; widows' negotiations always began with "No." "Actually, I am not proposing to buy anything," he said, wanting this to be clear at the start. "I am offering the hospitality of my gallery. It's a gamble I am willing to take because of my firm belief that the time—"

"What's the point of this show?"

"The point?" said Speck, his voice tightening as it did when Walter was being obtuse. "The point is getting Cruche back on the market. The time has come — the time to . . . to attack. To attack the museums with Hubert Cruche."

As he said this, Speck saw the great armor-plated walls of the Pompidou Art Center and the chink in the armor through which an 80 x 95 Cruche 1919 abstract might slip. He saw the provincial museums, cheeseparing, saving on light bulbs, but, like the French bourgeoisie they stood for, so much richer than they seemed. At the name "Cruche" their curators would wake up from neurotic dreams of forced auction sales, remembering they had millions to get rid of before the end of the fiscal year. And France was the least of it: London, Zurich, Stockholm, and Amsterdam materialized as frescoes representing the neoclassical façades of four handsome banks. Overhead, on a baroque ceiling, nymphs pointed their rosy feet to gods whose chariots were called "Tokyo" and "New York." Speck lowered his voice as if he had portentous news. Museums all over the world, although they did not yet know this, were starving for Cruche. In the pause that followed he seemed to feel Henriette's hand on his shoulder, warning him to brake before enthusiasm took him over the cliff.

"Although for the moment Cruche is just an idea of mine," he said, stopping cold at the edge. "Just an idea. We can develop the idea when we meet."

A week later, Speck parked his car between a ramshackle shopping center — survivor of the building boom of the sixties — and a municipal low-cost housing project that resembled a jail. In the space bounded by these structures crouched the late artist's villa, abiding proof in stucco that the taste of earlier generations had been as disastrous as today's. He recognized the shards of legal battle: center and block had left the drawing board of some state-employed hack as a unit, only to be wedged apart by a widow's refusal to sell. Speck wondered how she had escaped expropriation. Either she knows someone powerful, he thought, or she can make such a pest of herself that they were thankful to give up.

A minute after having pushed the gate and tugged the rusted wire bellpull, he found himself alone in a bleak sitting room, from which his hostess had been called by a whistling kettle. He sat down on a faded sofa. The furniture was of popular local design, garnished with marble and ormolu. A television set encrusted with gilt acanthus leaves sat on a sideboard, like an object d'art. A few rectangular shadings on the wallpaper showed where pictures had hung.

The melancholy tinged with foreboding Speck felt between seven and eight overtook him at this much earlier hour. The room was no more hideous than others he had visited in his professional quest for a bargain, but this time it seemed to daunt him, recalling sieges and pseudocourtships and expenditures of time, charm, and money that had come to nothing. He got up and examined a glass-fronted bookcase with nothing inside. His features, afloat on a dusty pane, were not quite as pinched as they had been the other night, but the image was still below par for a man considered handsome. The approach of a squeaking tea cart sent him scurrying back to the sofa, like a docile child invited somewhere for the first time.

"I was just admiring . . ." he began.

"I've run out of milk," she said. "I'm sure you won't mind your tea plain." With this governessy statement she handed him a cup of black Ceylon, a large slice of poisonous raisin cake, and a Mickey Mouse paper napkin.

Nothing about Cruche's widow tallied with the senator's description. She was short and quite round, and reminded Speck of the fat little dogs one saw being reluctantly exercised in Paris streets. The abundant red-gold hair of the senator's memory, or imagination, had gone ash-gray and was, in any case, pinned up. The striking fact of her person was simply the utter blankness of her expression. Usually widows' faces spoke to him. They said, "I am lonely," or "Can I trust you?" Lydia Cruche's did not suggest that she had so much as taken Speck in. She chose a chair at some distance from Speck, and proceeded to eat her cake without speaking. He thought of things to say, but none of them seemed appealing.

At last, she said, "Did you notice the supermarket next door?"

"I saw a shopping center."

"The market is part of it. You can get anything there now — bran, frozen pizzas, maple syrup. That's where I got the cake mix. I haven't been to Paris for three years."

Speck had been born in France. French education had left him the certainty that he was a logical, fair-minded person imbued with a culture from which every other Western nation was obliged to take its bearings. French was his first language; he did not really approve of any other. He said, rather coldly, "Have you been in this country long?"

"Around fifty years."

"Then you should know some French."

"I don't speak it if I don't have to. I never liked it."

He put down his cup, engulfed by a wave of second-generation distress. She was his first foreign widow. Most painters, whatever their origins, had sense enough to marry Frenchwomen — unrivaled with creditors, thrifty hoarders of bits of real estate, endowed with relations in country places where one could decamp in times of need and war.

"Perhaps, where you come from —" he began.

"Saskatchewan."

His tea had gone cold. Tannic scum had collected on its surface. She said, "This idea of yours, this show — what was it you called it? The hospitality of your gallery? I just want to say don't count on me. Don't count on me for anything. I don't mind showing you what I've got. But not today. The studio hasn't been dusted or heated for years, and even the light isn't working."

In Speck's experience, this was about average for a first attempt. Before making for civilization he stopped at a florist's in the shopping center and ordered two dozen roses to be delivered to Mme. Cruche. While these were lifted, dripping, from a plastic pail, he jotted a warm message on his card, crossing out the engraved "Dr. Sandor Speck." His title, earned by a thesis on French neo-Humanism and its ups and downs, created some confusion in Paris, where it was taken to mean that Speck could cure slipped discs and gastric ulcers. Still, he felt that it gave a grip to his name, and it was his only link with all the freethinking, agnostic Specks, who, though they had not been able to claim affinity by right of birth with Voltaire and Descartes, had probably been wise and intelligent and quite often known as "Dr."

As soon as he got back to the gallery, he had Walter look up Saskatchewan in an atlas. Its austere oblong shape turned his heart to ice. Walter said that it was one of the right-angled territories that so frequently contain oil. Oil seemed to Speck to improve the oblong. He saw a Chirico chessboard sliding off toward a horizon where the lights of derricks twinkled and blinked.

*

He let a week go by before calling Lydia Cruche.

"I won't be able to show you those roses of yours," she said. "They died right off."

He took the hint and arrived with a spray of pale-green orchids imported from Brazil. Settled upon the faded sofa, which was apparently destined to be his place, he congratulated his hostess on the discovery of oil in her native plain.

"I haven't seen or heard of the place since Trotsky left the Soviet Union," she said. "If there is oil, I'd sooner not know about it. Oil is God's curse." The iron silence that followed this seemed to press on Speck's lungs. "That's a bad cough you've got there, Doctor," she said. "Men never look after those things. Who looks after you?"

"I look after myself," said Speck.

"Where's your wife? Where'd she run off to?"

Not even "Are you married?" He saw his hostess as a tough little pagan figure, with a goddess's gift for reading men's lives. He had a quick vision of himself clasping her knees and sobbing out the betrayal of his marriage, though he continued to sit upright, crumbling walnut cake so that he would not have to eat it.

"My wife," he said, "insofar as I can still be said to have one, has gone to live in a warm climate."

"She run off alone? Women don't often do that. They haven't got that kind of nerve."

Stepping carefully, for he did not wish to sound like a stage cuckold or a male fool, Speck described in the lightest possible manner how Henriette had followed her lover, a teacher of literature, to a depressed part of French-speaking Africa where the inhabitants were suffering from a shortage of Racine. Unable to halt once he had started, he tore on toward the edge: Henriette was a hopeless nymphomaniac (she had fallen in love) who lacked any sense of values (the man was broke); she was at the same time a grasping neurotic (having sunk her savings in the gallery, she wanted a return with fourteen percent interest).

"You must be thankful you finally got rid of her," said Lydia Cruche. "You must be wondering why you married her in the first place."

"I felt sorry for Henriette," he said, momentarily forgetting any other reason. "She seemed so helpless." He told about Henriette living in her sixth-floor walkup, working as slave labor on a shoddy magazine. A peasant from Alsace, she had never eaten anything but pickled cabbage until Speck drove his Bentley into her life. Under his tactful guidance she had tasted her first fresh truffle salad at Le Récamier; had worn her first mink-lined Dior raincoat; had published her first book-length critical essay, "A Woman Looks at Edgar Allan Poe." And then she had left him — just like that.

"You trained her," said Lydia Cruche. "Brought her up to your level. And now she's considered good enough to marry a teacher. You should feel proud. You shouldn't mind what happened. You should feel satisfied."

"I'm not satisfied," said Speck. "I do mind." He realized that something had been left out of his account. "I loved her." Lydia Cruche looked straight at him, for once, as though puzzled. "As you loved Hubert Cruche," he said.

There was no response except for the removal of crumbs from her lap. The goddess, displeased by his mortal impertinence, symbolically knocked his head off her knee.

"Hube liked my company," she finally said. "That's true enough. After he died I saw him sitting next to the television, by the radiator, where his mother usually crouched all winter looking like a sheep with an earache. I was just resting here, thinking of nothing in particular, when I looked up and noticed him. He said, 'You carry the seed of your death.' I said, 'If that's the case, I might as well put my head in the oven and be done with it.' *'Non,'* he said, *'ce n'est pas la peine.'* Now, his mother was up in her room, making lists of all the things she had to feel sorry about. I went up and said, 'Madame,' because you can bet your boots she never got a 'Maman' out of me, 'Hube was in the parlor just now.' She answered, 'It was his mother he wanted. Any message was for me.' I said that if that was so, then all he needed to do was to materialize upstairs and save me the bother of climbing. She gave me some half-baked reason why he preferred not to, and then she *did* die. Aged a hundred and three. It was in *France-Soir.*"

The French she had spoken rang to Speck like silver bells. Everything about her had changed — voice, posture, expression. If he still could not see the Lydia Cruche of the senator's vision, at least he could believe in her.

"Do you talk to your husband often?" he said, trying to make it sound like an usual experience.

"How could I talk to Hube? He's dead and buried. I hope you don't go in for ghosts, Dr. Speck. I would find that very silly. That was just some kind of accident — a visitation. I never saw him again or ever expect to. As for his mother, there wasn't a peep out of her after she died. And here I am, alone in the Cruche house." It was hard to say if she sounded glad or sorry. "I gather you're on your own, too. God never meant men and women to live by themselves, convenient though it may seem to some of us. That's why he throws men and women together. Coincidence is God's plan."

So soon, thought Speck. It was only their second meeting. It seemed discourteous to draw attention to the full generation that lay between them; experience had taught him that acknowledging any fragment of this dangerous subject did more harm than good. When widows showed their cards, he tried to look like a man with no time for games. He thought of the young André Malraux, dark and tormented, the windblown lock on the worried brow, the stub of a Gauloise sending up a vagabond spiral of smoke. Unfortunately, Speck had been born forty years too late for the model; he belonged to a much reedier generation of European manhood. He thought of the pope. White-clad, serene, he gazed out on St. Peter's Square, over the subdued heads of one hundred thousand artists' widows, not one of whom would dare.

"So this was the Cruche family home," he said, striking out, he hoped, in a safe direction.

"The furniture was his mother's," said Lydia Cruche. "I got rid of most of it, but there was stuff you couldn't pay them to cart away. *Sa petite Maman adorable,*" she said softly. Again Speck heard the string of silver bells. "I thought she was going to hang around forever. They were a tough family — peasants from the west of France. She took good care of him. Cooked him sheep's heart, tripe, and onions, big beefsteaks they used to eat half raw. He was good-looking, a big fellow, big for a Frenchman. At seventy you'd have taken him for forty. Never had a cold. Never had a headache. Never said he was tired. Drank a liter of Calvados every other day. One morning he just keeled over, and that was that. I'll show you a picture of him sometime."

"I'd also like to see *his* pictures," said Speck, thankful for the chance. "The pictures you said you had upstairs."

"You know how I met Hube? People often ask me that. I'm surprised you haven't. I came to him for lessons."

"I didn't know he taught," said Speck. His most reliable professional trait was his patience.

"He didn't. I admired him so much that I thought I'd try anyway. I was eighteen. I rang the bell. His mother let me in. I never left — he wouldn't let me go. His mother often said if she'd known the future she'd never have answered the door. I must have walked about four miles from a tram stop, carrying a big portfolio of my work to show him. There wasn't even a paved street then — just a patch of nettles out front and some vacant lots."

Her work. He knew he had to get it over with: "Would you like to show me some of your things, too?"

"I burned it all a long time ago."

Speck's heart lurched. "But not his work?"

"It wasn't mine to burn. I'm not a criminal." Mutely, he looked at the bare walls. "None of Hube's stuff ever hung in here," she said. "His mother couldn't stand it. We had everything *she* liked — Napoleon at Waterloo, lighthouses, coronations, I couldn't touch it when she was alive, but once she'd gone I didn't wait two minutes."

Speck's eighteenth-century premises were centrally heated. The system, which dated from the early 1960s, had been put in by Americans who had once owned most of the second floor. With the first dollar slide of the Nixon era they had wisely sold their holdings and gone home, without waiting for the calamity still to come. Their memorial was an expensive, casual gift nobody knew what to do with; it had raised everyone's property taxes, and it cost a fortune to run. Tenants, such as Speck, who paid a fat share of the operation, had no say as to when heat was turned on, or to what degree of temperature. Only owners and landlords had a vote. They voted overwhelmingly for the lowest possible fuel bills. By November there was scarcely a trace of warmth in Speck's elegant gallery, his cold was entrenched for the winter, and Walter was threatening to quit. Speck was showing a painter from Bruges, sponsored by a Belgian cultural-affairs committee. Cost sharing was not a habit of his — it lowered the prestige of the gallery — but in a tight financial season he sometimes allowed himself a breather. The painter, who clearly expected Speck to put him under contract, talked of moving to Paris.

"You'd hate it here," said Speck.

Belgian television filmed the opening. The Belgian royal family, bidden by Walter, on his own initiative, sent regrets signed by aides-de-camp on paper so thick it would scarcely fold. These were pinned to the wall, and drew more attention than the show itself. Only one serious critic turned up. The rooms were so cold that guests could not write their names in the visitors' book — their hands were too numb. Walter, perhaps by mistake, had invited Blum-Weiler-Blochs instead of Blum-Bloch-Weilers. They came in a horde, leading an Afghan hound they tried to raffle off for charity.

The painter now sat in the gallery, day after day, smoking black cigarettes that smelled of mutton stew. He gave off a deep professional gloom, which affected Walter. Walter began to speak of the futility of genius — a sure sign of melancholia. Speck gave the painter money so that he could smoke in cafés. The bells of St. Clotilde's clanged and echoed, saying to Speck's memory, "Fascist, Fascist, Fascist." Walter reminded Speck that November was bad for art. The painter returned from a café looking cheerful. Speck wondered if he was enjoying Paris and if he would decide to stay; he stopped giving him money and the gallery became once more infested with mutton stew and despair. Speck began a letter to Henriette imploring her to come back. Walter interrupted it with the remark that Rembrandt, Mozart, and Dante had lived in vain. Speck tore the letter up and started another one saying that a Guillaumin pastel was missing and suggesting that Henriette had taken it to Africa. Just as he was tearing this up, too, the telephone rang.

"I finally got Hube's stuff all straightened out," said Lydia Cruche. "You might as well come round and look at it this afternoon. By the way, you may call me 'Lydia,' if you want to."

"Thank you," said Speck. "And you, of course, must call me — "

"I wouldn't dream of it. Once a doctor always a doctor. Come early. The light goes at four."

Speck took a pill to quiet the pounding of his heart.

In her summing-up of his moral nature, a compendium that had preceded her ringing "Fascist"s, Henriette had declared that Speck appraising an artist's work made her think of a real-estate loan officer examining Chartres Cathedral for leaks. It was true that his feeling for art stopped short of love; it had to. The great cocottes of history had shown similar prudence. Madame de Pompadour had eaten vanilla, believed to arouse the senses, but such recklessness was rare. Cool but efficient — that was the professional ticket. No vanilla for Speck; he knew better. For what if he were to allow passion for painting to set alight his common sense? How would he be able to live then, knowing that the ultimate fate of art was to die of anemia in safe-deposit vaults? Ablaze with love, he might try to organize raids and rescue parties, dragging pictures out of the dark, leaving sacks of onions instead. He might drop the art trade altogether, as Walter kept intending to do, and turn his talents to cornering the onion market. The same customers would ring at election time, saying, "Dr. Speck, what happens to my onion collection if the Left gets in? Shouldn't we try to unload part of it in New York now, just to be on the safe side?" And Speck, unloading onions of his own in Tokyo, would answer, "Don't worry. They can't possibly nationalize all the onions. Besides, they aren't going to win."

Lydia seemed uninterested in Speck's reaction to Cruche. He had expected her to hang about, watching his face, measuring his interest, the better to nail her prices; but she simply showed him a large, dim, dusty, north-facing room in which canvases were thickly stacked against the walls and said, "I wasn't able to get the light fixed. I've left a lamp. Don't knock it over. Tea will be ready when you are." Presently he heard American country music rising from the kitchen (Lydia must have been tuned to the BBC) and he smelled a baking cake. Then, immersed in his ice-cold Cruche encounter, he noticed nothing more.

About three hours later he came downstairs, slowly, wiping dust from his hands with a handkerchief. His conception of the show had been slightly altered, and for the better, by the total Cruche. He began to rewrite the catalogue notes: "The time has come for birth . . ." No — "for rebirth. In a world sated by overstatement the moment is ripe for a calm . . ." How to avoid "statement" and still say "statement"? The Grand Architect was keeping Speck in mind. "For avouchment," said Speck, alone on the stairs. It was for avouchment that the time had come. It was also here for hard business. His face became set and distant, as if a large desk were about to be shoved between Lydia Cruche and himself.

He sat down and said, "This is going to be a strong show, a powerful show, even stronger than I'd hoped. Does everything I've looked at upstairs belong to you outright? Is there anything which for any reason you are not allowed to lend, show, or sell?"

"Neither a borrower nor a lender be," said Lydia, cutting caramel cake.

"No. Well, I am talking about the show, of course."

"No show," she said. "I already told you that."

"What do you mean, no show?" said Speck.

"What I told you at the beginning. I told you not to count on me. Don't drop boiled frosting on your trousers. I couldn't get it to set."

"But you changed your mind," said Speck. "After saying 'Don't count on me,' you changed your mind."

"Not for a second."

"Why?" said Speck, as he had said to the departing Henriette. "Why?"

"God doesn't want it."

He waited for more. She folded her arms and stared at the blank television set. "How do you know that God doesn't want Hubert Cruche to have a retrospective?"

"Because He said so."

His first thought was that the Grand Architect had granted Lydia Cruche something so far withheld from Sandor Speck: a plain statement of intention. "Don't you know your Commandments?" she asked. "You've never heard of the graven image?"

He searched her face for the fun, the teasing, even the malice that might give shape to this conversation, allow him to take hold of it. He said, "I can't believe you mean this."

"You don't have to. I'm sure you have your own spiritual pathway. Whatever it is, I respect it. God reveals himself according to each person's mental capacity."

One of Speck's widows could prove she descended from Joan of Arc. Another had spent a summer measuring the walls of Toledo in support of a theory that Jericho had been in Spain. It was Speck's policy never to fight the current of eccentricity but to float with it. He said cautiously, "We are all held in a mysterious hand." Generations of Speck freethinkers howled from their graves; he affected not to hear them.

"I am a Japhethite, Dr. Speck. You remember who Noah was? And his sons, Ham, Shem, and Japheth? What does that mean to you?" Speck looked as if he possessed Old Testament lore too fragile to stand exposure. "Three," said Lydia. "The sacred number. The first, the true, the only source of Israel. That crowd Moses

led into the desert were just Egyptian malcontents. The true Israelites were scattered all over the earth by then. The Bible hints at
this for its whole length. Japheth's people settled in Scotland.
Present-day Jews are impostors."

"Are you connected to this Japheth?"

"I do not make that claim. My Scottish ancestors came from the
border country. The Japhethites had been driven north long before by the Roman invasion. The British Israelite movement, which
preceded ours, proved that the name 'Hebrides' was primitive
Gaelic for 'Hebrew.' The British Israelites were distinguished path-
finders. It was good of you to have come all the way out here, Dr.
Speck. I imagine you'll want to be getting back."

After backing twice into Lydia's fence, Speck drove straight to
Galignani's bookshop, on Rue de Rivoli, where he purchased an
English Bible. He intended to have Walter ransack it for contra-
Japhethite pronouncements. The orange dust jacket surprised
him; it seemed to Speck that Bibles were usually black. On the back
flap the churches and organizations that had sponsored this English translation were listed, among them the National Bible Society of Scotland. He wondered if this had anything to do with
Japheth.

As far as Speck could gather from passages Walter marked
during the next few days, art had never really flourished, even
before Moses decided to put a stop to it. Apart from a bronze
snake cast at God's suggestion (Speck underscored this for Lydia
in red), there was nothing specifically cultural, though Ezekiel's
visions had a certain surrealistic splendor. As Speck read the words
"the terrible crystal," its light flooded his mind, illuminating a
simple question: Why not forget Hubert Cruche and find an easier
solution for the cultural penury of the West? The crystal dimmed.
Speck's impulsive words that October night, "Cruche is coming
back," could not be reeled in. Senator Bellefeuille was entangled
in a promise that had Speck at one end and Lydia at the other.
Speck had asked if he might examine his lodge brother's collection and had been invited to lunch. Cruche *had* to come
back.

Believing Speck's deliverance at hand, Walter assailed him with
texts and encouragement. He left biblical messages on Speck's desk
so that he had to see them first thing after lunch. Apparently the
British Israelite movement had truly existed, enjoying a large and

respectable following. Its premise that it was the British who were really God's elect had never been challenged, though membership had dwindled at mid-century; Walter could find no trace of Lydia's group, however. He urged Speck to drive to the north of Scotland, but Speck had already decided to abandon the religious approach to Cruche.

"No modern translation conveys the word of Japheth or of God," Lydia had said when Speck showed her Walter's finds. There had been something unusual about the orange dust jacket, after all. He did not consider this a defeat. Bible reading had raised his spirits. He understood now why Walter found it consoling, for much in it consisted of the assurance of downing one's enemies, dashing them against stones, seeing their children reduced to beggary and their wives to despair. Still, he was not drawn to deep belief: he remained rational, skeptical, anxious, and subject to colds, and he had not succeeded in moving Lydia Cruche an inch.

Lunch at Senator Bellefeuille's was balm. Nothing was served that Speck could not swallow. From the dining room he looked across at the dark November trees of the Bois de Boulogne. The senator lived on the west side of Paris — the clients' side. A social allegory in the shape of a city separated Speck from Lydia Cruche. The senator's collection was fully insured, free from dust, attractively framed or stored in racks built to order.

Speck began a new catalogue introduction as he ate lunch. "The Bellefeuille Cruches represent a unique aspect of Cruche's vision," he composed, heartily enjoying fresh crab soufflé. "Not nearly enough has been said about Cruche and the nude."

The senator broke in, asking how much Cruche was likely to fetch after the retrospective. Speck gave figures to which his choice of socks and cufflinks lent authority.

"Cruche-and-the-nude implies a definition of Woman," Speck continued, silently, sipping coffee from a gold-rimmed cup. "Lilith, Eve, temptress, saint, child, mother, nurse — Cruche delineated the feminine factor once and for all."

The senator saw his guest to the door, took his briefcase from the hands of a manservant, and bestowed it on Speck like a diploma. He told Speck he would send him a personal invitation list for the Cruche opening next May. The list would include the estranged wife of a respected royal pretender, the publisher of an influential morning paper, the president of a nationalized bank, and the highest-ranking administrative official of a thickly populated area. Before driving away, Speck took a deep breath of westend air. It was cool and dry, like Speck's new expression.

That evening, around closing time, he called Lydia Cruche. He had to let her know that the show could go on without her. "I shall be showing the Bellefeuille Cruches," he said.

"The *what?*"

Speck changed the subject. "There is enormous American interest," he said, meaning that he had written half a dozen letters and received prudent answers or none at all. He was accustomed to the tense excitement "American interest" could arouse. He had known artists to enroll in crash courses at Berlitz, the better to understand prices quoted in English.

Lydia was silent; then she said, slowly, "Don't ever mention such a thing again. Hube was anti-American — especially during the war." As for Lydia, she had set foot in the United States once, when a marshmallow roast had taken her a few yards inside North Dakota, some sixty years before.

The time was between half past seven and eight. Walter had gone to early dinner and a lecture on lost Atlantis. The Belgian painter was back in Bruges, unsold and unsung. The cultural-affairs committee had turned Speck's bill for expenses over to a law firm in Brussels. Two Paris galleries had folded in the past month and a third was packing up for America, where Speck gave it less than a year. Painters set adrift by these frightening changes drifted to other galleries, shipwrecked victims trying to crawl on board waterlogged rafts. On all sides Speck heard that the economic decline was irreversible. He knew one thing — art had sunk low on the scale of consumer necessities. To mop up a few back bills, he was showing part of his own collection — his last-ditch old-age-security reserve. He clasped his hands behind his neck, staring at a Vlaminck India ink on his desk. It had been certified genuine by an expert now serving a jail sentence in Zurich. Speck was planning to flog it to one of the ambassadors down the street.

He got up and began turning out lights, leaving just a spot in the window. To have been anti-American during the Second World War in France had a strict political meaning. Any hope of letters from Louis Aragon and Elsa withered and died: Hubert Cruche had been far Right. Of course, there was Right and Right, thought Speck as he triple-locked the front door. Nowadays the Paris intelligentsia drew new lines across the past, separating coarse collaborators from fine-drawn intellectual Fascists. One could no longer lump together young hotheads whose passionate belief in Europe had led them straight to the Charlemagne Division of the Waffen-S.S. and the soft middle class that had stayed behind to make money on the black market. Speck could not quite remember why *pure* Fascism had been better for civilization than the other kind, but somewhere on the safe side of the barrier there was bound to be a slot for Cruche. From the street, he considered a page of Charles Despiau sketches — a woman's hand, her breast, her thigh. He thought of the senator's description of that other, early Lydia and of the fragments of perfection Speck could now believe in, for he had seen the Bellefeuille nudes. The familiar evening sadness caught up with him and lodged in his heart. Posterity forgives, he repeated, turning away, crossing the road on his way to his dinner.

Speck's ritual pause brought him up to St. Amand and his demon just as M. Chassepoule leaned into his window to replace a two-volume work he had probably taken out to show a customer. The bookseller drew himself straight, stared confidently into the night, and caught sight of Speck. The two greeted each other through glass. M. Chassepoule seemed safe, at ease, tucked away in a warm setting of lights and friends and royal blue, and yet he made an odd little gesture of helplessness, as if to tell Speck, "Here I am, like you, overtaxed, hounded, running an honest business against dreadful odds." Speck made a wry face of sympathy, as if to answer that he knew, he knew. His neighbor seemed to belong to an old and desperate breed, its back to the wall, its birthright gnawed away by foreigners, by the heathen, by the blithe continuity of art, by Speck himself. He dropped his gaze, genuinely troubled, examining the wares M. Chassepoule had collected, dusted, sorted, and priced for a new and ardent generation. The work he had just put back in the window was *La France Juive,* by Edouard Drumont. A handwritten notice described it as a classic study, out of print, hard to find, and in good condition.

Speck thought, *A few years ago, no one would have dared put it on display. It has been considered rubbish for fifty years. Edouard Drumont died poor, alone, cast off even by his old friends, completely discredited. Perhaps his work was always being sold, quietly, somewhere, and I didn't know.* Had he been Walter and superstitious, he might have crossed his fingers; being Speck and rational, he merely shuddered.

Walter had a friend — Félicité Blum-Weiler-Bloch, the owner of the Afghan hound. When Walter complained to her about the temperature of the gallery, she gave him a scarf, a sweater, an old flannel bedsheet, and a Turkey carpet. Walter decided to make a present of the carpet to Speck.

"Get that thing out of my gallery," said Speck.

"It's really from Félicité."

"I don't want her here, either," said Speck. "Or the dog."

Walter proposed spreading the carpet on the floor in the basement. "I spend a lot of time there," he said. "My feet get cold."

"I want it out," said Speck.

Later that day Speck discovered Walter down in the framing room, holding a vacuum cleaner. The Turkey carpet was spread on the floor. A stripe of neutral color ran through the pattern of mottled reds and blues. Looking closer, Speck saw it was warp and weft. "Watch," said Walter. He switched on the vacuum; another stripe of color vanished. "The wool lifts right out," said Walter.

"I told you to get rid of it," said Speck, trembling.

"Why? I can still use it."

"I won't have my gallery stuffed with filth."

"You'll never have to see it. You hardly ever come down here." He ran the vacuum, drowning Speck's reply. Over the noise Walter yelled, "It will look better when it's all one color."

Speck raised his voice to the right-wing pitch heard during street fights: "Get it out! Get it out of my gallery!"

Like a telephone breaking into a nightmare, delivering the sleeper, someone was calling, "Dr. Speck." There on the stairs stood Lydia Cruche, wearing an ankle-length fur coat and a brown velvet turban. "I thought I'd better have a look at the place," she said. "Just to see how much space you have, how much of Cruche you can hold."

Still trembling, Speck took her hand, which smelled as if she had been peeling oranges, and pressed it to his lips.

That evening, Speck called the senator: Would he be interested in writing the catalogue introduction? No one was better fitted, said

Speck, over senatorial modesty. The senator had kept faith with
Cruche. During his years of disappointment and eclipse Cruche
had been heartened, knowing that guests at the senator's table
could lift their eyes from quail in aspic to feast on *Nude in the
Afternoon.*

Perhaps his lodge brother exaggerated just a trifle, the senator
replied, though it was true that he had hung on to his Cruches
even when their value had been wiped out of the market. The only
trouble was that his recent prose had been about the capital-gains-
tax project, the Common Market sugar-beet subsidy, and the un-
informed ecological campaign against plastic containers. He wondered if he could write with the same persuasiveness about art.

"I have taken the liberty of drawing up an outline," said Speck.
"Just a few notes. Knowing how busy you are."

Hanging up, he glanced at his desk calendar. Less than six weeks
had gone by since the night when, by moonlight, Speck had heard
the senator saying ". . . hats."

A few days before Christmas Speck drove out to Lydia's with a
briefcase filled with documents that were, at last, working papers:
the list of exhibits from the Bellefeuille collection, the introduction,
and the chronology in which there were gaps for Lydia to fill. He
still had to draw up a financial arrangement. So far, she had
said nothing about it, and it was not a matter Speck cared to
rush.

He found another guest in the house — a man somewhat
younger than he, slightly bald and as neat as a mouse.

"Here's the doctor I was telling you about," said Lydia, introduc-
ing Speck.

Signor Vigorelli of Milan was a fellow-Japhethite — so Speck
gathered from their conversation, which took up, in English, as
though he had never come in. Lydia poured Speck's tea in an
offhand manner he found wounding. He felt he was being treated
like the hanger-on in a Russian play. He smashed his lemon cupcake, scattering crumbs. The visitor's plate looked cleaner than his.
After a minute of this, Speck took the catalogue material out of his
briefcase and started to read. Nobody asked what he was reading.
The Italian finally looked at his watch (expensive, of a make Speck
recognized) and got to his feet, picking up car keys that had been
lying next to his plate.

"That little man had an Alfa Romeo tag," said Speck when Lydia returned after seeing him out.

"I don't know why you people drive here when there is perfectly good bus service," she said.

"What does he do?"

"He is a devout, religious man."

For the first time, she sat down on the sofa, close to Speck. He showed her the introduction and the chronology. She made a number of sharp and useful suggestions. Then they went upstairs and looked at pictures. The studio had been cleaned, the light repaired. Speck suddenly thought, I've done it — I've brought it off.

"We must discuss terms," he said.

"When you're ready," she replied. "Your cold seems a lot better."

Inching along in stagnant traffic, Speck tried one after the other the FM state-controlled stations on his car radio. He obtained a lecture about the cultural oppression of Cajuns in Louisiana, a warning that the road he was now driving on was saturated, and the disheartening squeaks and wails of a circumcision ceremony in Ethiopia. On the station called France-Culture someone said, "Henri Cruche."

"Strange that it should be an Italian to discover an artist so essentially French," said the interviewer.

Signor Vigorelli explained that his admiration for France was second only to his intense feelings about Europe. His career had been consecrated to enhancing Italian elegance with French refinement and then scattering the result abroad. He believed that the unjustly neglected Cruche would be a revelation and might even bring the whole of Western art to its senses.

Speck nodded, agreeing. The interview came to an end. Wild jungle drums broke forth, heralding the announcement that there was to be a reading of medieval Bulgarian poetry in an abandoned factory at Nanterre. It was then and then only that Speck took in the sense of what he had heard. He swung the car in a wild U-turn and, without killing himself or anyone else, ran into a tree. He sat quietly, for about a minute, until his breathing became steady again, then unlocked his safety belt and got out. For a long time he stood by the side of the road, holding his briefcase, feeling neither shock nor pain. Other drivers, noticing a man alone with a wrecked car, picked up speed. He began to walk in Lydia's direction. A cruising prostitute, on her way home to cook her husband's dinner, finally agreed to drop him off at a taxi stand. Speck gave her two hundred francs.

Lydia did not seem at all surprised to see him. "I'd invite you to supper," she said. "But all I've got is a tiny pizza and some of the leftover cake."

"The Italian," said Speck.

"Yes?"

"I've heard him. On the radio. He says he's got Cruche. That he discovered him. My car is piled up in the Bois. I tried to turn around and come back here. I've been walking for hours."

"Sit down," said Lydia. "There, on the sofa. Signor Vigorelli is having a big Cruche show in Milan next March."

"He can't," said Speck.

"Why can't he?"

"Because Cruche is mine. He was my idea. No one can have my idea. Not until after June."

"Then it goes to Trieste in April," said Lydia. "You could still have it by about the tenth of May. If you still want it."

If I want it, said Speck to himself. If I want it. With the best work sold and the insurance rates tripled and the commissions shared out like candy. And with everyone saying Speck jumped on the bandwagon, Speck made the last train.

"Lydia, listen to me," he said. "I invented Hubert Cruche. There would be no Hubert Cruche without Sandor Speck. This is an unspeakable betrayal. It is dishonorable. It is wrong." She listened, nodding her head. "What happens to me now?" he said. "Have you thought about that?" He knew better than to ask, "Why didn't you tell me about him?" Like all dissembling women, she would simply answer, "Tell you what?"

"It might be all the better," she said. "There'll be that much more interest in Hube."

"Interest?" said Speck. "The worst kind of interest. Third-rate, tawdry interest. Do you suppose I can get the Pompidou Center to look at a painter who has been trailing around in Trieste? It had to be a new idea. It had to be strong."

"You'll save on the catalogue," she said. "He will probably want to share."

"It's my catalogue," said Speck. "I'm not sharing. Senator Bellefeuille . . . my biography . . . never. The catalogue is mine. Besides, it would look as if he'd had the idea."

"He did."

"But after me," said Speck, falling back on the most useless of all lover's arguments. "*After* me. I was there first."

"So you were," she said tenderly, like any woman on her way out.

Speck said, "I thought you were happy with our arrangement."

"I was. But I hadn't met him yet. You see, he was so interested in the Japhethite movement. One day he opened the Bible and put his finger on something that seemed to make it all right about the graven image. In Ecclesiastes, I think."

Speck gave up. "I suppose it would be no use calling for a taxi?"

"Not around here, I'm afraid, though you might pick one up at the shopping center. Shouldn't you report the accident?"

"Which accident?"

"To the police," she said. "Get it on record fast. Make it a case. That squeezes the insurance people. The phone's in the hall."

"I don't care about the insurance," said Speck.

"You will care, once you're over the shock. Tell me exactly where it happened. Can you remember? Have you got your license? Registration? Insurance?"

Speck sank back and closed his eyes. He could hear Lydia dialing; then she began to speak. He listened, while Lydia, her voice full of silver bells, dealt with creditors and dealers and Cruche's cast-off girlfriends and a Senator Bellefeuille more than forty years younger.

"I wish to report an accident," Lydia sang. "The victim is Dr. S. Speck. He is still alive — luckily. He was forced off the road in the Bois de Vincennes by a tank truck carrying high-octane fuel. It had an Italian plate. Dr. Speck was too shaken to get the number. Yes, I saw the accident, but I couldn't see the number. There was a van in the way. All I noticed was "MI.' That must stand for Milan. I recognized the victim. Dr. Speck is well known in some circles . . . an intimate friend of Senator Antoine Bellefeuille, the former minister of . . . that's right." She talked a few minutes longer, then came back to Speck. "Get in touch with the insurance people first thing tomorrow," she said, flat Lydia again. "Get a medical certificate — you've had a serious emotional trauma. It can lead to jaundice. Tell your doctor to write that down. If he doesn't want to, I'll give you the name of a doctor who will. You're on the edge of nervous depression. By the way, the police will be towing your car to a garage. They know they've been very remiss, letting a foreign vehicle with a dangerous cargo race through the Bois. It might have hit a bus full of children. They must be looking for that tanker all over Paris. I've made a list of the numbers you're to call."

Speck produced his last card: "Senator Bellefeuille will never allow his Cruches to go to Milan. He'll never let them out of the country."

"Who — Antoine?" said Lydia. "Of course he will."

She cut a cupcake in half and gave him a piece. Broken, Speck crammed the whole thing in his mouth. She stood over him, humming. "Do you know that old hymn, Dr. Speck — 'The Day Thou Gavest, Lord, Is Ended'?"

He searched her face, as he had often, looking for irony, or playfulness — a gleam of light. There floated between them the cold oblong on the map and the Chirico chessboard moving along to its Arctic destination. Trees dwindled to shrubs and shrubs to moss and moss to nothing. Speck had been defeated by a land-scape.

Although Speck by no means considered himself a natural victim of hard luck, he had known disappointment. Shows had fallen flat. Galleries had been blown up and torn down. Artists he had nursed along had been lured away by siren dealers. Women had wandered off, bequeathing to Speck the warp and weft of a clear situation, so much less interesting than the ambiguous patterns of love. Disappointment had taught him rules: the first was that it takes next to no time to get used to bad news. Rain began to fall as he walked to the taxi stand. In his mind, Cruche was already being shown in Milan and he was making the best of it.

He gazed up and down the bleak road; of course there were no taxis. Inside a bus shelter huddled a few commuters. The thrust of their lives, their genetic destiny, obliged them to wait for public transport — unlike Speck, thrown among them by random adventures. A plastic-covered timetable announced a bus to Paris every twenty-three minutes until four, every sixteen minutes from four to eight, and every thirty-one minutes thereafter. His watch had stopped late in the afternoon, probably at the time of the accident. He left the shelter and stood out in the wet, looking at windows of shops, one of which might contain a clock. He stood for a minute or two staring at a china tea set flanked by two notices: "Hand Painted" and "Christmas Is Coming," both of which he found deeply sad. The tea set had been decorated with reproductions of the Pompidou Art Center, which was gradually replacing the Eiffel Tower as a constituent feature of French design. The day's shocks caught up with him: he stared at the milk jug, feeling surprise because it did not tell him the time. The arrival of a bus replaced this perplexity with one more pressing. He did not know what was needed on suburban buses — tickets or tokens or a monthly pass. He wondered whether the drivers accepted banknotes, and gave change, with civility.

"Dr. Speck, Dr. Speck!" Lydia Cruche, her raincoat open and flying, waving a battered black umbrella, bore down on him out of the dark. "You were right," she said, gasping. "You were there first." Speck took his place at the end of the bus queue. "I mean it," she said, clutching his arm. "He can wait."

Speck's second rule of disappointment came into play: the deceitful one will always come back to you ten seconds too late. "What does it mean?" he said, wiping rain from the end of his nose. "Having it before him means what? Paying for the primary expenses and the catalogue and sweetening the Paris critics and letting him rake in the chips?"

"Wasn't that what you wanted?"

"Your chap from Milan thought he was first," said Speck. "He may not want to step aside for me — a humble Parisian expert on the entire Cruche context and period. You wouldn't want Cruche to miss a chance at Milan, either."

"Milan is ten times better for money than Paris," she said. "If that's what we're talking about. But of course we aren't."

Speck looked down at her from the step of the bus. "Very well," he said. "As we were."

"I'll come to the gallery," she called. "I'll be there tomorrow. We can work out new terms."

Speck paid his fare without trouble and moved to the far end of the bus. The dark shopping center with its windows shining for no one was a Magritte vision of fear. Lydia had already forgotten him. Having tampered with his pride, made a professional ass of him, gone off with his idea and returned it dented and chipped, she now stood gazing at the Pompidou Center tea set, perhaps wondering if the ban on graven images could possibly extend to this.

Speck had often meant to ask her about the Mickey Mouse napkins. He thought of the hoops she had put him through — God, and politics, and finally the most dangerous one, which was jealousy. There seemed to be no way of rolling down the window, but a sliding panel at the top admitted half his face. Rising from his seat, he drew in a gulp of wet suburban air and threw it out as a shout: "Fascist! Fascist! Fascist!"

Not a soul in the bus turned to see. From the look of them, they had spent the best Sundays of their lives shuffling in demonstrations from Place de la République to Place de la Nation, tossing "Fascist"s around like confetti. Lydia turned slowly and looked at Speck. She raised her umbrella at arm's length, like a trophy. For the first time, Speck saw her smile. What was it the senator had said? "She had a smile like a fox's." He could see, gleaming white, her straight little animal teeth.

The bus lurched away from the curb and lumbered toward Paris. Speck leaned back and shut his eyes. Now he understood about that parting shot. It was amazing how it cleared the mind, tearing out weeds and tree stumps, flattening the live stuff along with the dead. "Fascist" advanced like a regiment of tanks. Only the future remained — clean, raked, ready for new growth. New growth of what? Of Cruche, of course — Cruche, whose hour was at hand, whose time was here. Speck began to explore his altered prospects. "New terms," she had said. So far, there had been none at all. The sorcerer from Milan must have promised something dazzling, swinging it before her eyes as he had swung his Alfa Romeo key. It would be foolish to match the offer. By the time they had all done with bungling, there might not be enough left over to buy a new Turkey carpet for Walter.

I was no match for her, he thought. No match at all. But then, look at the help she had — that visitation from Cruche. "Only once," she said, but women always said that: "He asked if he could see me just once more. I couldn't very well refuse." Dead or alive, when it came to confusion and double-dealing, there was no such thing as "only once." And there had been not only the departed Cruche but the very living Senator Bellefeuille — "Antoine," who had bought every picture of Lydia for sixteen years, the span of her early beauty. Nothing would ever be the same again between Speck and Lydia, of course. No man could give the same trust and confidence the second time around. All that remained to them was the patch of landscape they held in common — a domain reserved for the winning, collecting, and sharing out of profits, a territory where believer and skeptic, dupe and embezzler, the loving and the faithless could walk hand in hand. Lydia had a talent for money. He could sense it. She had never been given much chance to use it, and she had waited so much longer than Speck.

He opened his eyes and saw rain clouds over Paris glowing with light — the urban aurora. It seemed to Speck that he was entering a better weather zone, leaving behind the gray, indefinite mist in which the souls of discarded lovers are said to wander. He welcomed this new and brassy radiation. He saw himself at the center of a shadeless drawing, hero of a sort of cartoon strip, subduing Lydia, taming Henriette. Fortunately, he was above petty grudges. Lydia and Henriette had been designed by a bachelor God who had let the creation get out of hand. In the cleared land of Speck's future, a yellow notebook fluttered and lay open at a new page. The show would be likely to go to Milan in the autumn now; it might be a good idea to slip a note between the senator's piece and the biographical chronology. If Cruche had to travel, then let it be with Speck's authority as his passport.

The bus had reached its terminus, the city limit. Speck waited as the rest of the passengers crept inch by inch to the doors. He saw, with immense relief, a rank of taxis half a block long. He alighted and strode toward them, suddenly buoyant. He seemed to have passed a mysterious series of tests, and to have been admitted to some new society, the purpose of which he did not yet understand. He was a saner, stronger, wiser person than the Sandor Speck who had seen his own tight smile on M. Chassepoule's window only two months before. As he started to get into a taxi, a young man darted toward him and thrust a leaflet into his hand. Speck shut the door, gave his address, and glanced at the flier he was still holding. Crudely printed on cheap pink paper was this:

FRENCHMEN!
FOR THE SAKE OF EUROPE, FIGHT
THE GERMANO-AMERICANO-ISRAELO
HEGEMONY!
Germans in Germany!
Americans in America!
Jews in Israel!
For a True Europe, For One Europe,
Death to the Anti-European Hegemony!

Speck stared at this without comprehending it. Was it a Chasse-poule statement or an anti-Chassepoule plea? There was no way of knowing. He turned it over, looking for the name of an association, and immediately forgot what he was seeking. Holding the sheet of paper flat on his briefcase, he began to write, as well as the un-steady swaying of the cab would let him.

"It was with instinctive prescience that Hubert Cruche saw the need for a Europe united from the Atlantic to the . . . That Cruche skirted the murky zone of partisan politics is a tribute to his . . . even though his innocent zeal may have led him to the brink . . . early meeting with the young idealist and future statesman A. Bellefeuille, whose penetrating essay . . . close collaboration with the artist's wife and most trusted critic . . . and now, posthu-mously . . . from Paris, where the retrospective was planned and brought to fruition by the undersigned . . . and on to Italy, to the very borders of . . ."

Because this one I am keeping, Speck decided; this one will be signed: "By Sandor Speck." He smiled at the bright wet streets of Paris as he and Cruche, together, triumphantly crossed the Alps.

WILLIAM H. GASS

The Old Folks

(FROM THE KENYON REVIEW)

WHO is not in league? The children waddle toward me, blue pants
on the bigger one, yellow on the other. I lift them on the train.
Away we go! We shall ride all day and eat lunches out of the same
sacks the kids keep their crayons in. Orange peels will enliven the
aisle, and our wan and bent reflections will float over a landscape
that streams behind us more rapidly than any river. We are going
to visit your father's family, Marty tells the children. How can they
know what that means? They cannot realize to what profound
degree the adults are conspiring against them.

It means heigho, and away we go! It will mean more later when
they stand in a strange stultifying room to stare at a cripple who
raises his hand in careful greeting like a liver-colored claw, while
grimacing at them through a row of colored bottles and muttering
"ah, then, there they are," or "well then where's the car?" or
something else they're not sure they should respond to, so they
become impassive as a pair of Indians or anyone who knows that
to reveal your feelings is to bare your breast for a blow you are
already too weak to receive or endure, much less manage to return.

It will mean more, but the low close meanness in the meaning
like a narrow door, old animosities like flies dead in the swatter's
screen, the nest of snakes and needles there, the clamping fear, the
lovelessness in the meaning like brackish tea, the serious signals in
the meaning (cancer coming like a train, foul prophecy, sour sugar,
star-crossed cards), and although grouped like a chorus of groans,
the bitter omens in the meaning will still pass them by like the
deadly angel, for had I not marked them with a bloody X? and
only the senselessness of it all will be evident, only the abrupt

unsocketing of their lives will be evident. The sudden outrage —
that will be evident. And my mother, her gray hair like a web she's
run into, will say, my, aren't they dear; how far along are they in
school? They're not in school, yet, mother. They're only two and
four. Well, four and a half, actually, and . . . My mother will sigh.
Too bad, poor things, not in school, so sad. A single fat tear will
run quickly across her cheek as though a blister had broken; and
we shall only that moment have crawled awkwardly from our cab,
the front door of the house will still be standing open, bags beneath
my hands like movie props, powder will be lying in the creases of
my mother's face like snow, her voice wet and wandering, blurry
as her gaze, Marty's eyes will ice, and I shall be . . . I shall be in a
rage.

I waddle down the hall through the dirty light of Sunday toward
what I hope will be an empty office, but I hear voices through the
gray glass and see a shadow — monstrous — that must be Planmantee, so I alter course to pass on down the stairs as secretly as
the rest of my dingy discipline does; and I realize, while I'm
bumping down the steps like a runaway ball, that as strange and
contradictory as my colleagues' views of history are, they each
think of time as something that rises like a kite, never as something
pulled out straight or stretched flat like dough, and certainly never
as seeking the sea like a river, thus running down as a watch would
either (for time is eternal to them, unlike the instrument), but that
was certainly how I saw it: not falling like a tower — nothing so
grand or dramatic, so thunderous or catastrophic — but sifting
and seeping, piddling itself away as one wastes a Sunday just as I
was doing, going for my mail and finding colleagues in conclave
before my box; so I suspect my sons will turn away from me less
abruptly than I did from my father, more like leaves revolve
toward the light through one cloud-spotted day.

And Oscar Planmantee, a colleague and my unsung theme song,
my nemesis, says suppose events were really more like things than
we think; suppose events could be broken in pieces like bread;
suppose, like when you break bread you reach a crumb you can no
longer credit, as if you'd gone past the beaten wheat, the yeast, into
the cell itself, then you'd have to back up, right? because you would
have sharpened your pencil past its point — haven't I put it precisely? — you'd have to adjust your sense of divisibility until you
got the right part into the right whole, right? you bet, Bill boy, and

then you'd have the ultimate element, and that's what we want, the basic bill, the changeless penny; that's what we need to secure for history an honest footing; and when I think back on these things (my summer spell of peace, those visits to the West and to the East, my birthplace in Iowa, home in Ohio, the brats we brought up, the succulent tits of my sow, this flood of bitterness that washes over me every seven minutes like plagues visited upon a speeded-up pharaoh), I wonder whether it is only pain that has parts, for my patches of happiness seem continuous, complete, so warmly substantial everywhere, like a mouth wet with wine, while my father's house is nothing but hunks, shards, tatters: rooms and parts of rooms, furniture falling to pieces like dry fruitcake, sun-faded draperies, raddled unretractable shades, cracked knickknacks, broken baskets, lifeless linens, small doughnut-holed cushions for resting the ass, wedge-shaped cushions for holding up the head, long broad pillows for propping up the back, cylindrical ones for raising the feet and legs, which Carl will promptly use to give his brother a whack, then plastic trays that stack and chairs with steel wheels and crowds of bottles we will have to watch like cops to keep the kids from sampling, each with little red-rimmed labels crossed with tiny typewritten symbols for hrs. and amts., along with words like *codeine* and *gold salts* and *cortisone,* the letter *o,* I notice, in each of them, with the plain white blank it circles, and then I think that maybe in there I won't feel anything, but my kids are bewildered by their surroundings, frightened, soon they are talking too loudly, and Carl's voice has a peculiar rising scoop to it that signifies hysteria.

I can't blame them, though I will hate them for vibrating at such a pitch when what I need is calm — actually, what I need is total obliteration, now — now that we have the bomb, we can all be blown back into our original pieces with one clean disintegration, instead of being pulled apart slowly with dental pliers. And what is the ultimate element in history but human life — human coupling, human pain? Planmantee grabs his nose. There's a bad smell coming from my mind, like a stopped drain. Human life? human suffering? simply a random set of deviations from a nonexistent norm. We average that out, he says.

Heigho! And we took our kids from their backyard where there was a little swing, from their friendly beds, and all their toys, and put them down — weren't we whirlwinds, really? — on this dusty threadbare rug, this small room crowded with furniture, footstools meeting in the middle like hills, say hello to your grandfather, Carl, and your grandmother, too, yes — hello, mother, do you remember the children's names? these are the pants that Auntie made, aren't they darling? and are you feeling any better, father? the weather too wet? gets the knees, I bet, fists and knuckles, crimps the elbows, turns up toes; and I suppose there were reasons for our coming — causes beyond guilt — the thought repeated like a lesson: but they want to see them, the Old Folks, sure, they have never seen their grandkids, all these years, though nobody asked mum how she was feeling because even falling down drunk she was supposed to be fine; her drinking was a secret from everybody, especially herself, because the gin got by her in the guise of tap water, swallowed gargle, as nasal spray unaccountably misdirected, under cover of cures for the nerves that steadily grew unsteadier, and thus required purer doses, longer swigs, more frequent spoons; and she mostly ate Life-Savers to sweeten her breath, and chewed limes, took tincture of iodine in prudent drops to ward off the goiter that wasn't coming, and to strengthen the blood that gushed out uncontrollably at her periods sometimes, the color of bourbon, one reason why we stayed away; but after all, Marty, we so rarely visit, and they have never seen our sons, and that's a shame; you've said hello once since our marriage, only once since our marriage, Marty, do you think that's often enough? even though the bloodstains on the rug drive you bats, and it's the first place you'll throw your eyes like a gauntlet when you barge with your shopping sack through the door to discover whether they're still there, which of course they will be, because things rot where they're dropped in that house, nature has taken over like lassitude in the tropics, anyhow the stains are not too noticeable against the worn wine border and the leaflike design so admired twenty years ago when it was laid out in Feeney's Fine Furniture like a work of Eastern art; nevertheless, how many times have we gone back to Iowa? even though we were both born there, you know perfectly well it's your clan that takes us in the way an elephant sucks up water with its trunk — so, say, half-a-dozen? since our marriage . . . our marriage that took place before thousands — relatives, connections, friends, the friends of friends, tradesmen, farmers — hordes heard us read over, saw the ring encircle your finger like a sore, witnessed the first connubial kiss, and hug too, delivered

like a package; and thus fortified with the Sacraments of Holy
Mother Church, June 1 (June 1, naturally), 1940 (to kiss off one
decade and kick off another), William Frederick Kohler, beloved
by nobody but dear son of Frederick Karl Kohler and Margaret
Phelps Finney, sometimes known as Feeney of Feeney's Fine Furniture, slid into the disembowered bed of Martha Krause Muhlenberg; dear daughter of Henry Heman Muhlenberg and Ruth
Dilschneider, sweet sister of Cramer and Catherine, the latter
younger by three years and already a Dallmeyer full of foal, and so
almost an aunt — yes — and certainly a dear sister-in-law who was
not yet enormous, with warm creamy flesh and moist parts; and
once there, even though they had fooled around with fooling
around before, so that neither felt obliged to play First Night,
Open Sesame, or Our Lady of Deflowers, as Culp called it, the
groom's penis pulsing as the bawdy books say . . .

> I once went to bed with a nun
> as a Master of Arts, not for fun.
> She was eager to learn,
> and had passion to burn,
> and was so apt in class,
> I put A on her ass;
> but she wouldn't take credit,
> though she smiled when she said it:
> your designs may be polished,
> Herr Prof, by your knowledge,
> but the smarts of your parts are homespun.

*And in that atmosphere, Herschel ventured the opinion that history was
the science of men in time. You blockhead, I thought, what do we know
about time? but Governali had already shouted SCI-ENCE? as if it were
pronounced* séance, *and Planmantee had brushed off mankind like a
piece of lint.*

Well, then Herr Husband proceeded to fuck her for all he was
worth, which wasn't much, with no house, no car, a salary of $3000
a year, a lousy job, no real prospects; and it wasn't much to ask,
either; it was little enough to do for the Old Folks, and they did
want to see the kids, they were grandparents, after all, and they
did want to see them — the prospering consequences of our care-

less encunting — even though dime-store photos in fancy frames
had arrived in time for unwrapping every Christmas season since
the first flash had gone off in baby's face, and somewhere in the
house there was a dresser where the years stood in brightly tinted
cemetery rows, their images smiling into a sickroom's dim medici-
nal distances; yet now the Old Folks spoke over the children's
heads and past their persons and rattled their words around them
impatiently the way you take a detour on a trip, to complete the *I-
told-you-so*s of their self-congratulations, recite litanies of community complaint, and utter their cries of international consternation;
dedicated, with the only pleasant absorption they knew, to a kind
of nondenominational kvetch, catholic in taste, Calvinist in ferocity,
which seemed as perpetual as promised cemetery care, though as
culturally confused as a big city street; and I must admit their
constant keening, though of course it did not spring into being in
a day but developed over years of practiced suffering and artful
emotional decay (and they weren't real *squeezers,* either, they
couldn't crush, they could only fuzz and smear, further bruise the
fruit they bitched about), has badly influenced me, even if I don't
complain much in public, and rarely go on about my own aches
and pains, although they're real enough, or bring up the wretched
lack of love I've had to endure my entire life, or cite the backbiting
of my colleagues, the professional jealousy that surrounds me like
a too-warm room, or the treachery of deans and other higher-ups
who have denied me the Commager Chair — those shit-resembling
administrators who wipe themselves with their memos and try,
then, to hold them under my nose, the excuses they hide behind,
bugs on the backside of leaves, as if the chair had to be occupied by
a specialist in American history, certainly not by a Nazi-nuzzler,
well, they're under their flimsy white reasons: toilet paper soaking
in the bowl like a great coil of cloudy sky, which I flush for fair
weather; anyway, they went right on about their illnesses, no matter how you tried to steer things, about their mutual exasperations
that thirty years of friction (like a religious war) had naturally
made cancerous, their aggravations with their neighbors (shitting,
barking, garbage-stealing dogs, mostly), mounting expenses (which
reminds me, so the mind slides, of a dumb joke by Culp), the
incompetence of all professions, including mine, the congenital
laziness of the poor, the insatiable greed of labor, the piracies of
business, the Communist menace, the collapse of moral standards,

and the dangerous spread of the spooks and kikes; although my mother, during her last quiet toot and ultimate toddle, was too muzzy-mouthed most of the time to form her words clearly, I gathered she was mostly remaking the past, enriching her family's coffers and raising their social status, pretending that she loved her father, and so on, and had once had a rich fine life, so that she could describe her marriage as a tragic comedown (which, in its way, it had been), while advancing reasons why I should give up my position at the university, my whole world and work, to return to live with her — with them — in her spoiled womb again, to become the local superintendent of schools (her gin-soaked eyes could see no higher than the same thin rim of cocktail onion might aspire to); forgetting, with a thoroughness Freud would have put in a footnote, how, in her schooldays, she had been called PP FinneyneeFeeney, over and over by chanting gangs of sweet-faced, pigtailed girls, until she often burst into tears, poor Peg; for no one could understand why her father had changed his name from Feeney to Finney in the first place, or why he retained the old name for his store in the second; though it was always perfectly clear to me that he was simply removing himself from the trade (he might be Feeney at the store but he was Finney at home), just as I am WFK sometimes, or Whiff Cough, or, as I used to be, Herr Rickler, in my prime; nor did she trouble to recall how humiliated she was to be dressed in upholstery remnants or the bolt-ends of drapes, for her father was famously stingy, as Peggy always accused my father of being when he bawled her out for spending money foolishly; and though she said she went to dances at the country club, and moved in circles too racy for my father's ears or under-standing, no one could say, looking at her lined, pale, and puffy face, the shapeless garish sack she had double-pinned around her, or the misfocusing eyes and slack wet mouth, that she had led the right life, and she knew it, not even with Freud's fist could she repress that, and so now in her whiskied age, my mother, Mar-garet, dreamed of fine parties and a large estate, long gowns and tall suitors, the handsome breasts of the girl she was, and enjoyed the anger of her husband, who understood the meaning of her lies — their thrust — without understanding the futility of arguing about them, as again and again he would inform her that there was no country club in the entire county during those schoolgirl days of hers, no dances, no romances, no roses; forcing his voice through the constrictions of his self-control till it rolled out flat as dough and dry as wash; but his hate had so melted his bones together he couldn't strike or throttle her while she ran on, speaking directly to Martha of her hopes for me and my return to the old hometown, as if my wife and the children no longer had that relation.

I am placed in the past by this journey, but my children find nothing here, not even the present, their father's world is too strange. They are making their memories, not living them, while Martha is resolved to let nothing in, her whole face a mask against poisonous gases. So the one-car cream and green garage does not look pitiful to them; there is no pathos to the barren patches beneath the trees or the single tulip frond that still pushes up each spring below the eave. I sense myself in that spent bulb, and let a little sadness overlay my rage. At the shaded bottom of the yard is a gathering of stones, mud, and meager weeds, which at one time was a garden made of ivy, moss, found rocks, and valley lilies we heaped up patiently. Soon now, I know, my family's simple house will empty and new life pour into it. Fresh hope will wash through the property like another rain; yet this skimpy lot and modest building will absorb these energies like China, and give only ruins in exchange.

I remember putting BBs through the bathroom window of the house immediately behind us. Was each BB an ultimate bit of the event as Planmantee might claim? I had fired into the air, exuberantly, like an Arab, and my father was consequently forced to redden my ears. So forty years later I remember the shots because I remember the shit that followed. It's what this house holds out to me: a plate of swallowed fruit.

I remember wheeling my bike from the garage and galloping away to school as though it were Arizona. I haven't cycled since I was siphoned off to war, and I've never been to Arizona.

I remember my many tame squirrels, and the hummingbirds at the honeysuckle, which climbed a trellis, broken then as now, to fill the early hours of the kitchen with a sweetness like fresh bread. Its vines are presently a dead web webbed with webs. I seldom see the birds I once saw — orioles and bluebirds, wrens — and watching the rubythroats (though rarely, as I said — the thrush is gone, that golden finch, the tanager like a healed wound) I am impressed by how they barely touch life, and therefore seem so Ariel and free, supping only through a straw. Into such beautifully flown mornings we would bring our nightfilled heads like loads of stinking garbage.

I remember waiting at the top of the basement stairs to surprise my father when he opened the door by planting my playful fist in his solar plexus, and feeling my breath rush away from what I'd done as his did. What will my children remember? Even less than I? Will Carl remember how I shook the crying out of him like salt, lifting his crib and hurling it as though I were the Hercules? And will even pleasant memories be shadowed by ambiguity the way these great oaks dim the grass?

I remember bolting through another door to encounter the gigantic nakedness of my mother, both of us too startled to be immediately ashamed, one of her hands scrabbling for a robe she'd just let fall; and I ran from the room with an awful slam, the sound coming after me like the clap of my own doom. I believed in doom in those days. Now, when the world ends, I doubt it will even whimper.

They weren't always Old Folks, of course, and I never thought of my father as my old man, despite the fact that he went in training to be Old Folks early. My mother declined the honor. Although it's easy for alkies to be someone's old man or lady (they have the necessary, broken-down, soft calf soul), they can't really make it as anybody's folks.

Old folk, old jokes, Culp claims.

The years were never an element, because my parents didn't age, they simply sickened. My father was mean and cocky like Cagney all the way to the dump. Flat on his back, his bones poking this way and that like the corpses in the camps, he still had a fiery eye, as though, but for those two coals, the grate held ash. There's no easy way out of this life, and I do not look forward to the day they put those tubes up my nose, and a catheter shows my pee the way out like some well-trained servant. I saw how my father's body broke his spirit like a match; and I saw how my mother's broken spirit took her body under the way a ship sinks after being disemboweled by an errant berg of ice.

My father suffered thirty years of pain. A continent could call it a war. It was an unjust fate. It was undeserved. And my mother drank for nearly the same, although she beat my father to the grave by a good five, having decayed for a decade before they lowered her away — a leftover spoiling in the light. Fare thee well, I say, now that the words have no designation.

My father taught me how to be a failure. He taught me bigotry and bitterness. I never acquired his courage, because I caught a case of cowardice from my mother — soft as cotton — and I was born with her desperate orality, her slow insistent cruelty — like quicksand — her engulfing love.

My mother drank to fill her life with the warmth that had long ago leaked out of it; and my father hurt like hell because his mother had, because he had inherited the wrong proclivities, his arthritis an arch between two sagging pillars.

My mother drank to let down her guard and allow her dreams to flood her like the cheap enamel basin they would later furnish her to puke in; while the aspirin my father fed on put a hole in his stomach like the one I have, having inherited the wrong proclivities, too, passivity like pavement over a storm.

My mother drank because, at the menopause, she missed the turn and struck a wall, her hormones went out of balance like the weights of a clock, and she couldn't tell time anymore; while my father held two jobs, one at his architect's office and another at the store, because the depression practically wiped out his practice, and Feeney's, also desperate, took him in at a family rate to let two others starve, and changed its name at the same time to Feeney's Family Furniture, not so much to honor my father's presence as to justify the junk the store now stocked; and there he worked long heartless hours, a foot backward in its shoe, filling the blankside of unused bills of sale with plans for gingerbread houses, garages too grand for their cars, gas stations disguised as castles, banks like forts, stores in the cute shapes of their specialties (often shoes), bars that were made entirely of glass brick, churches that were all spire, and little neighborhoods that were nothing but wall; then, as the world began to recover, my father's wasted efforts having bled his strength, he began to decline, and soon couldn't draw anymore, and soon couldn't sell sofas either, only sit in them, until they became too low and soft and mortal for him, his cane like a tree towering over him, his strength only in the grit of his jaws, in a mean streak now grown green and brave.

My mother had no steel. All puff — though sensitive — she was a cotton wad, and powdered her nose instead of washing it, and painted her nails instead of cleaning and cutting them, though when her hand shook, color crossed the cuticle, and sometimes the tips of her fingers were red. So she drank to the point of suicide, because a life that not only lacked love but couldn't even catch a little indifference, like a net to contain air, was intolerable; because she hadn't a single god, or god damn thing to do, or anything she could look back on as done — completed or accomplished — only one pleasureless screw that produced an ingrate and a monster upon whom she nevertheless pinned her hopes with exactly the same chance for success as anyone would who tried to drive a nail into a passing cloud — a son to whom she threw her soul at considerable peril, like a stone into a paper boat.

So my mother drank in order to die, but made her dying such a disagreeable, drawn-out business, and aimed it so deviously, like a draft or deep-sea current, that it became my father's dying, too. They must have both woke, if they slept, with the sense of imprisonment so strong in them (as though they had lain with a sachet of damp stones), what other sense — sound, sight, taste — could they have? tuned only to entrapment: she in her habit and household and husband, and he in himself, his wife's decay like the bad smell one employs to cover a bad smell.

Peg nursed at a poisonous nipple; she drank to fill herself with a milk malevolent enough to do her husband in if he ever thought to feed from her breasts again, in punishment for having suckled insufficiently before, and he ached in order not to Othello her with a whoopee cushion (or was I the object of their clever plans?); while my small aunt sat on her bed above them like a bird in a tree, boxes of nested boxes beneath her springs, and waited for both of them to melt away, and the weather to change. Well, so did I, though I was blunter and less hypocritical about it . . . I waited for them to leap from one another like cliffs; I waited for them to bludgeon one another into shapeless heaps, to stab with what points were left, to let go of life and sink inside each other like meeting seas or a struggling swimmer, to smother . . . I waited for them to die.

> I once went to bed with a nun,
> who had screwed every nation but one.
> I don't want to Russia,
> but your Pole feels like Prussia
> — far too Chile — to Finnish the pun.

And in that atmosphere, Herschel ventured the opinion that history was the self-knowledge of the mind. A birdcall on a wooden whistle, I thought, what do we know about knowledge? but Governali had already cried SELF? as if it were pronounced wealth, and Planmantee had buried mind like a mangy cat.

My kids will not come to visit me. We have broken the chain. And Governali says the Chinese were clever when they worshiped their ancestors, because they were really reverencing a true model of time — a model based on begetting, as Plato taught; but I did not become my children. I spat them out like pits and they grew up as near and yet apart from me as weeds in a row of beans.

My mother became me, though — that's true. She shrank as I grew large. Despite the fact that I was in Germany sharpening my claws, learning lessons she could not have begun to understand; nevertheless, I knew she referred to me incessantly, twisted her recollections of my now stout yet little knickered self like an anxious hankie. My activities had superseded and replaced hers; I was the principal figure in her fantasies, a shadow cast by her departed pride; so — yes, it was true — the life she had, such as it was, was only the life she dreamed for me, inaccurate and irrelevant as that was. I was her movie's movie star. When I stepped out of the cab, then, I came as the new superintendent of schools, parading in triumph down the avenues of my early education; and there were no lines in her script for these strangers she didn't want to see like flies beside me, whom she refused to acknowledge or focus on, and whom I'd brought along because of the wish I pretended she had like any conventional grandmomma or dad.

At first I was surprised by her designs, her hopes for me, as though a seamstress should dream her son would be a bank teller or a druggist. There appeared to be no connection. But when I allowed my thoughts to sink like a spoon in a pudding through the long cold evenings I spent with a then-unmuddled Margaret at our oilcloth-covered kitchen table, collecting cuttings for a scrapbook about Egypt or memorizing "The shades of night were falling fast" or doing sums, stumbling through Latin declensions or getting lost among the puzzling certainties of geometry or rushing through a novel's meaning like a train, the ground of her life with me seemed to dictate the building she envisioned; for it was my mother who was the architect in our family, and as I hammered another line of

Tennyson or Whittier in my head, turning up the silence in my sulks until my mother had to clap her hands over her ears and audibly protest, I was a window or a doorway or a wall that wouldn't stay in plumb, a leaning chimney, a poorly pitched roof, and she patiently redrew me, propped and pushed, until, through another day at school at least, I stood — indeed I peaked, I steepled on occasion. So when I left for college, she had nothing left, but had to linger on in that painful house, unfortunately more alone in my aunt's and father's company than ever in her own.

The fact that I was still in school, a professor of history in a huge if not distinguished university, with a Ph.D. like an abbreviation on one of my father's painkill bottles, was of no significance at all to her, because I was no longer in her educational system, the world she had helped me move through like a dancer's mum — no — I was far away in history, the ever-enlarging holocaust, the horrors of the human, as though it were another time and country, as it often was while I was studying the past, worshiping my heroes, or, later, warring on, then screwing in, Germany.

Eventually it came back to me like a letter I had no memory of writing, much less putting in the mail: that her father had been, among other things, a superintendent of schools in rural Iowa — the czar of something like two buildings and six rooms — and the historical force of this fact depressed me, as if an insignificant and innocent situation, by becoming the simplest sort of symbol, had triumphed despite its accompanying support, as if it were the one gun in the gang to coerce cash from the teller. Born blind, darkness follows forever; with a limp, one always perceives the world from aboard a ship; and was the wishbone, then, the single stanchion of the human spirit?

My own bones are old folks now. I remember how I faced the absurdity of my fate. I stood in a pool of cold and urine-yellow sunlight one early autumn afternoon, a sweater's empty arms around my neck, closing the family album on my children, one soft black page against another like the dark in which I'd mount my succeeding days; face dry, tight, smileless, smooth as an apple's skin, while I counted the overlapping shadows of their heavy steps when they went with their luggage to the car and drove away toward college as though it were Africa (it took ten strides, ten silhouettes like played cards); for I realized that I would never sleep straight through another night again; that my belly would

wake me, or my bladder, or my nose; that I would take my oblivion
henceforth in pinches like snuff; and that this intermittent dah-
dit-dah-dit, cutting up my consciousness in cubes, was the first
signal of senescence: C for ceasing, C for shutting shop. It wasn't
their leaving home, which I didn't mind at all, that made my frame
a codger. It was the pale stutter of their figures on the path, the
grass, the driveway, that convinced me. I'd be Old Folks now.

Who is not in league? The shadows of their skulls drifted across
the opaque glass — Culp and Planmantee, perhaps — so it seemed
so, and I drew back like a startled breath. I didn't dare eavesdrop
and risk hearing some opinion of me, yet I couldn't swing that
damn door in upon them, either, to gibe and josh as I had all week
and would again — lifelong, it seemed — Planmantee's huge
watch-chained shape against Culp's thin or Governali's woppy bulk
or Herschel's wispy gray — a libel of malicious lines like a cartoon
by Grosz.

Not your old pal, Boyle, Kohlee baby, but Bernoulli, Planmantee
says, saw the laws of history. Events are made of events, agree? but
we gotta find the right ones, the right elements. If I fall asleep in
church, and that puts a match to the ass of the preacher, why, then,
my somnolence is a part of the service; but if I surreptitiously
scratch my balls at a wedding (never mind the symbolism, Kohler,
never mind all that), my private itch, sneaked scratch, aren't atoms
of anything. O yeah, my glorious person is a part (I am expected
to attend the ceremony; I give a present to the happy pair; I kiss
the eager ugly bride), but otherwise my body — bones, fluids, cells,
physiognomy — does not matter a fart's worth. Ain't that a cri-
men-nently? Now those teeny little events, like thrown rice, right?
they collide, they rebound, they batter one another, passing the
heat of their motion around like biscuits at a banquet; so then the
total historical power of any event, see? it's simple! ah, such simplicity! a bubble up, the burp of a god! depends on the number
and violence of its random inner collisions and the good grip of
their container (the church, for instance, and its rites, right? holds
the wedding in its bounds); but chance is everything, isn't it, Kohler? and maybe as luck would have it there's a leak, you know, in
the little biosystem of my body — say I got the flu when I kiss her
— so then the bride starts to cough in four days, and the rest of
the wedding trip is ruined — she's sneezing all over the Falls, see?
and so the wedding, which was to make all the fucking legit, which

was ceremoniously, not causally, connected to their connections, correct? it sprang a leak, too, quite accidentally, and the bride is in bed with a bug, and hot from a different fever; yeah, Kohlee, that's how it goes.

I pulled out the shrunken drawers of my schoolboy desk to find perfumes, powders, and compacts, bracelets and skin-bracers and soap, utensils for a life nobody's led, because there's not a cranny in this house my aunt hasn't stuffed with something, often wrapped in its original tissue, still tagged, new however old it grows, however stale or out of style. The kids go for everything like squirrels, and I must get pointlessly cross before I take them for a stroll down those empty shady sidewalks I once triked, streets that still don't have sewers but are paralleled by weedy shallow ditches where I used to float boats after heavy rains and, with swagger and daring, leap.

Light has drained out of the windows like a sink. A radio is on. Carl is crying in an upstairs room. Martha is trying to conquer the kitchen. I remember the old stove — QuickCook, was it called? — a happy hen on its white enamel oven door, the blue flame like a dancing decoration when we warmed ourselves in front of it on cold mornings. Frost made the sun pink, and the kitchen table shook beneath its spill when I slid under. My aunt will soon be home from work, one hip hurrying a hop ahead of the rest of her. Mother is on the sofa in a caterwaul of clippings, all about me and my youthful academic exploits, columns she holds up to her watering eyes a moment before she mews with recognition and returns them to the tangle. My father is dressed in a thick green woodman's plaid wool shirt, so heavy with adjectives he can hardly lift his arms. I'm home, I say softly to myself. My father tips one large ear toward the speaker. The bottles on his table shudder slightly. He doesn't approve of the news. Heigho. I'm home. I'm home. I've brought us all here to my home.

And in that atmosphere . . .

I still see her feet, hanging out of the cloth of her gown like a pair of pulls. If I yank what will ring? and down the dark hall my mother wobbled toward my father's bed, and I realized then that they no longer slept in the same room — it should have been no surprise — and that normally she would be sleeping now where Martha and I lay together on the debris of my childhood, because the bell had gone off in my ear and I had risen as one called by the last trump to judgment — terrified — disoriented — Martha rolling toward me like a dislodged log. There were murmurs: my mother's and my father's voices, a broken moan from Martha, whimpers from the children sleeping in a corner full of pillow litter. The feet returned and slowly descended the stairs. She must be sleeping on the sofa — final bed of breadman's love, as I was expected to sleep on sheets of solitary vice, sheets I've filled since with notes on deportation procedures and other technicalities — to sleep above bedpans and chamber pots my mother had collected and shoved out of sight behind the tasseled chenille spread, inadequately rinsed — to sleep . . . well, I did not. I stared into the darkness until I could see my mother's ginny breath float by like night-sky clouds, waiting for the bell to ring again, my father's body passing its requests along a wire, not like Marconi's "What hath God . . ." but much less grandly: *bring a pot, I've got to pee*, or *please, I want to take a pill*, or *O, I've gotten stiff and need to turn*, turn over in my almost grave.

The breadman was the last love of my mother's life. She had begun by buying pies so thick with tapioca the filling stood without the crust, and these she would stack atop the refrigerator until I threw them out. His rolls grew slowly old and hard as I thought his rocks. The truck he drove had animals on it. His firm was the first with cracked wheat. Later on, he brought her bottles — the bastard — and for Christmas I was required to hand him a carton of cigarettes wreathed for the season in Lucky Strike green. He was a sturdy square-faced little man who knew how to blush but not how to stop — he couldn't or wouldn't talk — and not until now have I considered how her drunken negligence of dress must have seduced him, or what a pair they must have made: her gown open like a drape, his pants in a puddle about his ankles, their liquid kisses, doggy embrace.

> *I once wet my bed just for fun*
> *by soaking my sheet in my come.*
> *It was torn off in strips,*
> *and my mother's tight lips*
> *locked my deed in a heart that was numb.*

And in that atmosphere, Herschel ventured the opinion that history was, after all, a process through which human consciousness perhaps endeav-

ored to achieve self-contained existence. Bei-sich-selbst-seyn-scheiss, *I thought, we are as free to be of value as chewed gum; but Governali clapped Herschel on the back, shouting* bellissimo, *or some such Italian-ate slop, adding with great emotion that consciousness, of course, was simply Time in its bellissimist manifestation; while Planmantee glared at them both, scornfully denying such containment altogether (not even for the fruit bat, he said) and pronouncing their heady self-awareness a historical superfluity — the randy dance of light in a cake of melting ice.*

T. GERTLER

In Case of Survival

(FROM ESQUIRE FORTNIGHTLY)

LATE ONE NIGHT under the sliver of light from his bedside lamp, Harold Stein composed a letter he had long contemplated.

Dear Friends,

An accident is an accident, but what do you call an accident that gives a preview? My wife and I were supposed to take Flight 6 from New York to Miami four months ago. Because I had a premonition of some disaster, I kept us from getting on the plane, and this plane crashed, as you know. Maybe it would have been impossible to convince other people on the basis of the strong sort of nauseous feeling I had, but I think now I should have tried. All that could have happened would be that I would have made a fool of myself or the airline would have sued me for defamation of character. That would be nothing compared to saving twenty-seven lives and other injuries. I'm writing this letter to you to apologize if you lost a loved one or were yourself injured or just upset by being on that plane. It's not much, but it's all I can do.

Also, I have two shoe stores for ladies, Stein's Footwear in Bal Harbour and one on the Lincoln Road Mall and I would be very happy if you could stop by any time so I could fit you with a complimentary pair of shoes. This may sound foolish, but it would be something I can do. Since I am mainly in the Bal Harbour store, it would be better if you came there.

Again, I am deeply sorry.

Sincerely yours,

The next morning, his wife, Natalie, complained about a dream. "I can't remember it," she said. Though he wanted the list of passengers on the plane, he decided not to ask her where she kept her newspaper clippings about the crash. He folded the letter and put it behind his driver's license in his wallet.

There were nights when Harold slept well, nights when he stood poised on a peak ringed with clouds, then jumped easily, gracefully, into the sea below. He could feel the perfect arch of his body as he descended, could feel air rushing past him at just the right speed, in just the right places. This was how it had been for him years ago at swimming pools and once on a Caribbean island. He knew that he pierced the water precisely at a ninety-degree angle and that the surface showed not even a ripple as he passed beneath it.

There were other nights, nights when he stood on his cloud-ringed peak and looked down and saw nothing. And jumped blindly and could feel only terror as he plummeted down. He kept waking before he landed, dozing off and waking; each time he checked the shimmering blue-green face of the clock on his night table and felt the dreaming presence of Natalie beside him.

He would lie in the dark, his eyes open, and imagine the twenty-seven people who had died on the plane and the people who had been injured. He remembered faces from among the crowd at the gate: the black man in priest's clothing, a monochrome figure except for the slash of white collar; the thin, nervous girl of about eighteen with a nose like his older daughter Edith's original one, his own; the bent woman who for no reason other than great age reminded him of his mother before she died. He wondered if these people had survived, or the ones who had passed him in the boarding corridor as he was already hearing their screams and feeling his stomach contract with the plane's shuddering drop. In some equation he could not express, he knew he owed those passengers something, clearly more than shoes. It was on a night like this that he wrote his letter.

He suffered because his refusal to board the plane had made him, to his wife, a hero. The dread that had assaulted him in the boarding corridor was not heroic. The memory of it sent chills along the backs of his upper arms and calves. He had seen the plane fall. One minute it was gliding through gray sky; then, in unimaginable silence, it dropped, and the screaming inside the plane began. Someone called for God. Ice shot from a plastic glass and struck a window across the aisle. This vision seized him as he and his wife walked toward the plane. It was simple: You did not enter a plane that you knew was going to fall. Natalie said, "Let's go," when he halted. She pulled slightly at him; he pulled slightly back.

"C'mon," she said, and started to walk on. If she had said, "What is it?" or said nothing at all but waited for him to explain, he wouldn't have hit her. Transformed by his vision, in a burst of surrender to the certainty of a crash, he stopped her with a right hook to the jaw that kept her from going forward, that sent her, miraculously, down. His small and at times overpowering wife, whom he had never hurt before and would never hurt again, looked up at him for a moment with the new emotion of pure surprise before she blacked out. Later, telling and retelling the story to friends, she seemed to relish Harold's violence, as if that terrible act, which belied the courtesy of all their years together, proved the force of his love for her. The truth, as he understood it, was baser: He had hit her to keep her from entering the plane because he knew that if she entered the plane, he would have to go, too, and he did not want to go.

Shame and the helplessness of shame confused him; disloyal, he accepted Natalie's ignorance of his feelings as he had after a long-ago weekend with a woman in another city. Still, he felt he must confess something to his wife — if not that truth, then some other horrible truth that linked and yet separated them, like the coupling between train cars. He could not discover it. If, in refusing to board the plane, he had discerned the future, what was preventing him from reading the present?

Sometimes, when he looked at his lathered face in the mirror and saw the approaching razor, he felt he was going to cut himself. The blood mingling with soap and stray whiskers had not been drawn, but he saw it as clearly as if it had. He became lost in the different times, had to remember that the blood was not there, that he was still unshaved. Then he shaved and, no matter how careful he was, cut himself. The sting was doubly painful, carrying as it did the weight of future remembered and present past. And — "Damn, damn," he muttered as he fumbled through the medicine cabinet and sent the economy-size unwaxed dental floss flying into the toilet; he could never find a styptic pencil when he needed it.

Dr. Ira Blume, at the university, read about Harold in the *Miami Herald* and telephoned him. "I'd like to evaluate your potential paranormality," Blume's voice said. When Harold said nothing, Blume went on: "That's ESP we're talking about, Mr. Stein."

Harold said, "Forget it."

Blume: "You want to talk about guilt?"

Harold arrived at Blume's lab early, stayed late. Blume dazzled him with cards and patterns. Harold said, "We were going to talk."

Blume shuffled an oversize deck. "Your conception of yourself as having failed in a communal crisis evidences itself as guilt. You show survivor's syndrome. And you're terrified you may have had a psychic episode. Pick a card."

Harold: "It was a coincidence."

Blume: "Sounds reasonable. A hundred times a day in a hundred different airports some bozo is chickening out of a plane ride. Ninety-nine point X percent of those babies don't crash."

"Coincidence."

"Bet your ass. Can you come in next week?"

Blume submitted a paper to a learned journal. "Accuracy in measuring the unknown is essential to the methodology if we are to describe that unknown. Too often in too many statistics the ambiguous is classified and the merely coincidental masquerades as the phenomenal. How do we isolate psychic energy if all we can do is flip coins?" he wrote. Natalie put a copy of *American Parapsychological Review* on the coffee table. Harold had trouble finding *TV Guide,* which had always been on the coffee table before.

Natalie invited Blume to dinner, where he met the Steins' younger daughter, Cheryl.

"I'm minoring in psych," Cheryl told Blume, and for the first time it occurred to Harold that Blume was young and probably handsome.

Blume asked Cheryl if she'd like to undergo tests for ESP.

Harold said no.

Cheryl said yes.

Harold's friend and business partner, Mac Lishinsky, told him, "Relax. So you know you're going to cut yourself before you cut

yourself. I'll tell you something, you should know you're not alone.
Every night I know I'm gonna hate being home even before I get
home. So what do you think about that?"

Mac Lishinsky, Danny Silver, and Frank Merwitz refused to play
gin with Harold anymore.

"Can you or can you not tell me what's in my hand?" Danny
Silver demanded across the card table one evening in an exhalation
of peanut breath.

Harold said, "All you need is the six of clubs."

"I rest my case," Danny Silver said.

"You don't have to be psychic to know about the six of clubs."
Harold pointed at the discard pile. "I see what you throw away."

At the women's table, Fredelle Lishinsky, Myra Silver, Diane
Merwitz, and Natalie continued their canasta game. It was the last
weekly card party that the Steins attended.

Natalie laughed as they were driving home. "I won six dollars,
and the girls looked at me suspiciously. At *me!* And I was the one
who wanted to get on the plane."

The pebbles in the driveway looked familiar and welcoming as
the low beams passed over them. Harold felt the warm plastic grip
of the hand brake. He tried to turn off the ignition gently, so that
the change from noise to silence would not be abrupt, but it was.
The sound of crickets began to fill the silence. "I was with another
woman once," he wanted to say to Natalie in that narrow space. He
could smell the oversweet hair spray on her freshly done hair, the
fading presence of her perfume, the stale cigar aura that Frank
Merwitz conferred on them. Beneath or between these odors he
caught her scent, clean, modest, still — after all those years — inviting. He did not say "I was with another woman once" because
he could not foresee how her face would look when he told her.
He decided instead that the next day, in the privacy of his office,
he would type his letter to the passengers on the plane and to the
families of the victims.

Harold's office occupied a cubicle in the stockroom at the back of
the store. The top half of the partition walls was glass and afforded
Harold a vista of shoe boxes arranged in banks of metal shelves
from floor to ceiling. Each bank had a wooden ladder fixed on
tracks to the top row and equipped with wheels at its legs. Under
the purplish fluorescent lights, the ladders cast shadows on the

shelves, on the floor, on the round-backed salesmen walking past them. In places this view was obscured by papers taped to the glass: invoices with small windows punched by computer, an inventory of Italian shoes in a Brazilian shoe factory, yellowing black-and-white snapshots of Natalie and the children. One picture showed Edith and Cheryl standing near a lake at a summer camp on visitor's day, both of them squinting into the sun and waving good-bye. Another picture showed Natalie pointing at a mountain.

In his store Harold noticed the least adjustment of a showcase, the barest shine on a chair's scarlet velour seat. He knew the temperament of each of his salesmen, could register their day-to-day moods and manipulate them without a moment's thought. His customers gave him their frantic loyalty because he remembered them all by name, size, and style preference: "Now, Joe, I want you to take special care of Mrs. Mortimer here. Give her good support in her last and a nice narrow heel, seven with a triple A back there."

At home, though, he lost that certainty; in the wholeness of his family he struggled with details. If asked the color of the bedspread under which he slept — or lay awake — every night, he would have answered, "Yellow. No, wait, maybe orange. A kind of orange-yellow. Sort of gold, I think. A gold-and-green print." He thought that Natalie's bathrobe was white, with eyelets and ruffles, when in fact she had been wearing, under his gaze every morning at breakfast for six months, a blue kimono with yellow piping and frogs. He knew that Cheryl was in college, but in what year and for what purpose he couldn't say. He knew that Edith lived in either Denver or Detroit, but he wasn't sure whether she taught grade school or high school, and he had no idea why she lived so far away. Her infrequent letters clarified nothing for him: Though they were filled with descriptions of wonderful friends and parties, with little anecdotes about her job and apartment, he felt, when he held her blue stationery and saw her even brown script, the power of her unhappiness, a wild, unreasoning cry of "Help me, help me!"

"She really should do something with her talent," Natalie would say, handing him one of Edith's letters. "When I think of what they put in magazines . . ." And she would shake her head and turn to Cheryl. "And you, young lady, I'm expecting things from you too."

"Oh, Mom."

"I *am*, Cheryl. I most definitely am."

At night, Natalie would whisper into Harold's pajama collar, "Edith sounds happy, doesn't she?" "I guess," he would answer, and absently rub his wife's nylon back.

Blume's lab had been designed by a Formica freak. This was Cheryl's opinion, stated at dinner. She had wandered, barefoot, into the kitchen for a cup of yogurt and stayed while her parents ate. She watched the limp slice of pot roast on her father's plate shiver under the attack of his knife and fork. A slice of carrot slid away from the meat and traveled through gravy.

"I don't see how you can eat that stuff," Cheryl said.

Natalie murmured something about not imposing one's values on others. Harold said nothing.

Cheryl dragged the edge of a cracker across a tub of whipped cream cheese. "Doesn't anybody want to know what happened to me at Ira's place?"

"Ira?" Natalie asked.

"Blume," Harold said to her.

"Dr. Blume," Natalie said.

Cheryl pushed another cracker through cream cheese. "I went yesterday, after my Forms of Social Terror class, which, by the way, stinks."

"Cheryl," Natalie said.

"Sorry, Mom. Anyway, I went over to Ira's lab, Formica Heaven, and he gave me these tests, you know, funny cards and colors."

"Are you all right?" Natalie asked Harold.

Cheryl closed her mouth around a cream-cheese-laden cracker. For a moment she didn't chew, but held the cracker in her closed mouth, a habit that Harold remembered from her childhood. He was puzzled by her beauty. She seemed to resemble no one in the family.

Cheryl smiled at her father. "So guess what. Ira says that without a doubt, I am absolutely positively not psychic. I don't have even a little dot of ESP in my whole head."

Natalie began to clear the table. "You have other qualities. Hand me that plate."

Harold did not type his letter at the store. He sat at his cluttered metal desk and tenderly traced each scratch along its surface.

Mac Lishinsky opened a brown paper bag, peeled corned beef

from waxed paper. He said over the rustle, "You can't help it if some people died."

"I could have said something, I could have told them," Harold said.

"Oh, sure. A coupla hundred people're getting on a plane, and some nut says, 'Hey, don't go, this plane's gonna crash,' and you think they're all gonna get off the plane?"

"Look, what if it happens again? *Then* I didn't know what . . . what I was feeling. If I was crazy. But if it happens again . . ."

"So don't fly anywhere."

"I don't mean flying. I mean anything. Anything could happen, and what if I knew about it *before* it happened?"

Mac Lishinsky bit into a loud dill pickle. "Let me tell you something, something very helpful. Don't cross your bridges before you come to them."

Harold banged his desk, and a patent-leather pump waving an undone ankle strap fell over. "But that's the problem. What if I *can* cross my bridges before I come to them?"

Mac Lishinsky shrugged. "So what do you want? Don't look a gift horse in the mouth."

Blume said, "On a quantitative basis, your precognitive powers are indeterminable."

Harold asked, "I don't have ESP?"

"We need more tests. Your results are so borderline."

"Borderline ESP?"

"Borderline inconclusive."

"I'm too old for all this."

Blume did his imitation of a hearty chuckle. "A man's never too old to discover a new talent of his."

"A cancer is not a talent."

"Can you come in tomorrow?"

The next morning, while Natalie, her hair wrapped in two layers of gauze and an enormous plastic cap, sang "Strangers in the Night" under the shower, Harold sat at the desk in the living room and opened the bottom drawer. Beneath several blue envelopes from Edith and two gummy sheets of Green Stamps fused to a broken rubber band, he found the newspaper clippings about the crash. They were pasted in a red Woolworth's scrapbook that said

My Scrapbook on the cover. They filled ten pages, about a third of the book; Harold wondered if Natalie expected to fill the remaining pages with other instances of his recently erupted ability.

He looked again at the cover and saw faint writing that someone had tried to erase. He held it up to the morning light: "My Poems, by Edith Marcia Stein, 1966." The scrapbook had been Edith's, bought no doubt in one of her fits of organization. In 1966 she had been in high school. Something had happened, or something hadn't happened, and she had never assembled her poems. And Natalie, who hated waste, had saved the red scrapbook even after Edith left home: Someday it would be useful; someday there would be something to paste in it.

Careful not to read anything upsetting, he skimmed through several pages before finding what he wanted.

> *Estrellita Alvarez*
> *Mr. and Mrs. Mark Aronovitz*
> *Jack Bromberg*
> *Father Thomas Dennis*

The colored — the black priest, Harold thought.

> *Jorge Esposito*
> *Dr. William Evans*
> *Sean Goldman*
> *Michelle Goldstein*
> *Mr. Ronald Goldstein*
> *Mr. and Mrs. Harvey Jacoby*
> *Mr. and Mrs. Daniel Kincaid*

The names brought faces with them, faces he hadn't realized he knew. Particulars of strangers' lives assaulted him. Mr. and Mrs. Mark Aronovitz were honeymooners from Trenton. He was a lawyer. She was already beginning to dislike the red moles on his back. Dr. William Evans, an oncologist, was flying down to Miami to serve as consultant at a rich man's deathbed. Daniel Kincaid, a sandy-haired giant, preferred to be called Dan; his sparrow wife wore dark amethysts because no one had ever given her opals. Estrellita Alvarez was three days pregnant. Michelle Goldstein was in love.

Harold read down the list quickly, hoping that speed would obliterate empathy. "Now I know where Edith gets her imagination," he said out loud.

Natalie said, "Harold?" just as his eyes stopped at

Mr. and Mrs. Harold Stein.

She was standing in a bra and slip at the door to the living room. Talcum powder caked in the creases of her elbows, outlined the fine wrinkles on her neck. In one hand she held an uncapped eyebrow pencil.

"They have our name here," he said.

She came closer. One of her eyebrows had been penciled in; faint hairs described the ghost of the other. "Why are you reading that?" she asked. "It makes you nervous."

"I want to send a letter. I needed the names and addresses. But they have our name here."

"A letter?"

Her missing eyebrow troubled him; the eye beneath it seemed at once vulnerable and aggressive, introverted and probing, a microscope and a telescope. He had to look away to speak. "A letter. To explain to the people who were on the plane, or to their families."

"To explain what?"

"About me. About why I didn't, why I couldn't save them."

Natalie leaned against the desk and replaced the cap on her eyebrow pencil. She twirled the pencil between two fingers. "Harold, you can't send a letter like that —"

"Why not?"

"It doesn't make any sense. What can you say to those people?"

Reluctantly, he took the folded letter from his wallet and handed it to her. The rims of his ears flushed. "I was going to type it up and get it Xeroxed."

While she read, he closed the scrapbook and put it in the drawer. It crumpled one of Edith's letters, which he extracted and tried to smooth across his knee. His hand seemed clumsy to him as it patted the envelope. The postmark said Denver. That was where Edith was living.

A crackle of paper told him when Natalie turned the page. Her breathing lulled him; for a moment he felt sleepy.

She handed his letter back to him. Though he looked expectantly at her, she said nothing.

"Nat, you think I'm crazy?"

"No," she said automatically. "I love you."

"No, don't answer right away. Sit down, sit on the sofa and really think about it: Am I crazy?"

"Darling, I'm full of powder —"

"Natalie, please."

Powder settled on the sofa with her. She cleared her throat, avoided his eyes, then frowned, as if to show deep thought. The posturing ceased as real thought overtook her. Her face softened, her body assumed a quality of weightlessness on the green sofa.

Time, instead of moving forward, seemed to be spreading, bulging out at the sides, while an overflow streamed irresistibly backward. Harold's mother smiled, a sunburst of lines. Her skin was transparent, like the web of a thumb backlit by a burning candle. Blue veins beneath her skin showed their blurred, delicate network. Behind her wavered Harold's father, shadowed, bent over his sewing machine, singing. He looked up once and nodded before he and his wife disappeared.

Edith, still sleeping in her Denver bedroom, also lay curled up under her childhood quilt on the sofa, her head in Natalie's lap. Natalie stroked her daughter's fine brown hair with one hand and clutched the eyebrow pencil in the other. Edith murmured, "What time is it?" but her eyes stayed closed.

Cheryl, still taking notes in an early class at the university, sat cross-legged on the shag carpeting at Harold's feet. "Hi, Daddy." She wrote something down. "Listen to this." She began to read from her notes. " 'The shoe as an erotic symbol.' Did you ever think of that before?"

"What's neurotic about a shoe?" Harold asked.

" 'Erotic,' not 'neurotic.' Listen: 'The woman's shoe as a symbol of her sexual subservience to man — see the impossibly high shoe down through the ages. The chopines in sixteenth-century Venice. The traditional high clogs of Japanese courtesans.' "

"What course is this?"

"It's called The Self as a Free Entity: End of the Rainbow or Impossible Dream?"

"What's it for?"

"Three credits."

"No, why are you studying it? What do you want to be?"

Cheryl rolled her eyes. "*Uh*-oh. This is getting heavy."

"What time is it, darling?" Edith said in her sleep.

Cheryl said, "And heavier." She raised her voice. "I think you'd better wake up, Edith."

Edith opened her eyes. "Where's Michael?"

"In Denver, I guess," Cheryl said. "Hi."

"Who's Michael?" Harold asked.

Edith yawned, covered her mouth with a thin hand. "Daddy, I'm twenty-six." She stretched under the quilt, and her long pale toes wriggled at the end of the sofa. "I wrote you a letter a couple of days ago." She yawned again, and a tear ran from the corner of her right eye. "Oh, God, I'm talking and I've got morning mouth."

"Who's Michael?" Harold asked.

Natalie said, "Harold, you're shouting," and the girls disappeared, though Natalie's hand for a moment stroked the air where Edith's head had been.

"I'm shouting because no one's telling me who Michael is."

"What on earth makes you bring up Michael?"

"This," Harold shouted, and then he said in a lower voice, "this." He waved Edith's letter that he had been trying to uncrumple. "She says, 'Michael may come with me when I come home to visit.' "

Natalie rolled her eyes. Was she imitating Cheryl, or was Cheryl imitating her? "That's an old letter, you read it months ago. You know Michael is her . . . young man."

She stood up and slapped powder from the sofa cushions. Then she went over to him and kissed his forehead. "I've got to get dressed. Fight for Sight luncheon."

He was closing the desk drawer when Natalie returned to the living room, a pink silk dress fluttering over one arm. She had penciled in her missing eyebrow; both brows rose now when she spoke. "I almost forgot to tell you: No, I don't think you're crazy." She looked away shyly. "But then," she said as she left, "what do I know?"

He would have typed his letter at the store that day, but Mac Lishinsky wanted to calculate the merits of ESP in playing the market. The singer Eydie Gorme, or someone who looked just like her, came into the store in search of Guccis. She admired the travel poster of Florence, then asked directions to Neiman-Marcus, and laughed when she learned it was a few doors away. It must have been Eydie Gorme, because she had a very musical laugh.

After lunch, he climbed one of the wooden ladders in the stockroom and gazed down at his cubicle. He descended to commiserate with Fredelle Lishinsky, who came into the store looking for her husband and left with a consolation prize of chartreuse espadrilles.

Later in the afternoon, before closing, Harold drove to the university, where Dr. Blume introduced a machine and a set of electrodes.

"I been waiting a long time for this little mama," Blume said, patting the machine. "This will tell us something, we hope." He began to glue electrodes to Harold's temples.

Harold wrinkled his forehead; an electrode fell into his lap. "You're sure this isn't an electric chair?" he asked.

Blume lowered wounded eyes to Harold. "Mr. Stein, do you believe I feel any hostility toward you?"

Harold said, "It was only a joke."

"Or perhaps, Mr. Stein, you are projecting on me your own hostility."

A yawn pressed Harold's ribs. "I guess I just don't like you very much, Blume, even if you are a scientist. I'm sorry."

Blume finished attaching Harold to the electrodes. Then he said, "It's all right. You don't have to like me."

Expression shaped Harold's face; his forehead had already pleated gently before he stopped it. "So. When is there an end to this?"

"Mr. Stein, there's so much we don't know."

"Do you know how much longer I have to come here?"

Blume held up a tangle of bright wires. "Do you believe the slobs I have to share my equipment with?" He disappeared behind a white Formica construction.

Harold nodded slowly, to avoid disturbing the electrodes.

Blume muttered, "One second, Mr. Stein. I'm trying to get a reading here."

A flute whined at Harold as he opened the front door to his house. An orange reflection of sunset sprang at him from the living room: light deflected from a crystal vase.

"She's been playing that record over and over," Natalie said. "I'd go crazy, but I don't have the strength."

Harold knocked on Cheryl's door. When she didn't answer, he banged on the door. "Can I come in?"

She pushed the automatic-reject button as he entered. The tone arm swung through its maneuvers; the flute stopped in mid-note.

She was lying in bed, wrapped in zebra-striped sheets. Her brown hair spiraled over an arrangement of three large curlers; the scalp showed bloodless between the taut rolls. When she sat up, he noticed the shift of her small breasts beneath her T-shirt. A mystery paperback with a broken spine tumbled over stripes covering her knees. A balled-up paper towel rent by a protruding pear stem balanced in the sheeted valley created by her ankles. Tilting on the stereo near her bed, one of Natalie's good ashtrays held a gnarled yellow cigarette butt. The smell of sweet foreign tobacco clung to the curtains.

"It's off," she said, and he closed the door again.

In the kitchen, Natalie mashed potatoes. Her pink silk dress, unzipped down the back, billowed over her shoulders.

"How'd the luncheon go?" he asked her.

"Madeline Faye and Myra Silver squabbled all afternoon. I'm fed up. And then I come home to your daughter's eternal flute. Plus she 'forgot' to defrost the lamb chops." She rinsed the masher under steaming water at the sink. "We'll have to have eggs."

He lifted a glass of orange juice to her. "Madam Chairman."

"I want to change." She was unfastening the hidden clasp of her gold necklace. "There's a letter from your other daughter on the table," she announced from the living room. She might have been saying something else as she passed through the hall.

He left the letter where it lay, in the center of the kitchen table, a blue sheaf on yellow cloth, and he set two places on either side of it. After he laid a triangular-folded paper napkin under each fork, he sat down to read Edith's letter.

Feb. 8, 1977

Dear Mother & Dad,

I really don't see the point of writing anymore. We never tell each other anything. How many how-are-you-I-am-fine variations are there? Why should I keep writing about the weather in Denver and reading about the weather in Miami Beach? The store is doing well, the new David Evins line is a sellout — is this what you have to tell me?

Harold looked away from the letter, watched a palm-tree frond brushing against the kitchen window. Cheryl's flute record started again. He returned to the letter.

. . . you have to tell me? What are you thinking, what are you wondering about, what do you want?

Here's the truth about teaching. It's a daily battle against twenty-nine little cretins with the attention span of a guppy. All they want to know is how to get rich in a hurry. The school board decrees that I teach them Blake. When the classroom windows are closed, you could choke on the lethal fumes of Intimate and Clearasil. Their pimples are revolting. The idea of their sweaty, hopeful sex depresses me. The smartest kid in the class has a glimmering that something's wrong, but he doesn't know what and goes on quoting Paul Williams songs when he wants to make a point. Which is more than the rest of them do.

And that's just one of six classes. Try six times twenty-nine.

As for after school: For a while I loved having my own place. I was happy, you see, because I didn't know any better. I put a staghorn fern in a very expensive hanging basket. Then last year, Michael came along — well, as long as I'm ranting about the truth, Michael moved in with me.

Here Harold held his breath. Green spikes of palm frond, their edges blurred in twilight, scratched at the window. The flutist in Cheryl's bedroom played on. Harold gasped for air.

That's when I really loved the apartment. It wasn't a tastefully underfurnished expression of my soul; it was a messy, confusing home, with too many books for the bookshelves, too many shoes on the floor, not enough room for my makeup in the medicine cabinet, and always the wrong music on the radio.

Two months ago, Michael moved out. I hate this place now. It's still crowded — he hasn't carted away all his stuff yet, especially the ceremonial spears. And the boxes of cowrie-shell ornaments. You did know he's an anthropologist? I think I'm going to move.

Yesterday, after a profoundly unnerving day (one of the kids in English 12-2 described Kafka as "a guy who either needed a lay or a can of Raid" — this in a test paper), I came home and stood under the shower and cried for about forty minutes. Then I had a grilled-cheese sandwich, hot dinner of the lonely. Then I climbed into bed and read two books — sequentially, not simultaneously. I read until morning, this morning, time to go back to school. But I didn't go, just stayed in bed and kept reading. I read one favorite, *Gulliver's Travels,* and then I read one of Michael's books, *The Secret of the Hittites,* by C. W. Ceram, which I'd found in the laundry hamper last week. The Hittites were a Near Eastern people who were mentioned maybe three times in the Bible. The Hittite king had an enormous library and was the only one in his dominion who could hunt lions. Not exactly fantastic perks by today's standards, but I'm sure he had the equivalent of stock options too. Anyway, one day 3,000 years ago, someone wrote a letter to the Hittite king:

> So says Jakim-Addad, your servant: I wrote lately to my Lord in the following words: "A lion was captured upon the roof-balcony of the house belonging to Akkara. If this lion should remain on the roof until the coming of my Lord, let my Lord write this to me." Now the reply of my Lord has been delayed, and the lion has remained upon the roof a full five days. A dog and a swine have been thrown to him, and he also eats bread. I said: "This lion may cause a panic among the people." Then I became afraid and closed the lion in a wooden cage. I shall load this cage upon a barge and have it taken to my Lord.

Isn't it wonderful? After I read it, I cried. I've been crying a lot lately. But I know that feeling, the lion up there on the roof, waiting, and I in my house below him, listening to his pacing, wondering if he's hungry. And I ask for help, but no answer ever reaches me. And there's the solution — just ship the whole damn lion off to the only person you know who's allowed to kill lions. But who is that person? Where's the Hittite king? Do I check the classifieds under Position Wanted?

I'm all right, really. Even teachers can play hooky. I told you something. Now what?

Love to Cheryl.

Love,
Edith

P.S. I won't be coming home for Easter vacation. E.

P.P.S. Thank you for the birthday check. E.

Harold placed the letter in his plate. He stood up, noticed it was dark out. The pot of mashed potatoes on the counter was cold. He turned off the kitchen light; the darkness outside remained. He turned the light on again.

Bewildered, he wandered to the dining room, looking for Natalie. Then he remembered her hands on her gold necklace, and he walked down the hall, past Cheryl's closed door, to the bedroom.

Natalie, in the blue kimono, which he noticed for the first time, sat sewing. The lamp at her side lighted her work and left her face in shadow. With each rise her needle caught the light.

"What are you doing?" he asked her.

The needle sparkled. He thought he saw her lips press together.

"They're spoiled," she said.

"They're just cold," he answered, thinking that she meant the potatoes.

"Those girls. They're spoiled."

"Edith's letter?"

She nodded, and he thought he saw her crying. He wanted to touch her, but something in the way she sat prevented him.

"You're upset," he said.

She sniffled, put her sewing down. From her kimono pocket she drew a wadded tissue, which she held to her nose. "I'm insulted," she said.

"Because of what Edith wrote?"

"Yes. No."

"Then what?"

"Because she wrote it and *sent* it. To us." Natalie blew her nose, a small sad sound. "A thousand times a day I think things — a person thinks things — that you just don't say. You don't tell everything."

Images rushed at Harold, images supplanted one another. Edith, her eyes blue-ringed and swollen, touched a short finger to her bandaged nose. "What if I don't like it?" she asked. Natalie crossed her legs in a rustle of taffeta; one slender bare foot arched and flexed in time to faint music. He smelled roses. He stood at the top rung of a wooden ladder and looked down at himself as he sat working in his cubicle, a purple glow on the balding spot at the back of his head. Cheryl, squinting up at him, waved good-bye. "Save my comic books," she called, "till I get back from arts and crafts." Blume laughed mirthlessly and pointed at the ocean across a paper-strewn beach. An airplane wing floated alone on gray water. "Look into your wife's diamond," Blume said. The wind spun paper over mussel shells, carried paper out to the whitecaps. Natalie offered her familiar cool hand, and Harold bent over it to peer into a diamond. He saw through corridors of stone. Light and the angles of light did not deceive him; at the heart of the diamond he saw the absence of space, the place where light ended. He saw lamb-chop bones crusted with gristle and congealed fat as they slid over yellow-and-white porcelain. He saw bones that lay in earth, in the warm brown chaos of roots and insects. He saw bones that rested in weeds and water. He saw a skeleton, his own, standing in his bedroom.

He saw, with relief, that Natalie was whole and alive in her blue kimono. "Why don't you tell everything?" he asked her. He wanted to know the answer.

But she was crying now; even he could see it from where he stood. "Edith," she said, "Edith shouldn't have done that to us."

He went to her, carefully set her sewing on the carpet, then lifted her to his arms. "It's okay, it's okay. Don't."

"It hurts," she sobbed.

"What?" he asked, afraid that he'd injured her.

"Everything." She whispered this to him. A few of her tears trickled down his neck.

They swayed, locked together, in their French provincial bedroom. If he could have told her that everything would be all right, he would have. Comfort was not a vision; he had no access to it. He wondered if it, like his psychic gift, would occur to him one day. He listened to the thumping of his wife's heart.

"Is something wrong?" Cheryl asked, and the two of them looked up, still holding each other.

Their daughter, dressed, made up, and chained in gold, stood in the doorway to their room. Her hair swept over her shoulders, which were thin and narrow. Her mouth seemed an indivisible gleam of red. "I wanted to borrow your ivory hoops, Mom," she said. "Are you crying?"

"I was," Natalie said.

"Why?"

Natalie patted Harold's arms and released him. He felt his hands sliding from her body, felt the sudden absence of her heartbeat.

"I'm overtired," Natalie said to Cheryl. "The earrings are on my dresser."

Cheryl lifted the hoops from their blue velvet box. "I thought you were probably upset because of Edith's letter." She watched herself in the dresser mirror as she slid a gold post through the hole in her left earlobe, then fixed a gold backing in place on the post. "I thought it was a riot. All that stuff about the kids she's teaching and all. Real winners." She repeated the procedure for her right ear, then turned away from the mirror and faced her parents. "You shouldn't take what Edith says personally, you know. How do I look?"

"You look beautiful," Harold said. He sat down on his side of the bed, on a blue bedspread that startled him. "Where are you going?" he asked.

"To Ira's," Cheryl said. She kissed her mother. "Thanks for the earrings."

"To the lab?" Harold asked.

"No." Cheryl kissed her father.

Her lip gloss stuck to his cheek. Her perfume drifted into his eyes. "When will you be home?" he asked. He heard her open the front door. "Drive carefully," he shouted.

"I will," she shouted back. "G'night."

The front door closed.

"Well," Natalie said. In the dresser mirror, Harold could see moist ringlets deserting the upsweep of her hairdo. As if aware of his observation, she touched the back of her neck. "Let's have something to eat," she said.

He followed her, through dark rooms, to the kitchen. She tapped the pot of potatoes, then went to the table and took Edith's letter. She placed it, along with a fifty-cent coupon for instant coffee, in a correspondence folder she kept on the counter.

Harold knew that after he left for work the next morning or the morning after that, she would sit alone at the uncleared breakfast table and open the folder. Sipping warm coffee, she would reread Edith's letter. She would become upset again; distracted, she would burn her hand on the electric percolator when she went to pour a fresh cup.

The butter on her burned hand would glisten in sunlight as she sat writing at the desk in the living room. Her letter to Edith would be loving and almost without reference to Edith's letter. She would write about the family's health, about the stores, about the "really lovely mild winter" they were having. She would mention the Fight for Sight luncheon. She would add, toward the end, "Darling, if you must read two books at one sitting, I hope you are doing so in a proper light. Otherwise you could ruin your eyes."

Against the accustomed evening sounds of the teakettle boiling and water drumming against the stainless-steel sink, Harold heard the cycling of his own blood. He watched himself ruffling the eggs that were beginning to solidify in the frypan. Behind him, Natalie stood at the cutting board and carved radish roses for the salad. The thought of her poor burned hand made him careful as he stirred the eggs.

He closed his eyes. In the dark outside the kitchen window, dusk-colored chameleons scuttled over pebbles and hid beneath croton bushes; others, trapped on lamplit whitewashed walls, waited with throbbing throats for danger to pass. The house contracted in the coolness of the evening: The concrete foundation withdrew from the soil, wood beams diminished, paint flaked from the moving walls. On the flat roof, the bleached bones of a dog and a swine trembled.

"What kind of dressing do you want?" she asked.

Helplessness settled on Harold with the steam from reheated potatoes. He opened his eyes and breathed in homely odors. The kitchen offered itself to him: burners, counter, sink, dishwasher, refrigerator, table, chairs, all vibrating against yellow-and-white-and-silver-foil wallpaper. The salt and pepper shakers danced on the tile shelf above the sink. His wife, in a blue kimono, presented him with a bowl of chopped vegetables. He sighed. Questions of guilt and innocence fell away; he contemplated instead his endless, enduring helplessness. The knowledge of it soothed him as the kitchen dipped, shuddered, grew still.

"Whatever you want," he answered.

After dinner, if he took his bath quickly, he would have enough time before the ten o'clock news to make a neat copy of his letter to the air-crash survivors and the victims' families. Even if he never sent it to them, it was something, at last, that he could send to Edith.

ELIZABETH HARDWICK

The Faithful

(FROM THE NEW YORKER)

THE TRAVELS of youth, the cheapness of things, and one's intrepid poverty. "All ye who love the Prince of Orange take heart and follow me." So it was Holland that year, 1951. Descartes, more than three hundred years before, had spoken of himself as the only foreigner in Amsterdam not on business.

Everywhere we went in Europe that year, everywhere except for Amsterdam, there were Americans just like ourselves: those who had not been married long or were not married at all, most of us with fellowships and a little savings. We were to be seen now in December wearing winter coats pleated with the wrinkles of a long summer's rest in torn suitcases. Holland: led there by Motley's *The Rise of the Dutch Republic* and Fromentin's *The Masters of Past Time* in its neat little Phaidon edition.

An unfashionable *gracht* in the center of Amsterdam — the Nicolaas Witsenkade. A busy, bourgeois street bordering on sloppy waters, and the towers of the Rijksmuseum in view toward the west. Houses with stone steps and made of yellow or red brick were lined up in a businesslike, practical, nineteen-twenties decency and dullness. Autumnal tile decorations on the façades, and here and there fans of purple and amber glass over the doorways.

Housewives of centuries had created the pleasantly stuffy little rooms with their dark paneling, had hung round lamps, with shades of old tasseled silk, over the carpeted dining tables. The house was not handsome, and the landlady worried about the apartment because it had been her own and everything in it was dear to her. Anyway, he and I said as we met her anxious glance: What a triumph every country is.

We observed that the coziness of small countries could not always be expropriated by an invader. Yes, a squat, round, shiny black stove that had worked for years with the solemn obedience of an old donkey tormented our days and nights with its balky resentment of a new and ignorant hand. Perplexing dying of the embers so soon after they had been coaxed to blaze. We crept into the cold sheets under the ancient thick coverlets and were held at head and foot by the heavy frame of the bed, pierced by the sharp metal of carved leaves and fruits, acute reminders of spring. Daylight came in a rush and the whole town came alive at dawn. The baker and coal seller arrived with such swiftness they might have been dressed and waiting throughout the night. Greedy travelers, Americans, hail the dawn of a new experience!

In the winter, sleet blew through the beautiful town, graying the waters of the Amstel. In the spring, in daylight and in the early evening, we used to watch on the porch that faced us the life of the unemployed Indonesians. Their ancestors had been exiles, once flung out from the swamps of the Zuiderzee to the humid airs of Djakarta. Now their children were returned colons, geographical curiosities, back once more to the sluices and polders of home, the unfamiliar homeland that received them with the chagrin proper to what they were: a delayed bill, finally arriving.

The Indonesians gathered on their porch, sitting there as a depressed late testament to the great energy of the Dutch, to old mapmakers, shipbuilders, moneylenders, diamond cutters, receivers of Jews, Huguenots, Puritans. The unions we were staring at had taken place on unimaginable sugar plantations, in the deranging heat of exhausting empires. Beautiful, liquid-brown women — silky petite mother-in-law, dust-colored child — their little wrists and ankles delicate as chicken bones. And the heavy, dry, freckled, tufted Dutchmen, homely and reassuring.

The disasters of the war still lay over the country, and yet all of our Dutch friends were reading Valéry Larbaud's *A. O. Barnabooth: His Diary,* enjoying the sly chic of the fabulously rich hero and his addiction to "boutiqueism."

The crowds of Amsterdam, and even the countryside filled with people in their houses, each one a sort of declassed nobleman sharing the space as a tree would patiently accept the nightly roosting of flocks and flocks of starlings. All the knowledge of Europe seemed to be nesting there, too. And a certain sadness, a gasping for breath: No, no, the strain is nothing; take no notice of it; I have just had a wish for the mountains.

In Amsterdam we knew many people, and not a single one has slipped from memory. Just now, dreaming, I am drawn back to a woman painter named Simone and to her fervent romancer, the eternal husband, Dr. Z.

Dr. Z had the moderate, well-nourished egotism suitable to his small, learned group of colleagues and friends and proper to the educated professional world of Amsterdam. He had his success, some of it medical, as a specialist in blood diseases, and some of it amorous. Because of the time he devoted to women, he might be surprised to find himself remembered as a *husband*.

In Holland, the coziness of life is so complete it cannot even be disturbed by the violent emotional ruptures that tear couples and friends forever apart in other places. Instead, there first husbands and first wives are always at the same dinner parties and birthday celebrations with their second husbands and wives. Divorces and fractured loves mingle together as if the past were a sort of vinegar blending with the oil of the present. Where can one flee to? New alliances among this restless people are like the rearrangement of familiar furniture. Houses and lives are thus transformed — up to a point. My dear, look, there is the man who plays his violin in the street and there is his son with the saxophone. Coins are falling from the windows. The shadow has passed and everything is in order once more. She moves into his place.

The *Herengracht,* a great improvement. His wife settles someplace else, taking along her volumes of the existentialist philosophers. What a pleasure to be recombining and yet not going anyplace. The old map of the central city, with its faded tintings, catches the sunlight.

Dr. Z, all day in his white coat and in the evenings wearing a tie of bright red and blue stripes, was born in Amsterdam. But the blood of the East ran in his veins. There was something sheikish about him, and although there were more flamboyant men around, handsomer and younger, he occupied his space with a kindly, intense assurance. His personal life was rich in variety and yet thoughtful. His originality was that he did not shift so much as acquire.

Fidelity, consideration, sweet-natured uxoriousness were the marks of this faithless husband. In a way, he was like a cripple who yearly enters the hundred-yard dash. Bravo, everyone cried out when he scored. Of course, his exploits were not large in number and he was a busy, serious man who was often called to the platforms of universities and academies to receive honors. Still, he had his entanglements, rather plain and serious like himself, but worthy, intense, absorbing. Without ever leaving his only wife, he turned each of the women in his life into a wife. Have you paid your taxes? he would say; have you called your mother this week? Oh, dearest, I do not like the sound of that cough.

Many times, he was seized by the impulse to flee and thought himself ready or forced by love to "make a new life." But this was impossible for one who could not throw anything away. What a commitment intimacy always is, he would sigh. The sacred flow between men and women, in bed, conversing in a café, talking on the telephone, passing time. What didn't he know about the treacherous, beautiful, golden yoke of time?

Does one still enjoy his old schoolmates, his first cousins? That is not the point. They are one's schoolmates, one's cousins, and there is always something there, like the enduring presence of one's big toe.

Mevrouw Z: She had been there forever. They had been separated by the war, but managed to get back together in their same old house. Mevrouw Z liked to be called Madame Z, because she was French. Small, she must have become in her first youth one of those petite, compact persons who never change, who find a certain exterior style and accept it, as one accepts a piece of architecture for purchase. When her young black hair began to turn gray, she dyed it back to the old color and wore it in the short bob of her youth. The moment she got out of bed in the morning, she recolored her eyelashes with black mascara. She wore velvet berets and held firmly to her *look*, which announced like a trumpet that she was not Dutch, she was French. Otherwise, she did not conform to any of the notions of a Frenchwoman. She did not cook well, she was not interested in attracting men, she did not have a shrewd hand with household accounts. She let an old Dutchwoman from the country look after the house. Madame Z was idle except for the enormous amount of reading she did and except for her passion for the French theater. She read about the theater in French papers every day and went to Paris often, taking in a performance every night.

After you had seen her a few times, you found that she was vain but not argumentative. Little appeared to her as new in life, little came as a surprise. It was appealing. She had the idea that a gross, uncomplicated self-interest was the old truth that a new force or person was trying to disguise.

Dr. Z, who found the events of his own life flushed with the glow of the unique, the unexpected, the inexplicable, sometimes chewed his lip in annoyance when she expressed her belief in the principle of repetition. They lived in a profound intimacy nevertheless.

From Holland I wrote many complaining letters. Dear M: How cold the house is. How we fight after too much gin, etc., etc.

Complaining letters — and this one of the happiest periods of my life: With what gratitude I look back on Europe for the first time. So, that wraps up Verona. We take in the cracked windows and the brilliant dishevelment of Istanbul. And the long time in Holland: time to take trains, one to Haarlem to see the old alms-house governors painted in their unforgiving black-and-white misery by Frans Hals in his last days. The laughing cavaliers perhaps had eaten too many oysters, drunk too much beer, and died a replete, unwilling death, leaving the poor and their guardians, freed by a bitter life from the killing pleasures, to shrivel on charity, live on with their strong, blackening faces.

Antwerp and Ghent: what wonderful names, hard as the heavy cobbles in the square. Amsterdam, a city of readers. All night long, you seemed to hear the turning of pages: pages of French, Italian, English, and the despised German. Those fair heads remembered Ovid, Yeats, Baudelaire — and remembered suffering, hiding, freezing. The weight of books and wars.

Dr. Z had acquired the nurse in his office. A fresh-looking woman who had never married and who lived frugally outside the center — a long trip on her bicycle. She had her occasional afternoons with Dr. Z, afternoons now grown, according to gossip, as perfunctory and health-giving as a checkup. Oh, the burdens.

Dr. Z acquired Simone, the painter, after her husband left her. He nudged the other two to make room. Simone was often spoken of as the most independent woman in Amsterdam. She was also the only female painter anyone talked about, and it was from her long, anxious struggle to establish herself that the independence had arrived. If indeed it had. She did not display any special happiness or confidence from "doing something well."

Why should painting pictures make you happy? she said. It is not a diversion. Her nerves were frazzled and she had a strong leaning toward melancholy and exhaustion. Yet, worn down by life as she saw herself to be, she was always in movement, and always running up and down the stairs to her studio on the fifth floor. In her agitated fatigue, Simone was a striking figure in tattered, mysterious clothes that she apparently bought in junk shops on her travels. Skirts and blouses and jackets of satin or flowered cloth, Balkan decorations, old beads, capes, shawls, earrings. The effect was sometimes that of a deranged frugality, and other times she brought it off, like the church dignitaries in Florence when they go in their worn velvets and shredded furs to release the dove from the altar of the Duomo.

Perhaps if she had been a man she would have become a cardinal. She had been born a Catholic, and although this had been set aside in the libertarian Amsterdam intellectual world, which was a sort of archive of Trotskyist, Socialist, and anarchist learning, Simone was sometimes seen slipping into church, wearing several large shawls in pitiful disguise. It was whispered that perhaps she was praying for the soul of her brother, who had collaborated with the Nazis.

Simone's husband looked like an Alpine skier and was, instead, a professor of history. He actually went off alone on a long skiing holiday in Austria, and in about six months a new woman arrived in Amsterdam, an American. I've always wanted an American, the husband said.

Dr. Z was sympathetic to Simone and outraged by the husband's complacency, and more by his ridiculous happiness with the pretty American. The doctor would have managed differently somehow, in some way, man of binding memories that he was. He took to quoting the Russian folk song mentioned in Pushkin's story "The Captain's Daughter":

> *If you find one better than*
> *me — you'll forget me,*
> *If one who is worse — you'll*
> *remember.*

Worse? How does he know now, and if it turns out that way it will be too late, Madame Z insisted.

Slowly, or not so slowly, Dr. Z's duet became a trio. He and his wife had known Simone for years. Was that not favorable? Wasn't the ex-husband living with his American in the apartment below Simone's?

Dr. Z was a passive man *by nature;* that is, he was often led to actions and moods quite the contrary. Certainly at the beginning of his affairs, this natural passivity took flight. He began in a frenzy of passionate feeling. He fell in love; he drank too much; he rushed through his work as quickly as possible and got home very late for dinner and sometimes not until midnight. His nest was shaken by the new windstorm, and the squawking of birds began. His wife said that this was exactly what she had expected and that it did not interest her. Simone hesitated, but there was the infatuated Dr. Z with theater tickets. There he was holding fast to her arm as they passed her husband and the American girl at the door of the house. Soon she said with a disheartened sigh that she, too, was in love.

The nurse cried all day, even in front of the patients. When Simone sometimes called the office, the nurse abused and threatened her.

It is very poor medicine to have nurses in such a state, Simone said. Perhaps another position could be found for her.

Dr. Z was taken aback but quickly resumed his ground. It's all over with her, he insisted, but I cannot turn away someone I have known and worked with for seven years.

Dr. Z was jealous of Simone, and her silences filled him with terrible alarm. He pushed his love back a few years. Yes, he remembered being overcome with feeling years ago just at the sight of her buying a book in the square, and at a New Year's party when she was wearing green velvet shoes.

I don't remember anything of that sort. Right now is soon enough for me, she said.

At times, the doctor did not want to go home at night and announced that he was prepared to give his house to his wife or to set her up in France. For weeks, some new plan would seem to be working itself out. Yes, I am working it out, he said to everyone. But then the time came when his mood turned crestfallen and sad. He said Madame Z hated change.

No one likes change, Simone said. Dr. Z wept. But it has been more than twenty years. Think of that.

In Amsterdam, there were no celebrated expatriates living in the hills or set up in flowery villas near the sea. One week, a lot of snow. Where are we? we wondered. In Iowa City? Northern Europe — many times, it was as if all of the trams were leading back to America. At night, feeling uprooted because so much was familiar, we would tell each other the stories of our lives. The downy, musty embrace of the bed set us afloat, not as travelers but as ones somehow borne backward to the bricks and stuffs of home.

We went to the flower market. A thousand still lifes. People, rushing about on the Leidseplein, revealed ghostly similarities to those we had left behind. The stove died, the snow clung to the panes, the outline of our fringed lamps caught the light of the street. In the shadows, listening to the bells ringing the hours, we would lie smoking and talking. The hills of home in the flatness of Holland. Think of it, he would say, our parents were born in the last century. The czar was out chopping wood for exercise.

History assaults you, and if you live you are restored to the world of gossip. That is what it had been for Dr. Z. He was half Jewish and had spent time in a labor camp in Germany. This well-established Nederlands lover, with his nervous alliances and peculiar fidelities, had looked death in the eye, had lived through the extermination of his younger brother. This life, his *aura,* remained in his proud, olive-tinted eyes, in his researches on the devastations flowing in the blood stream, in his death-defying lovemaking. He was a small, shrewd European country, moving about carefully in peacetime, driven on by the force of ghastly memories.

So, life after death is to fall in love once more, to set up a little business, to learn to drive a car, take airplane trips, go to the sun for vacations.

It began to appear that Simone was not suited to the role of mistress. She said: This thing has brought a coarsening of my nature. I hate Madame Z. What is she — a general? She seems to be giving a great many orders to those of us behind the lines.

Hate? Dr. Z said. That's quite extreme. She has her qualities.

When Simone saw the wife on the street, she rushed off in the opposite direction. So fearful was she of a meeting that she would not go to her friends' houses without making careful inquiries.

The whole of their circle in Amsterdam was involved in the affair. This wish to oust Madame Z and the nurse is Simone's cardinal side, people decided. Yes, the little girl who held the hand of so many nuns cannot accept the purgatory of Dr. Z's confusing nature and intentions.

One time, Madame Z went to Paris for several weeks. With a round-trip ticket of course, Simone observed bitterly. But in the freedom she and the doctor went for a weekend to London to look at pictures. It was not a happy time. Dr. Z was always calling Paris to speak to his wife or calling his office to speak to the nurse. Telling them tremendous lies about a "conference." Simone spent most of her time in London saying: It will soon be over and we will be back where we started.

Dearest darling, do not rush to suffer future pain, the doctor said. But all went as she had predicted. Back once more, Simone could be seen several evenings a week at the window of her top floor, looking down on the street, waiting for the hurried approach of her lover. And late in the night, when he was returning to his wife, Simone would open the shutters and wave a long good-bye to the swarthy, badly dressed, vivacious man, now turning a corner and fading from sight.

Dr. Z was happy in his love pains. He adored to spend the evening in Simone's studio, smoking a cigarette, drinking coffee, eating little chocolate cakes, and sipping gin. He was honestly more and more in love, and the genuineness of his feelings often caused Simone to burst into tears of anger.

Dr. Z had studied the body and its workings and liked to say: We human beings are, *au fond*, put together quite simply. Yes, quite simply. The part that is complicated, even we as scientists are ignorant of that.

In matters of love he seemed to feel the same. His distressing trio caused him to be often fretful, sleepless, anxious, jealous, even drunken. But he also knew well the dejection of resignation and the torture of absence. So, tormented, accused, even guilty, there was still happiness to be found in reassuring the weeping nurse at the end of the day, in bringing home a pâté and cheese to his wife, in going down a dark canal on the arm of Simone and singing "In questa tomba oscura." Somehow he could lend to the noble composition a heartfelt flirtatiousness.

During our year in Holland, there was at last a movement of reclamation on the part of Simone. She broke off with the doctor and stayed in the house for weeks, for fear of meeting him and once more surrendering to his passion for her. He whistled below the window; potted tulips arrived. Look at the colors! A late Mondrian, no? his note would say.

He called upon the help of European poetry:

Alas for me, where shall I get the flowers when it is winter and where the sunshine and shadow of earth? The walls stand speechless and cold, the weather vanes rattle in the wind.

Simone was assisted by an attack of depression and did not turn back. She hurt the doctor's feelings by saying: I do not seem to care for anyone just now. Least of all myself.

The doctor's wife and the nurse were affronted by Simone's revolt. They accused her of triviality and shallowness, of heartlessness. The doctor's suffering fell alike upon them, as if it were a contagion. His alarm, his loss, his humiliation were an insult to themselves. And perhaps the two women, so accustomed to his ways, sensed that the singularity of endings may slowly gather into a plural.

Love affairs, with their energy and hope, do not arrive again and again forever. So you no longer play tennis, no longer move from place to place in the summer, no longer understand what use you can make of the sight of the Andes or the columns of Luxor. It gradually became clear that Simone would not be replaced. Poor Dr. Z, with his infidelities and agreeable lies, his new acquisitions and engaging disruptions: they vanished suddenly but so quietly and naturally he was the last to know.

As Raleigh said about Queen Elizabeth: Old age took her by surprise, like a frost.

In a few years, the nurse went home to retire, to look after her old mother in the country. Simone died. It turned out that she had done more than a dozen portraits of Dr. Z, and one was sold to an American museum for a fair price. In it Dr. Z is seen in a white jacket, and there are instruments of his profession about him. On the wall not one but three stylized skeletons are dangling from hooks.

*

Nineteen seventy-three. The doctor and his wife were in New York for a conference. I went to meet them at a shabby, depressing hotel in the West Seventies where Europeans who are not rich often stay. They were like two woolen dolls, and I could not decide whether the Frenchwoman had grown to the size of the Dutchman or whether he had, with a courteous condescension, simply inclined downward to the size of his little French wife. She was still wearing her black berets, and her fingernails shone with a wine-colored polish. She spoke in tongues: Dutch, German, French, and English, as if choosing cakes from a tray.

Dr. Z met a mild New York winter day clothed in Siberian layers. He was wearing a heavy black overcoat, a woolen vest, a dark-gray sweater, and when he sat down in the waiting room off the lobby, gray winter underwear appeared above his socks.

He talked: he told the Amsterdam gossip, he spoke of his work, of the fearful cost of things, of hippies in Vondel Park.

Madame Z smoked cigarettes and coughed. They were studying the map of the city, looking for subway and bus lines. The outstanding difficulties of thrift in New York bewildered them, and they sat there as if pulled down into the mud of a dismaying displacement, the confusion that afflicts unfashionable, elderly foreigners when they visit America. They who had been everywhere, from Djakarta to Tokyo to India and every country in Europe.

Dr. Z smiled and bowed and dashed about looking for chairs and a quiet corner. In fact, he seemed to be groping in the New York air for the supports of his life in Amsterdam, for his weathered little house on the Amstel, with his office on the first floor and the rooms above with the old patterned carpets, the comfort of the hideous abstract paintings given by patients, abstractions that covered the walls next to the stairs like so many colored water spots left over from an old leak.

Where is my life? he seemed to be saying. My plates of pickled mussels, the slices of cheese, the tumblers of lemon gin?

Still, importance flickered in his eyes — his olive eyes still shining with the oil of remembered vanity and threatening to water with the tears of all he had learned and forgotten in his long life.

We in Holland were the first to do certain important blood studies, he said. I no longer have my laboratory at the hospital, but I keep up with the developments in my field. How can one not? A life's work.

We in Holland kept appearing in his conversation. The vastness of the skies they had flown over and the large abyss into which they had fallen on the ground made him call forth his country — like an ambassador, one who stands for the whole.

You remember that he was well known there, his wife said without any special inflection. Oh, I know, I know. I remember well the well-known Dr. Z.

Enough of that, he said. Edam cheese is better known than any Dutchman. That it is well to recall also.

As it got to be near six o'clock, I asked if they wanted to go to a nearby Irish saloon for a drink. The doctor drew back with a frightened look, but his wife took up the suggestion vehemently. Indeed, yes, she would like a drink, she said with a peculiar insistence and defiance.

We sat in a dark booth, and Madame Z ordered a martini. An American martini, she said twice. The doctor crumpled and sagged over a beer — Heineken's.

Supporting home industries, his wife said.

Suddenly in the gloom, Madame Z began her lilting harangue, all of it pouring forth with an appalling energy. She did not use to talk very much, the doctor said, attempting a smile. See the unbeckoned, unpredicted changes of age, the sky full of falling stars!

It was clear that the recitation was not new and that in the midst of it she could pause only to order another drink.

I have always hated Holland. I am not Dutch. I am French, born in Paris.

There are many Frenchmen, the doctor interrupted. It is not what I would call a special distinction in itself.

She went on. There are many Dutchmen, too, and all alike. The men and the women. The provincialism. Can you imagine a country proud of skinny Indonesians, dark and slow and surly primitives, serving in red coats? *Rijsttafel* — a joke. Nuts and raisins and bananas. I would rather have herring, if the choice must be made . . . And it must be made or starve . . . But the worst thing is the ugliness of the people. Who can tell the men and the women apart in their rotten mackintoshes, their rubber-soled shoes . . . Look at the queen — a joke. And old Wilhelmina in her tweeds, like a buffalo . . . And the weather, steaming like hell in the summer and drizzling sleet the rest of the year . . . *Drizzling,* is that English? . . .

What is going on in Amsterdam, tell me? Someone playing the organ in a church. They think they are masters of culture when they speak French, but if you want to write something you write it in Dutch, which no one reads. And why should they? Even the Poles are better off. Warsaw is a real city, not a puppet-show setting like Amsterdam.

Her black, black hair, her tiny little black feet, her wine-colored fingers heavy with red and green semiprecious stones set in gold. She was like an old glazed vessel, veined and cracked, that nevertheless held water.

The doctor trembled. This is not what you would call a discussion, he said.

And, turning aside, he made an effort to change the awful flow. I am not a patriot, he said; still, couldn't I claim that the Dutch are a civilized people? A bit tiresome about the loss of Indonesia and all that, perhaps, but . . .

Indonesia! she shrieked, and the bartender shrugged. How all of you used to complain when you had to go out there to lecture — to advise, as you called it. To visit the rich men on their plantations. Little cries all night about the bugs and the humidity. The suffering sweat of the lordly Dutchman. Imagine Holland with colonies. Have you ever seen the so-called city of Paramaribo? It's a scandal, a joke.

Madame Z tottered to her feet, exhausted. The doctor took her arm and gave a sigh as deep as death itself. Out on the street, in the cold wind, he supported his little wife, who could not stand alone. She dangled on his arm like a black shopping bag. For the moment, she was quiet, and he attempted a lighthearted manner, a whispered addition.

As you can see, she has taken to drink in a disastrous fashion. A sigh, and then he bowed with something of his old sheikishness, drawing me into his memories.

It's all those love affairs — especially the darling Simone. They don't forgive you, after all. They have their revenge.

It seemed to soothe the doctor to try to take the blame, as if even the revenge brought him back to his younger days. It was not clear whether he believed what he was saying. The ruefulness of his smile.

As we neared the hotel, he said bitterly: It is only eight o'clock. But what can we do except go to bed without dinner? She will sleep it off and not remember a thing, the way they do. So mysterious. Yes, she must go to bed.

Bed! Madame Z cried out, calling upon her last breath. They are all terrible lovers. Frauds, every one of them. Fiascos!

They passed into the brown-and-gray lobby, old companions, sad but not quite miserable. They were waving good-bye. He was bowing and she was now winking and smiling.

She had hit the doctor like the Spanish Fury, but fortunately he was accustomed to the wind from the North Sea. Her hat askew and a strand of hair slanted down her cheek, Madame Z of Paris had at last become Dutch, needing only a few strewn oyster shells and a ragged dog to bring to mind those tippling, pipe-smoking women in the paintings of the seventeenth century, creatures of the common life the Dutch bourgeoisie were pleased to admire and purchase.

LARRY HEINEMANN

The First Clean Fact

(FROM TRIQUARTERLY)

GATHER HERE. Lean a good ear this way. Cup a curved hand around it if you have to.

Let's begin with the first clean fact, James: this ain't no war story. War stories are out — one, two, three, and a heave ho, into the lake you go with all the other alewife scuz and foamy harbor scum. But ain't it a pity. All those crinkly, soggy sorts of laid-by tellings crowded together as thick and pitiful as street cobbles, floating mushy bellies up like so much moldy shag rug (dead as rusty-ass doornails and smelling so peculiar and unchristian). Just isn't it a pity, because here and there and yonder among the corpses are some prizewinning, leg-pulling daisies — some real simple-ass, pop-in-the-oven muffins, so to speak, some real softly lobbed, easy-out line drives.

But that's the way of the world, James, or so the fairy tales go. The people with the purse strings and apron strings gripped in their hot and soft little hands denounce war stories — with perfect diction and practiced gestures — as a side-show geek-monster species of evil-ugly rumor. They stand bolt upright and proclaim with broad and timely sweeps of the arm that war stories put other folks to sleep where they sit. (When the contrary is more to the truth, James. Any carnie worth his cashbox — not dead or in jail or some county nuthouse — can tell you that most folks will shell out hard-earned greenback cash, every time, to see artfully performed and urgently fascinating, grisly and gruesome carnage.)

Other people (getting witty and spry, floor-of-the-Senate, let-me-read-this-into-the-*Congressional Record*, showboat-oratorical) slip one hand under a vest flap and slide one elegantly spit-shined wingtip shoe forward ever so clever, and swear and be damned if all that snoring at war stories doesn't rattle windows for miles around — all the way to Pokorneyville, or so the papers claim.

And a distinct, but mouthy, minority — book-learned witchcraft amateurs and half-savvy street punks and patriots for cash (for some piddling hand-to-mouth wage) — slyly hang their heads and secretly insinuate that the snoring (he-honk, he-honk the way a good, mean shake-shake-like-a-rag-doll snore snaps at you, James) is nothing if it isn't the Apocalypse choking on its own spit, trying to catch its breath for one more go-round.

(And the geeks and carnival freaks and side-show grifters of this world hear the yokels soaking up a shill like that, well, damned if they don't haul off and belly laugh — haw haw haw haw. They know a prizewinning shuck when they hear one, James. They lean way back in their folding lawn chairs lined up in front of their setups and shacks — the Skil-Throw and Ring-Toss and Guess-How-Many-Pennies-in-the-Jar-Bub? and such as that — and slap their thighs hard enough to raise welts, all the while whispering among themselves that the rubes of this world will never get the hang of things.)

According to some people, folks do not want to hear about busting jungle and busting cherries from Landing Zone Skater-Gator to Scat Man Do (wherever *that* is), humping and hauling ass all the way. We used French colonial maps back then — the names of towns and map symbols and such as that, crinkled and curlicued and mushed together, as incomprehensible as the Chiricahua dialect of Apache. We never could cipher a thing on those maps, so absolutely and precisely where Scat Man Do is tongue cannot tell; but we asked around and followed Lieutenant Stennett's nose — flashing through some fine fire-fight possibilities, pungi pits the size of copper mines, not to mention countless hog pens and chicken coops (scattering chickens and chicken feathers like so many wood chips). We made it to the fountain square in downtown Scat Man Do — and back to LZ Skater-Gator — in an afternoon, James, me singing snatches of arias and duets from "Simon Boccanegra" and "The Flying Dutchman" at the top of my socks. But what we went there for no one ever told us, and none of us — what was left of us that time — ever bothered to ask.

*

And folks don't especially want to hear about the night at Fire Base Sweet Pea the company got kicked in the mouth good and hard — streetfight hard — and wound up spitting slivers of brown teeth and mushy scabs for a fortnight. Lieutenant Stennett had us night-laagered on a lumpy, rocky slope down the way from high ground — his first (but by no stretch of your imagination his last) mistake. And you could hawk a gob of phlegm and spit on the woodline from your foxhole, James. And it was raining to beat the band. And no one was getting any sleep. And just after midnight — according to Gallagher's radium-dial watch — some zonked-out zip crawled up sneaky-close in the mangled underbrush and whispered in the pouring rain, "Hey, you! Rich-chard Nickzun is a egg suckin' hunk a runny owl shit!" Then Paco and me heard him and some other zip giggling — tee he he he — as though that was the world's worst thing they could think to say, and would provoke us into rageful anger. But before either of us could wipe the rain out of our eyes, Jonesy raised his head from his rucksack where he was taking one of his famous naps — fucking the duck, we called it — and stage whispered, "Listen, you squint-eyed spook, you ain't tellin' me annathing Ah don' know." Then they whispered back at us with one voice, as giggly and shivery cute as a couple smart-ass six-year-olds, "GI, you *die* tonight!" and then giggled some more. Paco blinked his eyes slowly, glanced at me out of the corners as if to say he didn't believe he heard what he knew he heard and shook his head, saying out loud, "What the fuck do these zips think this is, some kind of chickenshit Bruce Dern–Michael J. Pollard–John Wayne movie? *'GI, you* die *tonight!'* What kind of fucked-up attitude is that?" Then he leaned over his sopping-wet rucksack in the direction of the smirking giggles, put his hands to his mouth — megaphone-fashion — and said, "Hawk shit!" loud enough for the whole company to hear. "Put your money where your fucking mouth is, Slow Ped," he said. "Whip it on me!" And later that night they did. They greased half the fourth platoon and Lieutenant Stennett's brand new radioman, and we greased so many of them it wasn't even funny. The lieutenant got pissed at Paco for mouthing off, and getting his radioman blown away so soon — but that was okay, because the lieutenant wasn't "wrapped too tight," as Jonesy would say.

The next morning we got up, brushed ourselves off, cleared away the air-strike garbage — the fire-fight junk and jungle junk

— and dusted off the walking wounded and litter wounded, and the body bags. And the morning after that, just as right as rain, James, we saddled up our rucksacks and slugged off into the deepest, baddest part of the Goongone Forest north of our base camp at Phuc Luc, looking to kick some ass — anybody's ass (can you dig it, James?)— and take some names. Yesireebob! We hacked and humped our way from one end of that woods to the other — crisscrossing wherever our whim took us — feeling no more sophisticated or complicated or elegant than an organized gang, looking to nail any and all of that goddamned giggling slime we came across to the barn door. Then one bright and cheery morning when our month was up, Private First Class Elijah Raintree George Washington Carver Jones (Jonesy for short, James) had thirty-nine pair of blackened, leathery, wrinkly ears strung on a bit of black commo wire and wrapped like a garland around that bit of turned-out brim of his steel helmet. He had snipped the ears off with a pearl-handled straight razor just as quick and slick as you'd lance a boil the size of a baseball — snicker-snack — the way he said his uncle could skin a poached deer. Jonesy cured the ears a couple days by tucking them under that piece of elastic around his helmet, then toted them crammed in a spare sock. The night before Lieutenant Stennett called it quits, Jonesy sat up way after dark stringing the ears on that bit of wire and sucking snips of C-ration beefsteak through his teeth.

And the next afternoon, when we finally humped through the south gate at Phuc Luc, you should have seen those rear-area mother-fucking housecats bug their eyes and cringe every muscle in their bodies, and generally suck back against the buildings (you would have been right proud, James). Jonesy danced this way and that — shucking and jiving, juking and high-stepping, rolling his eyes and snapping his fingers in time — twirling that necklace to a fare-thee-well, shaking and jangling it (as much as a necklace of ears will jangle, James), and generally fooling with it as though it were a cheerleader's pompon.

And the Phuc Luc base-camp Viets couldn't help but look, too. The Viets worked the PX checkout counters (good-looking women who had to put out right smart and regular to keep their jobs) and the PX barbershop (where the barbers could run a 35¢ haircut into $6.50 in fifteen minutes) and the stylishly thatched souvenir shack (where a bandy-legged cripple sold flimsy beer coolers and zip-pity-do-da housecat ashtrays, and athletic-style jackets with maps of Vietnam embroidered on the back with the scrolled legend "Hot Damn — Vietnam" underneath). And, James, don't you know they were Viets during the day and zips at night (one zip we body-counted one time couldn't booby-trap a shithouse any better than he could cut hair).

Every Viet in the place crowded the doorways and the screened windows and such as that, gawking at Jonesy — and the rest of us, too. So he made a special show of shaking those ears at them, witch-doctor fashion, while booming out some gibberish mumbo jumbo in his best amen-corner baritone and laughing that cool, nasty, grisly laugh of his, acting the jive fool for *all* those housecats. And the rest of the company — what was left of us *that* time — had to laugh at him, too, even though we humped those last three hundred meters to the tents (up an incline) on mushy, bloody blisters with our teeth gritted, and the fraying rucksack straps squeezing permanent grooves in our shoulders. (A person never gets used to humping, James. When word comes, you saddle your rucksack on your back, take a deep breath and set your jaw good and tight, lean a little forward as though you're walking into a stiff and blunt nor'easter, and begin by putting one foot in front of the other. Then after a good while you've got two sharp pains straight as a die from your shoulders to your kidneys, but there's nothing to do but grit your teeth a little harder and keep humping. I swear, James, those last uphill three hundred meters were the sorriest, goddamnedest three hundred mother fuckers in all of Southeast Asia. Captain Courtney Culpepper, who never missed a chance to flash his West Point class ring in your face — that ring the size of a railroad watch — never once offered to send the trucks to meet us at the gate: said we had humped that far, might as well hump the rest.)

Nor do folks want to hear what a stone bore (and I do mean stone, James) sitting bunker guard could be. Now, some called it perimeter guard and some called it berm guard, but it was all the same. The bunkers, James: broad, sloping, sandbagged affairs the size of a forty-acre farm on the outside and a one-rack clothes closet inside, lined up every forty meters or so along the perimeter, within easy grenade range of the concertina wire and the marsh. You sit scrunched up, bent-backed and stoop-shouldered, on a plain pine plank, looking through a gun slit the size of a mail slot. You stare at a couple hundred meters of shitty-ass marsh that no zip in his right mind would try to cross, terraced rice paddy gone to seed, and a beat-to-hell woodline opposite. You stare at it and stare at it until the moonlit, starlit image of weeds and reeds and bamboo saplings and bubbling marsh slime burns itself into the back of your head in the manner of Daguerre's first go with a camera obscura. (I tell you, James, I can see that raggedy-assed woodline, the dead-smelling mist rising off the marsh slime at dawn — I can see all of that every now and again, in a vivid dream.) You peep through that skinny-ass embrasure with your M–16 on full rock and roll, a double armful of fragmentation grenades — frags, we called them — hanging above your head on a double arm's length of trip-flare wire, and every hour at the quarter hour you crank up the landline handphone and call in a situation report — sit-rep, we called it — to the main bunker up the hill in back of you fifty paces or so. "Hell-oh? Hell-oh, Main Bunker!" you say, extra friendly-like. "Yez," comes a sleepy, scrawny voice, mellowed by forty meters of landline commo wire. "This here is Bunker Number Seven," you say, and snatch one more glance downrange — everything bone-numb evil and cathedral quiet. "Everything is okey-dokey. Hunky-dory. In the pink and couldn't be sweeter." And that sleepy, scrawny voice takes a good long pause and takes a breath, and drawls right back at you, "Well okay, Cuz."

And between those calls up the hill — and taking a break every now and again to take a whiz, downrange — you have nothing better to do than stare at that marsh and twiddle your thumbs, and give the old pecker a few tugs for the practice — wet-dreaming about that Eurasian broad with the luscious, exquisite titties who toured with a Filipino trio and turned tricks for anyone of commissioned rank.

That Filipino trio, James, they were extra-ordinary. One guy played a rickety Hawaiian guitar, one guy played a banged-up tenor saxophone, and one guy played the electric accordion — and that dude could squeeze some *fine* accordion, James. That trio and the woman played every nickel-and-dime base camp, every falling-down mess hall and sleazy, scruffy Enlisted Men's Club south of the 17th parallel — as famous in their own way as Washing Machine Charlie, the legendary nightrider of Guadalcanal. So how come they never made the papers, you may ask?

Well, James, reporters — as a gang — acted as though our whole purpose for being there was to entertain them. They'd look at you from under the snappily canted brim of an Australian bush hat as though to say, "Come on, kid, *astonish* me! Say *something* fucked-up and quotable, *something* evil, something *bloody* and *nasty,* and be quick about it — I ain't got all day — I'm on a deadline." But mostly you'd see them with one foot on the lead pipe rail and one elbow on the stained plywood bar of the Mark Twain Lounge of the Hyatt-Regency Saigon, swilling ice-cold raspberry daiquiris and vodka sours by the pitcherful. The younger, "hipper" ones popped opium on the sly or sprinkled it on their jays and chewed speed like Aspergum, but their rap was the same — "Don't these grunts die *ugly!* It's goddamn bee-utiful." They lean sideways against the bar, drugstore-cowboy style — twiddling their swizzle sticks — and stare down at their rugged-looking L. L. Bean hiking boots or Adidas triple-stripe deluxe gym shoes, swapping bullshit lies and upcountry war stories. "Say, Jack," says this dried-up, milky-eyed old hack from the Pokorneyville *Volunteer-Register,* "I seen this goofy, wiggy-eyed, light-skinned spade up at Fire Base Gee-Gaw las' week. Had some *weird* shit scrawled on the back of his flak jacket, Jack: 'Rule 1. Take no shit. Rule 2. Cut no slack. Rule 3. Take no prisoners.' I ast 'im if he was octoroon — he looked octoroon to me! — and he says, 'I ain't octoroon, I'm from Philly.' Haw shit, buddy-boy, some of these nigras is awful D-U-M-B." Then Slush-eyes takes another he-man slug of raspberry daiquiri, smacking his lips and grinning to high heaven.

So, James, listening to conversation like that, how can anyone expect reporters and journalists and that kind to appreciate anything as subtle and arcane and pitiful as one puny three-piece USO band and the snazziest, hot-to-trot honey fuck to hit the mainland since the first French settlers? We cannot expect them to be everywhere, now can we?

Those Filipinos ha-wonked and razza-razzed and pee-winked, sharping and flatting right along for close to three hours down at the lighted end of our company mess hall. The whole charm of their music was the fact that they couldn't hit the same note at the same time at the same pitch if you passed a hat, plunked the money down, put a .45 to their heads, and said, "There! Now, damn it, play!" They played "The Orange Blossom Special" and "Home on the Range" and "You Ain't Nothing But a Hound Dog" and "I

Can't Get No Satisfaction"—after a fashion. And they played songs like "Good Night, Irene" and "I Wonder Who's Kissing Her Now?" and "I Love You a Bushel and a Peck"— music no one ever heard of except the grayheaded lifers. And that woman, who hardly had a stitch on (and she was one fluffy dish, James), wiggled those sweet-pea titties right in the colonel's mustache — Colonel Hubbel having himself a front-row kitchen chair — and she sure did sit him up straight all right, all right. And the rest of the battalion officers and hangers-on (artillery chaplains and brigade busybodies on the slum) sat shoulder patch to shoulder patch with the colonel in a squared-off semicircle just as parade-ground pretty as you please. They crossed their legs to hide their hard-ons, and tried to look as blasé and matter-of-fact — as officerlike and gentlemanly — as was possible, trying to keep us huns away from the honey. The rest of the company, us grunts, stood close-packed on the floor and the chairs and the tables, and hung one-armed from the rafters, our tongues hanging out, swilling beer from the meat locker and circle-jerking our brains out — our forearms just a-flying, James. Our forearms just a blur. And that broad shimmied and pranced around near-naked, jiggling her sweating titties like someone juggling two one-pound lumps of greasy, shining ham-burger and dry-humping the air with sure and steady, rhythmic thrusts of her snatch — ta-tada-ha-humpa, ta-tada-ha-humpa, ta-tada-ha-humpa, ha-who! Then a couple dudes from the third platoon's ambush began to clap their hands in time and shout, "Come on, Sweet Pea, twiddle those goddamned things in *my* mustache! Come on, Sweet Pea, why don'tcha sit on *my* face! Yaw haw haw!"

But most particularly, folks do not want to hear about the night at LZ Skater-Gator — down the way from Fire Base Harriette and within earshot of a rag-tag bunch of mud-and-thatch hootches everyone called Gookville — when the whole company, except for one guy, got killed. Fucked-up dead, James, scarfed up. Everybody but Paco got nominated and voted into the Hall of Fame in one fell swoop. The company was night-laagered in a tight-assed pe-rimeter up past our eyeballs in a no-shit fire fight with some headhunter NVA — corpses and cartridge brass and oily maga-zines and dud frags scattered around, and everyone running low on ammo. Lieutenant Stennett had been calling in air strikes and gunships and artillery and dust-offs like they were going out of style when all of a sudden — ZOOM — the air came alive and crawled and yammered and whizzed and hummed with the roar and buzz of a thousand incoming rounds. Everyone looked up — GIs and zips — and knew it was every incoming round left in creation, knew that the dirt under our bellies (and the woods and villes and us with it) was going to be pulverized to ash (and I do mean pulverized, James) — so you could draw a rake through it and not find the chunks — knew by the cool and quiet whispering those rounds were the size of houses. I don't know what the rest of the company did — or the zips for that matter — but the second squad of the second platoon swapped that peculiar look around that travels from victim to victim in any disaster. We ciphered it out right then and there that we couldn't dig a hole deep enough, fast enough — couldn't crawl under something thick enough, couldn't drop our rifles, and what not, and turn tail and beat feet far enough but that this incoming would catch us by the scruff of the shirt, so to speak, and lay us lengthwise. We looked around at one another as much to say, 'My man, this ain't your average, ordinary, everyday, garden-variety sort of incoming. This one's going to blow everybody down." I tell you, James, there are those days — no matter how hard you hump and scrap and scratch — when there is simply nothing left to do but pucker and submit. I leaned my M–16 against a fresh-cut stump, took off my steel helmet and sat down on it, and ran my hands and fingers through my hair to make myself as presentable as possible. Paco slipped off his bandanna and sprinkled the last of his canteen water on it, wiped his face and hands, then twirled it up again and tied it around his neck — the knot to one side. Jonesy laid himself out with his head on his rucksack getting ready to take one of his famous naps. And Gallagher, who had a red and black tattoo of a dragon on the inside of his forearm from his wrist to his elbow, buttoned his shirt sleeves and brushed himself off, and sat cross-legged with his hands folded meditatively in his lap. In another minute everyone within earshot was quiet, like the hush of anticipation that travels through any crowd. But a minute later the four of us couldn't help but snicker, because we could hear Lieutenant Stennett's asshole — clear as a bell, James — slamming open and shut with sharp puckery slaps — and he could pucker his asshole tighter than a white-knuckled fist. Then we heard the air rushing ahead of those rounds like a breeze through a cave — so sharp and cool on the face, refreshing and foul all at once — as though they were floating down to us as limp and leisurely as cottonwood leaves. The four of us looked each other up and down one more time, as much to say, "Been nice. See you around. Hang on, here that sucker comes."

And in less time than it takes to tell it, James, we screamed loud and nasty, and everything was transformed into Crispy Critters for half a dozen clicks in any direction you would have cared to point, everything smelling of ash and marrow and spontaneous combustion, everything — dog tags, slivers of meat, letters from home, scraps of sandbags and rucksacks and MPC scrip, jungle shit and human shit — *everything* hanging out of the woodline looking like so much rust-colored puke.

Yes sir, James, we screamed our gonads slam-up, squeeze-up against our diaphragms — screamed volumes of unprintable oaths. When the mother fuckers hit we didn't go POOF all of a piece, but rather like sand dunes in a stiff and steady offshore ocean breeze — one grain at a time. (Not that it didn't smart, James. Oh, it tickled right smart. At first it thumped ever so softly on the tops of our heads — like your fat-assed uncle pats you on the head, calm and soothing, telling you how proud he is of the way you do your chores. Then came the lung-busting rush — like the senior class's butterheaded peckerwood flashing around the locker room snapping the tattered, trademark corner of a sopping-wet towel upside everybody's head.)

I mean, *whooie!* we reared back and let her rip so loud and vicious that all the brothers and sisters at Parson Do-da's Meeting House Revival fled — I mean split, James, I mean they peeled the varnish off the double front doors in their haste. The good parson was stalking back and forth in front of the pulpit rail, shouting and getting happy, slapping his big meaty hands together, signifying those sinners — bim bam boom — and calling on the mercy of sweet Jesus. Our screams hit the roofing tin like the dictionary definition of a hailstorm and swooped down the coal-stove chimney — "Ahoo!" And those sinners jumped back a row or two as though Brother Do-da had thrown a tubful of something scalding in their faces. They threw up their arms and wiggled and wagged their fingers, shouting to high heaven, "Alle-lujah! A-men! Yes, Lord! Save me, Jesus!" Then they grabbed their dog-eared Bibles and hand-crocheted heirloom shawls, and what not, and hit the bricks. Yes sir, James, plenty of the good brothers and sisters got right and righteous that night. And Brother Do-da was left standing in the settling dust, slowly scratching his bald, shining head — pondering, wondering, just exactly how did he do that marvelous thing?

Oh, we dissolved all right, all right, but our screams burst through the ozone, burst through the rags and tatters and café-curtain-looking aurora borealis, and so forth and such-like: clean as a whistle, clean as a new car — unfucked-with and frequency-perfect out into God's everlasting Cosmos, out where it's hot enough to shrivel your eyeballs to the shape and color and consistency of raisins, out where it's cold enough to freeze your breath to resemble slab plastic.

And we're pushing up daisies for half a handful of millennia (we're *all* pushing up daisies, James) until we're powder finer than talc, *finer* than fine, as smooth and hollow as an old salt lick — but that bloodcurdling scream is rattling all over God's ever-loving Creation like a BB in a boxcar, only louder.

ROBERT HENDERSON

Into the Wind

(FROM THE NEW YORKER)

A LATE-SUMMER Friday afternoon. A scattering of yellow leaves already lies on the dark surface of a New Jersey lake. A west wind is rising. And a man named Richard Lucas is writing on the porch of a cabin that sits on a low bluff above the water. He is a slight, spare man in his mid-fifties — a professor of biology. He writes in pencil on a lined pad, writes and scratches out, writes and crumples and throws to the floor. He is composing a letter to a friend who heads a committee devoted to saving plant and animal life in a swamp that may soon give way to a housing development. Later, the committee plans to widen its protective work. Richard has been asked to join and advise the group, and he has accepted. After all, their concern is in his field. Now he is writing to withdraw his acceptance, and he is hard put to it to come up with a decent excuse.

Still, he must refuse. He is in sympathy with any effort to preserve the swamp; he has conducted field trips there and waded there alone. But ecologists thrive on confrontation, and confrontation is something that Richard shuns. Indeed, it seems to him that the committee may be better off without him. A challenge thrown down by him could easily prove infirm. He wishes he had not lunched the day before with his friend. The invitation had been urgently offered then. The lunch could have been avoided.

But Richard went to it in part because he knew that he has recently been too given to avoidance. More and more, since the death of his wife, he avoids whatever he can — simple tasks such as repotting his houseplants, larger ones such as studying new developments in biology. More and more, he avoids people. Jessie and he married late and, without children, were seldom more than a few begrudged hours apart. But Jessie has been dead for four years and the deepest grief should have passed, yet Richard is still despondent. All the more as time goes on, it seems to him. It is this that makes him reluctant even to rise in the morning.

The letter is going badly. He tosses his pencil aside. The cabin is a weekend retreat, and Richard, having come there that day, needs supplies from the village a half mile along the lake. He could drive, but this is the country. He will take his canoe. He locks his doors and goes down the bluff to where his canoe is lying beside a path that runs along the water's edge. He pushes the canoe into the water and jumps in.

The wind has grown stronger, making tiny whitecaps curl on the lake. Richard is sitting in the stern of the canoe, so its prow is high, catching the breeze. He tacks, making progress. He reflects that his arms will probably ache tonight; he has not felt like using the canoe much lately. Halfway to the village, a pier juts into the lake, and he must go around it. He paddles farther out — as far as the end of the pier, still a hundred yards ahead. But the canoe is light and exposed, and its upborne head is turned by the wind, so Richard is suddenly facing back toward his starting point. He swings the canoe around, and the same thing happens again. He could go ashore and take his car, but he is annoyed — with the wind and with himself. He grows stubborn. He tacks close to the pier, and, sheltered, paddles to the end of it, but out in the open the canoe whips around.

Resigned, Richard lets the canoe be blown homeward, only steadying it with the paddle. Then, with a sudden compulsion, he bends forward, sitting on his haunches, turns the canoe once more into the wind, and drives it hard and straight. Fiercely. Grimly. When he is almost around the pier's end, he feels exactly as if he were showing off for Jessie's admiration. He feels her watching him. He pushes on, grimacing at his own bravado, and then he is clear of the dock and into quieter water.

The exhilaration, the sense of victory that comes over him, is — as he knows at once — out of all proportion to the little feat. Still, he feels it with a genuine tingling of his back and scalp — a preposterous surge of triumph that stays with him the rest of the way to the village and buoys his walk to the stores.

The return trip, with the wind at Richard's back, is easy. The jutting pier is in front of the house of a large and feckless family. The Perrys. Chester, the father, does odd jobs for people around the lake when he is sober. His wife, small, with red hair that is always disheveled, has a faint air of lost gentility, of breeding that goes back generations; she is spoken of as "Mrs. Perry," though she has been known to chase her husband off the pier with a skillet. There are seven children. The oldest is sixteen, the youngest a year and a half. Laurie, fifteen and unmarried, has already had a baby. When a social worker came to try to arrange for adoption, the family put her out and Chester ostentatiously locked the door. Later, the baby died. One summer, out of some missionary impulse, Richard had hired Laurie to clean his cabin, but she stole some small bills from his wallet and he gave her up. But the boys keep coming to Richard's back door asking for drinks of water or sometimes money.

Paddling past the Perrys' house, Richard sees a state-police car parked beside it, and he wonders idly, though not for long, which member of the family is in trouble and what the trouble is. His high spirits have not faded, nor has the vision of his wife. For a long while after her death, he would speak to Jessie in his mind, though, as time has gone on, he has done this less and less — he has somehow lost touch with her; he is no longer as easy with her as he always used to be. But now he does speak to her silently, thinking, "I surely wouldn't be writing that letter if you were here."

When Richard met Jessie, they were both in their early forties. Neither had married. Richard taught (he still teaches) in a college in northeastern Pennsylvania. He had stayed deep in his work — a natural shield against the rush of a hurrying world. Jessie had left college years before to look after a disabled father, and only at his death had returned to finish her degree. Out of place, or feeling so, with the other students, she was at ease with the younger faculty, and it was at one of their gatherings that she and Richard met. She was slight, like him. Her hair was brown and already lightly touched with gray. She was popular; her darts of humor shot out unpredictably. Her smile seemed luminous to Richard, whose own was often tentative. Her love of nature was wholly unscientific, though she listened raptly when Richard explained obscure aspects of it that had eluded her. They would walk together in the woods near the campus. And it was after one of these walks, on an autumn evening, the sun low in the sky and glowing on her face, that they stood a long time looking silently at each other on her doorstep and it occurred to Richard that he was being invited to kiss her. He did so, and astounded himself by asking her on the spot to marry him. She astounded him further by saying at once, "Of course."

Later, she persuaded him to lighten the style of his lectures, of which she said she enormously admired the content. And for his part Richard began to enjoy a far more sociable life than he had ever known. He loved hearing his wife's laughter and, in her company, that of their friends.

Back at the cabin, Richard puts away his purchases, sits on the porch, and decides to postpone his letter. He wants to savor, and somewhat puzzle over, his unexpected elation. It no longer seems to come merely from his having won his battle with the wind. It comes from, it connects with, something deeper. With other times when he has felt it. It is, though less powerful, something akin to his feeling as he walked home after Jessie's "Of course." Crossing the campus, he had looked up into a long archway of elm branches moving in the evening breeze — moving in a sort of musical unison, up and down and around, over and over, linked in a grace he had never quite seen, or noticed, before. The sky above was streaked. The undersides of hurrying clouds were pale coral.

A car stops on the road up a slope behind his cabin, and Richard hears someone pushing down through the woods toward the water. It is a pair of state troopers. They go to the path along the shore and disappear eastward around a bend in the lake. Richard is curious, but he is still occupied with exploring his moments of ebullience. The source of the one he has just recalled is plain enough, but suddenly he remembers feeling something of the sort on a station platform in Naples the summer after Jessie died.

Richard had gone to Italy that summer to try to put a distance between himself and his loss. He did not succeed very well. He ate his meals in his hotels, as a rule, and dutifully visited museums and historic spots, alone.

He was to sail home from Naples. He was traveling light, with a single suitcase, which was just as well. His compartment on the train from Rome was jammed with the luggage of an Austrian family — a man and wife by the name of Messiner, and their little girl, blond, with large dark eyes. They were also on their way to Naples.

Richard's Italian came to a smattering, but his German was adequate, if rusty. After a while, when the train stopped at Formia, the child crossed the compartment, sat beside Richard, and announced that her name was Anna. Soon the conversation was general, and by the time the train reached Naples, Richard — in part because they were strangers whom he would not see again — liked them all immensely.

They each shook hands with him, and Richard, carrying his suitcase, left the train and glanced back to wave and saw Herr Messiner, deeply distressed, craning out of the compartment's window. No porters were in sight, the train was to make a short stop, and all the Messiners' luggage was still on board.

A man in a railway uniform was standing nearby. Richard hurried to him and asked in Italian for help — for a porter. The man shrugged. Richard switched to German. The man said in German that he would talk to him "after I start the train," and Richard was suddenly furious. The man walked away, and Richard dropped his suitcase and ran after him, caught his arm, and, swearing a little, threatened him with dire official consequences if his friends were not safely got off. The man finally said, "*Ich warte,*" and Richard hurried back, Herr Messiner handed the luggage out the window to Richard, and a lone porter appeared. The family emerged, hands were shaken once more, the Messiners and their luggage went off along the platform, and Anna ran back and kissed Richard, to his intense pride and delight.

There is a small flower garden in the back of Richard's cabin. Abandoning the letter a while longer, he goes there to weed. But first he leans over a railing at the far end of the garden, where lake water from a spillway near the cabin drains through a narrow channel. The water slips past with a tranquil sound, like rain late at night, he reflects, when one is safe at home. On the far side of the channel is a lilac bush. Thinking back to April, Richard remembers its blossoms, and then the fragrance of lilacs drenching a room three years before. He was there to return a book to a colleague. The man was not at home, so, with his landlady's assent, Richard went to leave the book in the man's study and found a cluster of lilacs on the desk. That day, soon after his return from Italy, he had been offered a promotion, to be head of his department. Looking at the lilacs, breathing their scent, he felt as if Jessie were witnessing his success. Later, after due thought, he turned down the offer. He did not feel up to dealing — having to deal constantly — with a teaching staff and a pair of secretaries. His superiors understood that his calling was to research, not administration. Jessie and the lilacs and the promotion had made a heady blend for a while, but such things are often ephemeral.

Richard lets the weeding go until Saturday; he must get his letter into the mail. He returns to the porch and sees Laurie Perry run by along the path the troopers had taken half an hour before. She seems to be crying, though with fluttering leaves in the way it is hard to tell. Richard has turned firmly to the letter, when Mrs. Perry, wearing an apron and carrying her latest baby, Mary-Sue, comes along the path. Meredith, who is twelve by Richard's guess, and Elspeth (ten) follow and disappear around the bend; then Laurie comes back and makes a beckoning gesture, and Omar (eight) and Delaney (four?) come into sight and follow Laurie. What's up, Richard wonders. And where are the old man and Tom? (Tom being the oldest, and the old man, Chester, being somewhere near forty but looking the worse for wear.)

Curiosity postpones the letter a bit longer, and in a few minutes the family comes back, single file, and stands in a cluster directly below the cabin. For once, they are silent, or largely so; Omar does push Elspeth toward the water and is pushed by her in return, but Laurie glares at them, hand raised, and they gape at her and stand still.

I have not known them quiet except at the funeral, Richard thinks. He is remembering the funeral of Laurie's baby. He had gone on an impulse, feeling it vaguely as a duty, dreading it. He had been shaken, seeing them all so sad and stiff in their good clothes, so solemn, so seemingly decent. There had been wildflowers on the coffin. At the end, Richard had passed Mrs. Perry. For lack of much else to say, he had told her the flowers were beautiful, and she had said that Pa had gathered them that morning.

Now, in retrospect, Richard is surprised at himself for having gone. The Perrys are less than nothing to him. He need not have put himself through it. Since Jessie's death, he has put himself through very little. She had had a friend called Joanna who lived in nearby Philadelphia. Richard knew her, but Joanna and Jessie were closer, having been high-school friends. The summer before Jessie's death, Joanna had come out of an auto crash with her nose and jaw hideously disfigured. Plastic surgery was delayed for medical reasons, and week after week Jessie — concerned and loyal, and managing, Richard was sure, to carry her laughter with her — had visited Joanna, never asking Richard to go along, coming home each time exhausted. Since then, Richard has seen Joanna only once.

Far down the lake, two rowboats have appeared, moving slowly across in a parallel course. Soon they turn back and again disappear from sight. On the path below the cabin, Mrs. Perry puts Mary-Sue down, and Laurie at once picks her up and caresses her, looking to Richard for all the world like a woman. Like a young mother. Mrs. Perry stares out at the water and rolls her apron up and lets it drop and rolls it up again. Laurie comes close and whispers in her ear.

Jessie had bought a present for Joanna — a calfbound early edition of *The Pickwick Papers*. She had not lived to deliver it. Richard, feeling that Joanna must have it, took it to her. He had not seen her since her accident. She let him into the apartment, wearing a scarf across the lower part of her face. She spoke, if thickly, repeating the condolences she had already written him. But when he gave her the book, she cried out in pleasure, and the scarf slipped down. Joanna sighed, slumped a little, and let the scarf stay as it was, and for the rest of his call Richard would look at her trying not to show his shock, then look away, knowing that he was signaling it. He never went back. He wrote once, and that was all.

The boats have come in sight again, a little closer. There are two men in each. A sort of ripple runs through the line of Perrys.

I failed Jessie, Richard thinks. *I don't even know that Joanna is alive. I should have gone again. I should have gone often. Jessie would have been quite certain that I would.*

He goes to get his binoculars from a shelf in the living room, and trains them on the boats. One man in each boat is rowing, the other repeatedly throws something heavy into the water and pulls it up again. There is a knock at the back door. Richard goes to open it. Tom, the oldest Perry boy, is outside. "I'm awful thirsty, Mr. Lucas," he says, mopping his brow. "Been workin' up the road."

Richard fetches a glass of water. "What's going on out there?" he asks.

"Lookin' for Papa," Tom says. "He been gone two days. Had a big fight with Mama. Then everybody got to fightin'. Papa took off in his boat. Nobody's seen him since. Boat came ashore upside down. I gotta go now. He coulda got too drunk, but I don't know." Tom starts away, then turns back. "He don't drink as much as folks think, Mr. Lucas," he says, and runs off down through the woods and stands beside his mother.

"Grappling," Richard says aloud. "Dragging the lake for Chester."

The afternoon is fading. Richard goes back to the porch. The boats are heading toward the cabin now. One of the state troopers is in one of them. Elspeth has begun to cry. Delaney is sucking his thumb, and Laurie gently pulls it out. The men in the boats shout to one another. *If there is — anything — in that lake, it will arrive here,* Richard says to himself. *The current comes over the spillway.*

One boat spins a little, as if a hook has caught. Tom waves the younger children away, but they go only a few steps and slip back, hiding behind trees. Mrs. Perry takes her apron off and pushes at her hair as if wanting to appear tidier. The boats move on. Nothing has been found.

They are a family, Richard thinks. *They are real. I suppose I never quite thought they were. Today, they are even close.* And he remembers that Meredith, the twelve-year-old, had once made a sketch of their house and the pier, and that Chester had taken it proudly to every cabin on the lake. The penciled lines had been concise, the perspective shaky but promising. *They are real,* Richard tells himself once more. *They are alive. All but — maybe — Chester. They are alive and facing death.*

And then it strikes him that he, too, is face to face with a sort of death. *My own,* he thinks, and winces inwardly. *I have been waiting for it. I invoke it. Day after day, I back away from life. I am not just grieving for Jessie. I am grieving because I fail her. I do not exactly believe that she knows what I have been doing, but I know, and I am surrogate for her.*

The boats are just about opposite the spillway. The nearest one spins again and stops, and the other pulls up beside it. Richard reaches for his binoculars. The men are conferring. The trooper appears to be giving them directions. The grappling iron has caught upon some object. Richard turns away. He lays his glasses down, locks his front door, goes out the back one and locks it, and walks toward his parked car. He will drive to the village, or, better, he will simply drive on home. He has no wish to witness the rest of the drama below his cabin. He reaches the car and unlocks its door, but though he has grasped the handle, he does not turn it.

For the strange thing is, he cannot. He stands confused, immobile. He shakes himself and impatiently tells himself aloud to get into the car. But — down beside the water, they are waiting. Waiting. Against his will, he turns away from the car and walks in a kind of trance back toward the cabin and around it and down the slope — on down until he is standing just back of Mrs. Perry. Apart from them all, but with them, one of them. One and not one, for along with a queer feeling of alliance is one of dreadful abashment. He has no right to be there, to intrude at such a time, but he has no choice — no choice at all but to share with them. Mrs. Perry glances at Richard, the children pay no heed. The boats are gently milling about, the hooks still in the water. And now, against and through the embarrassment and the tension, Richard feels a mounting warmth, a tiny exhilaration that, wildly unwarranted, will not be denied.

Someone is coming running along the path that follows the curve of the lake. The second trooper, hat in hand and panting, appears. He goes up to Mrs. Perry. "It's O.K., Ma'am," the trooper says. "I found him in a cabin way around the lake and back in the woods. Deserted cabin. He's asleep. I let him be. He looks as if he could use it." And the trooper waves to the men in the boats and tells them to go ashore.

The children straggle toward home. Mrs. Perry turns to Richard and holds out a hand. "You was good to come," she says.

Richard goes back up the slope and into his cabin. On the porch floor are all the discarded beginnings of his letter. He gathers them up. There are a lot of them. He puts them into the living-room fireplace and throws a lighted match in after them. The blaze flares briefly, and Richard decides he would like a proper fire; he has not bothered to build fires in this grate lately, but the evening coming on is cool. He lays a fire and lights it, and sits before it for a while, letting himself imagine his wife beside him, and being almost at ease with her again.

CURT JOHNSON

Lemon Tree

(FROM CONFRONTATION)

THE THIRD NIGHT in Cleveland — at the end of the day he gave the second of his four presentations — he took one of the room clerks to dinner and persuaded her to come back to his room with him. In his room she let him remove her brassiere, but she would not kiss him on the mouth, and she would not let him go further than kissing her breasts. She had large breasts with light-brown areolas larger than half dollars.

She was twenty-six and married, but her husband was out of town, finishing an EDP training course in Cincinnati. Her name was Kathleen, and after they had lain close to each other an hour, silent most of the time, she told him that her father had committed suicide three weeks before.

He lay there still silent and when she began to cry softly he knew why she had laughed so much earlier in the evening. He stroked her long hair.

"Can't it be all right again?"

"No," he said.

They had reconciled three days before their twentieth anniversary — reconciled after another four weeks of silence — and on their anniversary had gone to a French restaurant to celebrate and had sat three hours drinking and eating and talking. His wife enjoyed eating out.

But over his fourth after-dinner drink he mentioned their son — how at twelve, four years before, a girl had "broken the boy's heart, hadn't she . . . The rest of his life." He pointed his cigar at his wife for emphasis. "The rest of his life that heartbreak will be with him, won't it?"

"Nonsense," his wife said. "Sentimental nonsense."

And the old anger swelled in him and that ended their evening. Four days later he flew to Cleveland for the sales conference.

The night before he left for Cleveland he was in the kitchen finishing his notes for his presentations and his wife came down from their bedroom. She was wearing a short, sheer nightgown, and again he saw that she was attractive as a woman, still youthful even at thirty-eight.

"I think we should talk. It's no life like this."

"We have," he said. "For twenty years and not one thing ever changed." He had been thinking that he had to go away by himself somewhere — thinking that he must somehow change his whole life before it was too late and it was over, thinking he must somehow break the patterns.

The fourth night in Cleveland he took the room clerk out again, but this time to a pizza parlor — her choice. She had her car and they drove Memorial Shoreway and then went back to his room.

She let him kiss her breasts again and remove her skirt, but she would not let him remove her panties — bright blue, sheer panties. She had less pubic hair than most women he'd known. It was black and wiry, but the long long hair on her head was silky and brown. She did kiss him once.

After an hour he got up from the bed and got one of the two fifths of Beam from his suitcase and turned off the light and then came back to lie beside her. He was tired from talking for four days, and from late nights that seemed to stretch back to forever, and when he awoke it was morning and she was gone.

He remembered she had told him that she and her husband did not get along. And he remembered her stressing that people should be gentle with each other, that they should not hurt each other.

And he remembered saying, "They can't help it."

The night before he left for Cleveland he and his wife had talked for two hours in the kitchen. When he saw she was not going to leave him with his work and his thoughts, he got up from the table and poured himself some bourbon. *If I weren't so tired,* he thought, *we could go upstairs together and not have to talk.*

When he stood up to make a fourth drink, his wife stood, too.

"Sooner or later you always lose your temper when you've had something to drink," she said. "It's time for me to leave."

"It's time for *me*," he said. "That's the only way either one of us is going to get anything out of the rest of our lives." He believed that for himself, and had almost convinced himself it was true for her, as well — but he worried about his son and daughter.

"All right, leave then. But if you ever come back, your belongings will be out in the drive."

"Fair enough," he said, wishing it were not, or that at least he could find the old anger.

"Four years now you've done nothing but drink. What do you think the children think of you? Why do you think I won't talk to you? . . . In this house you're nothing but a drunk, and I can't stand to see you that way."

After she left he sat down, turned on the radio. *If she had only talked,* he thought, *it might have changed things . . . But no,* he thought then, *that's not true. You helped yourself or no one did.*

Four years, he thought, *yes: that was the year my mother died. And the year Ann took back her key and two months later got married.*

The radio was playing a song he knew. Under his breath he sang with it to the end and then he lifted his glass and finished the drink and stood up. A tear slid slowly down his cheek. He looked at the refrigerator. "Life is a very pretty pain in the ass," he said aloud to the yellow door. "So no need to cry about it."

He remembered the first time. She was short and blonde and he had known her for years, but never thought of her that way until she made the first move. And that night he had made love to his wife for an hour out of guilt and affection . . . But after the first time it was easy.

And always at the beginning with each new one he would remember walking with a girl, carrying his drawings under his arm, and a taller, heavier boy challenging him. He was losing, and then he saw that blood from his nose had spattered his drawings, and rage had filled him and he had lashed out at the bigger boy and beaten him. He did not know what the connection was.

*

The night of the last day of the conference he went walking with Kathleen. They walked several miles, then stopped for hamburgers and milkshakes — her choice again — and then started slowly back to the motel, taking side streets.

They walked slowly along under the trees, their fingers touching, but halfway back to the motel she began to slow her pace, and then her pace became slower still and then she stopped. He looked at her. Tears were in her eyes and glistening on her cheeks in the moon's light. Her mouth opened and he heard her sob. She put the fingers of one hand to her mouth and stood there, tears wet on her cheeks.

He stepped in front of her, put his hands on her shoulders, and she continued to sob, darkness all around, deep, animal sounds coming from her throat — "Unnh, *unnh, unnh.*"

Finally her sobs began to subside and she said, "I'm all right," and in another moment they were walking again. She took his arm and walked close to him now, her head against his shoulder.

When they got inside his room she clung to him, kissed him, running her hands up and down his back and shoulders and over his neck.

Now she was lying on her stomach beside him, nude except for her panties, her hands inside his pants.

"I'll take them off," he said, "if you'll do the same."

"Oh, is that the big deal?"

"I don't understand. You come here but you don't let me make love to you."

"Are you prepared?"

"I thought in this day and age that was no longer necessary."

"I don't want to get pregnant."

"That would be all right."

"Not for me. I don't want a baby, ever."

"Finish it then. With your hand."

"No. That would make me too horny."

"Well, then, I'll go out and get something."

"No. Not now."

"A blowjob then."

"No."

"*Why* won't you let me make love to you?"

She remained silent for a moment and then she said, "Because I like you, and want to see you again . . . But I had an idea. Why don't you stay over? My husband won't be back until Tuesday noon. That would give us three days."

Once with Ann he had fucked her twice and then, while he was mixing himself a drink, she said, "Third time is charm time," and he turned to her and said, "No, I don't want you or anybody, anymore, ever," and had meant it at that moment, but she only laughed.

He remembered saying then — and he only remembered it now, and this was six years ago — "Fuck you, I'm going to Mexico," and she laughed again, more loudly. But he had fucked her again. She didn't talk when she was fucking.

In the motel he told Kathleen, "I have one talent. I can spot a phony. By what they do after they're through talking. Very few people can do that very well."

She reached out and put her hand on the back of his neck and pulled his head slowly to hers and kissed him.

On the drive to her place, he said, "I think I should stay at the motel."

"I have room. Why?"

"Because if I were your husband, I wouldn't want some bastard moving in while I was gone — *staying* at my place."

She glanced at him. "Suit yourself," she said.

He *knew* his wife was wrong. The experience with the girl *had* marked their son — two children, neither of them knowing what was happening, and one had damaged the other. He knew because he had read the boy's letters to the girl, letters never sent, only crumpled on the desk.

And if his wife could not understand that, it justified whatever he finally decided to do, did it not?

He told Kathleen about his son and the girl.

"Right — fucked his head over," she said. "Kids feel. Most people think they don't, but kids really feel. They *really* feel."

Later she used the same expression again: her husband had "fucked her head over."

*

"I was close to my father. So close. I like men better than women anyway. Women really blow my mind. I can't talk to them. But men! — when I discovered boys in high school — wow!" She laughed, crinkled her eyes, darted her tongue at him, touched his arm. *"Wow!"* she repeated mockingly. Then she said, "Because for one thing, women don't talk straight with you. Like, I'll be wearing a klunk of a dress and *I* know it and *they* know it, and they'll say, 'That's cute.' "

She lived in a small, old, two-story brick house. The bricks needed tuckpointing and inside the house the floors sloped in all directions. She had two cats, a dog, and a black guinea pig she kept in the upstairs bedroom. She pointed to some chairs and then to a bookcase. "My husband made those. He's very talented. He can do *anything*. He's a genius, really. Really he is."

He went closer to one of the chairs, inspected it. *Genius or not,* he thought, *your husband is a rotten carpenter.*

"But he flunked out of school," she said. She pointed to a framed design on the wall. "He drew that, too," she said.

He made no comment. *A not especially gifted sixth-grader might have drawn that,* he thought.

She lit a stick of incense, blew on it. "If you stare at the smoke," she said, "these can really freak you out. The trouble is, there's only one thing he's interested in, he's losing interest in that. You see, I lived with him a year before we were married, so it's six years now."

They were waiting for one of her friends to stop by. The friend was a dishwasher at the motel. She had told her friend all about him. "You have two children in your family," she said. "My father had three."

He supposed he substituted for her father. Not a profound observation, considering their ages, but nevertheless he found it surprising to be taken on such terms, since his own father was still alive and did not seem particularly old to him, even at sixty-three.

He knew when he went back he must tell his wife something about his plans, since he *had* told her he was leaving.

"Richard has a good sense of humor and is always courteous and is sportsmanlike in work and play. He is a thoughtful, happy boy, neat and orderly in both personal appearance and in the work he produces. Richard has unusual reading ability and his language expression is very good. He shows special ability in interpersonal relationships and should be encouraged to develop this ability. His happy, cheerful, and orderly way of living and doing things accounts for his record this year and has earned him a double promotion. His success is due in no small part to his sense of responsibility." — MID-TERM REPORT — Grade Four, Nov. 13, 1938.

They were lying nude on the bed in the upstairs bedroom. They had been there an hour. Marty, her friend, had stayed for five hours and then the three of them had gone out for pizza and then they had driven Memorial Shoreway again and through two of the rich suburbs to admire sportscars in the driveways and then they had stopped for cokes and now he and Kathleen were alone again.

When he asked her if she wanted a drink, she told him that she did not smoke or drink, and never intended to. Neither had her father. They were Baptists.

He shifted himself so that his head was on her stomach. He tongued her navel, then lowered his head and began slowly to tongue her black hair. When she began to arch against him he started sucking the now-protruding inner lips. His hands were on her breasts. He raised his head and looked up. Her head was thrown back on the pillow, her long brown hair on either side, her mouth open, her eyes closed.

He raised himself on his arms. "Are you ready?"

"Do you have anything with you?"

He pushed himself abruptly to a kneeling position between her legs. "We've *been* together all day! Did we stop at a drugstore?"

"You blew it then," she said quietly, opening her eyes and smiling at him.

"Maybe your husband's supply . . ."

"My husband won't wear anything."

"What do you do? Does he deposit it there?" He touched her navel.

"When he comes, yes. It's all right if I like it. But Dave is funny. Most of the time he never comes. Sometimes we'll screw for two hours and still he doesn't come."

"Two *hours?*"

"Yes. I *like* to fuck . . . When we first lived together we'd stay in bed weeks at a time. Oh, we'd get up to eat and that, but . . ." She smiled and turned slowly over on her stomach. She had beautiful breasts and a beautiful ass and there was a layer of babyfat under her flesh all over her body, but especially on her back and shoulders, that felt like a pelt of soft, warm rubber.

She was staring out the window into the backyard, not looking at anything in the darkness, only staring. He had just begun to notice these dreamy spells. The expression around her lips was sad.

"My husband is only a kid," she said. "He has no understanding of people, none at all. David is only a little boy."

"I'll get dressed and use your car and get something."

"It's too late," she said. "The stores are all closed . . . He's only a kid, but he knows how to get *me* to do what he wants."

She turned her head to him and her eyes focused on his face and she smiled again, and at that moment behind him he heard the latch on the bedroom door click and he turned his head quickly and saw the door beginning to open. He stiffened, his eyes on the opening door.

She put her hand on his wrist. "Get me a Pepsi from the fridge, will you? It's only my dog."

Santa Cruz   Philadelphia   Mexico —
While he waited he made lists.

NEGATIVE: Promise faithfulness   Promise forever
           Sleep on a quarrel   Promises   Promises

He had been up since seven and now it was almost nine-thirty. For breakfast he had a Pepsi. Her refrigerator had contained two bottles of Pepsi-Cola, an opened half-pint of cream, and some carrots.

On the top of the upright piano in the living room were half a dozen framed photographs, but he avoided looking at them. He did not want to know what her husband looked like.

". . . he told me he didn't care — mess around if I wanted to. So that's why, when you put the hustle on . . . but just never let him know about it, he said. He told me that in January. I don't know why." Her tone was bewildered. "Hasn't your wife ever . . . ?"

"Not once. She doesn't believe in it. And doesn't have the time — or the imagination, maybe. And she still loves me, I think."

"That hasn't stopped you. Lack of the time, I mean."

She told him about her childhood, her going away to school, her lovers (four), her husband's accomplishments, her triumphs, her disappointments, her husband's many jobs ("Because I keep telling him to quit if he doesn't like it"), how the other girls at the motel all thought she was bitchy — and all the time she kept her hand moving slowly over his body, pulling herself closer to him — and tired as he was he did not weary of the sound of her voice. It was past three when he finally heard her steady breathing and knew she was asleep.

She had told him many things about herself, but from them all he could not decide whether she was a child or a woman. And she had not been shocked, as *he* had been at the time, that his first adulterous affair was with his wife's best friend. "David, too," she said quietly. "I think that's happening."

Well, everyone to his own line of bullshit — young sales reps, old sales managers — everyone, including motel-room clerks who burned incense and played the Who and the Jefferson Airplane twice too loud while you were trying to talk to their dishwasher friends.

He resented her friend Marty, and his headband and long hair and sports-car fanaticism and gentle voice talking about the "new" ways as if they were in the New Revolution. The boy had no idea of what power was or where it was or how, in this country, you got it. He resented the other friends she had told him about, too. And the lovers — and he knew they included Marty, even though she had not said so.

Once, five years ago, when he had thought of divorcing his wife and marrying Ann, he had asked one of the few men he trusted what he thought of the idea. "Doesn't matter. *Whatever* you do, you'll pay." And then he had asked another, Hal, and Hal had told him, "Do what you want, not what you should. Love it and leave it." . . . But now he felt he was at a time in his life when he was ready to do what he wanted to do, and he almost felt ready to pay — but he did not want others to pay, and he was certain that his children would.

When the doorbell rang he was relieved that he was up and dressed, because even if it were her husband he felt able to brazen it out. It was Marty.

"She's still sleeping," he said, opening the screen door.

"Oh — well, I thought I might take a bath," Marty said. There was a pained look around Marty's eyes. Marty began to back away across the porch. "I live here sometimes, you know," he said.

"Wait, I'll go with you. I've got to get shaving cream and a razor." In Marty's car he crumpled his list and threw it on the floor.

He remembered the girl he had been walking with when he had the fight in tenth grade. She died two years later, in her senior year. She had been born with a weak blood vessel in her brain, they discovered. It could have killed her in her first year, or her seventieth. Or it might have left her paralyzed.

The everlasting studs don't understand what love is, he thought, or fucking either . . . Though they may understand what most women want some of the time. But for that there were dildos. "Tell me," he said, his mouth next to her ear, her long hair tangling under his lips. "Tell me you want me to fuck you."

She was writhing under him, grunting, "Unnh-*unnh-unnh*," and now she said, "Fuck me," and then she repeated the words and he increased the speed of his thrusts and soon she was saying, "Good-good-good," softly under him, and he knew he had won, and the thought of her husband blurred from his mind and he went on to finish — though he was not quite sure that she did. Not quite sure.

"If you can type, if you can take shorthand, I can get you a job in Detroit. A good job. Or even if you can't."

"I don't know," she said. "I was going to take some courses at John Carroll this fall. I've already registered."

He took his wallet from the dresser, removed three twenties from it, extended them to her. "At least come for a weekend."

"I'll write and ask, if I do."

He put the money away and sat down at the dresser. He grasped the bottle of Beam by the neck and drank from it. Then he said, "I know there are all kinds of difficulties, but they don't matter. Not to me. But you see, I *had* the idea that you and your husband didn't get along, and now I don't know. Still, with all the qualifications, I'm asking you — come to Mexico with me."

She was lying nude on the bed, on top of the sheet. She patted the place beside herself with her hand. "I knew you would ask that," she said. "Come lie down by me again. Come on."

He lay down beside her and she began to talk, slowly and evenly, and when half an hour later she finished he realized that he had been given a definite No but such a gentle No that he could easily have interpreted it as Yes. What surprised him even more than being refused, however, was the maturity of her reasoning. She was older than he was. He lay there for a few minutes after she stopped talking and then he patted her thigh and stood up and went to the dresser and took a drink.

"Maybe you drink too much sometimes," she said. "I think you passed out one night at the motel."

"Thanks for the advice," he said, smiling at her.

They drove to the Western Reserve historical museum. "This is your vacation," she said. "We'll do whatever you want — whatever you feel like doing. But you'll like this place."

She clung to him as they strolled the halls, petted him, pulled him into empty hallways and gave him light kisses. His wife never touched him except in bed.

They stopped before an 1870 period room and she said, "Sometimes I come here and stare through that window for hours if no one is around. I pretend I'm living there." Her eyes had gotten dreamy again, but her face was not sad.

They ate in the museum's cafeteria and then drove aimlessly, and when they got back to her house he wanted to make love again but they couldn't because her friend Marty arrived.

It was midnight when Marty left, and he had had a number of drinks by then. "Let's go to bed," he said. "I want to fuck you. That was boring."

"No. Not tonight. In the morning. Marty is a good person. You shouldn't say that. He likes you. Why don't we go walking instead?"

So they walked. They walked six or seven miles, talking very little, walking slowly, their hands in each other's, and when they arrived back at the house it was two o'clock. She urged him to have a nightcap and because she insisted, he did, but he felt no need for it. They sat in the kitchen and as she sipped a Pepsi she told him about her father — what a gentle man he was, what a kind man — and talking about him did not seem to upset her.

In bed he realized that when her grief lessened for her father, so would whatever her feeling was for him. He stroked her thigh. "I thought you would go," he said.

"To Mexico?"

"I was sure you would. You complicated things, because if *you* had been willing, I would have done it."

"I didn't say I wouldn't," she said. "I just didn't say I would."

Hoping to get some kind of purchase on the future, or at least a token of the day and night they had had together, he closed his hand over her breast, put his mouth next to her ear. "I love you, Kathleen," he said.

"Mmmmm," she said sleepily, and patted his head.

He realized he was happy for the first time since his youth, and he could not think why.

He had known a man once who divorced his wife and married a girl his daughter's age, seventeen. Someone had told him — Hal had told him when they were talking about Ann five years ago — that every time the man started to screw his second wife he saw his daughter's face under him.

He thought about what he would say to his wife when he returned, but he could not decide because he still did not know what he was going to do.

He was drowsing off when suddenly he came awake. He looked at his watch: three-thirty.

She was crying. He reached behind himself for her hand and touched her stomach. Her body was next to his and he could feel her breasts against his back. "Kathleen?" he said.

She was crying, but not loudly. "I have to tell you," she said. "But never tell anyone else, promise?"

"All right."

He waited and finally she began speaking again, but now in an almost everyday tone of voice, her words coming evenly and steadily in the dark room, her body clasped to his, arms around his chest, her head just below his. He heard the guinea pig on the far side of the room rustling the paper in the bottom of its cage.

"My father killed himself because of something that happened that he never got over. You see, he had three children, three daughters — me and then my two baby sisters, they were four and six — and David and I had been married about a year and were staying with them because we had no money. But my mother and David couldn't get along. She wasn't well.

"She'd go for months and then one day we'd come home and she would be sitting in a chair by the living-room window, staring into the street, or lying upstairs on her bed without moving, staring at the ceiling. She wouldn't move for hours, sometimes for days — just lie and stare. And then when that would happen I'd get the meals and take care of my sisters and my father would talk to her and finally, after a while — but sometimes it lasted over a week — after a while she'd be all right then.

"But the littlest thing could put her into one of those. Once a gas-station man was rude to her, and once a woman said something nasty about some food she'd brought to a church supper — anything. I think that's why my father decided to have more children so long after me. He thought they would keep her mind on real things."

She shifted beside him. Outside he heard a plane overhead and from far away he thought he heard the noise of trucks on a highway. He felt her arms tighten on his chest and he felt her hair brush against his neck.

"So David and I were living with them, and David and my mother were always picking at each other, and one night at supper my sisters had left the table and my mother was telling us about a girl in the church who had gotten pregnant and had to go away because the boy wouldn't marry her and what a terrible thing it was for her parents and his, too, and how shameful it was. You see, even though she knew how that sort of talk bothered David, well, she was trying to get him to join the church. And that was when he told her that he and I had lived together a year before we were married.

"She said she had always suspected that but she never thought she'd live to hear anyone boast about it, and then she stood up and began to clear the table.

"That was on Sunday, at supper, and Monday everything seemed the same and all right and then on Tuesday my father called me at work and said that something had happened and would I meet him and then he told me what . . . what had happened."

She stopped speaking. When she did not resume, he turned slowly over and held her. He stroked her long hair slowly.

"I went to meet my father and it was like he was sleepwalking and so . . . well, I was the one then who had to take over, but it was so — and it wasn't until a long time after that when he told me what had happened, and . . . and it was so . . . it was so *horrible*. For him, for . . ."

He stroked her hair. "It's time to sleep," he said. "No more."

"I want to *tell* you. I *have* to tell you. My mother called him at the office, do you see? He had just gotten to the office. Only half an hour before he'd been sitting at the breakfast table with all of us, all three of them, you see — and she phoned him and she told him there was nothing he could do to stop her this time, no way he could talk her out of it, and that she was going to take my sisters away with her, that she wanted him to know she had always loved him and that she always would, forever, and that killing herself and my sisters was the only way, and then she hung up.

"My father called the police and they got to our house *right* away, but it . . . it wasn't in time . . . She had a knife, you see, and those little girls . . . my father . . . all of us."

She moved beside him.

"That broke his heart . . . do you see?"

And then, after a long silence, she said, "So I got what was coming to me, didn't I. I killed those girls and I killed my father. *And I knew it would happen.*"

They lay there silent a long while and then in a calm, even voice she said, "I had to arrange for the funerals. David left town. But Marty was there.

"And I had to wait for the relatives to come, and Marty was there. And I had to go to the church and the cemetery, but Marty went with my father and me.

"And three weeks ago, when my father . . . when my father . . . and Marty was there again, and once that week when I cried my husband slapped my face. He told me not to be so emotional."

The room was dark and outside it was silent, and at last he heard her steady breathing.

He was up at six-thirty, leaving her to sleep. He worked on his conference-evaluation report, because he did not want to think anymore about what she had told him two or three hours ago, and he did not want to think about how he had tried to give her money yesterday, and he did not want to think of her refusal to go with him to Mexico.

"What's left then?" he'd asked her yesterday while they were in the museum's cafeteria. "I'm going back to Detroit, and you'll be here." He had thought he'd been offering her an escape from a husband she was teaching herself to hate.

"You and me are left," she said. "I can talk to you. Even if we don't agree, we talk. I want to know you're there. I want you to come to see me. I want to come to see you." She bent over her chocolate pie and lifted topping from it and looked up at him with her tongue still out, the white whipped cream on the tip of her tongue, and let the corners of her mouth turn up.

It was raining outside now, the sky a greenish-gray, and when he had his report half-written he stood up and started for the kitchen. No sleep, he told himself. He looked at his watch: nine-thirty. He went to the refrigerator but there was no more Pepsi-Cola.

He went back upstairs and sat down by the dresser and had two deep swallows of Jim Beam, and then two more. They made him dizzy. He wished he had a cigar. No sleep, he told himself. His left leg jiggled and he took another swallow, looked at the sleeping guinea pig in its cage.

"Come here," he heard, and he looked at the bed and she had her arms out to him. He went to the bed, put the bottle beside it, and got under the sheets with her.

"I'm going back," he said.

"Why?"

"I'd just better."

"David won't be home till tomorrow."

"It's a feeling I have."

She put her finger on his lips. "Don't be mean," she said.

They kissed and he turned on the bed, throwing the sheet back, and began to lick her white stomach. In a few minutes his head was at her black hair and above him he felt her mouth on him. He looked up and saw her head bobbing over him and thought of what she had told him and he could not think of her as something to fuck, thinking of her mother, her sisters, so he pulled away and sat up in the bed and unrolled a condom while he was still rigid enough to get it on, but when he tried to make entry he was no longer rigid enough.

"Goddam," he said, and went back to tonguing her, hoping that would arouse him.

He labored for half an hour, and even thought of handling himself into readiness, but finally he gave up and finished it for her with three fingers.

She lay close to him, the palm of her hand sliding over his chest. "It's no big deal," she said.

He lifted the bottle from beside the bed and took a deep swallow, coughed. "It is for me," he said. The rain was coming down harder on the roof.

He set the bottle beside the bed and bent to her breasts. "Empty," he said. He laughed.

After a few minutes she said, "Why do you keep at me? We don't have to."

He took his mouth from her breast and looked up into her eyes, thinking, *I have to now because I couldn't.*

There was a noise in the backyard — a loud noise — and then the shifting of gears. He raised himself and she turned over and they lifted the shade and looked out. A garbage truck had stopped in the alley.

He turned over on his back, crossed his hands on his chest, looked up at the ceiling.

"I love the rain," she said. He turned his head and saw that her eyes were beginning to go dreamlike again as she stared down into the backyard. "I love it."

He picked up the empty bottle, tried not to think, and thought of what she had told him about her mother, her sisters.

She reached back with her hand, still looking out the window, and tangled the hair on his stomach. "That's all right. Marty says he really digs me, too, but can't get it up over me. Maybe I'm that kind of girl."

He saw her life. Eventually she would leave her husband and go with Marty, or someone like Marty who would probably be even less effective in dealing with the real world, and then there would be someone else and someone else and then she would be thirty-five and her flesh would begin to fatten and turn yellow and the light would start going out of her brown eyes.

Yet he knew that was no worse — no different — than any life he could offer her.

The thought of all the other men to come in her life saddened him. Everyone will drink from the dipper by the well, he thought, but no one will carry it home. It had something to do with that, as a warning for her, and it had something to do with making a choice, but he could never explain that to her because she looked at things so differently.

He thought of making a last attempt to persuade her to go away with him. You only had so much good time with anyone. If they could have six good months together, or six good years, with luck, what would be wrong with that?

He suddenly realized that the difference in their ages was exactly as long as he had been married.

He lay there and listened to her voice when she occasionally spoke and to the rain now quiet and steady on the roof and he could not bring himself to speak. He tried to convince himself that the sense of desolation he felt was brought on by whiskey for breakfast, but though he knew it was not that, he did not know what it was.

She took him to the airport at noon. She wanted to stay with him till his plane left, so he walked with her for half an hour, strolling slowly down the corridors with her, her hands in his arm, touching him, patting him, and then he told her to go to her car. "I don't like leavetakings," he said as she kissed him. "You have to go now."

.

"Be easy on your daughter," his wife told him. "She came in this afternoon and very brightly told me she'd just broken off with her boyfriend. She's taller than he is now, so I imagine it was inevitable, but she's been too cheerful ever since."

"I'm not going to do *anything* tonight," he said, "but get drunk. And then when the kids are in bed I'm going to screw the living bejesus out of you."

"You can make love to me," she said, "but I won't let you 'screw the living bejesus' out of me."

"There's a difference?"

"You know, I think you're having a nervous breakdown."

"You think too much," he said.

His wife came three times that night — and she had always maintained she was capable of only one orgasm, "no matter *what* the books say" — but when he finally rolled off and looked at the clock he saw that it had only taken forty-eight minutes.

He wakened at two in the morning and could not get to sleep again. About three he felt sick to his stomach and after that he felt cold — and it was warm in the bedroom — and then he began to sweat. At four-thirty he got up and showered and drove downtown. He let himself into the office, went through the mail and the messages and the sales reports, and finished his evaluation report, and by eight when the others began to arrive he felt all right.

One of the messages was from Ann. He had not heard from her in two years, so at nine-thirty he called. She was getting a divorce — would he like to stop in and console her, or "whatever."

After he called Ann, he placed a call to the motel in Cleveland, but Kathleen was not at work. He called her home and after six rings she answered.

"Are you all right? I mean you're all right, aren't you?"

"David got home in the middle of the night. He said he couldn't see any reason for staying in Cincinnati when he could be home, so he took a plane and got a taxi from the airport and at midnight he was home."

"Then the Lord does look after fools and drunkards."

"Oh . . . Yes, I see . . . We're going to a rock festival tomorrow — Dave and Marty and me. Jefferson Airplane."

"All right. Enjoy yourselves."

"Yes . . . Write me."

"That's Berlioz," Ann said. " 'Reveries and Passions.' It was supposed to put you in the right frame of mind, the right mood. But it doesn't seem to be working."

"I prefer Glenn Miller."

"You're such a hokey sentimentalist."

"I've got to get back, Ann. I've been away from the office more than a week." He poured himself half a glass. "But I hope things work out for you."

"No way, then?"

"No way." He was thinking of Kathleen, of her voice over the telephone.

"Why not? I won't make demands this time. I've learned my lesson. Why not?"

"I don't know. I guess I've come to an age where I like younger women. You know that age men come to?"

"You're such a bullshitter," she said.

He nodded, lifted the glass to his lips, thinking of how narrow the escape had been in Cleveland.

"Do the young women you like have more fun than we did?"

"I suppose they have their problems, too," he said. He was only half-listening, his glass at his lips, thinking of her husband arriving in the middle of the night, of this morning's conversation with her. He took a swallow, gagged, then took two swallows more. He remembered waking at two that morning feeling sick. Suddenly he felt sick again, felt the sweat on his temple, and this time he knew why.

He set the glass down. "Good-bye, Ann. Good luck."

"Well, that's the *first* time you ever left a drink unfinished. Or a poor girl unfucked."

He was getting a glass of water at the kitchen sink when his wife entered the room.

"*You're* home early," she said, and something in her voice caused him to turn and look at her. She was wearing a house robe.

"Why are you in that? Are you sick?"

"No. I was sewing."

"Are the kids home?"

"Hal's here. He was out this way, so he stopped in."

Behind her now he saw a big man in shirtsleeves and loosened tie. Something in her voice, he thought — wondering what it was, and then he knew and waited for the anger to come.

"I was out this way," the man said, "so I stopped to see if the three of us could have dinner tonight. Sound good?"

He looked at the white drainboard beside the sink, waited for the anger. *Well, fuck it,* he thought then, when the anger did not come, *none of this matters.* He looked up, saw the yellow refrigerator and beside it was his wife in her house robe. She was looking back at him. "You two go ahead," he said. "I'm beat."

He was still waiting for the anger, but he knew it would not come, because he realized now that he had decided sometime yesterday or the day before that he did not want to battle any longer . . . "Go on," he said. "Enjoy good company," thinking that if in this world the way it was you couldn't find anyone to be true to you, or anyone to be true to, then nothing mattered. Not even hurting children.

Three weeks later he got his first letter from Kathleen. He lit a cigar before he read it.

Her letter began: "My dear, sweet boy. I'm glad you like Mexico. I . . ."

He . . .

GRACE PALEY

Friends

(FROM THE NEW YORKER)

TO PUT US at our ease, to quiet our hearts as she lay dying, our
dear friend Selena said, Life, after all, has not been an unrelieved
horror — you know, I *did* have many wonderful years with her.

She pointed to a child who leaned out of a portrait on the wall
— long brown hair, white pinafore, head and shoulders forward.

Eagerness, said Susan. Ann closed her eyes.

On the same wall three little girls were photographed in a school-
yard. They were in furious discussion; they were holding hands.
Right in the middle of the coffee table, framed, in autumn colors,
a handsome young woman of eighteen sat on an enormous
horse — aloof, disinterested, a rider. One night this young woman,
Selena's child, was found in a rooming house in a distant city, dead.
The police called. They said, Do you have a daughter named
Abby?

And with *him,* too, our friend Selena said. We had good times,
Max and I. You know that.

There were no photographs of *him.* He was married to another
woman and had a new, stalwart girl of about six, to whom no harm
would ever come, her mother believed.

Our dear Selena had gotten out of bed. Heavily but with a comic
dance, she soft-shoed to the bathroom, singing "Those were the
days, my friend . . ."

Later that evening, Ann, Susan, and I were enduring our five-
hour train ride home. After one hour of silence and one hour of
coffee and the sandwiches Selena had given us (she actually stood,
leaned her big soft excavated body against the kitchen table to
make those sandwiches), Ann said, Well, we'll never see *her* again.

Who says? Anyway, listen, said Susan. Think of it. Abby isn't the only kid who died. What about that great guy, remember Bill Dalrymple — he was a noncooperator or a deserter? And Bob Simon. They were killed in automobile accidents. Matthew, Jeannie, Mike. Remember Al Lurie — he was murdered on Sixth Street — and that little kid Brenda, who O.D.'d on your roof, Ann? The tendency, I suppose, is to forget. You people don't remember them.

What do you mean, "you people"? Ann asked. You're talking to *us*.

I began to apologize for not knowing them all. Most of them were older than my kids, I said.

Of course, the child Abby was exactly in my time of knowing and in all my places of paying attention — the park, the school, our street. But oh! It's true! Selena's Abby was not the only one of the beloved generation of our children murdered by cars, lost to war, to drugs, to madness.

Selena's main problem, Ann said — you know, she didn't tell the truth.

What?

A few hot human truthful words are powerful enough, Ann thinks, to steam all God's chemical mistakes and society's slimy lies out of her life. We all believe in that power, my friends and I, but sometimes . . . the heat.

Anyway, I always thought Selena had told us a lot. For instance, we knew she was an orphan. There were six, seven other children. She was the youngest. She was forty-two years old before someone informed her that her mother had *not* died in childbirthing her. It was some terrible sickness. And she had lived close to her mother's body — at her breast, in fact — until she was eight months old. Whew! said Selena. What a relief! I'd always felt I was the one who'd killed her.

Your family stinks, we told her. They really held you up for grief.

Oh, people, she said. Forget it. They did a lot of nice things for me, too. Me and Abby. Forget it. Who has the time?

That's what I mean, said Ann. Selena should have gone after them with an ax.

More information: Selena's two sisters brought her to a Home. They were ashamed that at sixteen and nineteen they could not take care of her. They kept hugging her. They were sure she'd cry. They took her to her room — not a room, a dormitory with about eight beds. This is your bed, Lena. This is your table for your things. This little drawer is for your toothbrush. All for me? she asked. No one else can use it? Only me. That's all? Artie can't come? Franky can't come? Right?

Believe me, Selena said, those were happy days at Home.

Facts, said Ann, just facts. Not necessarily the *truth*.

I don't think it's right to complain about the character of the dying or start hustling all their motives into the spotlight like that. Isn't it amazing enough, the bravery of that private inclusive intentional community?

It wouldn't help not to be brave, said Selena. You'll see.

She wanted to get back to bed. Susan moved to help her.

Thanks, our Selena said, leaning on another person for the first time in her entire life. The trouble is, when I stand, it hurts me here all down my back. Nothing they can do about it. All the chemotherapy. No more chemistry left in me to therapeut. Ha! Did you know before I came to New York and met you I used to work in that hospital? I was supervisor in gynecology. Nursing. They were my friends, the doctors. They weren't so snotty then. David Clark, big surgeon. He couldn't look at me last week. He kept saying, Lena . . . Lena . . . Like that. We were in North Africa the same year — '44, I think. I told him, Davy, I've been around a long enough time. I haven't missed too much. He knows it. But I didn't want to make him look at me. Ugh, my damn feet are a pain in the neck.

Recent research, said Susan, tells us that it's the neck that's a pain in the feet.

Always something new, said Selena, our dear friend.

On the way back to the bed, she stopped at her desk. There were about twenty snapshots scattered across it — the baby, the child, the young woman. Here, she said to me, take this one. It's a shot of Abby and your Richard in front of the school — third grade? What a day! The show those kids put on! What a bunch of kids! What's Richard doing now?

Oh, who knows? Horsing around someplace. Spain. These days, it's Spain. Who knows where he is? They're all the same.

Why did I say that? I knew exactly where he was. He writes. In fact, he found a broken phone and was able to call every day for a week — mostly to give orders to his brother but also to say, Are you O.K., Ma? How's your new boy friend, did he smile yet?

The kids, they're all the same, I said.

It was only politeness, I think, not to pour my boy's light, noisy face into that dark afternoon. Richard used to say in his early mean teens, You'd sell us down the river to keep Selena happy and innocent. It's true. Whenever Selena would say, I don't know, Abby has some peculiar friends, I'd answer for stupid comfort, You should see Richard's.

Still, he's in Spain, Selena said. At least you know that. It's probably interesting. He'll learn a lot. Richard is a wonderful boy, Faith. He acts like a wise guy but he's not. You know the night Abby died, when the police called me and told me? That was my first night's sleep in two years. I *knew* where she was.

Selena said this very matter-of-factly — just offering a few informative sentences.

But Ann, listening, said, Oh! — she called out to us all, Oh! — and began to sob. Her straightforwardness had become an arrow and gone right into her own heart.

Then a deep tear-drying breath: I want a picture, too, she said.

Yes. Yes, wait, I have one here someplace. Abby and Judy and that Spanish kid Victor. Where is it? Ah. Here!

Three nine-year-old children sat high on that long-armed sycamore in the park, dangling their legs on someone's patient head — smooth dark hair, parted in the middle. Was that head Kitty's?

Our dear friend laughed. Another great day, she said. Wasn't it? I remember you two sizing up the men. I *had* one at the time — I thought. Some joke. Here, take it. I have two copies. But you ought to get it enlarged. When this you see, remember me. Ha-ha. Well, girls — excuse me, I mean ladies — it's time for me to rest.

She took Susan's arm and continued that awful walk to her bed.

We didn't move. We had a long journey ahead of us and had expected a little more comforting before we set off.

No, she said. You'll only miss the express. I'm not in much pain. I've got lots of painkiller. See?

The tabletop was full of little bottles.

I just want to lie down and think of Abby.

It was true, the local could cost us an extra two hours at least. I looked at Ann. It had been hard for her to come at all. Still, we couldn't move. We stood there before Selena in a row. Three old friends. Selena pressed her lips together, ordered her eyes into cold distance.

I know that face. Once, years ago, when the children were children, it had been placed modestly in front of J. Hoffner, the principal of the elementary school.

He'd said, No! Without training you cannot tutor these kids. There are real problems. You have to know *how to teach.*

Our PTA had decided to offer some one-to-one tutorial help for the Spanish kids, who were stuck in crowded classrooms with exhausted teachers among little middle-class achievers. He had said, in a written communication to show seriousness and then in personal confrontation to *prove* seriousness, that he could not allow it. And the board of ed itself had said no. (All this no-ness was to lead to some terrible events in the schools and neighborhoods of our poor yes-requiring city.) But most of the women in our PTA were independent — by necessity and disposition. We were, in fact, the soft-speaking tough souls of anarchy.

I had Fridays off that year. At about 11 A.M. I'd bypass the principal's office and run up to the fourth floor. I'd take Robert Figueroa to the end of the hall, and we'd work away at storytelling for about twenty minutes. Then we would write the beautiful letters of the alphabet invented by smart foreigners long ago to fool time and distance.

That day, Selena and her stubborn face remained in the office for at least two hours. Finally, Mr. Hoffner, besieged, said that because she was a nurse, she would be allowed to help out by taking the littlest children to the modern difficult toilet. Some of them, he said, had just come from the barbarous hills beyond Maricao. Selena said O.K., she'd do that. In the toilet she taught the little girls which way to wipe, as she had taught her own little girl a couple of years earlier. At three o'clock she brought them home for cookies and milk. The children of that year ate cookies in her kitchen until the end of the sixth grade.

Now, what did we learn in that year of my Friday afternoons off? The following: Though the world cannot be changed by talking to one child at a time, it may at least be known.

Anyway, Selena placed into our eyes for long remembrance that useful stubborn face. She said, No. Listen to me, you people. Please. I don't have lots of time. What I want . . . I want to lie down and think about Abby. Nothing special. Just think about her, you know.

In the train Susan fell asleep immediately. She woke up from time to time, because the speed of the new wheels and the resistance of the old track gave us some terrible jolts. Once, she opened her eyes wide and said, You know, Ann's right. You don't get sick like that for nothing. I mean, she didn't even mention him.

Why should she? She hasn't even seen him, I said. Susan, you still have him-itis, the dread disease of females.

Yeah? And you don't? Anyway, he *was* around quite a bit. He was there every day, nearly, when the kid died.

Abby. I didn't like to hear "the kid." I wanted to say "Abby" the way I've said "Selena" — so those names can take thickness and strength and fall back into the world with their weight.

Abby, you know, was a wonderful child. She was in Richard's classes every class till high school. Goodhearted little girl from the beginning, noticeably kind — for a kid, I mean. Smart.

That's true, said Ann, very kind. She'd give away Selena's last shirt. Oh, yes, they were all wonderful little girls and wonderful little boys.

Chrissy *is* wonderful, Susan said.

She *is*, I said.

Middle kids aren't supposed to be, but she is. She put herself through college — I didn't have a cent — and now she has this fellowship. And, you know, she never did take any crap from boys. She's something.

Ann went swaying up the aisle to the bathroom. First she said, Oh, all of them — just wohunderful.

I loved Selena, Susan said, but she never talked to me enough. Maybe she talked to you women more, about things. Men.

Then Susan fell asleep.

Ann sat down opposite me. She looked straight into my eyes with a narrow squint. It often connotes accusation.

Be careful — you're wrecking your laugh lines, I said.

Screw you, she said. You're kidding around. Do you realize I don't know where Mickey is? You know, you've been lucky. You always have been. Since you were a little kid. Papa and Mama's darling.

As is usual in conversations, I said a couple of things out loud

and kept a few structural remarks for interior mulling and right-
eousness. I thought: She's never even met my folks. I thought:
What a rotten thing to say. Luck — isn't it something like an insult?

I said, Annie, I'm only forty-eight. There's lots of time for me to
be totally wrecked — if I live, I mean.

Then I tried to knock wood, but we were sitting in plush and
leaning on plastic. Wood! I shouted. Please, some wood! Anybody
here have a matchstick?

Oh, shut up, she said. Anyway, death doesn't count.

I tried to think of a couple of sorrows as irreversible as death.
But truthfully nothing in my life can compare to hers: a son, a boy
of fifteen, who disappears before your very eyes into a darkness or
a light behind his own, from which neither hugging nor hitting can
bring him. If you shout, Come back, come back, he won't come.
Mickey, Mickey, Mickey, we once screamed, as though he were
twenty miles away instead of right in front of us in a kitchen chair;
but he refused to return. And when he did, twelve hours later, he
left immediately for California.

Well, some bad things have happened in my life, I said.

What? You were born a woman? Is that it?

She was, of course, mocking me this time, referring to an old
discussion about feminism and Judaism. Actually, on the prism of
isms, both of those do have to be looked at together once in a
while.

Well, I said, my mother died a couple of years ago and I still feel
it. I think *Ma* sometimes and I lose my breath. I miss her. You
understand that. Your mother's seventy-six. You have to admit it's
nice still having her.

She's very sick, Ann said. Half the time she's out of it.

I decided not to describe my mother's death. I could have done
so and made Ann even more miserable. But I thought I'd save that
for her next attack on me. These constrictions of her spirit were
coming closer and closer together. Probably a great enmity was
about to be born.

Susan's eyes opened. The death or dying of someone near or
dear often makes people irritable, she stated. (She's been taking a
course in relationships *and* interrelationships.) The real name of
my seminar is Skills: Personal Friendship and Community. It's a
very good course despite your snide remarks.

While we talked, a number of cities passed us, going in the

opposite direction. I had tried to look at New London through the dusk of the windows. Now I was missing New Haven. The conductor explained, smiling: Lady, if the windows were clean, half of you'd be dead. The tracks are lined with sharpshooters.

Do you believe that? I hate people to talk that way.

He may be exaggerating, Susan said, but don't wash the window.

A man leaned across the aisle. Ladies, he said, I do believe it. According to what I hear of this part of the country, it don't seem unplausible.

Susan turned to see if he was worth engaging in political dialogue.

You've forgotten Selena already, Ann said. All of us have. Then you'll make this nice memorial service for her and everyone will stand up and say a few words and then we'll forget her again — for good. What'll you say at the memorial, Faith?

It's not right to talk like that. She's not dead yet, Annie.

Yes, she is, said Ann.

We discovered the next day that give or take an hour or two, Ann had been correct. It was a combination — David Clark, surgeon, said — of being sick unto real death and having a tabletop full of little bottles.

Now, why are you taking all those hormones? Susan had asked Selena a couple of years earlier. They were visiting New Orleans. It was Mardi Gras.

Oh, they're mostly vitamins, Selena said. Besides, I want to be young and beautiful. She made a joking pirouette.

Susan said, That's absolutely ridiculous.

But Susan's seven or eight years younger than Selena. What did she know? Because: People *do* want to be young and beautiful. When they meet in the street, male or female, if they're getting older they look at each other's faces a little ashamed. It's clear they want to say, Excuse me, I didn't mean to draw attention to mortality and gravity all at once. I didn't want to remind you, my dear friend, of our coming eviction, first from liveliness, then from life. To which, most of the time, the friend's eyes will courteously reply, My dear, it's nothing at all. I hardly noticed.

Luckily, I learned recently how to get out of that deep well of melancholy. Anyone can do it. You grab at roots of the littlest future, sometimes just stubs of conversation. Though some believe you miss a great deal of depth by not sinking down down down.

Susan, I asked, you still seeing Ed Flores?

Went back to his wife.

Lucky she didn't kill you, said Ann. I'd never fool around with a Spanish guy. They all have tough ladies back in the barrio.

No, said Susan, she's unusual. I met her at a meeting. We had an amazing talk. Luisa is a very fine woman. She's one of the office-worker organizers I told you about. She only needs him two more years, she says. Because the kids — they're girls — need to be watched a little in their neighborhood. The neighborhood is definitely not good. He's a good father but not such a great husband.

I'd call that a word to the wise.

Well, you know me — I don't want a husband. I like a male person around. I hate to do without. Anyway, listen to this. She, Luisa, whispers in my ear the other day, she whispers, Suzie, in two years you still want him, I promise you, you got him. Really, I may still want him then. He's only about forty-five now. Still got a lot of spunk. I'll have my degree in two years. Chrissy will be out of the house.

Two years! In two years we'll all be dead, said Ann.

I know she didn't mean all of us. She meant Mickey. That boy of hers would surely be killed in one of the drugstores or whore-houses of Chicago, New Orleans, San Francisco. I'm in a big beautiful city, he said when he called last month. Makes New York look like a garbage tank.

Mickey! Where?

Ha-ha, he said and hung up.

Soon he'd be picked up for vagrancy, dealing, small thievery, or simply screaming dirty words at night under a citizen's window. Then Ann would fly to the town or not fly to the town to disentangle him, depending on a confluence of financial reality and psychiatric advice.

How *is* Mickey? Selena had said. In fact, that was her first sentence when we came, solemn and embarrassed, into her sunny front room that was full of the light and shadow of windy court-yard trees. We said, each in her own way, How are you feeling, Selena? She said, O.K., first things first. Let's talk about important things. How's Richard? How's Tonto? How's John? How's Chrissy? How's Judy? How's Mickey?

I don't want to talk about Mickey, said Ann.

Oh, let's talk about him, talk about him, Selena said, taking Ann's hand. Let's all think before it's too late. How did it start? Oh, for God's sake talk about him.

Susan and I were smart enough to keep our mouths shut.

Nobody knows, nobody knows anything. Why? Where? Everybody has an idea, theories, and writes articles. Nobody knows.

Ann said this sternly. She didn't whine. She wouldn't lean too far into Selena's softness, but listening to Selena speak Mickey's name, she could sit in her chair more easily. I watched. It was interesting. Ann breathed deeply in and out the way we've learned in our Thursday-night yoga class. She was able to rest her body a little bit.

We were riding the rails of the trough called Park Avenue-in-the-Bronx. Susan had turned from us to talk to the man across the aisle. She was explaining that the war in Vietnam was not yet over and would not be, as far as she was concerned, until we repaired the dikes we'd bombed and paid for some of the hopeless ecological damage. He didn't see it that way. Fifty thousand American lives, our own boys — we'd paid, he said. He asked us if we agreed with Susan. Every word, we said.

You don't look like hippies. He laughed. Then his face changed. As the resident face-reader, I decided he was thinking: Adventure. He may have hit a mother lode of late counterculture in three opinionated left-wing ladies. That was the nice part of his face. The other part was the sly out-of-town-husband-in-New-York look.

I'd like to see you again, he said to Susan.

Oh? Well, come to dinner day after tomorrow. Only two of my kids will be home. You ought to have at least one decent meal in New York.

Kids? His face thought it over. Thanks. Sure, he said. I'll come.

Ann muttered, She's impossible. She did it again.

Oh, Susan's O.K., I said. She's just right in there. Isn't that good? This is a long ride, said Ann.

Then we were in the darkness that precedes Grand Central.

We're irritable, Susan explained to her new pal. We're angry with our friend Selena for dying. The reason is, we want her to be present when we're dying. We all require a mother or mother-surrogate to fix our pillows on that final occasion, and we were counting on her to be that person.

I know just what you mean, he said. You'd like to have someone around. A little fuss, maybe.

Something like that. Right, Faith?

It always takes me a minute to slide under the style of her public-address system. I agreed. Yes.

The train stopped hard, in a grinding agony of opposing technologies.

Right. Wrong. Who cares? Ann said. She didn't have to die. She really wrecked everything.

Oh, Annie, I said.

Shut up, will you? Both of you, said Ann, nearly breaking our knees as she jammed past us and out of the train.

Then Susan, like a New York hostess, began to tell that man all our private troubles — the mistake of the World Trade Center, Westway, the decay of the South Bronx, the rage in Williamsburg. She rose with him on the escalator, gabbing into evening friendship and a happy night.

At home Anthony, my youngest son, said, Hello, you just missed Richard. He's in Paris now. He had to call collect.

Collect? From Paris?

He saw my sad face and made one of the herb teas used by his peer group to calm their overwrought natures. He does want to improve my pretty good health and spirits. His friends have a book that says a person should, if properly nutritioned, live forever. He wants me to give it a try. He also believes that the human race, its brains and good looks, will end in his time.

At about eleven-thirty he went out to live the pleasures of his eighteen-year-old nighttime life.

At 3 A.M. he found me washing the floors and making little apartment repairs.

More tea, Mom? he asked. He sat down to keep me company. O.K., Faith. I know you feel terrible. But how come Selena never realized about Abby?

Anthony, what the hell do I realize about you?

Come on, you had to be blind. I was just a little kid, and *I* saw. Honest to God, Ma.

Listen, Tonto. Basically Abby was O.K. She was. You don't know yet what their times can do to a person.

Here she goes with her goody-goodies — everything is so groovy wonderful far-out terrific. Next thing, you'll say people are darling and the world is *so* nice and round that Union Carbide will never blow it up.

I have never said anything as hopeful as that. And why to all our knowledge of that sad day did Tonto at 3 A.M. have to add the fact of the world?

The next night Max called from North Carolina. How's Selena? I'm flying up, he said. I have one early-morning appointment. Then I'm canceling everything.

At 7 A.M. Annie called. I had barely brushed my morning teeth. It was hard, she said. The whole damn thing. I don't mean Selena. All of us. In the train. None of you seemed real to me.

Real? Reality, huh? Listen, how about coming over for breakfast — I don't have to get going until after nine? I have this neat sourdough rye?

No, she said. Oh Christ, no. No!

I remember Ann's eyes and the hat she wore the day we first looked at each other. Our babies had just stepped howling out of the sandbox on their new walking legs. We picked them up. Over their sandy heads we smiled. I think a bond was sealed then, at least as useful as the vow we'd all sworn with husbands to whom we're no longer married. Hindsight, usually looked down upon, is probably as valuable as foresight, since it does include a few facts.

Meanwhile, Anthony's world — poor, dense, defenseless thing — rolls round and round. Living and dying are fastened to its surface and stuffed into its softer parts.

He was right to call my attention to its suffering and danger. He was right to harass my responsible nature. But I was right to invent for my friends and our children a report on these private deaths and the condition of our lifelong attachments.

JAMES ROBISON

Home

(FROM THE NEW YORKER)

PETER FLAHERTY was wrapping clear tape around a hinge on his eyeglasses. His hand was sure and the mend was nearly invisible. He sat on a piano bench in front of a scarred Baldwin that was angled at the corner of two walls of books.

"You know, Peter, I'm not certain that I can endure this much longer," his wife, Lily, said. She sat in a straight chair across the study from Peter. A gray cashmere coat was draped, cape style, on her shoulders, and she wore kid gloves and a bell-shaped soft wool hat. From a glass ashtray in her lap a filterless cigarette burned. Her legs were crossed. Her short white hair curled from under the edge of her hat, around button earrings.

"Might we freeze to death?" she asked Peter. "That's not a possibility, is it?"

"No," Peter said after a moment. It was the third day of an early February blizzard in Eastbury, Massachusetts. The Flaherty home had been without heat since the night before.

"When again did the gas-company man say he'd come?"

Peter didn't answer. He was using a razor blade on his spool of tape — slicing strips to patch his glasses.

"Peter?"

"Ten or fifteen minutes more," Peter said.

Lily picked up her cigarette carefully between two gloved fingers and took a deep drag. "Peter, would you care for tea now?" she said.

"Very much, dear." He looked up, squinting, and smiled absently at her. He was fifty-three, a small man, mostly bald, with fine red hair growing down from his temples. He had an elegantly pointed nose. "Unless the kitchen is too cold for you."

"Oh, no," Lily said. "Not at all."

Peter pulled the muffler that was wound at his throat a little tighter. "Tea, then," he said.

When Lily came back with a tray, Peter was wearing his repaired glasses and straddling the bench. Sheet music was unfolded in front of him, and he tapped the nail of his index finger on the bench wood as he studied the music.

The man from the gas company was big-shouldered and short-legged. His coat and pants were of quilted rayon stuffed with down. He stripped off a leather mitten and banged his boots in the foyer.

"Hard weather for us skinheads," he said. He patted Peter on top of the head and then he squeezed his own nose six or seven times. Peter smiled uneasily at the foot mat.

"You must be dying in here," the man said. "What is this, steam heat?"

"Yes, steam."

"It's happening all over the hill," the man said. "The whole east campus. Christ, I been blowin' around since five this morning and I'll still be out at midnight. I just been to your neighbor the dentist's. 'Pay me in fillings,' I told him." The gas man unsnapped one of the flap pockets on his coat and took out a thumb-size cigar. "I wish he'd agreed. He had a converted coal furnace that took me an hour to get chugging. Cost him enough to fix up my whole mouth. I got a head full of holes."

Peter led the gas man through to the study, which gave onto the kitchen and the basement steps. Lily stood up as they passed her chair, hugging herself. "I'm *Mrs.* Flaherty," she said. "So good to see you."

"I bet it is," the gas man said.

In a few minutes, Peter was back. "Are we saved?" Lily said.

"The pilot hadn't gone out," Peter said. "Something is clogged and needs to be tapped or drained. He said an hour perhaps."

"Feel the tip of my nose," Lily said. "You should put on a cap. You're losing heat from the top of your head."

"Don't concern yourself." Peter went to the side window of the study, which showed, through iced tree branches, the green copper roofs and spires of the university where he was chairman of the philosophy department and where Lily worked in the office of the dean.

"At least let me fetch your beret," Lily said.

"Please. Don't concern yourself," Peter said.

"What is burning?" she said. "Did you put something on the stove?"

"Our fellow downstairs has a cigar," Peter said. "Perhaps it's that."

Lily said, "Heavens." She sat down in the straight chair again.

Peter said, "Will you pay him? I want to go walking."

"If he'll take a check."

"I'll go see," Peter said.

He was back quickly. He got down into a cross-legged position at Lily's feet. "I was told to stay," he said, "for some reason."

"That's for the best. You shouldn't go out in this."

"In what?" Peter said. The storm windows groaned in the high wind and he said, "Oh."

"Did you know," he said, "that Delia keeps a diary?" Delia was their adopted daughter. They'd had her, officially, for six months, though she'd been living in the Flaherty home as a foster child off and on for nearly two years. When the heat had gone, they'd sent her to a neighbor's for the duration.

"A diary?" Lily said. She pulled hard on her cigarette and leaned toward her husband. "In fact?"

"Yes, and she has for a while. Since before we got her."

"She must be very clever to keep it hidden," Lily said. "I clean her room from drawer to dustbin."

"She keeps it at school, in her locker. She keeps *them* at school, I mean. There are two full books by now and she's starting on a third. She told me at the skating pond. She said that she 'writes things down.' "

Lily went to the piano and made herself tea from the kettle. She lit a fresh cigarette and came back to her chair. "Peter, you didn't pry?"

"No, no," he said. "We were having our chocolate after skating and she volunteered that she writes things down every day."

Lily said, "Yes?"

"Yes, and I said, 'That sounds like a diary.' "

"That was all right to say, I think."

"And she told me she'd started it at the orphanage because her roommate, Stacey Shear, had a diary. Delia's kept hers up through the foster homes and so forth, and she's still keeping it up."

Lily blew smoke and looked worried. "Good for her. I think a diary is a good thing to do, don't you, Peter?"

"Put the thermostat at ninety," the gas man yelled from the foot of the basement steps.

Peter used his hands to start to uncross one leg, and Lily said, "I'll do it. Hold my tea."

Peter was at the piano again, this time playing a little and humming to himself. He wore a red pullover and wine-colored corduroys. The front door sounded and he heard voices, and, after a minute, a thirteen-year-old girl ran into the room and did a long slide, on her knees, across the rug toward a white cat that was asleep in front of the radiator. The cat spurted away, but the girl twisted and, flopping on her side, caught the animal by its back legs. "Hey, hey, Bruce," the girl said to the cat. She gathered the cat into her arms as she sat up. "Bruce the big boy," she said.

She was slender, with a straight spine and long legs. Her hair was honey-blonde, going darker in bands, and she had a small, perfect face. She wore large, round glasses with thick lenses and thick, orange-tinted frames.

"Now you're home," Peter said to her.

The girl held the cat in front of her. "Hi, Dad," she said.

Lily came in, nose and cheeks burned pink with cold. She was still wearing her wool hat. "The Bonhams were so nice," she said. "I don't believe Delia wanted to leave."

"I did *so*," Delia said.

"Well, the cat was pining away here," Peter said. "He knew something was missing."

"He *was* acting queerly, wasn't he?" Lily said, seriously.

"Brucey-Bruce," Delia said, and let the cat go. She stood up and folded her arms and crossed one leg over the other. "It's hot in here," she said. She shifted the weight on her socked feet and whirled about.

"It feels good to Peter and me," Lily said. "And the entire house isn't back to normal yet. The upstairs is quite cold, and the kitchen . . ."

"How was school?" Peter said.

"It rots," Delia said.

"When the kitchen is a bit warmer, I'll need someone to help me with dinner and fudge."

"Well, Lily," Delia said, "can I go to my room?"

Lily looked at Peter, who was resting his chin in his palm. "If she can stand it," he said to Lily. To Delia he said, "You might want to think about a sweater."

"I know," the girl said, sprinting for the staircase. In the upstairs hall, under an oil landscape, was a tiny mahogany table serving as a stand for a heavy black phone with a long cord. Delia picked up the phone and carried it into her room. She pulled open drawers and put on a couple of sweaters and two more pairs of socks. From a linen chest she grabbed three folded blankets and fanned them across her high bed. She knocked some stuffed toys aside, getting into the bed, and hefted the phone onto her chest. She began to dial.

"She wants her dinner upstairs," Lily said, coming into the dining room.

Peter buried the long, two-pronged fork he was holding in the roast and set his carving knife down on the meat platter. He lowered himself into a Queen Anne chair that was at the head of the dining-room table.

"*I* don't mind," Lily said, "but what do we do?" She took a package of Lucky Strikes from the pocket of the apron she wore. The apron was decorated with fleurs-de-lis and was tied over her nicest wool skirt.

Peter pinched the bridge of his nose. "What was her reasoning?" he said.

"Well, she's tied up on the phone. She's very much enjoying being on the phone, and she asked politely to be served upstairs." Lily shook out a cigarette. She used a silver table lighter on some candles and then on her cigarette.

Peter went into the study and switched on a lamp by the davenport. He sat for a moment, and then turned to the end table and picked up a telephone identical to the one in the upstairs hall. He lifted the receiver and spoke quickly into it. "Dee, I'm on the line."

"What is this?" a young male voice said.

"Dad?" Delia's voice said. It rang unnaturally loud.

"It's rude of me to horn in, I know," Peter said. "I'm so sorry, Delia, but may I speak with you for a moment?"

"It's my dad," Delia said to the young man. "Do you mind?"

Peter waited, but there were no further sounds from the young

man's end of the line. Peter said, "Lily's prepared to bring you
your dinner, Dee, if you're sure this is a very important call. I must
tell you, I can't imagine what could be so important that you'd ask
to be waited on."

"You're miffed," Delia said, borrowing one of Lily's words.

"I'm not miffed. I'm playing fair and asking you to do the same.
If this is school work or something that can't be postponed . . . It's
none of my business and it's your decision . . ."

"Rob?" Delia said.

"Yeah," the young man said.

"Call you back. Be right down, Dad," she said, and she hung up
the phone.

Delia used her bread knife to put jam on a roll and then licked the
flat blade. She jiggled her right foot and chewed as she talked.
"Rob's so lucky. You know. But he talks, talks, talks. I can't make
him stop. No one can. He *thinks* he's unlucky because his father
had a stroke and died. But that was long ago and he doesn't even
remember. You know. It was, like, when he was seven. But he's so
lonely, so all he wants to do is talk to me. And I don't even have
the heart to say, 'Just shut up, Rob. At least you've got a *mother* and
a pool in the summer in your back yard.'"

Lily was clearing plates. The dining room was dark, except for
the candles and some light from the kitchen. Lily was smiling.

"So you couldn't cut him off?" Peter said.

"Right, and so I just asked Mom to bring me dinner. Which *was*
delicious, Mom."

Lily smiled.

"So," Delia said, "if he calls back or something, I'm not at home."

"All right," Peter said. "Will you join us for tea?"

"Umm," Delia said, thinking. "What flavor?"

"Peppermint or rose-hip," Lily said. She stood, with a china
gravy boat in one hand and a salad bowl in the other, and she
watched Delia.

"Hey, it's Bruce," Delia said. She squirmed sideways on her seat
and ducked under the table and came up holding the white cat.

"Tea?" Peter said. "Or what, Delia?"

Peter sat on the piano bench, gently twisting the wedding band on
his finger. His glasses were raised, resting on his forehead. Lily was

in the straight chair with her neck bent forward, her head tipped, her face down, asleep. The cat was sleeping as well, by Lily's pointed shoes. Peter rolled the ring on his finger and looked straight ahead.

"What are you doing?" Delia said. She came into the study wearing a yellow cotton nightgown. She wore frayed tennis sneakers for slippers.

Peter settled his glasses to look at her. "Lily's sawing logs," he said.

"At eight-thirty?" Delia yawned, opening her small mouth wide and pushing her shoulders back. "Do you want to watch television with me?" she said.

The two of them went into a room on the other side of the entrance foyer. It was papered in stripes and there were several deep chairs and a wooden rocker arranged before a tall fireplace, in front of which Peter had set an old black-and-white television on a chair seat.

Delia turned the set on, tapped a sneaker until the picture bloomed, and then twisted the rabbit-ear antenna violently until a police show was in focus. Peter sat in the rocker. Delia lay on her right hip, directly under the screen.

"I can, you know, tell when it's getting close to nine o'clock," she said.

"How is that?" Peter said.

"Well, because at nine o'clock you had to be either in recreation room with a staff person or in your own room, and then you had an hour before bed. So. Nearly all my life I knew when nine o'clock was coming. Even at the foster homes like the Taglios' and the Cuffs', I could tell." She pulled the nightgown high off her legs and scratched the back of an oblong thigh and then covered up again. "I could just tell, you know."

"Was that something you hated?"

"Just a minute," she said. She watched the screen for a while and then arched her back and looked at Peter upside down. "What?"

"Did you hate to see nine o'clock come?"

"I don't know. No. I can just tell when it's coming. Except for Christmas and Midnight Mass and a few times when I got to stay up." She watched the screen, and then said, "When you were a priest, did you say Midnight Mass?"

"Yes," Peter said.

"Did you get presents for Christmas? When you were a priest?"

"Not exactly. Not like this year, for example. When Lily gave me the blazer and you gave me the aftershave stuff."

"I know," Delia said. "Me, too. I got different presents this year."

They watched a commercial for cat food. Delia said, "Where *is* Bruce?" She scrambled up and headed for the study, calling the cat.

Peter was at the kitchen table, having coffee. The early-morning sun and the snow made the room very bright. Peter wore a suit with a small check, a bow tie with a small dot, and his black beret. Lily was at the long kitchen counter, cutting banana pieces into Delia's cereal bowl. She was dressed up, too, in dark wool clothes, and she had a silk scarf at her neck. "What else did she say?" Lily asked.

"It was just a conversation," Peter said. "She was feeling chatty, I guess. She told me about her gym class and the girls on her old floor and about going to sleep at ten every night."

"You didn't have to urge her on, did you?"

"No, Lily," Peter said. He adjusted his glasses. "It was just a conversation."

Lily put some slices of wheat bread into the toaster. "Why did she ask about your church days?" Lily said, and then turned from the counter and went, "Sh-h-h."

Delia was coming down the steps, making a lot of noise in boots. She thumped into the kitchen and went straight for Lily and kissed her on the cheek. "Morning, Mother. Morning, Father," she said. She slid into a chair on the other side of Peter. She was in a cable-stitch sweater that was much too large for her, and dungarees. Her hair was not brushed and there was a sheet print, like a scar, running a little way down her cheek. She wiped her glasses on the tablecloth. "Something smells good," she said.

Peter said, "The toast? The coffee?"

"Yeah, but something else." She was looking at Lily. "Something like flowers."

"It could only be my skin moisturizer," Lily said. "A gift from you."

"I thought so," Delia said. "Lily, I need a larger bra size. The ones I have are binding."

"We'll see to that later," Lily said. She gave Peter a quick smile, picked up the cigarette that was balanced on the edge of the counter, and puffed hurriedly before seeing to the toast.

Delia gulped her orange juice. "I'm so thirsty," she said. "Dad, Rob said he'd like to meet you."

"Whatever for?" Peter said.

"He wants to talk to people, I think. He's so sad." Delia licked her upper lip. "I told him you were — you used to be — a priest."

"I'm not anymore," Peter said. "Tell him that."

The offices for the philosophy department were in a wooden, three-story house on a mostly residential street that bordered the east campus. Peter's was on the top floor at the back of the building. From the room's single window Peter could see a section of the East Green, slate rooftops, and the bell tower of the Unitarian church. Lily had hung pictures and put some plants around, and there were two short, full bookcases with glass doors, but the furniture in the small room seemed sparse. Peter sat in a castered chair that he'd backed into a corner. His feet, still in galoshes with buckles, were propped up on an inverted metal waste can. He read a magazine.

There was a trembling at the office door, a faint disturbance on the surface of the wood. Peter said, "Come in, Lily."

The door opened and Lily's head appeared. "You're not with anyone?" she said.

"You don't have to knock, ever," Peter said. "Will you come in?"

Lily kept her coat on and her yarn gloves. She was shaking slightly. "Shall I fetch us some coffee?" she said.

Peter looked at his watch. "We're going to lunch in half an hour, aren't we?"

"I don't know, Peter," she said. She began to cry. For a short time, she stood in the center of Peter's office, biting the first knuckle of her right hand while tears ran over her face. Then she used the back of her glove to blot her eyes and smiled at her husband, who smiled back.

"I'll get us some coffee," Peter said.

When he stepped back into the office, carrying two foam cups, Lily was sitting on his desk, lighting a cigarette.

"Thank you kindly," she said to him.

"Aren't they missing you at the dean's office?" Peter said. "What's going on?"

"Well, Father, we have a problem with one of our flock," Lily said.

Peter sat down and cocked his galoshes on the waste can. "Don't be giddy, Lily," he said.

"When I got to work this morning, Mr. Cromwell called from Delia's school. She was absent without leave, he told me, and he was making a routine check, he said, and he said he suspected it had to do with the freezing spell."

"You told him it did."

"Yes. I lied for her and I went home then, because I couldn't reach you, because you had your class. And Delia and Robby whatever-his-name-is — with the teeth? They were on the couch in the study. When I came in, they were in a panic: buttoning shirts and fastening belts." Lily sipped coffee. "I left and came here without saying a word."

"Did you really?" Peter said, and grinned.

"Well, I stood in the foyer for a minute considering," Lily said. "I did call out to them, before I left, that they were to go back to school immediately."

Peter stood up and went to the desk and sat on it, beside Lily. He put his arm over her shoulder. "You handled that well," he said. "School's the important thing."

"They can't take her back, can they?" Lily said. "No matter how we bungle things. Even if we make horrible mistakes? They can't do that, can they?"

Peter was smiling and holding his wife. "No," he said. "She's ours now."

LEON ROOKE

Mama Tuddi Done Over

(FROM DESCANT)

YOU HAVE HEARD about Mama Tuddi. If you got eyes and ears or a brain in your head then you know that Mama Tuddi is a big celebrity, that she have her own show The Mama Tuddi Show on TV and radio where she sell soft drinks by the bottle and the crate, especially on TV where everyone know what she look like and how much she enjoy her work. On this day I am talking about, Mama Tuddi arrives at the doorstep of the house where Reno Brown have lived his life and said good-bye to it and there she pause and take a deep breath and think a final time about what it is she have to do. It is not right, that is what she think, but it is too late now to talk anybody out of it. Her sponsor have told her it is the right thing to do, she owe it to the public, that it is maybe in bad taste, a little on the obscene side, but it is good public relations all the same.

So she knocks on the door and waits. Somebody will come soon for sure because everybody must know it is Mama Tuddi at the door and she don't have all day, she got more important business elsewhere and she only have a little time to devote to the public service the Brown family and relatives and friends have ask for and apparently expect.

She is thirsty, Mama Tuddi is, waiting in the sun, and she wish she have swallowed down a soda pop or two before she start out on this job. Also it happen this afternoon that her teeth ache. She have time for this nonsense, but no, she have no time for her health, no one care if she ever find a minute to go to Dr. Pome and get her bad tooth knocked out. That is what Mama Tuddi think as she fidget at the door, how selfish everybody is. So this put her in a worse mood and she stand there beating on the door, grumbling to herself that it ain't right, all the time impatient for someone to come roll out the red carpet, give her the official greeting she expect.

But they don't come, it is like everybody inside — not just Reno — is dead.

Finally she say to herself *I be damned if I'm going to wait out here all day in the boiling sunshine,* and kick open the door and stride right in.

"Yoo-hoo!" she call, "Mama Tuddi have come!" But the room is empty, not a sound anywhere.

But she know she have the right address. Looking around, the first thing Mama Tuddi notice is that all the mirrors are turn to the walls, all the pictures on the walls and tables have a black cloth draped over them, all except the face of Jesus who is looking at her. She don't mind the look, it seem to her natural that Jesus is going to look over anyone who walk into the room and that he especially will want to take a long hard look at someone famous as Mama Tuddi. She even give him a little nod and a smile. It occur to her for her next show that maybe she can have a big picture of Jesus at the Last Supper and the sponsor can hire a man to paint in a picture of Double Ola in front of all the apostles at the table. That way, it seem to her, her work is done before she speak a single word. So the look of Jesus give pleasure to Mama Tuddi, it seem to her he have the same idea.

However, the black cloth hanging everywhere and the mirrors turn to the wall, that is another story. They send a shiver up Mama Tuddi's spine. It seem to her a tacky thing to do, what you'd expect from ignorant folks but not from anyone in the Mama Tuddi Fan Club. Not from anyone who like The Mama Tuddi Show. She hate it, that is what Mama Tuddi think to herself. She have a good mind to sail on out the door and never come back.

Still no one come and Mama Tuddi don't know what to do with herself.

It remind her of her early days in the Green Room when she was waiting to go on after the weatherman, a long time ago before she make a name for herself.

"Tooth, be quiet," she say to her tooth, but it go right on aching.

Mama Tuddi opens up her purse and takes out the aspirin bottle and she pick out a pill and put the top back on and goes to one of the mirrors on the wall which she take off the hook and turn around so she can see herself. Then she puts the mirror back up on the hook again. She hold her face real close so she can see inside her mouth. It is hard to tell which tooth hurt, so she does the best she can. She push the tablet down beside the most guilty-looking tooth, then she close her mouth to see what kind of bump the tablet make in her jaw.

"It look all right," she say to herself, "nobody notice a thing."

"I be good as new," she say, "soon as that pill dissolve."

Already she can feel the medicine flowing round her gum. It is on the sour side, but Mama Tuddi don't mind pills, she think it taste pretty good. She puts the aspirin bottle back in her purse and gets out her lipstick tube. Again she hold her face up close to the mirror, she scrunch up her nose and shape her mouth and paint on the red paint and licks her lips and backs up to look at herself. By now she is feeling pretty good, Reno Brown is the last thing on her mind. Her only regret is that in the rush to get here, the Double Ola man pushing and pulling her every which way she turn, she have not had time to black out her two front teeth which is how she always look on The Mama Tuddi Show and which is what her public have come to expect. She always feel much better when she know she have done all she can to please her public, when she spare not one iota of herself. It is proof to her mind of the kind of world we are living in and how bad things have got that the station people and the Double Ola man have not give her time to black out her front teeth, a Mama Tuddi trademark known far and wide. Be just as bad, she thinks, if she show up at the studio without her special Double Ola shoes or if she forget to put on her hat or get out her checkbook when she talk about the money a family save when they buy Double Ola by the case.

A smell was bothering Mama Tuddi, something in the air. She had got a whiff of it first coming in but now it was heavier, and if Mama Tuddi had a spray she would use it right here, she thought, her house or not. She liked a house where folks were not stingy on the spray, and she was beginning to have some second thoughts about these Brown folks and whether they were the right kind of people, the kind to appreciate a personal appearance from Mama Tuddi and know how much she was putting herself out for them, never mind their ignorance of how to run a clean, happy home.

Things was dusted, she could say that much for them.

And arranged nice, if you was to shove this studio couch back against the wall.

Mama Tuddi pulled the black cloth off a pair of bronze baby shoes resting atop a pile of maple leaves also in bronze. She poked her finger inside one and brought out a shriveled-up spider, which she flung with a gasp to the floor. Beside the shoes, under another cloth, was a picture of a boy with a flat nose and curls of tight black hair growing low over his forehead. He was spruced up smart in a Ben Blue short pants suit and to Mama Tuddi's mind he would have been a real heartbreaker but for his smart-alecky expression, which his mama ought to have smacked off his face before she let him step up to the camera. He had broomstick legs too and his socks was bunched up at his heels, what part hadn't been eat up by his shoes.

She wondered if this was the Reno Brown who had loved her so much.

She heard a giggle behind her and turned in time to see the same face jumped out of the picture frame to poke itself out at her from the doorway across the room. Mama Tuddi waved the picture at him, about to say "Well, your nose have improve!" but before she could get it out the boy's teeth flashed white and he have vaporized.

A minute later the whole back part of the house seem to blow up and people, men mostly, men in blue seersucker suits and men in nice sports jackets all yellows and blues, in stripes and in pinwheels like targets to be shooting at, were springing at Mama Tuddi from every side, their faces plastered with the biggest grins, running around her like a pack of dogs let loose suddenly from whatever was fencing them in, shouting out their welcomes to her, reaching for and shaking and then letting another of these creatures take her hand. Before Mama Tuddi know it she have been shove back against the wall, her breath all sucked out of her from so many faces to say "How you do?" to the way a lady would, with the dignity an entertainer of her standing have to maintain — but still they are coming, more men folks thrusting out their hands, beaming down on her, saying what an honor it is, while the few women who crowd in, as dowdy uninteresting females as Mama Tuddi have ever seen together under one roof, mill around the edge casting glances back and forth and smiling quick polite smiles when Mama Tuddi let her eyes light on them. "Now listen here," Mama

Tuddi find herself saying once the gentlemen have done pawing at her, "what is that smell I smell?" — which someone say is cabbage, just potluck, nothing special, only something the women folk have been cooking up for after the service. Mama Tuddi is about to inform them how a can of good spray can cut through a smell like sand stifling a fire when it strikes her that a man is standing over by the mirror she have turn around, just standing there with his mouth dropped open and a look of horror on his face. So Mama Tuddi forgets about the spray, the man with the open mouth have reminded her and she say, "Listen here, how come all these mirrors are turn and all the wall pictures except Jesus covered with this black cheesecloth double-folded over them like that, I never see the like of it to this day?" Everyone's look is blank followed by surprise, then they begin at once to jabber their response, saying "Sho-nuff, Mama Tuddi, you pulling a laig, don't you know what they is thataway faw!" or some such variation, while all through this time the struck-dumb man is staring from the mirror to Mama Tuddi as if he think his very life or hers is in peril.

"No, I do not," Mama Tuddi say, keeping her eyes off him for she is beginning to think maybe she have done something wrong judging by the few gasps she see, wishing these boisterous people would take her on in to see the dead boy so that she can get on back to the station for her evening broadcast and her TV Mama Tuddi Show which have an audience growing by leaps and bounds and which she have her duty to.

"Mama Tuddi," they say, "why Mama Tuddi how you do be a cutup, what a rascal, here pretending you don't know why they is thataway faw!" — poking each other in the ribs and swarming around her like they have lost the little mind they have. The man with the open mouth have put the mirror face-away back on the wall, and now he is bearing down on her, his face set like he is face to face with death. "Why, don't you know, Mama Tuddi, whoever see hisself in the glass a time like this don't you know the devil take his soul, Mama Tuddi, we surprised at you!"

"Hogwash," Mama Tuddi say once she find her voice. Someone is pushing behind Mama Tuddi and a little child is down between her legs trying to crawl through after another one on the floor. She want to kick both of them and tell the man behind her to get his hands off her, but before she can someone else have take her arm while another person shove in front and swing open the door so it seem to her finally that they are ready to get on with what they have ask her here for; in some way-off part of the house she can hear a tin-can piano making feeble notes of reverence. Mama Tuddi have a rush of mixed thought, not wanting to go in to see the laid-out body of Reno Brown she presume, not wanting to look on anybody dead, not even if he have love her like a mother, which is what the program manager and the Double Ola man have told her when they say she have to come here for the public service of the thing. Mama Tuddi's hands and feet in fact have gone cold, her legs are stiff and in fact she would not be moving at all but for the elbow pushing her in the back. Her throat have gone dry too for want of a soda pop or even a drink of water now that she think of it. She lick her tongue over the two front teeth which ought to been blacked out because that is the Mama Tuddi trademark, though she glad these people recognize her all the same. She glad at least she have remembered to wrap the foxtail around her neck, never that she have yet gone a place without it. She crane her head round to catch sight of Reno Brown or to see where the music is coming from and what kind of creature must be propped up on the stool playing it so bad with his bony fingers that have no weight on the keys. She can see nothing but the sway of shoulders and backs and ugly-women faces turning to study her as she enter through the held-open door and move slowly down the aisle that is being cleared for her. Now some wretch can't control himself and he catch at her arm. Without looking Mama Tuddi smack out at his hand, she struggle to go on, but he have arms like an octopus, he catch her again. Turn out it is the struck-dumb man, now climbing over someone to root his worried face up close to Mama Tuddi, his eyes lit up like orange peel, tugging at her to get a firm hold and spitting his saliva into her eardrum. He is screaming something at Mama Tuddi, she can't tell what because other folks are hugging the aisle wanting Mama Tuddi to touch them, but Mama Tuddi know it is not good news he bring. People in her walk of life, people above the crowd, then have to put up with so much from the unruly mob, from crazy people in the mob, that sometime Mama Tuddi rue the day she ever start The Mama Tuddi Show, she wish she back at home in her rocking chair maybe dipping a little snuff, talking quiet with neighbors, seeing the best in people. *It wear her out all this public-service stuff,* that is what she think as she try her best to sweep on down the aisle, *it plumb tire her out and ain't worth the effort no how.*

"*Pray!*" the man is screeching. "*Pray.* Mama Tuddi, for you have look in the mirror and Satan himself will run amuck inside your soul!"

"Shoo!" Mama Tuddi say. "Shoo!" — fanning her arms like she have walk into a nest of bees. One of the men beside her says, "Shut your mouth, Rufus, what you want to be upsetting Mama Tuddi faw?" and another one push the man called Rufus back while a third person whispers into Mama Tuddi's ear, "That's Rufus, he got the devil on his brain, don't you mind Rufus, he just a stupid superstitious type." Mama Tuddi does not know what to say to this, she hardly know what to think. Clearly the man have religion, he wearing a nice tie and is no lazy driftabout, all the same Mama Tuddi think they be doing everyone a favor they lock this Rufus creature up. Still, she don't mind, a person in her position have to learn to take the icing with the cake, or they sink back under the mud. The pain in Mama Tuddi's bad tooth have vanish thanks to the aspirin tablet, her hands and feet are no longer cold and her limbs can function normal now, she have conquered her vexation and is as a matter of fact beginning to be glad she stoop to come, she glad to do these folks a favor, their good friendly feelings and the love they have for Mama Tuddi remind her of the time she first set foot on a naked stage, with hot lights around her and the little red light on the camera she have to look at for the zoom. It remind her of the joy she feel the first time she sit down with a Double Ola on the table and her front teeth blacked in good, and the wonderful way she have scored a big hit with the public, who have tune in not even knowing in them days who she was. She got no time now, she tell herself, to be bothering about no trashy Rufus, she in no mood for ignorant superstition, folks will stay ignorant no matter how many times you tell them what's what.

It never cross Mama Tuddi's mind that a crowd this large will be on hand for the service of Reno Brown, she guess it is news of her presence which have bring them out, maybe a hundred or so with not near enough chairs to go around, the windowsills full too and everyone squirming for a place to put their knees. She give these onlookers her best smile, her Double Ola smile, which keep the station phone ringing every time she do her show. These folks are all smiling too, whispering, "Dare she is, dare Mama Tuddi, lookadare, son, dare she is, our own Mama Tuddi!"

Mama Tuddi keep her poise, she have a rule never to let cheers go to her head: she walk with the same regal bearing she have learn by heart at the poise clinic she have attended for one day, her head kind of thrown back, her chin stiff and erect, not walking like her legs made of rubber, like some tarty women do. Mama Tuddi know she have sex appeal, if you got it flaunt it, that is what Mama Tuddi say. Over in a side room Mama Tuddi spots where the music coming from, a piano with a dark oak frame, and playing it is the most skinny woman Mama Tuddi have ever seen this side of a pickling jar, though to give the music lady credit she have on a stunning hat in black layers like a wedding cake, which Mama Tuddi very much admire. But she got her fox collar and her jewels, Mama Tuddi ain't worried none. Down near the front row Mama Tuddi see a man standing, pointing out his arm at her, shouting "Lookadare! What I tell you? Mama Tuddi is got tooths, I tole you she have tooths!" and the man next to him dig in his pocket and it look to Mama Tuddi like he pass the first man a dollar bill.

It is at this point that Mama Tuddi observe at the front a tiny coffin stretched over two sawhorses there. "Is that Reno?" she ask, and a figure near her nod in a somber voice, "Dat's old Reno, bless the poor chile's heart," and Mama Tuddi can't take her eyes off the coffin, which thank the Lord have a lid on it.

Suddenly her escorts touch her elbows, they do a little dip, and a second later to Mama Tuddi's astonishment they have fade away.

Suddenly the room fill up with total quiet.

Mama Tuddi licks her lips, she have a mild case of nerves, wondering if now is the time to do her speech in praise of the dead boy. That is all she have been told she have to do, maybe cry a little as she read off the credits for Reno Brown and tell how he is bound for heaven on the glory train.

Mama Tuddi feel a tug on her skirt but she have her poise and won't look down.

The music lady play three quiet notes on a new song.

Suddenly a low groan begin in the room:

Ummmmmmmmmmmmm . . .

It stretch out on the same key and commence to grow:

UmmmmmmmmmmmmmmMMMMMMMMMMMMMMMM . . .

It hold on for the longest time, then it advance up a note and swell, it keep on swelling, sending a shiver up Mama Tuddi's spine.

MMMMMMMMMMMMMMMMMMMMMMMMMMMMM . . .
The floor under Mama Tuddi shake, she got goose bumps on
her arm: it the most beautiful singing Mama Tuddi have ever
heard, she think for a second God himself is lifting her out of her
shoes. *MMMMMMMMMMMMMMMMM* . . . Then the sound just
explode out of these folk's popping jaws, it wham into Mama
Tuddi most to knock her down, in the split instant before it sweep
on past her like a mighty wave:

> *Bringing in the sheep*
> *Bringing in the sheep*
> *We be here rejoicing*
> *Bringing in the sheep*

Mama Tuddi unhook her fox, she close her mouth and sit down.
  Amen, murmur a soft voice next to Mama Tuddi. *Amen. De Lawd
is bringing in de sheep, de Lawd is taking Reno home.* Then the woman
whose voice it is begin to wail, she begin to wail and shriek, and
Mama Tuddi hold her mouth tight, she look straight ahead over
the coffin lid, correctly figuring in her head that the brokenhearted
woman beside her must be the bereft mother of the child. They
have give Mama Tuddi the seat of honor but although she think
the world of motherhood Mama Tuddi wish they give her another
chair.
  A few other women join Reno's mother in the tribute to her son,
their moans kind of snake around the room, but the grief does not
get very far. It seem the outburst have been premature, for one
thing Mama Tuddi overhear a remark that the preacher have not
yet come, he held up in traffic on the freeway. This cause Mama
Tuddi some concern since it have always seem to her that preaching ain't now what it was in her day, that their heads are too big,
they ought to take their lesson from her and be on time, that is
what she think.
  A heavy hand fall on Mama Tuddi's knee, and although she give
a little jump of surprise it does not go away. She look at the man's
big hand and slowly turn her head meaning to give the hand's
owner a cut of her tongue, it rile her the familiar ways certain men
have who are so full of themselves they think they can get away
with anything. But she see the man in question have a friendly
smile, he have a certain charm to him. "I'se LeRoy," he say teas-

ing-like, fixing on her a half-wink. "You was Reno's favorite to the end." He have nice black hair all straighten-out and smooth on his head, he a handsome man, Mama Tuddi can see, with winning ways, and she hear a small voice inside her head saying *Mama Tuddi you watch out for him.*

For some reason Mama Tuddi gets it in her mind he is Reno Brown's daddy. "Pardon me," she say, "I assume you are the departed boy's father?"

LeRoy just grin. "No'm," he say, "I'se the boy friend."

"The boy friend," Mama Tuddi repeat, not knowing what else she can say.

"Of Mrs. Brown," LeRoy explain, leaning forward to poke his head in the direction of Reno's mother on her other side. And Reno's mother come out of her crying spell long enough to look Mama Tuddi in the eye and present her hand, saying, "So please you could come, me and LeRoy was worried on Reno's account, this mean all the world to him."

"He was a dear little boy, I'm sure," Mama Tuddi say.

"Old Reno," observe LeRoy, "they break the mold when they make him."

Scrunched up in the seat on the other side of Mrs. Brown, with his hands covering his face and looking out at Mama Tuddi between split fingers, is a small boy. Mrs. Brown smack at his hands, saying, "This here be Reno's twin brother Lasvegas, he the man in the family now." The boy give Mama Tuddi a grin and once more hide his face. Then he wrench around and whisper something in Mrs. Brown's ear.

"He say to tell you he's older," Mrs. Brown informs Mama Tuddi. "He older by three minutes, to tell the truth. You knock me over with a feather when the doctor tells me another one knocking at the gate."

Although Mama Tuddi nod and think to say she never have a child herself and proud of it, her mind is elsewhere. LeRoy's hand have crept up her thigh, it continue to rest there, and Mama Tuddi have her hands full trying to decide what to do with it. He certainly a forward type, she think, and it strange to her that Mrs. Brown don't appear to mind. He a flashy dresser, this LeRoy, he is too young too, and plainly Mrs. Brown have snatched the cradle to get him. Mama Tuddi puzzle to herself how Mrs. Brown have manage to bring this off. She is not an overly smart-looking woman, sorry to say, with not much meat on her bones and none of the savoir-faire a man appreciate. She is over the hill, Mama Tuddi would say. And in the wardrobe category she is running a pretty bad race. The black mourning dress is all right, but it have a three-inch hem of fancy lace, which have no place at a funeral. Not to mention black net stockings. At the moment Mrs. Brown have one leg crossed over her knee and she is swinging it pretty good. Also she have something flashing there. Mama Tuddi reach down to scratch her own ankle, wondering what it is. Turn out it is a gold anklet Mrs. Brown have on, with a big moon disc which have inscribed on it the word *mine.*

Pretty tacky stuff, Mama Tuddi theorize.

"LeRoy give it to me," the woman now say, leaning close. "He a cutup from the word *go.*" Then she hook up her dress and show Mama Tuddi her other ankle, which have the word *his.*

Although Mama Tuddi is interested and she nod, she have her mind elsewhere. LeRoy have lifted his hand from her leg and now either a fly have landed on her neck or that Romeo have put his hand there. She hope it is his hand. Mama Tuddi have a fear of little fly feet walking all over her neck, getting his dirt and disease everywhere. Now the little feet are walking around, it tickle and tingle until it drive Mama Tuddi almost to distraction. She clamp her knees together and hold her body straight, wondering where it going to walk next. She hears the little boy whine, "Mama, I wants a drink," and "Mama, I wants to go to the bafroom" and "Mama, I'se hongry," and Mama Tuddi wish Mrs. Brown would tell him to hush up. The piano lady starts up another tune, and another woman pass in front of Mama Tuddi, saying back to someone that she think she best go stir up the runnin beans. Mama Tuddi wish all these people would hush up so she could give her attention to the thing on her neck. She no longer think it is LeRoy's hand on her neck because he have both his hands down in front of him looking for "The Old Rugged Cross," which is the song the piano lady is playing. Although the fly have now stopped walking it have not gone away, and Mama Tuddi think standing still is worse than moving because she cannot bear the thought of what the fly might do next. She think to herself that if they kept this place clean they wouldn't have so many flies around here, and it seem to her that was the least they could do since they knew she was coming. Reno Brown may have love her like everybody say, he may have believe the sun and moon rose and set on Mama Tuddi, but there is a limit to what she will put up with, whether from him or somebody else.

The fact is Mama Tuddi have sunk so deep in thought she have failed to observe that the audience is now getting up and filing by the box which hold the remains of Reno Brown, the lid lifted and held up by a red broomstick, the folks who have already had their last look at the boy now crowding around Mrs. Brown to tell her what their last look at Reno have meant to them, telling her that he look so peaceful you would swear he was only sleeping, telling her they never seen him looking so good, he the prettiest child they ever sat eyes on, he is safe at rest in the arms of the Lord — hugging her and patting her hands and sort of being swept along until they come to Mama Tuddi, where they bend their knees and take a close look at her foxtail with the head of the fox still on it and at her two front teeth, which they know now is real, and at her dyed-orange hair and even at her shiny black purse, which have the word *Double Ola* in big letters on the flap — then to slouch on by and return to their seats or their standing place and join in on another verse of "The Old Rugged Cross," which is the cross Jesus and Reno and everyone in this room have to wear until they exchange it for a crown.

The song goes on and everybody files by to pay Reno their last respects. Then the music lady half-lifts from her stool, she fix a look on Mama Tuddi, who is slapping at her neck, she lets her eyes go bong-bong and roll around in her head, then she shrug to show her confusion and sit down again to play "The Old Rugged Cross" all over again in the hope that Mama Tuddi will stand up and do what's right, that being the same hope others have, which is why they are beginning to whisper and shuffle about and wonder aloud why Mama Tuddi will not pay her last respects to Reno, wondering if maybe she have something up her sleeve.

Mrs. Brown in the meantime know nothing of this, she is up by the coffin sobbing and moaning, crying for her dead child, now and then letting fly a big shriek which go through the room like a fast curve ball which send others down on their knees weaving and moaning and shrieking back. Mrs. Brown is telling Reno that Mama Tuddi have come, that old LeRoy have come, that Lasvegas is standing by, that Reno be happy to learn all his close friends and loved ones are here paying their last respects, that the preacher will be here to say a few kind words soon as his car gets off the freeway jam, that they are all praying for his soul and never forget him till their dying day. She is looking up through the ceiling and flailing her arms to get her message through to heaven, reminding the Lord to look after His humble servant Reno, her poor beloved son Reno, to place a chair for Reno close-by to God's own chair, to watch over his growth the way a mama would because she know in her heart Reno would have make something of himself if he had the chance, a nice bright boy like Reno who didn't have a hurtful bone in his body, a believer who commit his heart to Jesus on the very day he was born, who turn a helping hand to his mama anytime she ask and who love his daddy and treat him with respect even if his daddy was a sorry worthless no-count snake who never walk God's road a day in his life, that worm who also gone to his reward praise be to God, taken away by the Grim Reaper and none too soon if God want to know the sorry truth of the case. His daddy burning in hell where he ought to be, Mrs. Brown cry out, but her precious lamb Reno he will walk right out of the valley of death into the stretched-out arms of Jesus, GLORY GLORY, to ride around heaven in the golden chariot God have carved out of ebony bone for all the innocent children of the world, "GLORY GLORY!" she say, "LIVE AGAIN!"

"*Thine the glory!*" come the chorus behind Mrs. Brown; "*Hallelujah Amen!*" the chorus shout, now drumming their feet on the floor in a quick rhythm that makes the whole building shake, that cause the sawhorses on which Reno's coffin repose to quiver and bounce as if old Reno himself want to climb out and show these folks how grateful he is, to show them the power of God's love, that His power have no end, that God Himself have climbed down on Jacob's ladder from heaven to show He approve, to show the poor people's welfare is ever close to his heart. Mrs. Brown now have a grip on the coffin, her head momentarily disappear as she stoop down to give her boy one final kiss on his sorrowful closed eyes, now emerging with tears streaming down her ravaged face, her body twisting about, her mouth opening and closing though silence have the day, her feet lifting and lifting as if she have set them down in a bed of burning coal, while her friends in the audience look on with half-envy, with their hearts caught up in their throats, for it is plain to them that Mrs. Brown is now in the rapture of God's strong embrace, that God Himself have taken hold of her tongue, that He have come to claim this hour for His own. And they is proud in fact that this have happen, for in no other way can it be explain why this innocent boy have been plucked away in his tender years, poor Reno who have never done no harm to no one, as nice a boy as you ever hope to see, with always a kind word for the old and the lame and the sick, who give his last dime to any stranger ask it of him. This is why they have come in the first place, it is why they are thumping their feet so hard against this wood, and clapping their hands, and twisting about themselves, and aiding Mrs. Brown with their shouts as best they can — all to urge God on, to argue Him into showing His face or showing His presence with a sign like He have give to Moses with the burning bush, or to them with their tents pitched by the Red Sea. If you love God He will not let you down, that is what they think and know and believe, and they have not doubted He will show up today because God have plucked out of a mother's arms an innocent child, and even God would not do this without some good excuse. He have a reason for it just as He have a reason for the sun and moon and for resting on the seventh day. God's power is awesome, it is both a terrible and beautiful thing, it take the breath away, all the same He will not take an innocent child less He have to, and it is clear this time He have been force to for how else can He remind them they are a sorry bunch and evil live in their hearts, the eyes they see with are blind as wheelbone, the mouth they talk with is bitter as a snake's tooth, their soul is slick as marble, they come to Truth slow as a wheelbarrow. They are sinners all. Only by plucking away poor Reno have God been able to make them face up to the error of their ways, only by this pilgrimage through a mother's grief can He guide their footsteps after His into the everlasting Hereafter. "Gone!" Mrs. Brown cry out. "My baby gone, done gone, first he here and then he gone, out of my arms he stolen like a thief in the night, my poor baby gone on High, gone on ahead to Gloryland!"

Throughout this Mama Tuddi sits high in her seat, her backbone straight as a barber pole, even so her breath quickening as if hurried along by the drumming of feet. Except for sheer willpower and reminding herself who she is her own feet would be beating against the floor. But she have her dignity to uphold so she hold herself steady and oppose the tide that sweep the rabble along. She blink her eyes and hold on tight to her fox, fearing for her personal mortal safety as this untidy crowd invoke the Lord and exalt this doomed child Reno above any station she expect he might have truly achieve. It do no harm she guess but still to her mind it is a tacky show, it hardly the sort of performance to go down well on TV. All the same it have a point, she kind of like it to tell the truth, it have the hocus-pocus that keep her on the edge of her seat, some of it have hit like something from a slingshot, she too have felt a stirring in her breast. Now she see Mrs. Brown pulling at the red stick which hold up the coffin lid, yanking it away with fire in her eyes, slamming the lid down with a loud crack while she shout over Mama Tuddi's head and everyone else's loud enough to cause anyone walking by in the street to stop and think: *"Gone! Gone! My sweet baby gone!"* — and she sink down in a puddle, which LeRoy leap up and bring back to its seat.

"Mama Tuddi," someone calls, "Mama Tuddi, for shame!"

And Mama Tuddi cannot believe her ears, it have been ages since she hear anyone speak her name in vain. She rise in her seat and glare around, she search these faces looking at her with accusation and reproof, these looks that say *Mama Tuddi you have let us down.* Mama Tuddi is in a dither close to outrage as she look perplexed at a man standing in the rear who jab out his finger and keep on jabbing it her way, yelling "She in league with the Devil, pray sinners pray!" and it is the man Mama Tuddi recognize as the man who have said Mama Tuddi in her vanity and pride have looked at herself in the mirror, thereby prompting Satan to enter her skin, the man who have first accused her with his stinging eyes. LeRoy have Mrs. Brown back in her seat now and Mama Tuddi swing on her, she wanting Mrs. Brown to tell this man he is a fool, that Reno have wanted Mama Tuddi to come here because he love her so, which Mama Tuddi have done as a public service on her own time with no question of money in the bank, she wants Mrs. Brown to tell this buffoon that very thing.

But Mrs. Brown shrink away, it looks like she is angry too, that she too believe Mama Tuddi have not done right by her departed child. Mama Tuddi switch to LeRoy, she gets his ear and whispers to him "What went wrong?" but Leroy only give her a quick sad smile, he duck his head toward the close coffin and that is all he do before he go back to tending Mrs. Brown, now a weeping ghost of her former self. Suddenly it come to Mama Tuddi what she have done wrong, it hit her like a flash; she have been too high and mighty in the eyes of these people to give a last look at the remains of Reno Brown. She have remain in her seat fussing about flies and thinking of the pleasures of the flesh while others have paid tributes to his name.

Something scrunch up in the brain of Mama Tuddi, it form a tight ball and pulse there to gather strength, it seem to get down on its hind legs awaiting the perfect moment to fly forth — that is what everyone feel watching Mama Tuddi, and a sigh of relief goes up, you can see it and feel it rising dense as a cloud, the tension leave these folks for they can see now that Mama Tuddi mean to make matters right, she have only been jiving them, she have something up her sleeve sure as night be night and day be day and dream be something in between. They see Mama Tuddi square her shoulders back, they see the way her tongue is licking over her front teeth like she intend to black them out, they see the blood swelling in her face. They hold their breath as she stride around Reno's coffin, as she position herself behind it on her spread-out legs, her both hands gripping the foxtail and pulling at each end like she mean to tear it in two. They fall silent, waiting in a hush for what it is Mama Tuddi will say to them.

Indeed Mama Tuddi have at last got into the spirit of things. She glaring out at these folks, she is letting them see she have poise and dignity and above all she have nerve. She letting them know she don't like it that they have even for a minute give up on her. She stroke the coffin slowly as she stare them down, she sweeps her body over the lid and both her hands now move over it like she is washing this body of Reno Brown, bathing Reno with her own hands for this holy trip. LeRoy comes out of his spell, he the first one to sense what Mama Tuddi require, and he leap up to retrieve the stick which have propped up the lid, he is all business as he pass it to Mama Tuddi who reward him with a stern nod of her head.

Mama Tuddi props up the lid though she don't yet look down. She is looking out into this sea of faces, compelling them to admit the personal wrong they have done to a celebrity of her importance. Now she lick her lips, she take a breath way down so folks know that when she speak she is someone to be listen to. The cords thicken in her neck, she let out a big groan sweeping up both her arms. "*Now let me see,*" thunders Mama Tuddi's TV voice — "*Let me see this heah Reno Brown!*" Her eyes rake on past everyone, they roll over the ceiling, then they drop and settle peacefully on Reno Brown.

"Praise the Lawd," someone murmur nearby. "Praise the Lawd."

And the spirit pass around, it multiplies as Mama Tuddi study the face of Reno Brown, her own face softening as she study his tender remains. Mama Tuddi is in fact quite a bit surprised that Reno is as he seem: so young, so composed, yet so small, so tiny, so shrunken almost to nothing in the Ben Blue suit which lie flat on his bones. For a second she let her eyes dart over the space in that box, space which to her seem horrible, more than a person can understand or cope with and which she hates to believe — a terrible thing, that is what Mama Tuddi sees. It is like doom stretching all around, defeating not just this shriveled child; not something simply lying in wait for Mama Tuddi and everyone else sharing this globe, but just bigger, bigger, so big one almost want to hang the head, condemn God, cuss Him out, say "It ain't right, God, this little space You let us have, how can we live it well when death loom so large?" But Mama Tuddi falter only for a second, no one in fact realize she falters at all; quite the other story, for in fact everyone is amazed. Mama Tuddi bends right down, her orange hair descend inside the coffin with Reno Brown. Then she straighten up and suddenly both are there, Mama Tuddi with her arms around Reno, Reno with his head stiff against her breast.

In that position she look down on him, she stroke his hair. Her voice when she speak is quiet as a lamppost at first dark, it have the soft lick of a single flame under glass. *"This heah be Reno Brown,"* she intone.*"This heah be Reno Brown who adore his mama and his poppa and who love LeRoy and all you folks. He dead now but Mama Tuddi say he not dead, he live forever in the Book and in The Mama Tuddi Show. I now rename this child, I rename him Calvary, for Mama Tuddi can do what she please and it please me to name him that. Now I say adios to Reno Brown renamed Calvary from this moment on. I say to you that this boy Calvary alias Reno have withstood the birth, he have withstood the pain, he have stood off the infidels and let his light shine wherever he go. Now he gone like his mama say. She right insofar as she know but she don't know yet Mama Tuddi going to speed him safe and sound on his way."*

That is all Mama Tuddi say. She grip the boy's shoulders firm in each hand. It seem a marvel to everyone that Reno's head don't fall back but indeed it stay there flat and indeed it seem to some that Reno lifts his head to meet Mama Tuddi as she come down to put a kiss on his mouth.

"Glory!" some folks cry, *"now he riding fast!"*

"Lickety-split! Look out Lawd, here he come!"

Mama Tuddi complete that kiss pretty soon, she give a smart look all around and stand a minute patting her foot. It seem she still have more to do. She suck in her breath through her nose, she unwrap her fox fur and stretch it out full-length over Reno. Then she give it one last look good-bye and close the lid.

The man in the back row who have accuse Mama Tuddi can only shake his head and try to drop down out of sight. Everybody else too stunned with happiness to do anything but sit and look. It a long minute before they collect themselves and give Mama Tuddi her earned applause. Then you can see them exchanging smiled-at remarks, saying as how Mama Tuddi have sure speed him up to heaven with her kiss — laughing at the thought of old Reno — old Calvary — streaking from star to star like a fox. "From now on," one of them suggest, "I reckon it will be the swish of his tail making them blink." "If he don't make it to heaven," LeRoy tell Mrs. Brown, "at least we know he have made it that far."

After that it seem the people have enough and they breaks up, though milling around, still waiting for the preacher to come. For good as Mama Tuddi have done — and she have done more than they bargain for — it take the preacher to make Reno's passage complete. Folks pass on to the kitchen to get their food, they pass on through and eat in the yard, after first seeing to it that Mama Tuddi have started in on hers. She is the guest of honor and they don't eat nothing Mama Tuddi haven't tasted of first. She eats the ham biscuits and she eats the corn, she eats the mashed potatoes and pokes at the succotash. She eats the cornbread and the yams and she have a bite or two of the greens. She pass up for some reason, maybe not seeing them or because her plate is limber and won't hold no more, the runnin beans. Everybody else have no choice but to pass them up too, which riles somewhat the woman who have cooked them up. But she is a forgiving sort and is the first to let Mama Tuddi know she don't hold no grudge.

It is out in the yard by the honeysuckle vines that Mama Tuddi learn the story of Reno Brown and what have happen to him; there too that she learn what LeRoy have done when the boy's daddy out of spite and meanness thought to put the killing stick to him. It is hard telling some of this to Mama Tuddi because much as they regret it and hope the misfortune here will end, the plain truth of it is Reno's death have a bearing on her. So they mostly leave that

part out, that part about Reno looking in the mirror at the burying
for his daddy that took place. His daddy had been whupped fair in
a knife fight with LeRoy, which nobody could blame LeRoy for
doing since it was a case of doing it or having it done to him. Reno's
daddy was no good, the wonder of it was it hadn't been done to
him long before. He like his drink that man did and whenever he
had it he lit up real good and nobody could do a thing with him,
he as soon light into a person as look at him. Usually who he lit into
was Reno or Lasvegas or their mama because she wouldn't give in,
she'd stand between him and them daring that drunk fool to raise
his hand to her own flesh and blood. She had any sense she would
of run but she never did. So he'd pour it on, or try to, even if he
couldn't stand up. You never saw a man so keen on beating the
daylights out of what was closest to him. Everybody have seen the
licks that poor woman receive fighting him off her boys. Nor did
they blame her for taking up with LeRoy. LeRoy was young and
high of blood but he was dependable where it count. He wasn't
about to let nobody walk over him. Or over those what were dear
to him. Mrs. Brown was older but she know her own mind and
LeRoy make it plain that he like a woman who is mature in her
views. And she have a warm way with him, she know how to please
a man who return her love. That is all she was looking for, that and
a man who is soft with her boys. She don't mind taking a stick to
them herself when they do something low-down and deserve it,
but she don't like it when her husband just takes up a stick to them
for no good reason.

So yes she is with LeRoy one night trying to have a good time
and forget for a minute her bad homelife when her husband catch
up with her. He calls that woman names no one here will repeat,
for no need to offend Mama Tuddi with name-calling she no doubt
have heard herself, being a woman who have got around and not
one who hide her head under a stone. He calls her names and
starts beating up on her and on Reno who it happens is tagging
along. He pulls out a knife he have obviously brought with him
intending to do bodily harm and he start swinging it around.

LeRoy is not going to stand for that. He lays into him and somebody throws him a tool just to even it up. Her husband don't even
have the excuse of drinking this time, he's just mean. He just want
to carve on someone, it don't matter who. LeRoy he don't mean for
it to happen most likely, he just want the man to come to his senses

and stop but he don't so after LeRoy take a nick or two on the wrist
and have that blade switching over his throat when he is down,
after that he gets down to business, throwing Brown off. They
tumble in the grass, they roll in the bushes, folks looking on hold
their breath — in a minute it's LeRoy who crawl out. He's looking
for Mrs. Brown, who is standing over under a shed hiding Reno
under her dress so he can't see, and LeRoy get them and take them
on home. I guess he stayed on after that.

Some folks claim the law ought to be called but anyone with eyes
could see it happened too fast. LeRoy was scratched up bad, he
must of lost a gallon of blood. Brown he was dead, nothing anybody could do to change that. He got what was coming to him,
what he been asking for. The truth is everybody breathes a little
easier around here with him gone. Nobody like him. Everybody
know he worse than dirt. We glad to be rid of him.

Anyway, it ain't right that a man, bad as he is, be left to rot so we
have a notion to give him a decent turn in the ground. We hold
the service right here, after all she is his wife. We try to think of
something good to say about him. We hedge a little on his virtues
is what I mean. Some of the women say he was a right good-looking
man, for he was that. And sometimes he would work, though naturally he throw it all away. No need grieving, that's just how some
folks are. He was one of them: plain no good.

He stupid, that what the trouble was.

So that part they tell Mama Tuddi and glad to get it off their chest.
The part that more directly concern Reno is the part they attempt
to skate around. How he raise the black cloth which he knew better
than to touch and which he had been told a dozen times to keep
away from. Reno was a good boy but nobody ever deny he have a
hard head. Stubborn as the day is long. A service for the dead no
time to be primping, he told that time and time again. Still he look.
He in one of his know-everything jackass moods and he do it anyway. He took sick pretty soon after. Nothing anybody can do, he
have done it to himself. He hung on for five days, wasting away,
wasting down to skin and bones. No use to call in a doctor but they
call in one for lack of any better idea and the doctor all he can do
is throw up his hands. He bring LeRoy and Lasvegas and Mrs.
Brown into the kitchen and he says, "I throw up my hands." He
say this boy have been looking into mirrors, and the family have to

agree. "All I can do," the doctor say, "is give him something to stop
his foaming at the mouth. If the devil have walked in you will be
seeing a lot of that." Mrs. Brown cry, what other relief she have?
Lasvegas cry, LeRoy cry too I guess. Mrs. Brown blame herself,
thinking she have not parade the danger enough across Reno's
brain. That don't do no good. LeRoy blame the husband, he gets
to feeling low just when he was bouncing back from what he have
to do to him. LeRoy ain't killed nobody before. Mrs. Brown she
comforts him, LeRoy he comforts her. Lasvegas he a little short
when the brains passed out, he don't much seem to know what is
going on. He just a nice fella, he do the best he can. LeRoy and
Mrs. Brown they get their heads together, they agree they doing
nobody no good, so they figure out what they can do to help Reno
pass the time in his final days. They pools their money and come
up with enough to buy Reno a little twelve-inch TV set. That is
how Mama Tuddi come into the picture. Reno never have no TV
of his own to watch before. Still nothing cheer him up, he don't
care a hoot about no wagon train or shootumup cops nor none of
that soapy doctor stuff.

Then one night Lasvegas have turn in and LeRoy and Mrs.
Brown are drinking tea in the kitchen when they hear a shriek
from Reno. They run in fearing he is dying on the spot, but what
they see is Reno rolling on the floor, giggling and wheezing himself
blue in the face, getting up to point at Mama Tuddi on the screen
then rolling on the floor again. Old solemn-faced Reno who is on
his sickbed, at death's door, yet they have never seen him having
so much fun before.

"I going to marry her," Reno say. "She going to be my bride.
What her name?"

"Why shore," Mrs. Brown answer him. "You know her! That's
Mama Tuddi. Everybody know Mama Tuddi."

Reno drag himself up to the tiny screen, he get close enough to
look Mama Tuddi in the eyes and trace out her face with his finger
on the glass. "She don't have no tooths," he say, "that woman have
no tooths," and he laughs hard and kicks his thin legs into the air
with a loud whoop that wake Lasvegas in a yonder room.

"You never seen Mama Tuddi before?" his mother ask. "Land
sakes alive, Mama Tuddi is a household name."

"No tooths," Reno repeat, and he clutch his sides laughing all
the more.

"Yes, she is," LeRoy say, "she got tooths all right, they just blacked out because that her trademark."

"No she ain't. If she had 'um I could see 'um, you trickin' me."

"You watch," his mother say, "we prove it to you."

Mama Tuddi is talking about her sponsor Double Ola, a bottle in her hand with the other hand pointing to it while she tell them how good it is. The camera come in full-face on her, she opens her mouth wide and recline her head and put the bottle between her lips. The liquid go chug-chug in the narrow bottle neck, Mama Tuddi hold it there a long time, her eyes growing bigger with every swallow she take. They count fifteen swallows and Mama Tuddi bring the bottle down, she say "AHHHHHHHHHHHHH!" and with the backside of her hand wipe the spittle from her mouth. Then she tilt the bottle back between her lips, she swallow fifteen times more and then she say "AHHHHHHHHHHHHH!" and hold the bottle straight out in her hand and study it awhile, her head shaking as if she cannot believe her luck. Then she hold her head way back and hold the bottle upside down, the liquid go chug-chug down the neck, and when she have finish the last of it Mama Tuddi again cries "AHHHHHHHHHHHHHHH!", smacking her lips and rubbing her belly and standing with her shaking head and winking eyes so that everybody watching The Mama Tuddi Show will know that Mama Tuddi love Double Ola and they will too the first chance they have to go out and get some.

"Now look here," Reno's mother say.

For right there the camera come in on Mama Tuddi's mouth alone — wide open, smiling, inviting anyone who want to have a look — and Reno lets out a shout, "SEE! SEE! I TOLE YOU, SHE GOT NO TOOTHS," Mrs. Brown and LeRoy at the same time screaming, "SEE! SEE! SHE HAVE!", Lasvegas also yelling from his part of the house for them to hush their mouths, he sleepin' — while in the meantime it seem the camera have gone right on through Mama Tuddi's mouth to come out on the other side where it turn so that Mama Tuddi's hindside can be seen as she throw her fox fur over her shoulder and maybe pin a small hat on her head and pick up her Double Ola shopping bag, on her way out now to get some more.

The screen fade to black and that is all of Mama Tuddi for this hour.

"I loves Mama Tuddi," Reno say. "I going to marry her."

There is no other way around it either, that boy have fallen head over heels. He keep the TV set running 128 hours straight, he will let no one turn off the thing for fear he miss a minute of her show. Even when later in the week he can't hardly walk or crawl or see his own hand in front of him he have somehow drag himself in front of the box and laugh for joy as he trace out her picture on the screen.

"I saving up my money," Reno say. "Her hand gone be mine one day." Then he die.

Mama Tuddi, hearing this tale told, is sure it is the saddest tale she have heard since her own daddy's mule have run away with him and broken three legs. "Hush up now," she say to Mrs. Brown, "you have my heart clanging and twisting like someone have taken a meat cleaver to it. You have me wanting to go back in there and lift the lid and give that sweet boy these very shoes I have on, my best walking pair. I wants to take off these jewels from my neck and string them around his."

"They nice jewels," Reno's mother agree. A sorrowful look reclaim her face, and she add: "He was a sweet thing. No one ever take his place."

They with some others are now sitting out in the yard, enjoying a leisurely chat while the debris — white paper plates and Dixie Cups — is being cleaned away. Plates and cups blow about the yard and dogs chase after them, pouncing with their front legs to lick at them.

Everybody getting a little drowsy after this fine feed. From time to time a family will step up to shake Mama Tuddi's hand and give Mrs. Brown a good hug, to say what they have to say before heading on home.

LeRoy is over by the rose bushes kicking a tin can with Lasvegas who now seem a kind of dreamy child.

"I hopes you don't mind him," Mrs. Brown confide, meaning LeRoy. "His hand on your leg, he don't mean a thing, it just his way of showing he like you."

"I hardly notice," Mama Tuddi reply. Her heart have been moved today but now the juice have gone out of her and she is beginning to wonder how she is ever going to get out of here.

"Well, maybe not, but I see lots of women slap his face. First month I know LeRoy he walk around with my handprint on his face six or seven times a day. I say to him 'Listen LeRoy if you see something you like if you like it enough it is worth waiting for.' Finally he ask me if I see anything I like, and it was his saying that that baked the cake. It don't pay to argue with LeRoy."

Mama Tuddi have a watch on a dog's wagging rear end. She feel somehow she is slowing down, getting tired — "Losing my zip," that is what go through her mind. She feel a mite woozy in the sun and come close to asking if there is a place she can use for lying down. But her doubts save her in time. One person is already here lying down and that to her way of thinking is enough. It occur to her that some prankster have put a spike in her tea. The top layer of her head seem to be floating away from the rest of her.

She is aware of the peculiar way Mrs. Brown is looking at her. Of how she keep leaning forward to ask "Is something wrong, is something troubling you?" To be sure, something is. Mama Tuddi have a notion that the air have thicken between them. She can hear a bluejay prattling in a tree, she can even see the limb the bird is sitting on, but it seem to her the bird's song come from another place.

"I was just thinking," Mrs. Brown confess, "I like you better off the air than on. It seem to me you have more poise." More "paws," she say.

Mama Tuddi nod. She try to focus on one part of the woman's face the way she have to learn to look at the red button on the camera box.

"Your dignity come through."

"That my trademark in life," Mama Tuddi agree. She turn her head to look out over the yard and down to a leaning shed which LeRoy with Lasvegas is standing beside. It appear the two are trying to plant a tree. The tree to her eyes is nothing, maybe three feet tall, a couple of scraggly limbs which the foliage have drop away from or it never have.

"That a fruit tree," Mrs. Brown explain. "Apple, could be. Reno was partial to apples. He had it in his head that one day he like to plant one."

"I like trees," Mama Tuddi say to keep her end of the conversation going. Her voice sound strange to her, like it have entered her ear from some distance far away. She switch her head back to notice Mrs. Brown have her leg crossed over one knee, swinging that free leg hard. The gold anklet catch a glitter from the sun and Mama Tuddi see she have on her face a wayward smile.

Mrs. Brown catch Mama Tuddi looking and laughs out loud. "My motor running," she say. "It a disgraceful thing to be feeling in this time and place with my Reno not yet in the ground, but it have a way of coming over me when I looks at that man." She hitch her head off LeRoy's way, wanting herself plainly understood.

Mama Tuddi give a little push and her head wag slowly up and down. "He have any other women?" she ask.

"Could be he do but they don't have him."

"You lucky, I guess."

"I guess. I have my cross to bear but cross ain't all."

Mama Tuddi at a loss to understand what have come over her. It been ages — since way before she embark on a career — since she have sat rocking in a chair out in the yard talking to another person like she have all day. She observe Mrs. Brown and think to herself she could like this woman, she could be friends with her. She is part trash, maybe more trash than she let on, but Mama Tuddi find herself admiring her. It sadden her, now that she think of it, to realize she never have any woman friends, never have the time, always from the minute her alarm clock ring it is a case of get up and go. Get up and go because if you don't whatever you are after won't be there.

Yet now she surprise herself by wondering what it all come to. She wonder if maybe she ought not to gone into politics, since she get along so well with people. She wonder what the Double Ola people say if she march in and tell them, "You can get yourself another Mama Tuddi, this one's retiring."

The roof, she is sure, would cave right in, they would have a fit.

She wonder if she can chalk the fox fur up to her expense account.

A chill suddenly steal through Mama Tuddi. The sun is shining bright on Mrs. Brown, the sun shine all over the yard, but it seem to her as if dark shade have suddenly envelop her chair. Her bad tooth begin to ache again, the throb spreading all through her mouth. She feel weak clear through to her bones.

Now there be fresh excitement in the yard. Folks scurrying this way and that, relating that the preacher have come, he have escaped with his life from the freeway jam. Mama Tuddi looks off at the gate where five men are turning through single file like they are playing a Choo-Choo game. The one in front she take to be the preacher since he have a Bible in his hand. She spots right away he have back trouble because of his stiff legs with the feet pointing off opposite each other and the way his shoulders are slung back like they can't quite catch up with the rest of him. He have a pointy head, Mama Tuddi can tell even though he have a hat on.

The train come right on up to her chair. The man behind the preacher step out from the line, coughing a few times while Mama Tuddi scramble to get her shoes on. Then he grin and say, "Mama Tuddi, this heah be Preacher Teebone who express a pleasure to meet you."

"T-Bone?" Mama Tuddi inquire.

The preacher's eyebrows, trimmed to a boomerang shape and pomaded down, now shoot up, which make his pointy head more extreme.

"T-E-E-Bone," the preacher say, spelling it out. He have an expression of doom which never change and he stares deep into Mama Tuddi's eyes, which is why she can't stand preachers in the first place. "I heah," Preacher Teebone say, "you have kiss the boy and give him a fur coat. My feelings is you be best off kissing the Holy Book but I ain't against kissing in the circumstance, irregardless of which wherever he go thet coat ain't liable to hep him none."

Mama Tuddi stay quiet. Her experience at the station have taught her that the preachers of the world are engaged in an international conspiracy to take over every second, minute, and hour of TV time. And if they doing it, she tells herself, you can bet this T-Bone is in on it.

The minister abruptly turn on his heels and him and his train wheel along inside the house.

Wouldn't you know it, everybody out in the yard, having a perfectly nice time up to this point, toot along after him.

After a minute or two of sober thought during which time Mama Tuddi expect someone to come superintend her needs, she gets up and follows them. The preacher is already down at the front wiping a white handkerchief over his face. One of his aides takes away his hat while another one is setting up a speaker's stand which have draped from it a red cloth with a gold fringe which have stamped on it the words ONE GOD and something like a lightning bolt shooting down the middle. The music woman is taking her seat at the piano and Lasvegas have been set up with a candle on a plate and told where to stand up by the coffin. Curtains are being pulled and it is almost dark by the time Mama Tuddi is able to claim her front seat. LeRoy's seat is empty and for all Mama Tuddi know he have gone for good. It gives her a funny feeling that empty chair beside her, and a second chill come over her when she is surrounded on both sides by empty chairs because Mrs. Brown is now being led up to the coffin also, she and her boy now standing with lit candles at both ends like a pair of watchdogs. That is Mama Tuddi's view of the matter and it is all *tacky tacky tacky,* that is the only word she have for it. Preacher Teebone himself lights up a row of candles on the coffin lid.

The whole room then plunge into darkness except for the light up there. Preacher Teebone, standing behind the coffin, stretches out his arms and his hands fall square on top the heads of Mrs. Brown and her living son. His face have a yellow glow, his ears stand out from his head like he would flap right on up to heaven unless he have this duty to hold him down. He have not yet spoken a word but the sweat is already pouring off him and Mama Tuddi is beside herself thinking *tacky tacky tacky, I could do better with my hands tied behind me and my feet in a bucket of concrete.*

"LAWD GOD IN HEAVEN," rings out the preacher's voice, "PROP THESE HEAH TWO PEOPLE UP ON THEIR WEAK AND LEANEST SIDES IN THEIR HOUR OF SACRIFICE FOR THEY ARE BUT THE CHILDREN OF YOUR HANDIWORK." Mama Tuddi almost falls out of her chair since it comes to her such a big surprise that this pointy-headed man with his bad back can speak so loud.

"Prop 'um up!" replies a few in the back. "Preach on, Reverend," another says.

The preacher withdraws into the darkness and the music lady does a roll on her piano. When next he appears, behind the rostrum, his suit is washed in shiny magenta and he have his head thrown back so that all Mama Tuddi can see of his face is mouth. "*Friends,*" he begins . . .

Something crawls over Mama Tuddi's skin, first up her legs and over her knees then wrapping her thighs and hips and finally settling like a feathery waked-up thing that thinks to play possum in her lap.

And suddenly the preacher's voice have leaped out at her, forcing Mama Tuddi's spine straight back against her chair: FRIENDS WHEN YOU GO TO SHECAGO YOU KNOW WHAT TIME YO BUS DEPART

AND WHEN YOU GOT YO TICKET TO BATON ROUGE OR FOWT WAYNE
OR IF YOU GOING TO NU YAWK OR MONTRAWL OR WHETHER YOU
GOING TO DEETROIT OR THE YUKON TERRITORY YOU KNOW WHAT
TIME THE BUS LEAVE AND WHAT TIME SHE GET THERE AND SO YOU
GOT YO BAGS PACKED AND YOU GOT YO SKIVVIES IN ORDER AND YOU
WOMENS GOT YO FACE MADE AND YO HAIR CURLED AND YOU ALL SET
CAUSE YOU KNOW —

— CAUSE YOU KNOW THE HOUR AND THE MINUTE AND THE DAY
YO BUS GON GO CAUSE YOU DONE SEEN THE TIMETABLE OR YOU
DONE ASK OVER THE TELEPHONE AND THE VOICE DONE TOLE YOU
THAT BUS LEAVE AT NINE FAWTY FIVE OR TWELVE PM OR ON THE
BUTTON AT SIX O'CLOCK AND YOU IS HAD TIME FRIENDS —

Tacky tacky, Mama Tuddi think. Yet even as she say this to herself
the thing in her lap darts up its head, listening to her, and Mama
Tuddi's scalp tightens as once more it begin to crawl.

— YOU IS HAD TIME FRIENDS TO MAKE YO PREPARATION COMPLETE!

"*Amen!*" someone cried.

"*My baby gone,*" moan Mrs. Brown, "*he gone.*"

"*Gone!*" everybody say.

BUT BROTHERS AND SISTERS WHEN YOU TAKE THE TRIP THAT RENO
BROWN TAKE WHICH IS ONE THE QUICKEST RIDES YOU GON EVER
HAVE — WHEN YOU TAKE THE GLORY RIDE YOU AIN'T GOT NO TIME
TO PUT THE CURL IN YO HAIR —

"No, you ain't!"

OR TO SLICK IT DOWN —

"No, you ain't!"

OR TO POLISH UP YO SHOES OR PAINT UP YO LIPS —

"No, you ain't!"

CAUSE THERE AIN'T NO TIMETABLE OF THE LAWD'S PLAN AND THERE
AIN'T TELEPHONE POLE OR FREEWAY TO THAT FAR KINGDOM —

"No, you ain't!"

AND SO MY FRIENDS UNLESS YOU CAREFUL AND GOT YO FINGERS
CROSSED YOU GONNA HAVE TO MAKE THAT TRIP WITHOUT YO PREP-
ARATION COMPLETE CAUSE THAT ONE TRIP WHAT RUN BY NO SKA-
DULE YOU LIKELY TO UNDERSTAND —

"Praise the Lawd!"

YOU GONE BE CAUGHT WITH THE WINE IN YO MOUTH AND YO FOOT
IN THE TRAP! YO BED OF PLEASURE GONE BE YO BED OF PAIN, YO PATH
OF SIN GONE BE YO PATH OF WOE, THE DEVIL HIMSELF GONE COME AND
SWEEP YOU UP LIKE A WOMAN WITH A BROOM, YES MY FRIENDS THE
HIGH AND THE LOW!

"The high and the low!"

The room is aquiver with this preacher's work, in the din Mama
Tuddi cannot hear herself think. Teebone's eyes are boring in on
her from his face gone slick, she can see the flash of his gold teeth
and the sweep of his arms as he grab the red banner and flaps it
hard and fast, like he mean to shake out the words ONE GOD and
hurl them around her neck. Mrs. Brown and her boy are down on
their knees, bent over like two melted piles. Candle flames jump
off their wicks and spin through the black air, clearing a path for
Reno's spirit to follow. His spirit is climbing out of the box. Mama
Tuddi sees it clear as day passing on up through the lifted lid,
walking barefoot through the throbbing air. Mama Tuddi sucks in
her breath, she grind her teeth together and sucks again. She press
her hands tight between her legs, whining all the time, whining
despite all her desire to maintain her dignity and poise, for the
crawly thing have twisted down over her stomach and is hissing out
its tongue and she can feel its rough nose pushing cold and wet
under her hands, aiming to slide up through her woman's trough
to lodge inside of her. "*How many?*" Teebone asks . . .

The snake thing slides in.

HOW MANY OF YOU FOLKS BEEN TO THE RIVER?

"We been there, preacher!"

HOW MANY OF YOU POOR SINNERS HAVE BEEN TO THE RIVER?

"The river, amen!"

I SEE SOME OF YOU FOLKS HAVE BEEN TO THE RIVER AND I KNOW
YOU HAVE BEEN THERE AND JUMPED RIGHT IN —

"Right in!"

— WHILE OTHERS OF YOU HAVE STOOD ON THE SHORE AND WAITED
FOR THE WATER TO DIVIDE SO YOU COULD WALK A DRY BOTTOM
RIGHT INTO GLORY LAND NOW AIN'T THAT THE TRUTH?

"It's the truth!"

YOU HAVE STOOD ON THE SHORE BIDING YOUR TIME AND WHILE
YOU HAVE BEEN BIDING YO TIME THE DEVIL HAVE CUT THROUGH
THE WATER LIKE A SILVERFISH AND HE HAVE COME RIGHT ON UP
INSIDE. YOU HAVE STOOD ON THE SHORE WATCHING YO FACE IN THE
WATER AND LIKING WHAT YOU SEE AND THINKING YOU ARE ABOVE
GOD'S PLAN AND THE DEVIL'S HUNGRY FISH HAVE JUMPED OUT OF
THE WATER AND DROVE HIMSELF SMACK-DAB INSIDE YO EVIL HEART.

"Save us, preacher!"

I SAY TO YOU THE SAME AS I HAVE SAID TO THAT BOY IN THE BOX,

I SAY BROTHERS AND SISTERS IF YOU WENT TO THE RIVER WHY WERE YOU NOT BAPTIZED? I SAY TO YOU IF YOU WENT TO THE RIVER WHY DID YOU NOT JUMP RIGHT IN AND SWIM RIGHT ON HOME?

"Show us how, preacher!"

"You bring us home!"

MAYBE YOU THINK YO FUR COAT OR YO TV GONE GET YOU THERE —

"No, we don't!"

MAYBE YOU THINK YO DEEP FREEZE OR YO POCKETBOOK OR YO LOOSE WAYS GONE GET YOU THERE —

"No, we don't!"

MAYBE YOU THINK YO SODA POP GONE SWING IT WITH JESUS MAYBE YOU THINK YOU CAN GIT OUT ON THE FREEWAY AND THAT GONE TAKE YOU THERE OR MAYBE YOU THINK THIS BOY GONE GO ON AHEAD AND PUT IN A GOOD WORD AND THAT GONE GET YOU THERE BUT I SAY TO YOU THE SAME AS I WOULD SAY TO A MAN BLIND IN ONE EYE AND UNABLE TO SEE OUT OF THE OTHER FRIENDS I SAY THERE IS BUT ONE GOD ONE HEAVEN AND ONE WAY OF GETTING THERE WHILE THE WAY OF THE DEVIL IS LEGION AND HE CAN CLIMB INTO YO HEART AND TAKE CHARGE WITH NO MORE SECOND THOUGHT THAN A VAIN WOMAN HAVE WHEN SHE APPROACH THE LOOKING GLASS!

"Amen!"

"Thine the glory!"

Preacher Teebone speaks on. The music woman's fingers roll over the keys like someone stripping bark from a living tree; the voices in the room shake the roof with their song and one by one the long line form to head down to Teebone, who have a bucket of water to sprinkle from, saying "Sister, I baptize thee."

Going home, we going home, the song goes.

But Mama Tuddi can see through her heart and she like what she see. She like what she feel. The thing inside her is warm and quiet, he have come inside and curled up and it seem to her he have brought her peace. He have taken her a long way from these people, she hardly aware of them. She have her hands full just thinking she feel so satisfied. The thing inside her is sleeping now. But she have a notion he is going to wake up when she want him to, she going to have new strength for her show; this thing going to lead her out of this backwoods town into the bright lights of bigger places and more important work: pretty soon all the world going to know Mama Tuddi's name and bow down to her esteem.

JOHN SAYLES

At the Anarchists' Convention

(FROM THE ATLANTIC MONTHLY)

SOPHIE calls to ask am I going to the Anarchists' Convention this year. The year before last I'm missing because Brickman, may he rest in peace, was on the committee and we were feuding. I think about the Soviet dissidents, but there was always something so it's hard to say. Then last year he was just cooling in the grave and it would have looked bad.

"There's Leo Gold," they would have said, "come to gloat over Brickman."

So I tell Sophie maybe, depending on my hip. Rainy days it's torture, there isn't a position it doesn't throb. Rainy days and election nights.

But Sophie won't hear no, she's still got the iron, Sophie. Knows I won't be caught dead on the Senior Shuttle so she arranges a cab and says, "But Leo, don't you want to see *me?*"

Been using that one for over fifty years.

Worked again.

We used to have it at the New Yorker hotel before the Korean and his Jesus children moved in. You see them on the streets peddling flowers, big smiles, cheeks glowing like Hitler Youth. High on the Opiate of the People. Used to be the New Yorker had its dopers, its musicians, its sad sacks and marginal types. We felt at home there.

So this year the committee books us with the chain that our religious friends from Utah own, their showpiece there on Central Park South. Which kicks off the annual difficulties.

"That's the bunch killed Joe Hill," comes the cry.

"Not to mention their monkey business with Howard Hughes and his will—"

"And what about their stand on blacks and Indians?"

Personally, I think we should have it where we did the year the doormen were on strike, should rent the Union Hall in Brooklyn. But who listens to me?

So right off the bat there's Pinkstaff working up a petition and Weiss organizing a countercommittee. Always with the factions and splinter groups those two, whatever drove man to split the atom is the engine that rules their lives. Not divide and conquer but divide and subdivide.

First thing in the lobby we've got Weiss passing a handout on Brigham Young and the Mountain Meadows Massacre.

"Leo Gold! I thought you were dead!"

"It's a matter of days. You never learned to spell, Weiss."

"What, spelling?"

I point to the handout. "Who's this Norman? 'Norman Hierarchy,' Norman Elders.' And all this capitalization, it's cheap theatrics."

Weiss has to put on his glasses. "That's not spelling," he says, "that's typing. Spelling I'm fine, but these new machines — my granddaughter bought an electric."

"It's nice she lets you use it."

"She doesn't know. I sneak when she's at school."

Next there's the placard in the lobby — WELCOME ANARCHISTS — and the caricature of Bakunin, complete with sizzling bomb in hand. That Gross can still hold a pen is such a miracle we have to indulge his alleged sense of humor every year. A malicious man, Gross, like all cartoonists. Grinning, watching the hotel lackeys stew in their little brown uniforms, wondering is it a joke or not. Personally, I think it's in bad taste, the bomb-throwing bit. It's the enemy's job to ridicule, not ours. But who asks me?

They've set us loose in something called the Elizabethan Room and it's a sorry sight. A half-hundred old crackpots tiptoeing across the carpet, wondering how they got past the velvet ropes and into the exhibit. That old fascination with the enemy's lair, they fit like fresh kishke on a silk sheet. Some woman I don't know is pinning everyone with name tags. Immediately the ashtrays are full of them, pins bent by palsied fingers. Name tags at the Anarchists' Convention?

Pearl is here, and Bill Kinney in a fog and Lou Randolph and Pinkstaff and Fine and Diamond tottering around flashing his new store-boughts at everyone. Personally, wearing dentures I would try to keep my mouth shut. But then I always did.

"Leo, we thought we'd lost you," they say.

"Not a word, it's two years."

"Thought you went just after Brickman, rest his soul."

"So you haven't quit yet, Leo."

I tell them it's a matter of hours and look for Sophie. She's by Baker, the committee chairman this year. Always the committee chairman, he's the only one with such a streak of masochism. Sophie's by Baker and there's no sign of her Mr. Gillis.

There's another one makes the hip act up. Two or three times I've seen the man since he set up housekeeping with Sophie, and every time I'm in pain. Like an allergy, only bone deep. It's not just he's CP from the word go — we all had our fling with the Party, and they have their point of view. But Gillis is the sort that didn't hop off of Joe Stalin's bandwagon till after it nose-dived into the sewer. The deal with Berlin wasn't enough for Gillis, or the purges, no, nor any of the other tidbits that started coming out from reliable sources. Not till the Party announced officially that Joe was off the sainted list did Gillis catch a whiff. And him with Sophie now.

Maybe he's a good cook.

She lights up when she sees me. That smile, after all these years, that smile and my knees are water. She hasn't gone the Mother Jones route, Sophie, no shawls and spectacles, she's nobody's granny on a candy box. She's thin, a strong thin, not like Diamond, and her eyes, they still stop your breath from across the room. Always there was such a crowd, such a crowd around Sophie. And always she made each one think *he* was at the head of the line.

"Leo, you came! I was afraid you'd be shy again." She hugs me, and tells Baker that I'm like a brother.

Sophie who always rallied us after a beating, who bound our wounds, who built our pride back up from shambles and never faltered a step. The iron she had! In Portland they're shaving her head, but no wig for Sophie, she wore it like a badge. And the fire! Toe to toe with a fat Biloxi deputy, head to head with a Hoboken wharf boss, starting a near riot from her soapbox in Columbus Circle, but shaping it, turning it, stampeding all that anger and energy in the right direction.

Still the iron, still the fire, and still it's "Leo you're like a brother."

Baker is smiling his little pained smile, looking for someone to apologize to, Blum is telling jokes, Vic Lewis has an aluminum walker after his stroke, and old Mrs. Axelrod, who knew Emma Goldman from the Garment Workers, is dozing in her chair. Somebody must be in charge of bringing the old woman, with her mind the way it is, because she never misses. She's our museum piece, our link to the past.

Not that the rest of us qualify for the New Left.

Bud Odum is in one corner trying to work up a sing-along. Fifteen years younger than most here, a celebrity, still with the denim open at the chest and the Greek sailor cap. The voice is shot though. With Harriet Foote and old Lieber joining they sound like the look-for-the-Union-label folks on television. Determined but slightly off-key. The younger kids aren't so big on Bud anymore, and the hootenanny generation is grown, with other fish to fry.

Kids. The room is crawling with little Barnard girls and their tape recorders, pestering people for "oral history." A pair camp by Mrs. Axelrod, clicking on whenever she starts awake and mutters some Yiddish. Sophie, who speaks, says she's raving about the harness-eyes breaking and shackles bouncing on the floor, some shirt-factory tangle in her mind. Gems, they think they're getting, oral-history gems.

There are starting to be Rebeccas again, the little Barnard girls, and Sarahs and Esthers, after decades of Carol, Sally, and Debbie. The one who tapes me is a Raisele, which was my mother's name.

"We're trying to preserve it," she says with a sweet smile for an old man.

"What, Yiddish? I don't speak."

"No," she says. "Anarchism. The memories of anarchism. Now that it's served its dialectical purpose."

"You're a determinist."

She gives me a look. They think we never opened a book. I don't tell her I've written a few, it wouldn't make an impression. If it isn't on tape or film it doesn't register. Put my name in the computer, you'll draw a blank.

"Raisele," I say. "That's a pretty name."

"I learned it from an exchange student. I used to be Jody."

Dinner is called and there's confusion, there's jostling, everyone wants near the platform. The ears aren't what they used to be.

There is a seating plan, with place cards set out, but nobody looks. Place cards at the Anarchists' Convention? I manage to squeeze in next to Sophie.

First on the agenda is fruit cup, then speeches, then dinner, then more speeches. Carmen Marcovicci wants us to go get our own fruit cups. It makes her uneasy, she says, being waited on. People want, they should get up and get it themselves.

A couple minutes of mumble-grumble, then someone points out that we'd be putting the two hotel lackeys in charge of the meal out of a job. It's agreed, they'll serve. You could always reason with Carmen.

Then Harriet Foote questions the grapes in the fruit cup. The boycott is over, we tell her, grapes are fine. In fact grapes were always fine, it was the labor situation that was no good, not the *fruit.*

"Well I'm not eating *mine,*" she says, blood pressure climbing toward the danger point, "it would be disloyal."

The Wrath of the People. That's what Brickman used to call it in his articles, in his harangues, in his three-hour walking diatribes. Harriet still has it, and Carmen and Weiss and Sophie and Bill Kinney on his clear days and Brickman had it to the end. It's a wonderful quality, but when you're over seventy and haven't eaten since breakfast it has its drawbacks.

Baker speaks first, apologizing for the site and the hour and the weather and the Hundred Years' War. He congratulates the long travelers — Odum from L.A., Kinney from Montana, Pappas from Chicago, Mrs. Axelrod all the way from Yonkers. He apologizes that our next scheduled speaker, Mikey Dolan, won't be with us. He apologizes for not having time to prepare a eulogy, but it was so sudden.

More mumble-grumble, this being the first we've heard about Mikey. Sophie is crying, but she's not the sort you offer your shoulder to or reach for the Kleenex. *If steel had tears,* Brickman used to say. They had their battles, Brickman and Sophie, those two years together — '37 and '38. Neither of them known as a compromiser, both with healthy throwing arms, once a month there's a knock and it's Sophie come to borrow more plates. I worked for money at the movie house, I always had plates.

The worst was when you wouldn't see either of them for a week. Phil Rapf was living below them then and you'd see him in Washington Square, eight o'clock in the morning. Phil who'd sleep through the Revolution itself if it came before noon.

"I can't take it," he'd say. "They're at it already. In the morning, in the noontime, at night. At least when they're fighting the plaster doesn't fall."

Less than two years it lasted. But of all of them, before and after, it was Brickman left his mark on her. That hurts.

Bud Odum is up next, his Wisconsin accent creeping toward Oklahoma, twanging on about "good red-blooded American men and women," and I get a terrible feeling he's going to break into "The Ballad of Bob La Follette" when war breaks out at the far end of the table. In the initial shuffle Allie Zaitz was sitting down next to Fritz Groh and it's fifteen minutes before the shock of recognition. Allie has lost all his hair from the X-ray treatments, and Fritz never had any. More than ever they're looking like twins.

"*You*," says Allie, "you from the Dockworkers!"

"And you from that yellow rag. They haven't put you away from civilized people?"

"They let *you* in here? You an *an*archist?"

"In the fullest definition of the word. Which you wouldn't know. What was the coloring book you wrote for?"

At the tops of their voices, in the manner of old Lefties. What, old, in the manner we've always had, damn the decibels and full speed ahead. Baker would apologize but he's not near enough to the microphone, and Bub Odum is just laughing. There's still something genuine about the boy, even if he does get all weepy when you mention Eleanor Roosevelt.

"Who let this crank in here? We've been infiltrated!"

"Point of order! Point of order!"

What Allie is thinking with point of order I don't know, but the lady from the name tags gets them separated, gives each a Barnard girl to record their spewings about the other. Something Fritz said at a meeting, something Allie wrote about it, centuries ago. We don't forget.

Bud gets going again and it seems that last year they weren't prepared with Brickman's eulogy, so Bud will do the honors now. I feel eyes swiveling, a little muttered chorus of "Leoleoleo" goes through the room. Sophie knew, of course, and conned me into what she thought would be good for me. Once again.

First Bud goes into what a fighter Brickman was, tells how he took on Union City, New Jersey, singlehanded, about the time he organized an entire truckload of scabs with one speech, turning them around right under the company's nose. He can still rouse an audience, Bud, even with the pipes gone, and soon they're popping up around the table with memories. Little Pappas, who we never thought would survive the beating he took one May Day scuffle, little one-eyed, broken-nosed Pappas stands and tells of Brickman saving the mimeograph machine when they burned our office on Twenty-seventh Street. And Sam Karnes, ghost pale, like the years in prison bleached even his blood, is standing, shaky, with the word on Brickman's last days. Tubes running out of him, fluids dripping into him, still Brickman agitates with the hospital orderlies, organizes with the cleaning staff. Then Sophie takes the floor, talking about spirit, how Brickman had it, how Brickman was it, spirit of our cause, more spirit sometimes than judgment, and again I feel the eyes, hear the "Leoleoleo," and there I am on my feet.

"We had our troubles," I say, "Brickman and I. But always I knew his heart was in the right place."

Applause, tears, and I sit down. It's a sentimental moment. Of course, it isn't true. If Brickman had a heart it was a well-kept secret. He was a machine, an express train flying the black flag. But it's a sentimental moment, the words come out.

Everybody is making nice then, the old friendly juices flowing, and Baker has to bring up business. A master of tact, a genius of timing. A vote — do we elect next year's committee before dinner or after?

"Why spoil dinner?" says one camp.

"Nobody will be left awake after," says the other. "Let's get it out of the way."

They always started small, the rifts. A title, a phrase, a point of procedure. The Chicago Fire began with a spark.

It pulls the scab off, the old animosities, the bickerings, come back to the surface. One whole section of the table splits off into a violent debate over the merits of syndicalism, another forms a faction for elections *during* dinner, Weiss wrestles Baker for the microphone, and Sophie shakes her head sadly.

"Why, why, why? Always they argue," she says, "always they fight."

I could answer, I devoted half of one of my studies to it, but who asks?

While the argument heats another little girl comes over with used-to-be-Jody.

"She says you're Leo Gold."

"I confess."

"*The* Leo Gold?"

"There's another?"

"I read *Anarchism and the Will to Love.*"

My one turkey, and she's read it. "So you're the one."

"I didn't realize you were still alive."

"It's a matter of seconds."

I'm feeling low. Veins are standing out in temples, old hearts straining, distemper epidemic. And the sound, familiar, but with a new, futile edge.

I've never been detached enough to recognize the sound so exactly before. It's a raw-throated sound, a grating, insistent sound, a sound born out of all the insults swallowed, the battles lost, out of all the smothered dreams and desires. Three thousand collective years of frustration in the room, turning inward, a cancer of frustration. It's the sound of parents brawling with each other because they can't feed their kids, the sound of prisoners preying on each other because the guards are out of reach, the sound of a terribly deep despair. No quiet desperation for us, now while we have a voice left. Over an hour it lasts, the sniping, the shouting, the accusations and countercharges. I want to eat. I want to go home. I want to cry.

And then the hotel manager walks in.

Brown blazer, twenty-dollar haircut, and a smile from here to the Odessa Steps. A huddle at the platform. Baker and Mr. Manager bowing and scraping at each other, Bud Odum looking grim, Weiss turning colors. Sophie and I go up, followed by half the congregation. Nobody trusts to hear it secondhand. I can sense the sweat breaking under that blazer when he sees us coming, toothless, gnarled, suspicious by habit. Ringing around him, the Anarchists' Convention.

"A terrible mistake," he says.

"All my fault," he says.

"I'm awfully sorry," he says, "but you'll have to move."

Seems the Rotary Club, the Rotary Club from Sioux Falls, had booked this room *before* us. Someone misread the calendar. They're out in the lobby, eyeballing Bakunin, impatient, full of gin and boosterism.

"We have a nice room, a smaller room," coos the manager, "we can set you up there in a jiffy. Much less drafty than this room, I'm sure the older folks would feel more comfortable."

"I think it stinks," says Rosenthal, every year the committee treasurer. "We paid cash, the room is ours."

Rosenthal doesn't believe in checks. "The less the Wall Street boys handle your money," he says, "the cleaner it is." Who better to be treasurer than a man who thinks gold is filth?

"That must be it," says Sophie to the manager. "You've got your cash from us, money in the bank, you don't have to worry. The Rotary, they can cancel a check, so you're scared. And maybe there's a little extra on the side they give you, a little folding green to clear out the riffraff?"

Sophie has him blushing, but he's going to the wire anyhow. Like Frick in the Homestead Strike, shot, stomped, and stabbed by Alexander Berkman, they patch him up and he finishes his day at the office. A gold star from Carnegie. Capitalism's finest hour.

"You'll have to move," says the manager, dreams of corporate glory in his eyes, the smile hanging onto his face by its fingernails, "it's the only way."

"Never," says Weiss.

"Out of the question," says Sophie.

"Fuck off," says Pappas.

Pappas saw his father lynched. Pappas did three hard ones in Leavenworth. Pappas lost an eye, a lung, and his profile to a mob in Chicago. He says it with conviction.

"Pardon?" A note of warning from Mr. Manager.

"He said to fuck off," says Fritz Groh.

"You heard him," echoes Allie Zaitz.

"If you people won't cooperate," huffs the manager, condescension rolling down like a thick mist, "I'll have to call in the police."

It zings through the room like the twinge of a single nerve.

"Police! They're sending the police!" cries Pinkstaff.

"Go limp!" cries Vic Lewis, knuckles white with excitement on his walker. "Make 'em drag us out!"

"Mind the shuttles, mind the shuttles!" cries old Mrs. Axelrod in Yiddish, sitting straight up in her chair.

Allie Zaitz is on the phone to a newspaper friend, the Barnard girls are taping everything in sight. Sophie is organizing us into squads, and only Baker holding Weiss bodily allows Mr. Manager to escape the room in one piece. We're the Anarchists' Convention!

Nobody bickers, nobody stalls or debates or splinters. We manage to turn the long table around by the door as a kind of barricade, stack the chairs together in a second line of defense, and crate Mrs. Axelrod back out of harm's way. I stay close by Sophie, and once, lugging the table, she turns and gives me that smile. Like a shot of adrenalin. I feel fifty again. Sophie, Sophie, it was always so good just to be at your side!

And when the manager returns with his two befuddled street cops to find us standing together, arms linked, the lame held up out of their wheelchairs, the deaf joining from memory as Bud Odum leads us in "We Shall Not Be Moved," my hand in Sophie's, sweaty-palmed at her touch like the old days, I look at him in his brown blazer and think *Brickman,* I think, *my God if Brickman was here we'd show this bastard the Wrath of the People!*

ISAAC BASHEVIS SINGER

The Safe Deposit

(FROM THE NEW YORKER)

SOME FIVE YEARS back, when Professor Uri Zalkind left New York for Miami after his wife Lotte's death, he had decided never to return to this wild city. Lotte's long sickness had broken his spirit. His health, too, it seemed. Not long after he buried her, he fell sick with double pneumonia and an obstruction of the kidneys. He had been living and teaching philosophy in New York for almost thirty years, but he still felt like a stranger in America. The German Jews did not forgive him for having been raised in Poland, the son of some Galician rabbi, and speaking German with an accent. Lotte herself, who was German, called him *Ostjude* when she quarreled with him. To the Russian and Polish Jews he was a German, since, besides being married to a German, for many years he had lived in Germany. He might have made friends with American members of the faculty or with his students, but there was little interest in philosophy at the university, and in Jewish philosophy in particular. He and Lotte had no children. Through the first years they still had relatives in America, but most of the old ones had died and he never kept in touch with the younger generation. Just the same, this winter morning Dr. Uri Zalkind had taken a plane to New York — a man over eighty, small, frail, with a bent back, a little white beard, and bushy eyebrows that retained a trace of having once been red. Behind thick-lensed glasses, his eyes were gray, permanently inflamed.

It was a bad day to have come to New York. The pilot had announced that there was a blizzard in the city, with gusting winds. A dark cloud covered the area, and in the last minutes before landing at LaGuardia an ominous silence settled over the passengers. They avoided looking one another in the eye, as if ashamed beforehand of the panic that might soon break out. Whatever happens, I have rightly deserved it, Dr. Zalkind thought. His Miami Beach neighbors in the senior-citizens apartment complex had warned him that flying in such weather was suicide. And for what was he risking his life? For the manuscript of a book no one would read except possibly a few reviewers. He was glad that he carried no other luggage than his briefcase. He raised the fur collar of the long coat he had brought with him from Germany and, clutching his case in his right hand and holding on to his broad-brimmed hat with his left, he went out of the terminal to look for a taxi. From sitting three hours in one position his legs had become numb. Snow fell at an angle, dry as sand. The wind was icy. Although he had made a firm decision that morning to forget nothing, Professor Zalkind now realized that he had left his muffler and rubbers at home. He had planned to put on his woolen sweater in the plane and this he had forgotten, too. By the time a taxi finally stopped for him, he could not tell the driver the address of the bank to which he wanted to go. He remembered only that it was on Fifty-seventh Street between Eighth Avenue and Broadway.

Professor Zalkind had more than one reason for undertaking this journey. First, the editor of the university press that was to publish his book, *Philo Judaeus and the Cabala,* had called to tell him that he would be visiting New York in the next few days. According to the contract, Professor Zalkind was to have delivered the manuscript some two years ago. Because he had added a number of footnotes and made many alterations in the text, he decided he should meet with the editor personally rather than send the manuscript by mail. Second, he wanted to see Hilda, the only living cousin of his late wife. He hadn't seen her for five years, and her daughter had written to him that her mother was seriously ill. Third, Professor Zalkind had read in the *Miami Herald* that last Saturday thieves had broken into a bank in New York and by boring a hole in the steel door leading to the vault they had stolen everything they could. True, this theft had not occurred in the bank where Zalkind rented a safe-deposit box. Still, the news item, headlined "How Safe Is a Safe?," disturbed him to such a degree that he could not sleep the whole night after he read it. In his box were deposited Lotte's jewelry, his will, and a number of important letters, as well as a manuscript of essays on metaphysics he had written when he was young — a work he would never dare publish while he was alive but one he did not want to lose. In addition to the safe-deposit box, he had in the same bank a savings account of some seventeen thousand dollars, which he intended to withdraw and deposit in Miami. It was not that he needed money. He had a pension from his years of teaching at the university. He had been receiving a Social Security check each month since he became seventy-two; regularly, reparation money came from Germany, which he had escaped after Hitler came to power. But why keep his belongings in New York now that he was a resident of Florida?

Another motive — perhaps the most important — brought the old man to New York. For many years he had suffered from prostate trouble, and the doctors he consulted had all advised him to have an operation. Procrastination could be fatal, they told him. He had made up his mind to visit a urologist in New York — a physician from Germany, a refugee like himself.

After crawling in traffic for a long time, the taxi stopped at Eighth Avenue and Fifty-seventh Street. No matter how Professor Zalkind tried, he couldn't read the meter. Lately, the retinas of his eyes had begun to degenerate and he could read only with a large magnifying glass. Assuming that he would get change, he handed the driver a ten-dollar bill, but the driver complained that it was not enough. Zalkind gave him two dollars more. The blizzard was getting worse. The afternoon was as dark as dusk. The moment Zalkind opened the door of the taxi, snow hit his face like hail. He struggled against the wind until he reached Seventh Avenue. There was no sign of his bank. He continued as far east as Fifth. A new building was being constructed. Was it possible that they had torn down the bank without letting him know? In the midst of the storm, motors roared, trucks and cars honked. He wanted to ask the construction workers where the bank had moved, but in the clang and clamor no one would hear his voice. The words in the Book of Job came to his mind: "He shall return no more to his house, neither shall his place know him anymore."

Now Zalkind had come to a public telephone, and somehow he got out a dime and dialed Hilda's number. He heard the voice of a stranger, and could not make out what was being said to him. Well, everything is topsy-turvy with me today, he thought. Presently it occurred to him that he had looked only on one side of the street, sure that the bank was there. Perhaps he was mistaken? He tried to cross the street, but his glasses had become opaque and he couldn't be sure of traffic-light colors. He finally made it across, and after a while he saw a bank that resembled his, though it had a different name. He entered. There was not a single customer in the place. Tellers sat idly behind the little windows. A guard in uniform approached him and Zalkind asked him if this was indeed his bank. At first the guard didn't seem to understand his accent. Then he said it was the same bank — it had merged with another one and the name had been changed.

"How did it come that you didn't let me know?"

"Notices went out to all our depositors."

"Thank you, thank you. Really, I began to think I was getting senile," Dr. Zalkind said to the guard and himself. "What about the safe-deposit boxes?"

"They are where they were."

"I have a savings account in this bank, and a lot of interest must have accumulated in the years I've been away. I want to withdraw it."

"As you wish."

Dr. Zalkind approached a counter and began to search for his bankbook. He remembered positively that he had brought it with him in one of the breast pockets of his jacket. He emptied both and found everything except his bankbook — his Social Security card, his airplane ticket, old letters, notebooks, a telephone bill, even a leaflet advertising a dancing school, which had been handed to him on the street. "Am I insane?" Dr. Zalkind asked himself. "Are the demons after me? Maybe I put it into my case. But where is my case?" He glanced right and left, on the counter and under it. There was no trace of a briefcase. "I have left it in the telephone booth!" he said with a tremor in his voice. "My manuscript too!" The bank suddenly became dark, and a golden eye lit up on a black background — otherworldly, dreamily radiant, its edges jagged, a blemish in the pupil, like the eye of some cosmic embryo in the process of formation. This vision baffled him, and for some time he forgot his briefcase. He watched the mysterious eye growing both in size and in luminosity. What he saw now was not altogether new to him. As a child, he had seen similar entities — sometimes an eye, other times a fiery flower that opened its petals or a dazzling butterfly or some unearthly snake. Those apparitions always came to him at times of distress, as when he was whipped in cheder, was attacked by some vicious urchin, or was sick with fever. Perhaps those hallucinations were incompatible forms that the soul created without any pattern in the Ideas, Professor Zalkind pondered in Platonic terms. He leaned on the counter in order not to fall. *I'm not going to faint,* he ordered himself. His belly had become bloated and a mixture of a belch and a hiccup came from his mouth. This is my end!

Dr. Zalkind opened the outside door of the bank with difficulty, determined to find the telephone booth. He looked around, but no telephone booth was in sight. He choked from the blast of the wind. In all his anguish his brain remained playful. *Is the North Pole visiting New York? Has the Ice Epoch returned? Is the sun being extinguished?* Dr. Zalkind had often seen blind men crossing the streets of New York without a guide, waving a white stick. He could never understand where they acquired the courage for this. The wind pushed him back, blew up the skirts of his coat, tore at his hat. No, I can't go looking for the phantom of a telephone booth in this hurricane. He dragged himself back to the bank, where he searched again for his briefcase on the counters and floor. He had no copy of the manuscript, just a pile of papers written in longhand — actually, not more than notes. He saw a bench and collapsed onto it. He sat silent, ready for death, which, according to Philo, redeems the soul from the prison of the flesh, from the vagaries of the senses. Although Zalkind had read everything Philo wrote, he could never conclude from his writings whether matter was created by God or always existed — a primeval chaos, the negative principle of the godhead. Dr. Zalkind found contradictions in Philo's philosophy and puzzles no mind could solve as long as it was chained in the errors of corporality. "Well, I may soon see the truth," he murmured. For a while he dozed and even began to dream. He woke with a start.

The guard was bending over him. "Is something wrong? Can I help?"

"Oh, I had a briefcase with me and I lost it. My bankbook was there."

"Your bankbook? You can get another one. No one can take out your money without your signature. Where did you lose it? In a taxi?"

"Perhaps."

"All you have to do is notify the bank that you lost the bankbook and after thirty days they will give you another one."

"I would like to go to the safe-deposit boxes."

"I'll take you in the elevator."

The guard helped Dr. Zalkind get up. He half led him, half pushed him to the elevator and pressed the button to the basement. There, in spite of his confusion, Professor Zalkind recognized the clerk who sat in front of the entrance to the safe-deposit boxes. His hair had turned gray, but his face remained young and ruddy. The man also recognized Zalkind. He clapped his hands and called, "Professor Zalkind, whom do I see! We already thought that . . . you were sick or something?"

"Yes, no."

"Let me get the figures on your account," the clerk said. He went into another room. Zalkind heard his name mentioned on the telephone.

"Everything is all right," the clerk said when he returned. "What you owe us is more than covered by the interest in your account." He gave Zalkind a slip to sign. It took some time. His hand shook like that of a person suffering from Parkinson's disease. The clerk stamped the slip and nodded. "You don't live in New York anymore?"

"No, in Miami."

"What is your new address?"

Dr. Zalkind wanted to answer, but he had forgotten both the street and the number. The heavy door opened and he gave the slip to another clerk, who led him into the room holding the safe-deposit boxes. Zalkind's box was in the middle row. The clerk motioned with his hand. "Your key."

"My key?"

"Yes, your key, to open the box."

Only now did it occur to Dr. Zalkind that one needed a key to get into a safe-deposit box. He searched through his pockets and took out a chain of keys, but he was sure they were all from Miami. He stood there perplexed. "I'm sorry, I haven't the key to my box."

"You do have it. Give me those keys!" The man grabbed the key chain and showed Professor Zalkind one that was larger than the others. He had been carrying a key to his safe-deposit box with him all those years, not knowing what it was for. The clerk pulled out a metal box and led Zalkind into a long corridor, opened a door to a room without a window, and turned on the light. He put the box on the table and showed Zalkind a switch on the wall to use when he had finished.

After some fumbling, Zalkind managed to open the box. He sat and gaped. Time had turned him sick, defeated, but for these objects in the box it did not exist. They had lain there for years without consciousness, without any need — dead matter, unless the animists were correct in considering all substance alive. To Einstein, mass was condensed energy. Could it perhaps also be condensed spirit? Though Professor Zalkind had packed his magnifying glass in his briefcase, he recognized stacks of Lotte's love letters tied with ribbons, his diary, and his youthful manuscript with the title "Philosophical Fantasies" — a collection of essays, feuilletons, and aphorisms.

After a while he lifted out Lotte's jewelry. He never knew that she possessed so many trinkets. There were bracelets, rings, earrings, broaches, chains, a string of pearls. She had inherited all this from her mother, her grandmothers, perhaps her great-grandmothers. It was probably worth a fortune, but what would he do with money at this stage? He sat there and took stock of his life. Lotte had craved children, but he had refused to increase the misery of the human species and Jewish troubles, he had said. She wanted to travel with him. He deprived her of this, too. "What is there to see?" he would ask her. "In what way is a high mountain more significant than a low hill? How is the ocean a greater wonder than a pond?" Even though Dr. Zalkind had doubts about Philo's philosophy and was sometimes inclined toward Spinoza's pantheism or David Hume's skepticism, he had accepted Philo's disdain for the deceptions of flesh and blood. He had come to New York with the decision to take all these things back with him to Miami. Yet, how could he carry them now that he had no briefcase? And what difference did it make where they were kept?

How strange. On the way to the airport that morning, Zalkind still had some ambitions. He planned to make final corrections on his manuscripts. He toyed with the idea of looking over "Philosophical Fantasies" to see what might be done with it. He had sworn to himself to make an appointment with the urologist the very next day. Now he was overcome by fatigue and had to lean his forehead on the table. He fell asleep and found himself in a temple, with columns, vases, sculptures, marble staircases. Was this Athens? Rome? Alexandria? A tall man with a white beard, dressed in a toga and sandals, emerged. He carried a scroll. He recited a poem or a sermon. Was the language Greek? Latin? No, it was Hebrew, written by a scribe.

"Peace unto you, Philo Judaeus, my father and master," Dr. Zalkind said.

"Peace unto you, my disciple Uri, son of Yedidyah."

"Rabbi, I want to know the truth!"

"Here in the Book of Genesis is the source of all truth: 'In the beginning God created the heaven and the earth. And the earth was without form, and void; and darkness was upon the face of the deep. And the Spirit of God moved upon the face of the waters.' "

Philo intoned the words like a reader in the synagogue. Other old men entered, with white hair and white beards, wearing white robes and holding parchments. They were all there — the Stoics, the Gnostics, Plotinus. Uri had read that Philo was not well versed in the Holy Tongue. What a lie! Each word from his lips revealed secrets of the Torah. He quoted from the Talmud, the Book of Creation, the Zohar, Rabbi Moshe from Córdoba, Rabbi Isaac Luria. How could this be? Had the Messiah come? Had the Resurrection taken place? Had the earth ascended to Heaven? Had Metatron descended to the earth? The figures and statues were not of stone but living women with naked breasts and hair down to their loins. Lotte was among them. She was also Hilda. One female with two bodies? One body with two souls?

"Uri, my beloved, I have longed for you!" she cried out. "Idolators wanted to defile me, but I swore to be faithful."

In the middle of the temple there was a bed covered with rugs and pillows; a ladder was suspended alongside it. Uri was about to climb up when a stream of water burst through the gate of the temple. Had Yahweh broken his covenant and sent a flood upon the earth?

Uri Zalkind woke up with a start. He opened his eyes and saw the bank clerk shaking his shoulder. "Professor Zalkind, your briefcase has been found. A woman brought it. She opened it and on top there was your bankbook."

"I understand."

"Are you sick?" the clerk asked. He pointed to a wet spot on the floor.

It took a long while before Dr. Zalkind answered. "I'm kaput, that's all."

"It's five minutes to three. The bank will be closing."

"I will soon go."

"The woman with the briefcase is upstairs." The clerk went out, leaving the door half open.

For a minute, Dr. Zalkind sat still, numbed by his own indifference. His briefcase was found but he felt no joy. Beside the box, Lotte's jewelry shimmered, reflecting the colors of the rainbow. Suddenly Dr. Zalkind began to fill his coat pockets with the jewels. It was the spontaneous act of a cheder boy. A passage from the Pentateuch came into his mind: "Behold, I am at the point to die: and what profit shall this birthright do to me?" Zalkind even repeated Esau's words with the teacher's intonation.

The clerk came in with a woman who carried a wet mop and a pail. "Should I call an ambulance?" he asked.

"An ambulance? No."

Zalkind followed the clerk, who motioned for the key. It was underneath Lotte's jewelry, and Zalkind had to make an effort to pull it out. The clerk took him up in the elevator, and there was the woman with his briefcase — small, darkish, in a black fur hat and a mangy coat. When she saw Zalkind, her eyes lit up.

"Professor Zalkind! I went to make a telephone call and saw your briefcase. I opened it and there with your papers was your bankbook. Since you use this bank, I thought they would know your address. And here you are." The woman spoke English with a foreign accent.

"Oh, you're an honest person. I thank you with all my heart."

"Why am I so honest? There is no cash here. If I had found a million dollars, the *Yetzer Hora* might have tempted me." She pronounced the Hebrew words as they did in Poland.

"It's terrible outside. Maybe you should take him somewhere," the guard suggested to the woman.

"Where do you live? Where is your hotel?" she asked. "I heard that you just arrived from Miami. What a time to come from Florida in your condition. You may, God forbid, catch the worst kind of cold."

"I thank you. I thank you. I have no hotel. I had planned to stay over with the cousin of my late wife, but it seems her telephone is out of order."

"I will take you to my own place for the time being. I live on 106th and Amsterdam. It is quite far from here, but if we get a taxi it won't be long. My dentist moved to this neighborhood and that is why I'm here."

One of the bank employees came over and asked, "Should I try to get a taxi for you?"

Even though it wasn't clear whom he addressed, Zalkind replied, "Yes — I really don't know how to express my gratitude."

Other clerks came over with offers of help, but Zalkind noticed that they winked at one another. The outside door opened and one of them called, "Your taxi!"

The snow had stopped, but it had got colder. The woman took Zalkind's arm and helped him into the taxi. She got in after him and said, "My name is Esther Sephardi. You can call me Esther."

"Are you a Sephardi?"

"No, a Jewish daughter from Lodz. My husband's surname was Sephardi. He was also from Lodz. He died two years ago."

"Do you have children?"

"One daughter in college. Why did you come in such a weather to New York?"

Dr. Zalkind didn't know where to begin.

"You don't need to answer," the woman said. "You live alone, huh? No wife would allow her husband to go to New York on a day like this. You won't believe me, in frost worse than this I stood in a forest in Kazakhstan and sawed logs. That's where the Russians sent us in 1941. We had to build our own barracks. Those who couldn't make it died, and those who were destined to live lived. I took your briefcase with me to the Automat to get a cup of coffee and I looked into your papers. Is this going to be a book?"

"Perhaps."

"Are you a professor?"

"I was."

"My daughter studies philosophy. Not exactly philosophy but psychology. What does one need so much psychology for? I wanted her to study for a doctor but nowadays children do what they want, not what their mother tells them. For twenty years I was a book-keeper in a big firm. Then I got sick and had to have a hysterectomy. Dr. Zalkind, I don't like to give you advice, but what you have should not be neglected. An uncle of mine had it and he delayed until it was too late."

"It's too late for me, too."

"How do you know? Did you have tests made?"

The taxi stopped in a half-dark street, with cars buried under piles of snow. Dr. Zalkind managed to get a few bills from his purse and gave them to Esther. "I don't see so well. Be so good — pay him and give him a tip."

The woman took Zalkind's hand and led him up three flights of stairs. Until now, Professor Zalkind had believed that his heart was in order, but something must have happened — after one flight he was short of breath. Esther opened a door and led him into a narrow corridor, and from there into a shabby living room. She said, "We used to be quite wealthy, but first my husband got sick with cancer and then I got sick. I'm working as a cashier during the day in a movie theater. Wait, let me take off your coat." She weighed it in her hands, glanced at the bulging pockets, and asked, "What do you have there — stones?"

After some haggling she took off his shirt and pants as well. He tried to resist, but she said, "When you are sick, you can't be bashful. Where is the shame? We are all made from the same dough."

She filled the bathtub with hot water and brought him clean underwear and a robe that must have been her late husband's. Then she made tea in the kitchen and warmed up soup from a can. Professor Zalkind had forgotten that he had had nothing to eat or drink since breakfast. As she served him, Esther kept on talking about her years in Lodz, in Russia, in New York. Her father had been a rich man, a partner in a textile factory, but the Poles had ruined him with their high taxes. He grew so distraught that he got consumption and died. Her mother lived a few years more and she, too, passed away. In Russia Esther became sick with typhoid fever and anemia. She worked in a factory where the pay was so low that one had to steal or starve. Her husband was taken away by the N.K.V.D., and for years she didn't know if he had been killed in a slave-labor camp. When they finally reunited, they had to wait two years in Germany in a D.P. camp for visas to America. "What we went through in all those years only God the merciful knows."

For a moment, Professor Zalkind was inclined to tell her that even though God was omniscient, the well of goodness, one could not ascribe any attribute to Him. He did not provide for mankind directly but through Wisdom, called Logos by the Greeks. But there was no use discussing metaphysics with this woman.

After he had eaten, Dr. Zalkind could no longer fight off his weariness. He yawned; his eyes became watery. His head kept dropping to his chest. Esther said, "I will make you a bed on the sofa. It's not comfortable, but when you are tired you can sleep on rocks. Ask me."

"I will never be able to repay you for your kindness."

"We are all human beings."

Dr. Zalkind saw with half-closed eyes how she spread a sheet over the sofa, brought in a pillow, a blanket, pajamas. "I hope I don't wet the bed," he prayed to the powers that have the say over the body and its needs. He went into the bathroom and saw himself in a mirror for the first time that day. In one day his face had become yellow, wrinkled. Even his white beard seemed shrunken. When he returned to the living room, he remembered Hilda and asked Esther to call her. Esther learned from an answering service that Hilda had gone into a hospital the day before. *Well, everything falls to pieces,* Zalkind said to himself. He noticed a saltshaker that Esther had neglected to take from the table, and while she lingered in the bathroom he put some of the salt on his palm and swallowed it, since salt retains water in the body. She returned in a house robe and slippers. *She's not so young anymore,* he thought appraisingly, *but still an attractive female;* in spite of his maladies he had not lost his manhood.

The instant he lay down on the sofa he fell into a deep sleep. This is how he used to pass out as a boy on Passover night after the four goblets of wine. He awoke in the middle of the night with an urgent need to urinate. Thank God, the sheet was dry. The room was completely dark; the window shades were down. He groped like a blind man, bumping into a chest, a chair, an open door. Did it lead to the bathroom? No, he touched a headboard of a bed and could hear someone breathing. He was overcome with fear. His hostess might suspect him of dishonorable intentions. Eventually, he found the bathroom. He wanted light but he could not find the switch. On the way back, in the corridor, he accidentally touched the switch and turned on the light. He saw his briefcase propped against the wall, his coat hanging on a clothes tree. Yes, Lotte's jewelry was still there. He had fallen into honest hands. It had become cold during the night, and he put the coat on his shoulders over his pajamas and took the briefcase with him in order to place the jewelry in it. He had to smile — he looked as if he were going on a journey. *I will give it to this goodhearted woman*, he resolved. *At least a part of it. I have no more need for worldly possessions. If some part of Lotte's mind still exists, she will forgive me.* Suddenly his head became compressed with heat and he fell. He could hear his body thud against the floor. Then everything was still.

Professor Zalkind opened his eyes. He was lying on a bed with metal bars on both sides. Above the bed a small lamp glimmered. He stared in the semidarkness, waiting for his memory to return. An ice bag rested on his forehead. His belly was bandaged and his hand touched a catheter. "Am I still alive?" he asked himself. "Or is it already the hereafter?" He felt like laughing, but he was too sore inside. In an instant everything he had gone through on this trip came back to him. Had it been today? Yesterday? Days before? It did not matter. Although he was aching, he felt a rest he had never known before — the sublime enjoyment of fearing nothing, having no wish, no worry, no resentment. This state of mind was not of this world and he listened to it. He was granted the revelation he yearned for — the freedom to look into the innermost secret of being, to see behind the curtain of phenomena, where all questions are answered, all riddles solved. "If I could only convey the truth to those who suffer and doubt!"

A figure slid through the half-opened door like a shadow — the woman who had found his briefcase. She bent over his bed and asked, "You have wakened, huh?"

He did not answer and she said, "Thank God, the worst is over. You will soon be a new man."

RICHARD STERN

Dr. Cahn's Visit

(FROM THE ATLANTIC MONTHLY)

"How FAR is it now, George?"

The old man was riding next to his son, Will. George was his brother, dead the day after Franklin Roosevelt.

"Almost there, Dad."

"What does 'almost' mean?"

"It's Eighty-sixth and Park. The hospital's at Ninety-ninth and Fifth. Mother's in the Klingenstein Pavilion."

"Mother's not well?"

"No, she's not well. Liss and I took her to the hospital a couple of weeks ago."

"It must have slipped my mind." The green eyes darkened with sympathy. "I'm sure you did the right thing. Is it a good hospital?"

"Very good. You were on staff there half a century."

"Of course I was. For many years, I believe."

"Fifty."

"Many as that?"

"A little slower, pal. These jolts are hard on the old man."

The cabbie was no chicken himself. "It's your ride."

"Are we nearly there, George?"

"Two minutes more."

"The day isn't friendly," said Dr. Cahn. "I don't remember such — such—"

"Heat."

"Heat in New York." He took off his gray fedora and scratched at the hairless, liver-spotted skin. Circulatory difficulty left it dry, itchy. Scratching had shredded and inflamed its soft center.

"It's damn hot. In the nineties. Like you."

"What's that?"

"It's as hot as you are old. Ninety-one."

"Ninety-one. That's not good."

"It's a grand age."

"That's your view."

"And Mother's eighty. You've lived good, long lives."

"Mother's not well, son?"

"Not too well. That's why Liss and I thought you ought to see her. Mother's looking forward to seeing you."

"Of course. I should be with her. Is this the first time I've come to visit?"

"Yes."

"I should be with her."

The last weeks at home had been difficult. Dr. Cahn had been the center of the household. Suddenly, his wife was. The nurses looked after her. And when he talked, she didn't answer. He grew angry, sullen. When her ulcerous mouth improved, her voice was rough and her thought harsh. "I wish you'd stop smoking for five minutes. Look at the ashes on your coat. Please stop smoking."

"Of course, dear. I didn't know I was annoying you." The ash tumbled like a suicide from thirty stories, the butt was crushed into its dead brothers. "I'll smoke inside." And he was off, but, in two minutes, back. Lighting up. Sometimes he lit two cigarettes at once. Or lit the filtered end. The odor was foul, and sometimes his wife was too weak to register her disgust.

They sat and lay within silent yards of each other. Dr. Cahn was in his favorite armchair, the *Times* bridge column inches from his cigarette. He read it all day long. The vocabulary of the game deformed his speech. "I need some clubs" might mean "I'm hungry." "My spades are tired" meant he was. Or his eyes were. Praise of someone might come out "He laid his hand out clearly." In the bedridden weeks, such mistakes intensified his wife's exasperation. "He's become such a penny-pincher," she said to Liss when Dr. Cahn refused to pay her for the carton of cigarettes she brought, saying, "They can't charge so much. You've been cheated."

"Liss has paid. Give her the money."

"Are you telling me what's trump? I've played this game all my life."

"You certainly have. And I can't bear it."

In sixty marital years, there had never been such anger. When

Will came from Chicago to persuade his mother into the hospital, the bitterness dismayed him.

It was, therefore, not so clear that Dr. Cahn should visit his wife. Why disturb her last days? Besides, Dr. Cahn seldom went out anywhere. He wouldn't walk with the black nurses (women whom he loved, teased, and was teased by). It wasn't done. "I'll go out later. My feet aren't friendly today."

Or, lowering the paper, "My legs can't trump."

Liss opposed his visit. "Mother's afraid he'll make a scene."

"It doesn't matter," said Will. "He has to have some sense of what's happening. They've been the center of each other's lives. It wouldn't be right."

The hope had been that Dr. Cahn would die first. He was ten years older, his mind had slipped its moorings years ago. Mrs. Cahn was clearheaded, and, except near the end, energetic. She loved to travel, wanted especially to visit Will in Chicago — she had not seen his new apartment — but she wouldn't leave her husband even for a day. "Suppose something happened." "Bring him along." "He can't travel. He'd make an awful scene."

Only old friends tolerated him, played bridge with him, forgiving his lapses and muddled critiques of their play. "If you don't understand a two bid now, you never will." Dr. Cahn was the most gentlemanly of men, but his tongue roughened with his memory. It was as if a lifetime of restraint were only the rind of a wicked impatience.

"He's so spoiled," said Mrs. Cahn, the spoiler.

"Here we are, Dad."

They parked under the blue awning. Dr. Cahn got out his wallet — he always paid for taxis, meals, shows — looked at the few bills, then handed it to his son. Will took a dollar, added two of his own, and thanked his father.

"This is a weak elevator," he said of one of the monsters made to drift the ill from floor to floor. A nurse wheeled in a stretcher and Dr. Cahn removed his fedora.

"Mother's on eight."

"Minnie is here?"

"Yes. She's ill. Step out now."

"I don't need your hand."

Each day, his mother filled less of the bed. Her face, unsupported by dentures, seemed shot away. Asleep, it looked to Will as if the universe leaned on the crumpled cheeks. When he kissed them, he feared they'd turn to dust, so astonishingly delicate was the flesh. The only vanity left was love of attention, and that was part of the only thing that counted, the thought of those who cared for her. How she appreciated the good nurses, and her children. They — who'd never before seen their mother's naked body — would change her nightgown if the nurse was gone. They brought her the bedpan and, though she usually suggested they leave the room, sat beside her while, under the sheets, her weak body emptied its small waste.

For the first time in his adult life, Will found her beautiful. Her flesh was mottled like a Pollock canvas, the facial skin trenched with the awful last ditches of self-defense; but her look melted him. It was human beauty.

Day by day, manners that seemed as much a part of her as her eyes — fussiness, bossiness, nagging inquisitiveness — dropped away. She was down to what she was.

Not since childhood had she held him so closely, kissed his cheek with such force. "This is mine. This is what lasts," said the force.

What was she to him? Sometimes, little more than the old organic scenery of his life. Sometimes she was the meaning of it. "Hello, darling," she'd say. "I'm so glad to see you." The voice, never melodious, was rusty, avian. Beautiful. No actress could match it. "How are you? What's happening?"

"Very little. How are you today?"

She told her news. "Dr. Vacarian was in, he wanted to give me another treatment. I told him, 'No more.' And no more medicine." Each day, she had renounced more therapy. An unspoken decision had been made after a five-hour barium treatment that usurped the last of her strength. (Will thought that might have been its point.) It had given her her last moments of eloquence, a frightening jeremiad about life dark beyond belief, nothing left, nothing right. It was the last complaint of an old champion of complaint, and after it, she had made up her mind to go. There was no more talk of going home.

"Hello, darling. How are you today?"

Will bent over, was kissed and held against her cheek. "Mother, Dad's here."

To his delight, she showed hers. "Where is he?" Dr. Cahn had waited at the door. Now he came in, looked at the bed, realized where he was and who was there.

"Dolph, dear. How are you, my darling? I'm so happy you came to see me."

The old man stooped over and took her face in his hands. For seconds, there was silence. "My dearest," he said; then, "I didn't know. I had no idea. I've been so worried about you. But don't worry now. You look wonderful. A little thin, perhaps. We'll fix that. We'll have you out in no time."

The old man's pounding heart must have driven blood through the clogged vessels. There was no talk of trumps.

"You can kiss me, dear." Dr. Cahn put his lips on hers.

He sat next to the bed and held his wife's hand through the low rail. Over and over he told her she'd be well. She asked about home and the nurses. He answered well for a while. Then they both saw him grow vague and tired. To Will he said, "I don't like the way she's looking. Are you sure she has a good doctor?"

Of course Mrs. Cahn heard. Her happiness watered a bit, not at the facts but at his inattention. Still, she held on. She knew he could not sit so long in a strange room. "I'm so glad you came, darling."

Dr. Cahn heard his cue and rose. "We mustn't tire you, Minnie dear. We'll come back soon."

She held out her small arms, he managed to lean over, and they kissed again.

In the taxi, he was very tired. "Are we home?"

"Almost, Dad. You're happy you saw Mother, aren't you?"

"Of course I'm happy. But it's not a good day. It's a very poor day. Not a good bid at all."

BARRY TARGAN

The Rags of Time

(FROM SOUTHWEST REVIEW)

Awake, O north wind; and come, thou South; blow upon my garden, that the spices thereof may flow out. Let my beloved come into his garden, and eat his pleasant fruits.
                                                             —SONG OF SOLOMON

TWICE A WEEK Thomas Wilkens's passion raged up and in him, pounding and beating against his ribs like a violent bird that, even after weeks of captivity, could not comprehend or abide its cage.

At 1:30, Tuesday and Thursday afternoons, Fay Lester would slam her way, always nearly late, into his class in Seventeenth-Century English Poetry, her hips moving in a flippant bounce of scorn for the way flesh goes.

Why me? Wilkens had wondered to himself when the first hot blast of his infatuation had blown across the decorous, well-tended garden of his life and withered it. He had held up the hands with which he had tended that garden to the mid-afternoon sun and brought them close to his eyes so that he could see the blood-red light through the edges of the fingers. His hands, like his career, like his life, were thin and translucent, soft but precise, well defined. Until now. He had clapped his fingers to his eyes against what he saw, but nothing could darken the self-illuminating madness he tumbled in now. Or was it love?

Love? What had he to do with love? A man of calm and propriety, he had fallen to a slow but enormous poison, that was all; so who was he, Thomas Wilkens, to ask, "Why me?" Who, he asked, are any of us to ask such questions of flesh, especially when the flesh brazenly announced itself to be Fay Lester?

Wilkens sat in his gracious carpeted office in the new faculty building and looked out across the neat, groomed campus sloping down to the bordering village of Cobbton. Between the village and the campus, in the thick buffering band of maples, was his house, near and far enough to bike between when the weather was right, a sedate rider erect on his old three-speed Raleigh, his muffler streaming out behind him in the downhill wind, nearly an anachronistic picture of the professor that he had preserved from an old English film he had once seen, a slight affectation, the smallest permission of whimsy.

In November, when all the leaves were gone, he could make out which house was his, for in Cobbton the houses were elegantly old and individually conceived and far apart. He could see the high, turreted room in which Neil, his elder son, sixteen, crashed about in his life just now, arrogant and befuddled by fits and starts as his body thickened and his thoughts turned.

He and Mildred had wanted the large round turreted room for themselves. A hundred years before, the room had been designed for the masters, and when they had purchased the house ten years ago, the year after he had gotten tenure and been promoted to associate professor, it was that room with all its windows and difficulties (where did anything go in a round room) that had convinced them. The boys slept together then on the second floor.

But at fourteen, Neil had won the room from them, his need for a private territory driving them out. On the other hand, it was their way of containing, of isolating, him. Let his music and his banners and his fantasies be in one place. Let there be a precise boundary between Neil's maddening life and their own so that there could continue to *be* a life of their own. For the tale was too old for telling.

In his own high-school days there had been a cheerleader taller, blonder, prettier than the rest, who answered to the crowds she exhorted as though it was she they cheered rather than the Egremont High School football team out there on the muddy field behind her. And she was right. Nor was this a vain and conscious egotism; she was as lovely and alive, as destined to adulation as swirling hawks and yellowing oaks and summer sunsets are destined. She was an epitome of what all the lesser girls prancing beside her were supposed to be, what women everywhere were aimed at. And the crowds that lived vicariously in the warriors clashing on the field lived vicariously in her as well.

She alone of all the others wore earrings to the game, droplets of gold dangling on delicate chains, and when she swung her head to the rhythm of the chanting ritual cadences, the eye was attracted, as to a bait, to the flickering gold and to her.

For six months the young sophomore Wilkens prowled the halls of Egremont High School for daily glimpses of her. He never spoke to her. She was a senior and possessed by others. In all his masturbatory fantasies she fumed about like an ether making him drunk, knocking him out.

On the day he had given in to Neil he had thought about that girl. Had there been others? He could not remember others, only her. By Mildred he had not been possessed. Mildred he had come to love naturally, as a man ready for life looks up one day at a pretty graduate student in the carrel across from him in the library and decides, *is* decided. He had always loved Mildred tenderly and intelligently, but never fiercely.

On the day he gave the room to Neil he had wanted to say something that would open them to each other, but what could he say? The urgency of youth is too outrageous to be considered carefully like a poem, and even to recognize it is an embarrassment. And what could there have been to say? That time and chance happeneth to all men? What would that have meant to Neil? *Did* it mean anything? But if there was nothing that he could have said to his son then, there was surely even less that he could say now. Not that Neil was asking or talking. Not that he was.

Wilkens looked out of his office window at the pretty picture of his life. It looked just as he had hoped it would when, twenty years ago, he awoke to his last conclusion: that he was lucky and was pleased to be lucky and to know, at twenty-four, what he wanted the rest of his life to be like, to know already the sweetness of contentment, leaping over the riotous excursions of youthful ambition directly into lucidity and peace. If his vision was small, at least it was well lighted.

He could remember the day, at least the sensation, when, one week after he had marched in the commencement for his Master's degree at Syracuse University, old Martinson, the department chairman, had called him and asked him if he could come to his home that afternoon at five o'clock. At their meeting Martinson gave him a drink and offered him a summer-school teaching job that had suddenly developed: one freshman composition course and one survey of British literature course.

He had accepted at once, although he had made elaborate plans for a free summer, his first ever, before returning to graduate school, this time to Brown and to the truly solemn ceremony of the doctorate program. But Europe could be postponed. He accepted the summer job at once because he was overwhelmed by his desire and his long clear view of himself that to go to the library and prepare classes, to find and organize his thoughts and words for the six weeks to come, and then for the years after, was exactly, perfectly, what he wanted to do. What Martinson offered him in the afternoon was his future now — to build fine edifices and then to explain them, to organize and educate, to try and see life steadily and whole through the prismatic imagination of other men who had taken the chances. He was glad he was himself not a writer, had never had any disposition to be one.

Teaching, of course, was what he had always expected he would do, at least from his sophomore year in college. But it was more than just teaching — a calling or a career — that he had leaped to in Martinson's living room, it was a *condition,* the graceful and lucid design of a professor's life as he conceived it. That afternoon, his Master's finished and nothing pending, a magma from deeper than all he knew about himself had had the chance to rise to his surface for Martinson to imprint with his massy seal. And then to cool and solidify.

And that is the way it had been from then to now, a sweetly reasonable succession of life's events arranged in a languid upward curve of pleasant small accomplishments. If there was any major prospect for Wilkens to consider, other than promotion to a full professorship — and even that would come, as had everything else, in time — it was the maintenance of the way things were now and had been; of staying what he was, becoming more of that: a stable man, clearheaded, a *student* of mysteries, not a participant. He understood that about himself, the dry refinement of his mind, the limited extension he would permit it, and that was O.K., fine. He was just how he wanted to be, not smugly so, but contentedly. And there was nothing wrong with that. He made no apologies for the adequacy of his existence. Wrong, if it came to that, was the failure to live your life in the terms that you could handle. Or afford. Wrong was what was going on now.

Fay Lester was neither ignorant nor rough, though after her she left that feeling in the air she had disturbed, just as she left a vital scent, though she wore none.

The conference about her midterm exam had gone on for fifteen increasingly uneasy minutes, though not for her.

"But I just don't know quite what to make of this," he said. "On the first question you write well enough. You seem to understand the impact of the history of the time, of the culture, upon poetry. You seem to understand that the literature is about the . . . the human condition as it exists at a particular moment."

He tried not to look directly at her. He would lose his way if he did that, would change the subject, become friendly, ask her about herself, about college in general, about where she came from, about books she might be reading. Drown.

"Dr. Wilkens," she said.

"What?"

"You were saying?"

But he had wandered. Halfway between question one and question two, he had fatigued, been turned from his proper path off toward what brightly beckoned but which he could not name. Dare name. Though it had drawn him.

"The second question," he came back. "How could you manage the insights of the first question about Donne and Herbert and miss them so completely in the second?"

"It's Vaughan," she said. "Crashaw. Traherne. It's them," she explained. Then stopped as though she had, as though he understood.

"Yes," he urged, "go on."

"I don't like them."

"But you don't have to like them. Just to understand them. That's what the exam is about — a test to see what you know to help direct you to what you should . . ."

"It's all that religion," Fay Lester said as though he had been saying nothing. "To tell you the truth it's hard for me to take, grown men believing in God and religion and all that the way they do. It just turns me off." And then, before he could answer, she added: "It just seems silly."

"Silly?"

She nodded.

He was thrilled and appalled. Whatever else they had been called, praised or blamed for, he had never heard poets of such canonical stature as Henry Vaughan or Richard Crashaw or Thomas Traherne called *silly*. He could not have imagined it happening. But there it was, Fay Lester's judgment, and what was he to do with it? Teach her? Change her mind? Defend Traherne? *Do his job for civilization and the English language?*

"Dr. Wilkens?" He had wandered off again.

"Yes, yes. Your comment, it . . ." He raised his eyebrows and turned his mouth down and lifted his hands, palms up, to imply . . . what? Where were his words today? His weapons? "But what about Donne and Herbert? You like them. You like them a lot." He tapped her bluebook on the desk between them. "And they were religious, lord knows. Donne was dean of St. Paul's. Herbert was a priest in the Church of England. You know that."

"Yes," Fay Lester said, not inching back at all, "but Donne and Herbert, they were better poets."

In that splendid non sequitur, all, not reason least, stood indicted.

"But Donne?" He lifted his lance against her again, but weakly. "He was a cleric. His sermons are immortal testaments to his religious belief. He was always a believer in God."

"Not in the beginning he wasn't," she came right back, instinctively prepared, alert to the nuances of a terrain that she knew well. "For God's sake hold your tongue, and let me love," Fay Lester shouted at him. She filled his office with the victory she assumed.

> Come live with me, and be my love,
> And we will some new pleasures prove
> Of golden sands and crystal brooks;
> With silken lines, and silver hooks.

"That's no priest," she explained to him.

> Love, all alike, no season knows, nor clime,
> Nor hours, days, months, which are the rags of time.

"That's no metaphor for the *spirit* he's talking about, sir. He's talking about the *real thing.*"

The real thing. He staggered under the weight of her instruction. He glanced at his watch to avoid her. He could bear no more. There were spasms in him already that he feared.

"It's late," he said. "It's four o'clock." He leaned forward slowly and then stood up, and was surprised to find that his legs were shaky. And not surprised. But Fay Lester stayed seated. He sat down.

"To tell the truth, Dr. Wilkens, I never did think too much of priesthood and nunship. It's not natural. So the poetry that comes out isn't natural too."

"There's a body of criticism that agrees with you. In some respects. But it's not a strong argument."

"I'm not surprised," she said, overriding him again. She rose at last. "See you Thursday, Dr. Wilkens." And then Fay Lester left but was not gone.

Wilkens stayed in his chair and turned in it to look out of his window at the night coming on, struggling to float down, to release himself, to be still.

He had managed by easy stratagems to see her out of class at least once a week, casual encounters in the library or the bookstore, the college coffee hours, English Club meetings, passings between classrooms and laboratories and dorms. Three weeks ago he had begun to calculate more exactly: he had obtained from the registrar a listing of her class schedule, and wherever it was possible for him to do so, he arranged to be somewhere near enough to see her or hear her voice or to say hello or even stop and talk a moment. This afternoon he had been more privately with her for longer than ever before. He had intended that their meeting should have lasted longer yet, but he could not stand it — the possibilities bred of his imagining, the impossibilities asserted by his life.

Fay Lester had first appeared, though not as the blinding mote in his eye that she became, the year before, and by hearsay. He had been told at some party or other about this prince's daughter for whom Dimitri Varnov, the young Russian instructor, had cut his academic throat so far as staid Cobbton College was concerned. He, Varnov, had fallen too demonstratively in love with her, clearly enough so that his ardor became a factor that had to be considered in the college community life, which it did not want to consider.

Varnov was not rehired, although what had happened to him had happened to most of them once or from time to time: the fall into an infatuation with a student, to look up one ordinary day from his lecture notes at a girl whom he suddenly looks anxiously forward to seeing again when the class meets next.

She becomes the irritant seed around which he constructs the pearl of his first vague and then specific erotic musings and dreams, the protagonistic foil to himself in his symbolic scenarios: the two of them careening off together across some empty white beach by some blue sea somewhere free of everything. The banality of the dream itself is enticing. At last he imagines her when making love to his wife. Until one day when she is standing next to his lectern after a class, he notices some pimples on her forehead or crusts of sleep in the corners of her eyes, a spray of dandruff, a breath made human by pizza and cigarettes. And there are parts of her still molten, not yet fixed, not yet womanly. She is only a little girl. Nothing like the dream-sleek maiden after all. In class she eats Mallo Cups washed down by Pepsi. And paints her fingernails blue.

By the end of the semester he cannot always remember her name.

That was not the invariable pattern, Wilkens knew. Sometimes infatuation stumbled into love, and wives were discarded and girls made wives. And sometimes the infatuation grew into little earthly dalliances. But mainly the sexual impulsiveness was just one of the small, quiet, abrading elements in the professorial life, a slight infection one always ran a risk of just as medical doctors ran comparable risks in the wards.

But Wilkens now was locked into something other than any of these, and so old resolutions were not available to him. He knew that Fay Lester would not pass away into chimera as others had. And certainly he did not want to leave his wife, even for a moment. And he did not want to have an affair, a complicating and difficult liaison. What he wanted was for all this Fay Lester business to go away and leave him be, for her to get out of his body and his mind so that he could get back to the trim arrangement of his life, so that he could have back his time and energy to go on compiling the little notes and gentle observations about literature that he had used, like currency, to buy his existence.

He did not need Fay Lester and he did not want her. He was even angry that she had come upon him this way, unbidden, unexplained. But where could he direct his anger? And he could not be free of this passion that was larger than desire by a simple act of will, either. Even if he had had such a will. He thought back to the golden high-school cheerleader. Even now, across the decades, the throb of that recalled madness drummed in him a bruising tattoo. And surprised him.

So here I am again, he thought, half a lifetime later. GO DONNE GO! HIP HIP FOR HERBERT! C-R-U-S-H CRASHAW! TRAMPLE TRAHERNE! Fay Lester, my metaphysical cheerleader. Wilkens groaned at the bitter portents in the bone. You cannot fight with flesh.

Outside, across the darkness, the lights of Cobbton twinkled as in a fairy-tale village. He distinguished the lights in Neil's high turreted room burning bright. Like a beacon.

"Look at him. Look at that ox," Uncle Norman said, grabbing Neil in a great hug.

Norman Wilkens, three years younger than his brother, had come from Elmira for Thanksgiving, with his springy wife Elaine and their three children: Stephanie, at fifteen, nearly passed beyond earliest angular adolescence to the edges of a comely young womanhood; Joseph, Peter's age; and Fred, at ten, the baby.

Norman took Neil by the shoulders and held him away like a sweater.

"Just look at him, will you. He's grown a foot at least." And then, elaborately, looking all around, "So where is she? Thanksgiving and you didn't invite your girl friend over to meet us? What's the matter? You're ashamed? Or maybe you couldn't decide which one to bring, huh? Is that it? Tough luck, Steph," he shouted over to his daughter, who watched him with practiced blankness, determined to be inured to her outrageous father. "I can see this Adonis is up to here with the girls."

Neil shuddered that his uncle would suddenly, characteristically, show them all where he thought "here" was. But Norman pulled him back into his arms again and squeezed, then let him be, going on now to Peter in his grand exuberant ceremony of love and greeting.

Neil stood his ground, but his father watched the writhing in him that he could see, the boy impaled now upon a sensitivity to his sex so exquisite that he could bear nothing public about it, like a sufferer from one of those rare diseases in which any sunlight upon the skin at all can scorch and blister. It would take more than Uncle Norman's jostling affection and the kidding about his girls to make him bolt out of a room, a house, his skin. But not much more.

And so it went. Norman Wilkens in an endless touching and bustling in and about the children, them, and the past year's events. Elaine dissolving into the kitchen with Mildred. The younger boys rattling in and out of everything. Stephanie with a book in the bay window of the den, doomed to these two days. Neil was nowhere.

At four, colleagues appeared for a couple of hours of easy drinks. And then they left. And after that came the ritual of the feast, which took them into the evening and into the profound structure that arranged them happily.

The next day, from mid-morning to mid-afternoon, the day bright and November-mild enough to walk in, they visited teaching friends who lived on a farm twenty miles from Cobbton. Others visited too, arriving and leaving constantly, making a circuit of the genuine barnyard, standing by the edge of the large fireplace, drinking warm punch, admiring the mountains already capped with a dust of early snow. They talked about books, projects, vacations to come, children visiting from college. This was the soft and gentle and unstressed world where he belonged and must stay. The hard winds beating and flickering at his existence for the past two months must be stilled, driven off. Must be. And here in the midst of his central pleasures he would find the talisman and strength to do it. He could tell. Already it was easier.

The youngest Wilkens children roamed the farm, its fields and woodlot and stream, from time to time returning, brambly and muddied, to report whatever they could remember to bring back. Stephanie and Neil stayed as far from each other as they did from their parents, circling like satellite moons but bent on a comet's course, waiting for gravity to lessen and the great chance to come for them to speed into their expanding universe, to rush into and after it before it got away.

When the time for the Wilkenses to leave came, the boys found Stephanie gazing by the stream side, Neil in the barn's private loft.

At three, Thomas Wilkens took his brother to his health club in the Y. He lent him equipment and they played briefly at handball.

"At your age, this is the stuff that kills you, you know," Norman said, stripping off the sweat-sodden clothes.

"I work out three times a week. I ride a bike or walk almost every day. My weight is perfect." Thomas Wilkens slapped his reasonably flat belly. "Hell, there are guys my age playing pro football." He walked into the shower room.

"Yeah," his brother said after him. "Two. And five hundred

more our age in coronary care units every day from handball or something like it."

After the shower they sat in the steam room, then showered again and then sat in the dry heat of the sauna.

"If handball kills, this saves," Norman said resting back against the redwood walls, his eyes closed as the heat unraveled his muscles, fiber by fiber. "This is glorious. I've got to do something like this. I should take the time. I should force myself. I'm forty-one, Tommy."

"You make it sound like a terminal disease."

"So? Isn't it?"

"What's the matter, Norman? Have you got trouble?"

"No. I don't think so. Nothing I can name, anyway, or describe." The heat pressed into his brains. "Last year, when I turned forty, I thought I was going to be depressed or something. You know? Forty? Middle-aged? That? But I wasn't. It was more like a joke, everyone kidding. But it's like I must have thought that, O.K., forty. Enough is enough. That's it. And now I'm forty-one, sooner than I thought." He laughed. "This is very typical, isn't it?"

"Yes," his brother said. "I think so. Typical, which also means natural. A shock of recognition. But forty isn't sixty, and even sixty isn't so bad any more, I hear."

"I'm not depressed. It isn't that," Norman Wilkens said. "It's just what it obviously is." He opened his eyes and blinked the heavy sweat out of them and glanced over at his brother, alike enough in looks to be twins. "Tommy, is it tough teaching with all those girls around?"

"Not so tough," he said quickly. He looked back at his brother. "It's not such a glamour thing. From the outside, I know it looks like a . . . a harem. And sure, things go on. But altogether not much. Not as much as the public likes to think. Coeds, after all, have always had a strong sexual connotation in the culture. But you get used to it. To see what they look like, many of them, at a nine o'clock class in the winter, it's not so hard to avoid temptation of either thought or deed." He was trying to make his voice inflect with humor and lightness much as he might as a lecturer.

"Were you ever tempted?" Norman Wilkens asked his brother.

"Yes," he said, then quickly, "sure. More than once. But tempted more by the *idea* of something than anything else. Like an aesthetic consideration. Do you understand that, an aesthetic consideration of temptation? More interested in the mechanism of lust than in screwing? The way a theologian can explore the dazzling ramifications of Divinity without actually, personally, believing in a religious God?" He was teaching now and felt safe.

He was strong and certain about everything now. His brother, their families, a Thanksgiving together, his friends and their stability — it had all been the anodyne of order that he had needed, the scruple weight of ritual upon the balance beam that had brought him back to equilibrium. He breathed in deeply the superheated air of the sauna, the air expanding his lungs, *him*, to a giddiness of well-being. He had sweated her out of him as easily as that. He got up. They had had enough heat.

"Sometimes I think of my daughter," Norman Wilkens said to his brother. "I worry about her. I think about what men must think when they look at her now. And what they'll think in a couple more years."

"What my Neil is thinking now?"

"Yeah. And middle-aged men."

"Sure. Right. Sometimes. But this is such a mystery? Something that never occurred to you till now?"

"No. What's new is that I think about it now at all. A lot."

"Well," Thomas Wilkens said, moving to the sauna door, tired of the conversation, of the weight of it, the heat sapping at him now, "let's say it's human. The human condition. It's what we're about." He left the sauna.

"But nothing else?" his brother shouted after him, but his words were quickly broken into molecules of heat.

Monday bloomed. The day itself was edged and sharp like a new-whetted knife, and cold enough to startle but not hurt. A good time for waking up, or for homestretch bursts to the end of the semester; or for some, fresh starts altogether. Wilkens resonated to the day like a crystal of the correct frequency, and the day echoed him back.

His early classes sparkled, both he and the students thinking up to some levels beyond, so that a teacher could believe that the previous slogging weeks had been worth it after all. In the eleven o'clock mail he received notice that an article he had worked on now and again for the past two years had been accepted for publication by the prestigious *Seventeenth Century Studies*. The article,

"Metrical Systems in Crashaw and Traherne: Catholic and Protestant Sensibilities," would be printed in thirty months. Lunch in the faculty dining room surprised them all — crisp shrimp, avocado salad. And in the afternoon, student after student came well prepared to present and discuss topics for the major course paper. By four o'clock he whooped as he soared down to home.

All the day long Fay Lester never crossed his mind. He had not even had to pretend not to be thinking of her; no more sudden looking up out of a colossal reverie; no more scurrying around the campus; no more tumbling mixture of desire and chagrin. So he was free at last, and would, in time, lean back leisurely into this aberration and consider it, recollect it in tranquillity as he might do with some book or poem that had, in its progress, grasped him fiercely about the heart. He would, when the time for it came, consider this whole incident with meticulous and maybe even scholarly detachment and interest, measuring the larger ambiguities of life and his little adventure as best he could.

But not now. Now he was free. He let his bicycle dive through the darkening streets and whooped again, even to his own doorstep.

He was ready for Fay Lester Tuesday afternoon, but she did not come to class, the first she had missed that semester. He had prepared against her, the vaccine of life's neat joys his shield, but he had not prepared for her absence, and the momentum of his defense, the anticipation of his victory over her, carried him through and beyond the resistance he had gauged for into nothing, and he fell, like one of the Three Stooges who rushes to break down the door that opens at the last moment; or, too, like Lucifer and his mighty host cast over the battlements of Heaven, falling farther than time through viscous Chaos into rock-hard Hell. He could have fought *her*, but not the unexpected memory of her, for in memory there is substance greater than objects, and in memory there is longing. By the end of the class he could hardly breathe, suffocating in a delirium of Fay Lester. How could this be happening? He clenched himself into a fist against his life just then and shook himself at it.

In his own college days one Christmas vacation he went skiing in Utah, and in the middle of the second day he followed friends out onto a cornice of snow that collapsed. He never knew how far he fell, and all the time he was falling he was within the snow that was falling too, which stayed tight and heavy around him. When he hit he dug straight into a snowbank and was buried. Later they told him he was only buried for five minutes, but he could never tell that from what he felt while falling and buried, only that he was in terror and yet amazingly beyond time all at once. And he remembered that it was not the terror of dying and death he felt but the terror of hopelessness: the terror that he would *not* die and would not change either out of the entombing whiteness.

And that was what he felt now in his office seated by his window trembling when Fay Lester knocked at his door and opened it and asked if she could enter.

"I'm sorry I missed class, but I had a lot of trouble getting back from where I was."

"That's O.K."

"I was marooned. There were six of us. We spent the weekend in this guy's father's lodge in New Hampshire and we got snowed in. Which wasn't the worst of it."

"Well, I'm glad you made it back O.K. I suppose you came to talk about your paper?"

"It wasn't easy. This guy was from Dartmouth and I think those guys from Dartmouth are a little crazy. Hanover is too far away from anything." He did not want to know. He did not want to hear.

"Your paper?"

"I don't know what I want to do a paper on."

"Have you thought about it?"

"To tell the truth, not much. I thought maybe something about love. They all write about love a lot. I don't know." She was swinging about, trying to hit something, obliged to go on but not much caring.

"Love in seventeenth-century poetry is a pretty broad topic, don't you think? You would have to narrow it down considerably. Religious love? Secular love? Love as a symbol? The Convention of Love Poetry?"

"Yes."

"Yes? Yes *what*? Do you have any more specific ideas?" But what was he asking her? There was a roaring in him.

"No. I thought maybe you could make some suggestions."

"Would you rather come back another day? Think about it and then come back? You seem, well, not into the subject." He began to hit his hand on his desk softly.

"It was this weekend. You wouldn't believe it." And then Fay Lester laughed like it wasn't trouble she had had in high New Hampshire or had brought back with her to his office. "No, Dr. Wilkens." She came back to what was at hand. "I think it would be better for you to assign me something to write about. It's late, only three weeks left to the semester. I'd learn more if you'd just tell me what to look for and I got right down to doing it."

"But selecting a topic is supposed to be part of the learning process. What you select helps me to understand what you've learned." He waited for her response, but she sat still, watching him. And then he wanted her to see deeply enough, wanted her to see his anger and to understand it, as if by her knowing she would draw back out of his life and leave him to return to peace. But what could he expect, that she could in some way *quench* herself? Cease in her nature? Get to a nunnery? He expected nothing; he hoped.

"You could write on *carpe diem*. You remember that, don't you? My lecture?" She nodded. "That would keep you away from Crashaw and Traherne. You'd like to stay away from them, wouldn't you?" She nodded again. She opened her notebook and prepared to take notes. "You'd get to read and think about the good stuff. Remember Herrick, 'To the Virgins, to Make Much of Time'? 'Gather ye rosebuds while ye may,/Old time is still aflying'? Remember that? Or 'Corinna's Going A-Maying'? 'Come, let us go while we are in our prime,/And take the harmless folly of the time.' And Waller's magnificent 'Go, Lovely Rose'? And, of course, Marvell's 'To His Coy Mistress.' Did you read all those poems, Miss Lester? They are on the syllabus, as well as others." He stood up and walked around the desk. He could sit no longer, as if he could not willingly go over his precipice in a padded office chair. "Do you know what *carpe diem* is about, Miss Lester?" He listened to the anger, the accusation, in his voice, the snarl in it.

"Yes." She pushed back against what she heard, the anger. And more.

"What?" He thought he was shouting. Would Billings in the next-door office hear him?

"*Sex,*" she told him, almost ready to stand herself.

"*Death,*" he corrected her, nearly a shriek.

"*What's wrong with you?*" she shouted. And then she did stand up to face him.

"You don't want to write this paper, do you?"

"NO. I DON'T. But I've got to, don't I?"

He turned away and walked back to his desk.

They both sat down. He turned in his chair more than sideways from her. He looked obliquely out toward Cobbton. The concluding line to Herrick's trivial tinkling couplet clanged in him like a curfew knell: the folly of the time, the folly of the time.

The folly of time.

At last he heard her gently say, as if she had been talking to him but he had not heard, "But I *don't* have to write this paper, do I?"

He said nothing for as long as he could continue to believe that he was going to answer her question as he always thought he would answer such questions, and when he gave that up he stepped into space and said, "Perhaps not."

Then he waited for the room and then the building and then his life to crack into pieces. For Billings listening in the next office to come running out denouncing him to the faculty as a hypocrite and liar, for the atoms of what he had always said and believed about life's moral necessities and balances to coalesce into a fissionable mass of personal holocaust. But he was elated instead, and stunned to discover that he was elated. "Perhaps not," he repeated, and turned to look at her whose beauty and allure, which had to this moment astonished him, now reached out more like the soft promise it was and maybe had always been.

"What do I say now?" he asked her. "What do I say next?" Having gone so far toward his perdition as this, he could be whimsical, like Hamlet, clowning by the graveside, clarified by what he had already dared even though trapped into a strict course. So are mountaineers sometimes elated and eased in attaining a desperate ledge upon which they can rest and recoup but from which they cannot descend. It isn't the way they want to go; it is the only way that is left.

But of course Wilkens still had options, if he chose.

"I have a friend who has an apartment I can get," Fay Lester said, taking his options away. "Listen," she said, "let me handle this. I guess you've got to be careful."

He wondered if she mocked him. But no. Her experience with Dimitri Varnov must have schooled her. Certainly it must have been the impetuous Russian and not this efficient girl who had disvalued the world's opinion to his own loss. Fay Lester knew, kindly and firmly, what she was about. Increasingly he was charmed by what was precisely happening more than he was excited by what would.

And so it was arranged. On the Friday after this coming Friday, he would go to an address in Cobbton village that she gave him. At three in the afternoon. It was reasonably safe.

Standing by the office door she said, "Dr. Wilkens, you don't know what a load off my mind this is."

So it could not be his desire for her that compelled him. Not now.

When we set off across a chartless sea toward a landfall we can only dimly surmise, and even that doubtfully, as in a dreamscape where there is no port we can count on, only at best a far shore and the oceanic sweep, then every act becomes a tactic, a response to the universe. We sail *when* we have wind, we sail *where* there is leeway. We dodge squalls and run in troughs of heavy seas; staying afloat and heading into the western airs is all that matters. So Wilkens sailed through his week and a half of voyage, uncertain where he was taking himself or why, but certain that he was in motion again, no longer trapped in the mad latitudes of the past few months, and that seemed enough. The order he had wanted to wrest back from Fay Lester he had, now that he had made his pact. His life was less feverish again. There might be shoals out there awaiting him, but he commanded his own ship. He was vibrant with perception, keen with curious insight, as long as he kept moving, an actor, a participant. Only when he sometimes thought to call it off would the old leering panic and confusion in his body start to throb. Committed, he was safe. If that was the price he had to pay, then he could.

He met his classes and his students in conferences, worked on faculty committee assignments, wrote on his review of a book for *Renaissance Studies,* played handball at the Y, drove with Peter to a high-school basketball game away at Marlton, dined with Mildred Saturday at the Brookshires, spent Sunday happily with the *Times.*

The week was firm. Even when Fay Lester came into class he did not falter. Instead he considered, and with odd pleasure in the belittling irony, that what had seduced him was an Idea after all and not passion itself; it was a fate not unfit for a scholar/acolyte of the ghostly poet Traherne, who had of his own human predicament written:

I knew not that there was a Serpents Sting,
Whose Poyson shed
On Men, did overspread
The World: nor did I dream of such a Thing
As Sin; in which Mankind lay Dead.

And then it was Friday and time. He showered thoroughly and dressed with special care — new undershorts and T-shirt, no holes in his socks — ate his usual thin breakfast and then went about his day, as ordinary a Friday as he had ever spent. At one-thirty he returned home. Mildred, an audiologist, was somewhere out in the country testing grade-schoolers for hearing difficulties. For an hour he sat in his study, his mind traveling around and around the edges of a contemplation.

He did not want Fay Lester; his blood did not rage for her as in the earlier months of the college year it had, as years ago it had raged for his golden cheerleader. He had never made great sexual demands upon his life, nor had Mildred; they had been on that point as well as most others satisfied and well mated. What he wanted from Fay Lester he decided over and over again as he circled about in the vagaries of such measuring, what he wanted was to do what he was going to do, to do this outrageous and nearly irrational thing. It was all as simple and as complex as that. He looked at his walls; four hundred square feet of books, he had once calculated. And so had all their knowledge come to this.

At two-thirty he started off. He walked down to the denser part of the village. The day was cold but not hard, clear but not gleaming, as winter days could be in January after snowstorms in the reflecting sun. This was early December, that time of year without equilibrium, when days as late as autumn can come back, or overnight deep winter burst like a bomb. He turned left at Lamont Street, the nearest Cobbton could come to a *quarter:* three blocks of closer houses that had been converted into apartments. Some young faculty lived in this area, and students from the college who, in their senior year, could live off campus if they wanted; and people between college and whatever was to come after lived there; and single workers in the marble quarries twenty miles away; and older pensioners. An art gallery, two bars, a bookstore, some lunchrooms and assorted shops.

Wilkens had been into the area often enough. It would not appear unusual for him to be there now. He walked up the wide wooden stairs at 327 Lamont Street, into the foyer, up to the second floor landing and, as she had directed him, immediately into the front apartment.

She sat deeply in a very old high-backed, thickly stuffed reading chair, her legs tucked beneath her, her long golden-white hair a mantle, the light from the window sculpting the high, tight curve of her breasts. If he had not come here under the lash of appetite, looking at her now he wished he had. All about softly played a folk-rock song about mountains and trees.

"Hi," she said, getting up. "You're on the dot. Find this place O.K.?"

"Yes." He took off his muffler, gloves, overcoat, and dropped them on the arm of a sofa. He looked around at the apartment, but he could not tell from what he saw who might live here, who Fay Lester's friend was — someone like him more permanently based, or just a student perhaps like her. And waiting in the closet to charge out with a camera when they were in each other's arms? Were there tape recorders scattered about? Old jealous boy friends lurking (Dimitri Varnov)?

But Wilkens had dealt with his apprehensions over the past ten days, and he had quickly learned not to think about what would happen and what he would do if he were caught. There was too much he could terrify himself with that way and no solution either. And once he stopped thinking of catastrophe, the dread of anticipation nearly went away. What he was left with was the proper view; he was taking a chance but not so great a one. And that, more than her, was what he wanted.

In the middle of the room they stood looking at each other. Had he expected her to talk? What *had* he expected from her? Or from himself? That he would amuse her with witty discourse? My vegetable love should grow/Vaster than empires and more slow?

"Well," she said, "let's go." She walked into the bedroom.

She stripped herself quickly and stood naked across from him before he had gotten out of his shoes and socks.

"I thought you might want to look at me."

He worked at his clothes more quickly. And then he was naked with her too. They got into the bed together and he enwrapped her and began to kiss her. She reached down between them and took him into her hand. Her hand was ice. After a time he rose above her. Before he entered her, she said, "Listen. I don't have to take the final exam either, do I?"

"No," he said. "No." And down he went.

He walked back from the village to the campus, nearly three miles. All the way he waited for his thoughts, but the heavy words like *adultery* did not come. Nothing did, neither *tristesse* nor guilt nor exuberance nor gaiety. If he felt anything to which he could give a name it would be accomplishment, achievement, but not as in a triumph. All he could compare it to was how he felt when his article had been accepted for publication by *Seventeenth Century Studies*. Then and now his life seemed stronger, better balanced, affirmed, prospective, as if his life was running on evenly, well tuned, which was all that life was supposed to do.

In his office, between the writing of one letter to a friend and the writing of another, the actual statement "contented with life" occurred to him. What a minimal way of expressing what that means, he thought. But then, he was no poet nor was meant to be. Was rather an attendant to events. At five-fifteen he started home.

Parked in front of his house was a state-police car. He ran into the house. A trooper, large and gray, was speaking to Mildred. Whatever he had said to her she had not comprehended yet. Even as Wilkens rushed to her he saw her absorb it like the recoil of a branch in a terrible wind.

"No," she said. "Oh no." She did not see her husband next to her. She was sliding quickly into shock.

"That is the charge, Ma'am. Would you please call him?" The trooper was gentle.

"What? What is it?" Wilkens demanded.

"I have a warrant for the arrest of Neil Wilkens on the complaint of Cecily Grant and her father, Frederick Grant," the trooper opened his paper and began to read from it, "who alleges that on December the . . ."

"What?" Wilkens broke in. "Tell me what?"

"Rape," the trooper said, lowering the paper. What could the details mean now? "In the first degree. If your son is at home would you please call him?" Mildred's hands were knotted into her hair, frozen between ripping and screaming. Peter stood, had been standing, halfway up the stairs.

"Is Neil home?" he asked his second son, who nodded, wide with fear. "I'll get him," he said to the trooper. "Let me get him. There will be no trouble. Just let me get him," as if he imagined violence. He ran quickly to the stairs and up them to the high dark turret. The door was open.

"Neil?" He turned on the light and looked about. The boy lay on his bed. "Neil, there's a state trooper downstairs who has a warrant . . ."

"I heard," the boy said. "It's a lie."

"You'll tell me about it, but right now we have to go down and go with the trooper. Now listen to me, Neil. *Neil, sit up!*" The boy rose slowly.

"She's a goddamn liar," he said.

"Good. Fine. Just listen to me. Don't talk to the police about this, do you hear? We'll go down and you'll get arraigned and I'll get a lawyer and bail and you'll be home in an hour. Then we'll talk, O.K.? Neil, are you listening? For christsake, Neil, *are you listening?*"

"Yes."

Downstairs the trooper had led Mildred to a chair. Wilkens phoned Jean Lipson, their nearest friend, and told her enough to get her over to the house to stay with Mildred until he could return.

"Pete," his father said to him at the door. "Go sit by your mother. Hold her hand." By the curb, as he and Neil got into the back of the police cruiser, a cage, he knew how much of Cobbton must already be reporting this. They drove off, slowly, with no siren or whirling lights.

Neil was not arraigned. In an hour charges had been dropped. During that afternoon Neil and three of his friends went with Cecily Grant and one by one did with her what half of Cobbton's high-school males had done. What Frederick Grant had discovered that afternoon was not the act but the size of it; he may have known even before, but only now could he abide his daughter no longer, and called the cops, as much to stop her as to stop the boys of Cobbton whom she had helped along their way.

In the substation, officials bustled around Frederick Grant. From time to time his rage and confusion spumed up. Wilkens and the three other fathers sat together silently on a bench on the other side of the room. The high-school principal, two guidance counselors, the school psychologist appeared, nodded at the four fathers, and went to talk to Grant. Policemen, lawyers, even a clergyman none of them knew. At last Grant relented. His daughter had more to lose of what was left than to gain in proceeding with the action. He put on his coat. Before he left the station he passed by the four fathers and paused and looked at them. Whatever anger he had had was gone. They were all in this together. Daughters, fathers, sons.

It was difficult for Wilkens to comprehend that, only little more than an hour later than usual, the four of them were eating supper together as if the last hours had only been a gimmicky device of technique in a manneristic French film where the real is definable only in flickering glimpses of its underside, the way photographic negatives become positives when held at the proper angle to light. Wilkens had immediately called Mildred to tell her Neil was safe, that it was all over. They were coming home. He would stop on the way for a bucket of fried chicken. "Make a salad," he told her. "And make me a very large martini." Mildred had broken into laughter and tears. By the time they got home, she would be solid again.

Was this a celebration, he wondered at the table? Should he open champagne and make a playful toast? It was not the kind of victory you crow about exactly. Or do you? Wilkens considered his son. There was no repentance in him. Nor embarrassment. He had undergone his rite of passage and survived it, more narrowly than most. But if his danger had turned out to be greater, so too would be his reward tomorrow when the feral pack he roamed with would howl his praises.

The telephone rang frequently throughout the evening, and he and Mildred took turns delicately explaining to their friends what had happened. To every single one's amusement.

He could not fall asleep at once that night. The day hovered over him; it had been such a day. He tried to make distinctions, to force these rare events into an insight or a judgment, to make something out of these prodigies. But it all blurred, collapsed as if he were building with soft concrete where he needed brick. His last thought before sleep did finally come was that there was perhaps nothing special to be understood; that nothing extraordinary had happened. Only that it had happened to him. That time and chance happeneth to all men.

*

Monday began the week of final exams and the windstorm of term papers, excuses, pleas for incompletes, and all the other crises that the young can invent for themselves. But the true weather held good. Wilkens rode his bicycle to school and waded into the last high tide of the semester.

Tuesday afternoon he gave the final exam in the Seventeenth Century course and collected the term papers. He announced, "I'll read the papers and grade the exams and you can pick them both up from me next semester. If you want your final grade as soon as possible, give me a stamped, self-addressed postcard." And then he set them to scribbling work.

Fay Lester was in the classroom. She wore the same sweater and skirt that she had worn on Friday. To remind him? She bent to apparent work over a bluebook and turned it in with the rest of the class. She left no term paper, but no one noticed or would have.

After class, in his office, he went through the pile of exams until he came to hers. He opened it. It was blank. Inside was a postcard addressed to her at her home somewhere on Long Island.

Through the rest of the week he read exams and term papers and dutifully wrote comments between the lines and in the margins, and a concluding paragraph or two at the end. He held no great illusions about what was accomplished by his responding in this reasonably labored detail; few students considered in any significant depth what he said. The grade at the end of the comment loomed too large. But he felt responsible to his function and to his own knowledge. He would do his part, let them make of it what they may.

Monday again and the campus was mostly empty, all but a few students gone for their long Christmas vacation. Wilkens settled in, after the cushion of the weekend, to fairly deciding final grades. After lunch that day he got to the Seventeenth Century. In his grade book, by Fay Lester's name, there was a C for her midterm exam. In the column for the term paper he wrote "accepted." For the final exam he put a noncommittal check, to keep at least the record straight. For the final grade he put a C. He marked her postcard and mailed it along with all the others late that afternoon. He signed the grade sheets for his classes and turned them in to the registrar. And that was the end of that.

For the rest of the week he arranged his files, began to look over his lecture notes for the course he would teach next semester, and worked on his review article. It was a gentle moment, one of the periods in the academic year that he enjoyed most, like a deep breath, like time-out in a game. That Friday afternoon they would drive down to New York to visit for a week their oldest friends, a couple who went back to their own graduate-school days. It was a week they all gave each other every year, like a gift, a time for absorbing the city, for shows, for restaurants, shopping, bookstores, and long evenings of talk. It was a good week right now for Wilkens to look forward to, light and buoying as he knew it would be.

Not that he was sinking. His days and nights fit well enough to suit him. Fay Lester had not seeped through unexpected fissures in his soul to poison his dreams. His life was as abundant as he could want it to be, and as much more of it as he had had already stretched out before him waiting. But he could not place what he had done in a sufficient context. The act, which settled so much that was turbulent, yet did not feel completed. He had explained himself to himself in every way, and every way was right but not *enough*, as if he would pour a cup of water into a bucket and the level would rise with every cup but the bucket would never fill.

But what most disturbed him was the recurrence of the memory of his falling through the cornice of snow and being buried. He would think about Fay Lester in controlled and rational terms, like the exegesis of a poem; but then unbidden would come the memory of that nearly fatal accident of so long ago. After a few moments he could drive the memory away, but he could not stop it from arriving when it chose. Twice now in four months his mind determined him against his conscious will: first his virulent agony for Fay Lester, and now this memory. He looked forward to his New York visit, which would scrub all of this away.

Fay Lester stood in the open door of his office.

"You son of a bitch!" she screamed. He turned into air, all the atoms of him spinning off in all directions. He could exactly feel them go. "You rotten miserable son of a bitch."

"Close the door," he managed. But she did not.

"A *C*. You gave me a *C*. My mother told me on the phone."

"Please. Close the door." She could not hear him; her anger burned away everything as she advanced.

"How could you do it? A *C*? Listen, you. I was probably the best thing you ever had. And you . . . you stink. I'd give you an . . . F.

An F *minus!*" He got his body together and stumbled from behind his desk to the door to get it closed just before she said, "What are you trying to do, blackmail me? Extort me? A *C* for a lay? What next? A *B* for going down on you? Jesus, what do I have to do for an *A,* tricks?" She wept as only rage can weep.

"I wasn't grading you," he tried to explain, his throat so suddenly constricted that it was raw. "I didn't think you cared about the grade. I was trying to be safe, to avoid suspicion. You can understand that, can't you?" He wanted to touch her shoulder, to soothe her, but he did not dare. "Suppose someone who worked for an A found out that you got an A? What would happen?"

"What do I care? What difference is that to me? And let me remind you, Dr. Wilkens, I *did* work for my grade. You didn't talk about different work when you made the deal." She wept harder yet. "You son of a bitch."

"Please," he said. "Don't take it personally. I wanted to protect both of us. I didn't want to take a chance."

"But you *did.* You *did* take a chance." She raised her arms, her fists, and shook them as if he did not understand and she would batter down his ignorance.

But they meant different things.

"*Another* chance," he said. And then he added, softly, rasping, "Any *more* chances." But then he was looking somewhere else, at long vistas that had unexpectedly begun to open, a view so vast he could have fainted from it, and over or through it all a bloom of light rising and widening and rushing toward him, intensifying until his eyes seared. He staggered. Vaughan swept through him as what he saw must once have swept through Vaughan:

> *I saw Eternity the other night,*
> *Like a great ring of pure and endless light,*
>   *All calm, as it was bright;*
> *And round beneath it, Time in hours, days, years,*
>   *Driven by the spheres*
> *Like a vast shadow moved; in which the world*
>   *And all her train were hurl'd.*

And then it darkened, snapped out like an electric bulb. By small but absolute degrees he let drift out of him Vaughan's hallucinated universe that he had peeked at. In the blackness, over his heaving breath, he heard her say, "Then you won't do it?" She had sobbed down.

"Do what?" She sounded distant, far away, as if his eardrums had been pressured, muffled. The darkness changed into a dull, unilluminated whiteness like the inside of a cloud. "Do what?" he repeated.

"Change my grade?"

Her grade? "I can't," he said. "I . . ." He could not keep a steady train of thought. "I'd have to write a reason for the registrar." The soft white helpless dream of the snow packed in around him blurring everything. "It would — could — draw attention . . ." He stopped. What difference did explanations make now? What explanations were there? "No. I'm sorry. I can't."

"You could." She flared up again a little. "You could. You're just afraid."

"Yes," he said. "I am."

When she was gone he sat quite still and let the first terror she had brought in with her subside. He let fade the jagged collage of public accusation and denial that had first sprung through him, the tumult of fear that he would lose . . . what? Everything? But what could that mean? No. The loss he had sustained would be a small one, something he would hardly notice in his life as it had been and would be lived hereafter. There would be no more chances.

At last he was empty.

Tomorrow they would drive down to the city. That evening, the reservations already made, they would eat at Normandie de Soire on 53rd Street. Vichyssoise, artichoke vinaigrette, escargots, coq au vin, a 1969 St. Julien. A supper you could count on.

PETER TAYLOR

The Old Forest

(FROM THE NEW YORKER)

I WAS already formally engaged, as we used to say, to the girl I was going to marry. But still I sometimes went out on the town with girls of a different sort. And during the very week before the date set for the wedding, in December, I was in an automobile accident at a time when one of those girls was with me. It was a calamitous thing to have happen — not the accident itself, which caused no serious injury to anyone, but the accident plus the presence of that girl.

As a matter of fact, it was not unusual in those days — forty years ago and a little more — for a well-brought-up young man like me to keep up his acquaintance, until the very eve of his wedding, with some member of what we facetiously and somewhat arrogantly referred to as the Memphis demimonde. (That was merely to say with a girl who was not in the Memphis debutante set.) I am not even sure how many of us knew what the word *demimonde* meant or implied. But once it had been applied to such girls it was hard for us to give it up. We even learned to speak of them individually as demimondaines — and later corrupted that to demimondames. The girls were of course a considerably less sophisticated lot than any of this sounds, though they were bright girls certainly and some of them even highly intelligent. They read books, they looked at pictures, and they were apt to attend any concert or play that came to Memphis. When the old San Carlo Opera Company turned up in town, you could count on certain girls of the demimonde being present in their block of seats, and often with a score of the opera in hand. From that you will understand that they certainly weren't the innocent, untutored types that we generally took to dances at the Memphis Country Club and whom we eventually looked forward to marrying.

These girls I refer to would, in fact, very frequently and very frankly say to us that the M.C.C. (that's how we always spoke of the club) was the last place they wanted to be taken. There was one girl in particular, not so smart as some of the others perhaps and certainly less restrained in the humor she sometimes poked at the world we boys lived in, an outspoken girl, who was the most vociferous of all in her disdain for the country club. I remember one night, in one of those beer gardens that became popular in Memphis in the late thirties, when this girl suddenly announced to a group of us, "*I* haven't lost anything at the M.C.C. That's something you boys can bet your daddy's bottom dollar on." We were gathered — four or five couples — about one of the big wooden beer-garden tables with an umbrella in its center, and when she said that, all the other girls in the party went into a fit of laughter. It was a kind of giggling that was unusual for them. The boys in the party laughed, too, of course, but we were surprised by the way the girls continued to giggle among themselves for such a long time. We were out of college by then and thought we knew the world pretty well; most of us had been working for two or three years in our fathers' business firms. But we didn't see why this joke was so very funny. I suppose it was too broad for us in its reference. There is no way of knowing, after all these years, if it was too broad for our sheltered minds or if the rest of the girls were laughing at the vulgar tone of the girl who had spoken. She was, you see, a little bit coarser than the rest, and I suspect they were laughing at the way she had phrased what she said. For us boys, anyhow, it was pleasant that the demimondaines took the lighthearted view they did about not going to the M.C.C., because it was the last place most of us would have wished to take them. Our *other* girls would have known too readily who they were and would not willingly or gracefully have endured their presence. To have brought one of those girls to the club would have required, at any rate, a boy who was a much bolder and freer spirit than I was at twenty-three.

To the liberated young people of today all this may seem a corrupting factor in our old way of life — not our snobbery so much as our continuing to see those demimonde girls right up until the time of marriage. And yet I suspect that in the Memphis of today customs concerning serious courtship and customs concerning unacknowledged love affairs have not been entirely altered. Automobile accidents occur there still, for instance, the reports of which in the newspaper do not mention the name of the driver's "female companion," just as the report of my accident did not. If the driver is a "scion of a prominent local family" with his engagement to be married already announced at an M.C.C. party, as well as in the Sunday newspaper, then the account of his automobile collision is likely to refer to the girl in the car with him only as his "female companion." Some newspaper readers might, I know, assume this to be a reference to the young man's fiancée. That is what is intended, I suppose — *for* the general reader. But it would almost certainly not have been the case — not in the Memphis, Tennessee, of 1937.

The girl with me in my accident was a girl whose origins nobody knew anything about. But she was a perfectly decent sort of girl, living independently in a respectable rooming house and working at a respectable job. That was the sort of girl about whom the Memphis newspapers felt obliged to exercise the greatest care when making any reference to her in their columns. It was as though she were their special ward. Such a girl must be protected from any blaze of publicity. Such a girl must not suffer from the misconduct of any Memphis man or group of men — even newspaper publishers. That was fine for the girl, of course, and who could possibly resent it? It was splendid for her, but I, the driver of the car, had to suffer considerable anguish just because of such a girl's presence in the car, and suffer still more because of her behavior afterward. Moreover, the response of certain older men in town to her subsequent behavior would cause me still further anguish and prolong my suffering by several days. Those men were the editors of the city's two newspapers, along with the lawyers called in by my father to represent me if I should be taken into court. There was also my father himself, and the father of my fiancée, *his* lawyer (for some reason or other), and, finally, no less a person than the mayor of Memphis, all of whom one would ordinarily have supposed to be indifferent to the caprices of such a girl. They were the civic leaders and merchant princes of the city. They had great matters on their minds. They were, to say the least, an imposing group in the eyes of a young man who had just the previous year entered his father's cotton-brokerage firm, a young man who was still learning how to operate under the pecking order of Memphis's male establishment.

The girl in question was named Lee Ann Deehart. She was a quite beautiful, fair-haired, hazel-eyed girl with a lively manner, and surely she was far from stupid. The thing she did that drew attention from the city fathers came very near, also, to changing the course of my entire life. I had known Lee Ann for perhaps two years at the time, and knew her to be more levelheaded and more reserved and self-possessed than most of her friends among the demimondaines. It would have been impossible for me to predict the behavior she was guilty of that winter afternoon. Immediately after the collision, she threw open the door on her side of the car, stepped out on the roadside, and fled into the woods of Overton Park, which is where the accident took place. And from that time, and during the next four days, she was unheard from by people who wished to question her and protect her. During that endless-seeming period of four days no one could be certain of Lee Ann Deehart's whereabouts.

The circumstances of the accident were rather complicated. The collision occurred just after three o'clock on a very cold Saturday afternoon — the fourth of December. Although at that time in my life I was already a member of my father's cotton firm, I was nevertheless — and strange as it may seem — enrolled in a Latin class out at Southwestern College, which is on the north side of Overton Park. (We were reading Horace's Odes!) The class was not held on Saturday afternoon, but I was on my way out to the college to study for a test that had been scheduled for Monday. My interest in Latin was regarded by my father and mother as one of my "anomalies" — a remnant of many "anomalies" I had annoyed them with when I was in my teens and was showing some signs of "not turning out well." It seemed now of course that I had "turned out well" after all, except that nobody in the family and nobody among my friends could understand why I went on showing this interest in Latin. I was not able to explain to them why. Any more than I was able to explain why to myself. It clearly had nothing to do with anything else in my life at that period. Furthermore, in the classroom and under the strict eye of our classics professor, a rotund, mustachioed little man hardly four feet in height (he had to sit on a large Latin dictionary in order to be comfortable at his desk), I didn't excel. I was often embarrassed by having to own up to Professor Bartlett's accusation that I had not so much as glanced at the assigned odes before coming to class. Sometimes other members of the class would be caught helping me with the translation, out in the hallway, when Professor Bartlett opened his classroom door to us. My real excuse for neglecting the assignments made by that earnest and admirable little scholar was that too many hours of my life were consumed by my job, by my courtship of the society girl I was going to marry, and by my old, bad habits of knocking about town with my boyhood cronies and keeping company with girls like Lee Ann Deehart.

Yet I had persisted with my Horace class throughout that fall (against the advice of nearly everyone, including Professor Bartlett). On that frigid December afternoon I had resolved to mend my ways as a student. I decided I would take my Horace and go out to Professor Bartlett's classroom at the college and make use of his big dictionary in preparing for Monday's test. It was something we had all been urged to do, with the promise that we would always find the door unlocked. As it turned out, of course, I was destined not to take the test on Monday and never to enter Professor Bartlett's classroom again.

It happened that just before I was setting out from home that afternoon I was filled suddenly with a dread of silence and the peculiar isolation of a college classroom building on a weekend afternoon. I telephoned my fiancée and asked her to go along with me. At the other end of the telephone line, Caroline Braxley broke into laughter. She said that I clearly had no conception of all the things she had to do within the next seven days, before we were to be married. I said I supposed I ought to be helping in some way, though until now she had not asked me so much as to help address invitations to the wedding. "No indeed," said my bride-to-be, "I want to do everything myself. I wouldn't have it any other way."

Caroline Braxley, this capable and handsome bride-to-be of mine, was a very remarkable girl, just as today, as my wife, she seems to me a very remarkable woman of sixty. She and I have been married for forty-one years now, and her good judgment in all matters relating to our marriage has never failed her — or us. She had already said to me before that Saturday afternoon that a successful marriage depended in part on the two persons' developing and maintaining a certain number of separate interests in life. She was all for my keeping up my golf, my hunting, my fishing. And, unlike my own family, she saw no reason that I shouldn't keep up my peculiar interest in Latin, though she had to confess that she thought it almost the funniest thing she had ever heard of a man of my sort going in for.

Caroline liked any sort of individualism in men. But I already knew her ways sufficiently well to understand that there was no use trying to persuade her to come along with me to the college. I wished she would come with me, or maybe I wished even more she would try to persuade me to come over to her house and help her with something in preparation for the wedding. After I had put down the telephone, it even occurred to me that I might simply drive over to her house and present myself at her front door. But I knew what the expression on her face would be, and I could even imagine the sort of thing she would say: "No man is going to set foot in my house this afternoon, Nat Ramsey! *I'm* getting married next Saturday, in case the fact has slipped your mind. Besides, you're coming here for dinner tonight, aren't you? And there are parties every night next week!"

This Caroline Braxley of mine was a very tall girl. (Actually taller than she is nowadays. We have recently measured ourselves and found that each of us is an inch shorter than we used to be.) One often had the feeling that one was looking up at her, though of course she wasn't really so tall as that. Caroline's height and the splendid way she carried herself was one of her first attractions for me. It seems to me now that I was ever attracted to tall girls — that is, when there was the possibility of falling in love. And I think this was due in part to the fact that even as a boy I was half in love with my father's two spinster sisters, who were nearly six feet in height and were always more attentive to me than to the other children in the family.

Anyhow, only moments after I had put down the telephone that Saturday, when I still sat with my hand on the instrument and was thinking vaguely of rushing over to Caroline's house, the telephone underneath my hand began ringing. Perhaps, I thought, it was Caroline calling back to say that she had changed her mind. Instead, it was Lee Ann Deehart. As soon as she heard my voice, she began telling me that she was bored to death. Couldn't I think of something fun she and I could do on this dreary winter afternoon? I laughed aloud at her. "What a shameless wench you are, Lee Ann!" I said.

"Shameless? How so?" she said with pretended innocence.

"As if you weren't fully aware," I lectured her, "that I'm getting married a week from today!"

"What's that got to do with the price of eggs in Arkansas?" She laughed. "Do you think, old Nat, *I* want to marry you?"

"Well," I explained, "I happen to be going out to the college to cram for a Latin test on Monday."

I could hear her laughter at the other end. "Is your daddy going to let you off work long enough to take your Latin test?" she asked with heavy irony in her voice. It was the usual way those girls had of making fun of our dependence on our fathers.

"Ah, yes," I said tolerantly.

"And is he going to let you off next Saturday, too," she went on, "long enough to get married?"

"Listen," I said, "I've just had an idea. Why don't you ride out to the college with me, and fool around some while I do my Latin?" I suppose I didn't really imagine she would go, but suddenly I had thought again of the lonely isolation of Dr. Bartlett's classroom on a Saturday afternoon. I honestly wanted to go ahead out there. It was something I somehow felt I had to do. My preoccupation with the study of Latin poetry, ineffectual student though I was, may have represented a perverse wish to experience the isolation I was at the same time dreading or may have represented a taste for morbidity left over from my adolescence. I can allow myself to speculate on all that now, though it would not have occurred to me to do so at the time.

"Well," said Lee Ann Deehart presently, to my surprise and delight, "it couldn't be more boring out there than sitting here in my room is."

"I'll pick you up in fifteen minutes," I said quickly. And I hung up the telephone before she could possibly change her mind.

Thirty minutes later, we were driving through Overton Park on our way to the college. We had passed the art gallery and were headed down the hill toward the low ground where the park pond is. Ahead of us, on the left, were the gates to the zoo. And on beyond was the point where the road crossed the streetcar tracks and entered a densely wooded area that is actually the last surviving bit of the primeval forest that once grew right up to the bluffs above the Mississippi River. Here are giant oak and yellow-poplar trees older than the memory of the earliest white settler. Some of them surely may have been mature trees when Hernando de Soto passed this way, and were very old trees indeed when General

Jackson, General Winchester, and Judge John Overton purchased this land and laid out the city of Memphis. Between the art gallery and the pond there used to be, in my day, a little spinney of woods that ran nearly all the way back to what was left of the old forest. It was just when I reached this spinney, with Lee Ann beside me, that I saw a truck approaching us on the wrong side of the icy road. There was a moderately deep snow on the ground, and the park roads had, to say the least, been imperfectly cleared. On the ice and the packed snow, the driver of the truck had clearly lost control of his vehicle. When he was within about seventy-five feet of us, Lee Ann said, "Pull off the road, Nat!"

Lee Ann Deehart's beauty was of the most feminine sort. She was a tiny, delicate-looking girl, and I had noticed, when I went to fetch her that day, in her fur-collared coat and knitted cap and gutta-percha boots she somehow seemed smaller than usual. And I was now struck by the tone of authority coming from this small person whose diminutive size and whose role in my life were such that it wouldn't have occurred to me to heed her advice about driving a car — or about anything else, I suppose. I remember feeling something like: This is an ordeal that I must and that I want to face in my own way. It was as though Professor Bartlett himself were in the approaching truck. It seemed my duty not to admit any weakness in my own position. At least I *thought* that was what I felt.

"Pull off the road, Nat!" Lee Ann urged again. And my incredible reply to her was "He's on *my* side of the road! Besides, trucks are not allowed in the park!" And in reply to this Lee Ann gave only a loud snicker.

I believe I did, in the last seconds, try to swing the car off onto the shoulder of the road. But the next thing I really remember is the fierce impact of the two vehicles' meeting.

It was a relatively minor sort of collision, or seemed so at the moment. Since the driver of the truck, which was actually a converted Oldsmobile sedan — and a rather ancient one at that — had the good sense not to put on his brakes and to turn off his motor, the crash was less severe than it might have been. Moreover, since I *had* pulled a little to the right it was not a head-on meeting. It is worth mentioning, though, that it was sufficiently bad to put permanently out of commission the car I was driving, which was not my own car (my car was in the shop, being refurbished for the honeymoon trip) but an aging Packard limousine of my mother's, which I knew she would actually be happy to see retired. I don't remember getting out of the car at all and I don't remember Lee Ann's getting out. The police were told by the driver of the truck, however, that within a second after the impact, Lee Ann had thrown open her door, leaped out onto the snow-covered shoulder, jumped the ditch beyond, and run up the incline and into the spinney. The truck driver's account was corroborated by two ice skaters on the pond, who also saw her run through the leafless trees of the spinney and on across a narrow stretch of the public golf course that divides the spinney from the old forest. They agreed that, considering there was a deep snow on the ground and that she was wearing those gutta-percha boots, she traveled at a remarkable speed.

I didn't even know she was out of the car until I got around on the other side and saw the door there standing open and saw her tracks in the snow, going down the bank. I suppose I was too dazed even to follow the tracks with my eyes down the bank and up the other side of the ditch. I must have stood there for several seconds, looking down blankly at the tracks she had left just outside the car door. Presently I looked up at the truck driver, who was standing before me. I know now his eyes must have been following Lee Ann's progress. Finally he turned his eyes to me, and I could tell from his expression that I wasn't a pleasant sight. "Is your head hurt bad?" he asked. I put my hand up to my forehead and when I brought it down it was covered with blood. That was when I passed out. When I came to, they wouldn't let me get up. Besides the truck driver, there were two policemen and the two ice skaters standing over me. They told me that an ambulance was on the way.

At the hospital, the doctor took four stitches in my forehead; and that was it. I went home and lay down for a couple of hours, as I had been told to do. My parents and my two brothers and my little sister and even the servants were very much concerned about me. They hovered around in a way I had never before seen them do — not even when somebody was desperately sick. I suppose it was because a piece of violence like this accident was a very extraordinary thing in our quiet Memphis life in those years. They were disturbed, too, I soon realized, by my silence as I lay there on the daybed in the upstairs sitting room and particularly by my being reticent to talk about the collision. I had other things on my mind.

Every so often I would remember Lee Ann's boot tracks in the snow. And I would begin to wonder where she was now. Since I had not found an opportunity to telephone her, I could only surmise that she had somehow managed to get back to the rooming-house where she lived. I had not told anyone about her presence in the car with me. And as I lay there on the daybed, with the family and servants coming and going and making inquiries about how I felt, I would find myself wondering sometimes how and whether or not I could tell Caroline Braxley about Lee Ann's being with me that afternoon. It turned out the next day — or, rather, on Monday morning — that the truck driver had told the two policemen and then, later, repeated to someone who called from one of the newspapers that there had been a girl with me in the car. As a matter of fact, I learned that this was the case on the night of the accident, but as I lay there in the upstairs sitting room during the afternoon I didn't yet know it.

Shortly before five o'clock Caroline Braxley arrived at our house, making a proper sick call but also with the intention of taking me back to dinner with her parents and her two younger sisters. Immediately after she entered the upstairs sitting room, and almost before she and I had greeted each other, my mother's houseboy and sometime chauffeur came in, bringing my volume of Horace. Because Mother had thought it might raise my spirits, she had sent him down to the service garage where the wrecked car had been taken to fetch it for me. Smiling sympathetically, he placed it on a table near the daybed and left the room. Looking at the book, Caroline said to me with a smile that expressed a mixture of sympathy and reproach, "I hope you see now what folly your pursuit of Latin poetry is." And suddenly, then, the book on the table appeared to me as an alien object. In retrospect it seems to me that I really knew then that I would never open it again.

I went to dinner that night at Caroline's house, my head still in bandages. The Braxley family treated me with a tenderness equal to that I had received at home. At table, the serving man offered to help my plate for me, as though I were a sick child. I could have enjoyed all this immensely, I think, since I have always been one to relish loving, domestic care, if only I had not been worrying and speculating all the while about Lee Ann. As I talked genially with Caroline's family during the meal and immediately afterward before the briskly burning fire at the end of the Braxleys' long living room, I kept seeing Lee Ann's boot tracks in the snow. And then I would see my own bloody hand as I took it down from my face before I fainted. I remember still having the distinct feeling, as I sat there in the bosom of the Braxley family, that it had not been merely my bloody hand that had made me faint but my bloody hand plus the tracks in the deep snow. In a way, it is strange that I remember all these impressions so vividly after forty years, because it is not as though I have lived an uneventful life during the years since. My Second World War experiences are what I perhaps ought to remember best — those, along with the deaths of my two younger brothers in the Korean War. Even worse, really, were the deaths of my two parents in a terrible fire that destroyed our house on Central Avenue when they had got to be quite old, my mother leaping from a second-story window, my father asphyxiated inside the house. And I can hardly mention without being overcome with emotion the accidental deaths that took two of my and Caroline's children when they were in their early teens. It would seem that with all these disasters to remember, along with the various business and professional crises I have had, I might hardly be able to recall that earlier episode. But I think that, besides its coming at that impressionable period of my life and the fact that one just does remember things better from one's youth, there is the undeniable fact that life *was* different in those times. What I mean to say is that all these later, terrible events took place in a world where acts of terror are, so to speak, all around us — everyday occurrences — and are brought home to us audibly and pictorially on radio and television almost every hour. I am not saying that some of these ugly acts of terror did not need to take place or were not brought on by what our world was like in those days. But I am saying that the context was different. Our tranquil, upper-middle-class world of 1937 did not have the rest of the world crowding in on it so much. And thus when something only a little ugly did crowd in or when we, often unconsciously, reached out for it the contrasts seemed sharper. It was not just in the Braxleys' household or in my own family's that everything seemed quiet and well ordered and unchanging. The households were in a context like themselves. Suffice it to say that though the Braxleys' house in Memphis was situated on East Parkway and our house on Central Avenue, at least two miles across town from each other, I could in those days feel perfectly safe, and *was* relatively safe, in walking home many a night from Caroline's house to our house at two in the morning. It was when we young men in Memphis ventured out with the more adventurous girls of the demimonde that we touched on the unsafe zones of Memphis. And there were girls still more adventurous, of course, with whom some of my contemporaries found their way into the very most dangerous zones. But we did think of it that way, you see, thought of it in terms of the girls' being the adventurous ones, whom we followed or didn't follow.

Anyhow, while we were sitting there before the fire, with the portrait of Caroline's paternal grandfather peering down at us from above the mantel and with her father in his broad-lapeled, double-breasted suit standing on the marble hearth, occasionally poking at the logs with the brass poker or sometimes kicking a log with the toe of his wing-tipped shoes, suddenly I was called to the telephone by the Negro serving man who had wanted to help my plate for me. As he preceded me the length of the living room and then gently guided me across the hall to the telephone in the library, I believe he would have put his hand under my elbow to help me — as if a real invalid — if I had allowed him to. As we passed through the hall, I glanced through one of the broad, etched sidelights beside the front door and caught a glimpse of the snow on the ground outside. The weather had turned even colder. There had been no additional snowfall, but even at a glance you could tell how crisply frozen the old snow was on its surface. The serving man at my elbow was saying, "It's your daddy on the phone. I'd suppose he just wants to know how you'd be feeling by now."

But I knew in my heart it wasn't that. It was as if that glimpse of the crisp snow through the front-door sidelight had told me what it was. When I took up the telephone and heard my father's voice pronouncing my name, I knew almost exactly what he was going to say. He said that his friend the editor of the morning paper had called him and reported that there had been a girl in the car with me, and though they didn't of course plan to use her name, probably wouldn't even run the story until Monday, they would have to *know* her name. And would have to assure themselves she wasn't hurt in the crash. And that she was unharmed after leaving the scene. Without hesitation I gave my father Lee Ann Deehart's name, as well as her address and telephone number. But I made no further explanation to Father, and he asked me for none. The only other thing I said was that I'd be home in a little while. Father was silent a moment after that. Then he said, "Are you all right?"

I said, "I'm fine."

And he said, "Good. I'll be waiting up for you."

I hung up the telephone, and my first thought was that before I left Caroline tonight I'd have to tell her that Lee Ann had been in the car with me. Then, without thinking almost, I dialed Lee Ann's roominghouse number. It felt very strange to be doing this in the Braxleys' library. The woman who ran the roominghouse said that Lee Ann had not been in since she left with me in the afternoon.

As I passed back across the wide hallway and caught another glimpse of the snow outside, the question arose in my mind for the first time: *Had* Lee Ann come to some harm in those woods? More than the density of the underbrush, more than its proximity to the zoo, where certain unsavory characters often hung out, it was the great size and antiquity of the forest trees somehow, and the old rumors that white settlers had once been ambushed there by Chickasaw Indians, that made me feel that if anything had happened to the girl it had happened there. And on the heels of such thoughts I found myself wondering for the first time if all this might actually lead to my beautiful, willowy Caroline Braxley's breaking off our engagement. I returned to the living room, and at the sight of Caroline's tall figure at the far end of the room, placed between that of her mother and that of her father, the conviction became firm in me that I would have to tell her about Lee Ann before she and I parted that night. And as I drew nearer to her, still wondering if something ghastly had happened to Lee Ann there in the old forest, I saw the perplexed and even suspicious expression on Caroline's face and presently observed similar expressions on the faces of her two parents. And from that moment began the gnawing wonder that would be with me for several days ahead: What precisely would Caroline consider sufficient provocation for breaking off our engagement to be married? I had no idea, really. Would it be sufficient that I had had one of those unnamed "female companions" in the car with me at the time of the accident? I knew of engagements like ours that had been broken with apparently less provocation. Or would it be the suspicious-seeming circumstance of Lee Ann's leaping out of the car and running off through the snow? Or might it be the final, worst possibility — that of delicate little Lee Ann Deehart's having actually met with foul play in that infrequently entered area of underbrush and towering forest trees?

Broken engagements were a subject of common and considerable interest to girls like Caroline Braxley. Whereas a generation earlier a broken engagement had been somewhat of a scandal — an engagement that had been formally announced at a party and in the newspaper, that is — it did not necessarily represent that in our day. Even in our day, you see, it meant something quite different from what it had once meant. There was, after all, no written contract, and it was in no sense so unalterably binding as it had been in our parents' day. For us it was not considered absolutely dishonorable for either party to break off the plans merely because he or she had had a change of heart. Since the boy was no longer expected literally to ask the father for the girl's hand (though he would probably be expected to go through the form, as I had done with Mr. Braxley), it was no longer a breach of contract between families. There was certainly nothing like a dowry any longer — not in Memphis — and there was only rarely any kind of property settlement involved, except in cases where both families were extraordinarily rich. The thought pleased me — that is, the ease with which an engagement might be ended. I suppose in part I was simply preparing myself for such an eventuality. And there in the Braxleys' long living room in the very presence of Caroline and Mr. and Mrs. Braxley themselves I found myself indulging in a perverse fantasy, a fantasy in which Caroline had broken off our engagement and I was standing up pretty well, was even seeking consolation in the arms, so to speak, of a safely returned Lee Ann Deehart.

But all at once I felt so guilty for my private indiscretion that actually for the first time in the presence of my prospective in-laws, I put my arm about Caroline Braxley's waist. And I told her that I felt so fatigued by events of the afternoon that probably I ought now to go ahead home. She and her parents agreed at once. And they agreed among themselves that they each had just now been reflecting privately that I looked exhausted. Mrs. Braxley suggested that under the circumstances she ought to ask Robert to drive me home. I accepted. No other suggestion could have seemed so welcome. Robert was the same serving man who had offered to help my plate at dinner and who had so gently guided me to the telephone when my father called. Almost at once, after I got into the front seat of the car beside him — in his dark chauffeur's uniform cap — I fell asleep. He had to wake me when we pulled up to the side door of my father's house. I remember how warmly I thanked him for bringing me home, even shaking his hand, which was a rather unusual thing to do in those days. I felt greatly refreshed and restored and personally grateful to Robert for it. There was not, in those days in Memphis, any time or occasion when one felt more secure and relaxed than when one had given oneself over completely to the care and protection of the black servants who surrounded us and who created and sustained for the most part the luxury that distinguished the lives we lived then from the lives we live now. They did so for us, whatever their motives and however degrading our demands and our acceptance of their attentions may have been to them.

At any rate, after my slumber in the front seat beside Robert I felt sufficiently restored to face my father (and his awareness of Lee Ann's having been in the car) with some degree of equanimity. And before leaving the Braxley's house I had found a moment in the hallway to break the news to Caroline that I had not been alone in the car that afternoon. To my considerable surprise, she revealed, after a moment's hesitation, that she already knew that that had been the case. Her father, like my father, had learned it from one of the newspaper editors — only he had learned it several hours earlier than my father had. I was obliged to realize as we were saying good night to each other that she, along with her two parents, had known all evening that Lee Ann had been with me and had fled into the woods of Overton Park — that she, Caroline, had as a matter of fact known the full story when she came to my house to fetch me back to her house to dinner. "Where is Lee Ann now?" she asked me presently, holding my two hands in her own and looking me directly in the eye. "I don't know," I said. Knowing how much she knew, I decided I must tell her the rest of it, holding nothing back. I felt that I was seeing a new side to my fiancée and that unless I told her the whole truth there might be something of this other side of her that wouldn't be revealed to me. "I tried to telephone her after I answered my father's call tonight. But she was not in her room and had not been in since I picked her up at two o'clock." And I told Caroline about Lee Ann's telephoning me (after Caroline and I had talked in the early afternoon) and about my inviting her to go out to the college with me. Then I gave her my uncensored version of the accident, including the sight of Lee Ann's footprints in the snow.

"How did she sound on the telephone?" she asked.

"What do you mean by that?" I said impatiently. "I just told you she wasn't home when I called."

"I mean earlier — when she called you."

"But why do you want to know that? It doesn't matter, does it?"

"I mean, did she sound depressed? But it doesn't matter for the moment." She still held my hands in hers. "You do know, don't you," she went on after a moment, "that you are going to have to *find* Lee Ann? And you probably are going to need help."

Suddenly I had the feeling that Caroline Braxley was someone twenty years older than I; but, rather than sounding like my parents or her parents, she sounded like one or another of the college teachers I had had — even like Dr. Bartlett, who once had told me that I was going to need outside help if I was going to keep up with the class. To reassure myself, I suppose, I put my arm about Caroline's waist again and drew her to me. But in our good-night kiss there was a reticence on her part, or a quality that I could only define as conditional or possibly probational. Still, I knew now that she knew everything, and I suppose that was why I was able to catch such a good nap in the car on the way home.

Girls who had been brought up the way Caroline had, in the Memphis of forty years ago, knew not only what was going to be expected of them in making a marriage and bringing up a family there in Memphis — a marriage and a family of the kind their parents had had — they knew also from a fairly early time that they would have to contend with girls and women of certain sorts before and frequently after they were married: with girls, that is, who had no conception of what it was to have a certain type of performance expected of them, or girls of another kind (and more like themselves) who came visiting in Memphis from Mississippi or Arkansas — pretty little plantation girls, my mother called them — or from Nashville or from the old towns of west Tennessee. Oftentimes these other girls were their cousins, but that made them no less dangerous. Not being on their home ground — in their own country, so to speak — these Nashville or Mississippi or west Tennessee or Arkansas girls did not bother to abide by the usual rules of civilized warfare. They carried on guerrilla warfare. They were marauders. But girls like Lee Ann Deehart were something else again. They were the Trojan horse, more or less, established in the very citadel. They were the fifth column, and were perhaps the most dangerous of all. At the end of a brilliant debutante season, sometimes the most eligible bachelor of all those on the list would still remain uncommitted, or even secretly committed to someone who had never seen the inside of the Memphis Country Club. This kind of thing, girls like Caroline Braxley understood, was not to be tolerated — not if the power of mortal women included the power to divine the nature of any man's commitment and the power to test the strength and nature of another kind of woman's power. Younger people today may say that that old-fashioned behavior on the part of girls doesn't matter today, that girls don't have those problems anymore. But I suspect that in Memphis, if not everywhere, there must be something equivalent even nowadays in the struggle of women for power among themselves.

Perhaps, though, to the present generation these distinctions I am making won't seem significant, after all, or worth my bothering so much about — especially the present generation outside of Memphis and the Deep South. Even in Memphis the great majority of people might say, Why is this little band of spoiled rich girls who lived here forty years ago so important as to deserve our attention? In fact, during the very period I am writing about it is likely that the majority of people in Memphis felt that way. I think the significant point is that those girls took themselves seriously — girls like Caroline — and took seriously the forms of the life they lived. They imagined they knew quite well who they were and they imagined that that was important. They were what, at any rate, those girls like Lee Ann were not. Or they claimed to be what those girls like Lee Ann didn't claim to be and what very few people nowadays claim to be. They considered themselves the heirs to something, though most likely they could not have said what: something their forebears had brought to Memphis with them from somewhere else — from the country around Memphis and from other places, from the country towns of west Tennessee, from middle Tennessee and east Tennessee, from the Valley of Virginia, from the Piedmont, even from the Tidewater. Girls like Caroline thought they were the heirs to something, and that's what the other girls didn't think about themselves, though probably they were, and probably the present generation, in and out of Memphis — even the sad generation of the sixties and seventies — is heir to more than it thinks it is, in the matter of manners, I mean to say, and of general behavior. And it is of course because these girls like Caroline are regarded as mere old-fashioned society girls that the present generation tends to dismiss them, whereas if it were their fathers we were writing about the story would, shocking though it is to say, be taken more seriously by everyone. Everyone would recognize now that the fathers and grandfathers of these girls were the sons of the old plantation South come to town and converted or half-converted into modern Memphis businessmen, only with a certain something held over from the old order that made them both better and worse than businessmen elsewhere. They are the authors of much good and much bad in modern Memphis — and modern Nashville and modern Birmingham and modern Atlanta, too. The good they mostly brought with them from the old order; the bad they mostly adopted from life in cities elsewhere in the nation, the thing they were imitating when they constructed the new life in Memphis. And why not judge their daughters and wives in much the same way? Isn't there a need to know what they were like, too? One thing those girls did know they were heirs to was the old, country manners and the insistence upon old, country connections. The first evidence of this that comes to mind is the fact that they often spoke of girls like Lee Ann as "city girls," by which they meant that such girls didn't usually have the old family connections back in the country on the cotton farms in west Tennessee, in Mississippi, in Arkansas, or back in Nashville or in Jonesboro or in Virginia.

When Robert had let me out at our side door that night and I came into the house, my father and mother both were downstairs. It was still early of course, but I had the sense of their having waited up for me to come in. They greeted me as though I were returning from some dangerous mission. Each of them asked me how the Braxleys "seemed." Finally Mother insisted upon examining the stitches underneath the bandage on my forehead. After that, I said that I thought I would hit the hay. They responded to that with the same enthusiasm that Mr. and Mrs. Braxley had evidenced when I told them I thought I should go ahead home. Nothing would do me more good than a good night's sleep, my parents agreed. It was a day everybody was glad to have come to an end.

After I got upstairs and in my room, it occurred to me that my parents both suddenly looked very old. That seems laughable to me now almost, because my parents were then ten or fifteen years younger than I am today. I look back on them now as a youngish couple in their early middle age, whose first son was about to be married and about whose possible infidelity they were concerned. But indeed what an old-fashioned pair they seem to me in the present day, waiting up for their children to come in. Because actually they stayed downstairs a long while after I went up to bed, waiting there for my younger brothers and my little sister to come in, all of whom were out on their separate dates. In my mind's eye I can see them there, waiting as parents had waited for hundreds of years for their grown-up children to come home at night. They would seem now to be violating the rights of young individuals and even interfering with the maturing process. But in those times it seemed only natural for parents to be watchful and concerned about their children's first flight away from the nest. I am referring mainly to my parents' waiting up for my brothers and my sister, who were in their middle teens, but also as I lay in my bed I felt, myself, more relaxed, knowing that they were downstairs in the front room, speculating upon what Lee Ann's disappearance meant and alert to whatever new development there might be. After a while, my father came up and opened the door to my room. I don't know how much later it was. I don't think I had been to sleep, but I could not tell for sure even at the time — my waking and sleeping thoughts were so much alike that night. At any rate, Father stepped inside the room and came over to my bed.

"I have just called down to the police station," he said, "and they say they have checked and that Lee Ann has still not come back to her roominghouse. She seems to have gone into some sort of hiding." He said this with just the slightest trace of irritation in his voice. "Have you any notion, Nat, why she *might* want to go into hiding?"

The next day was Sunday, December 5th. During the night it had turned bitterly cold. The snow had frozen into a crisp sheet that covered most of the ground. At about nine o'clock in the morning, another snow began falling. I had breakfast with the family, still wearing the bandage on my forehead. I sat around in my bathrobe all morning, pretending to read the newspaper. I didn't see any report of my accident, and my father said it wouldn't appear till Monday. At ten o'clock, I dialed Lee Ann's telephone number. One of the other girls who roomed in the house answered. She said she thought Lee Ann hadn't come in last night and she giggled. I asked her if she would make sure about it. She left the phone and came back presently to say in a whisper that there was no doubt about it: Lee Ann had not slept in her bed. I knew she was whispering so that the landlady wouldn't hear . . . And then I had a call from Caroline, who wanted to know how my head was this morning and whether or not there had been any word about Lee Ann. After I told her what I had just learned, we were both silent for a time. Finally she said she had intended to come over and see how I was feeling but her father had decreed that nobody should go out in such bad weather. It would just be inviting another automobile wreck, he said. She reported that her parents were not going to church, and I said that mine weren't either. We agreed to talk later and to see each other after lunch if the weather improved. Then I could hear her father's voice in the background, and she said that he wanted to use the telephone.

At noon the snow was still falling. My father stood at a front window in the living room, wearing his dark smoking jacket. He predicted that it might be the deepest snowfall we had ever had in Memphis. He said that people in other parts of the country didn't realize how much cold weather came all the way down the Mississippi Valley from Minneapolis to Memphis. I had never heard him pay so much attention to the weather and talk so much about it. I wondered, if, like me, he was really thinking about the old forest out in Overton Park and wishing he were free to go out there and make sure there was no sign of Lee Ann Deehart's having come to grief in those ancient woods. I wonder now if there weren't others besides us who were thinking of the old forest all day that day. I knew that my father, too, had been on the telephone that morning — and he was on it again during a good part of the afternoon. In retrospect, I am certain that all day that day he was in touch with a whole circle of friends and colleagues who were concerned about Lee Ann's safety. It was not only the heavy snow that checked his freedom — and mine, too, of course — to go out and search those woods and put his mind at rest on that possibility at least. It was more than just this snow, which the radio reported as snarling up and halting all traffic. What prevented him was his own unwillingness to admit fully to himself and to others that this particular danger was really there; what prevented him and perhaps all the rest of us was the fear that the answer to the gnawing question of Lee Ann's whereabouts might really be out there within that immemorial grove of snow-laden oaks and yellow poplars and hickory trees. It is a grove, I believe, that men in Memphis have feared and wanted to destroy for a long time and whose destruction they are still working at even in this latter day. It has only recently been saved by a very narrow margin from a great highway that men wished to put through there — saved by groups of women determined to save this last bit of the old forest from the axes of modern men. Perhaps in old pioneer days, before the plantation and the neoclassic towns were made, the great forests seemed woman's last refuge from the brute she lived alone with in the wilderness. Perhaps all men in Memphis who had any sense of their past felt this, though they felt more keenly (or perhaps it amounts to the same feeling) that the forest was woman's greatest danger. Men remembered mad pioneer women, driven mad by their loneliness and isolation, who ran off into the forest, never to be seen again, or incautious women who allowed themselves to be captured by Indians and returned at last so mutilated that they were unrecognizable to their husbands or who at their own wish lived out their lives among their savage captors. I think that if I had said to my father (or to myself), "What is it that's so scary about the old forest?" he (or I) would have answered, "There's nothing at all scary about it. But we can't do anything today because of the snow. It's the worst snow in history!" I think that all day long my father — like me — was busily not letting himself believe that anything awful had happened to Lee Ann Deehart or that if it had it certainly hadn't happened in those woods. Not just my father and me, though. Caroline's father, too, and all their friends — their peers. And the newspapermen and the police. If they waited long enough, it would come out all right and there would be no need to search the woods even. And it turned out, in the most literal sense, that they — we — were right. Yet what guilty feelings must not everyone have lived with — lived with in silence — all that snowbound day.

At two o'clock, Caroline called again to say that because of the snow her aunt was canceling the dinner party she had planned that night in honor of the bride and groom. I remember as well as anything else that terrible day how my mother and father looked at each other when they received this news. Surely they were wondering, as I had to also, if this was but the first gesture of withdrawal. There was no knowing what their behavior or the behavior of any of us that day meant. The day simply dragged on until the hour when we could decently go to bed. It was December, and we were near the shortest day of the year, but that day had seemed the longest day of my life.

On Monday morning, two uniformed policemen were at our house before I had finished my breakfast. When I learned they were waiting in the living room to see me, I got up from the table at once. I wouldn't let my father go in with me to see them. Mother tried to make me finish my eggs before going in, but I only laughed at her and kissed her on the top of the head as I left the breakfast room. The two policemen were sitting in the very chairs my parents had sat in the night before. This somehow made the interview easier from the outset. I felt initially that they were there to help me, not to harass me in any way. They had already, at the break of dawn, been out to Overton Park. (The whole case — if case it was — had of course been allowed to rest on Sunday.) And along with four other policemen they had conducted a full-scale search of the old forest. There was no trace of Lee Ann Deehart there. They had also been to her roominghouse on Tutwiler Avenue and questioned Mrs. Troxler, whose house it was, about all of Lee Ann's friends and acquaintances and about the habits of her daily life. They said that they were sure the girl would turn up but that the newspapers were putting pressure on them to explain her disappearance and — more particularly — to explain her precipitate flight from the scene of the accident.

I spent that day with the police, leaving them only for an hour at lunchtime, when they dropped me off at my father's office on Front Street, where I worked. There I made a small pretense of attending to some business for the firm while I consumed a club sandwich and milkshake that my father or one of my uncles in the firm had had sent up for me. At the end of the hour, I jogged down the two flights of steep wooden stairs and found the police car waiting for me at the curb, just outside the entrance. At some time during the morning, one of the policemen had suggested that they might have a bulldozer or some other piece of machinery brought in to crack the ice on the Overton Park Pond and then drag the pond for Lee Ann's body. But I had pointed out that the two skaters had returned to the pond after the accident and skated there until dark. There was no hole in the ice anywhere. Moreover, the skaters had reported that when the girl left the scene she did not go by way of the pond but went up the rise and into the wooded area. There was every indication that she had gone that way, and so the suggestion that the pond be dragged was dismissed. And we continued during the rest of the morning to make the rounds of the roominghouses and apartments of Lee Ann's friends and acquaintances, as well as the houses of the parents with whom some of them lived. In the afternoon we planned to go to the shops and offices in which some of the girls worked and to interview them there concerning Lee Ann's whereabouts and where it was they last had seen her. It seemed a futile procedure to me. But while I was eating my club sandwich alone in our third-floor walkup office I received a shocking telephone call.

Our office, like most of the other cotton factors' offices, was in one of the plain-faced, three- and four-story buildings put up on Front Street during the middle years of the last century, just before the Civil War. Cotton men were very fond of those offices, and the offices did possess a certain rough beauty that anyone could see. Apparently there had been few, if any, improvements or alterations since the time they were built. All the electrical wiring and all the plumbing, such as it was, was "exposed." The wooden stairsteps and the floors were rough and splintery and extremely worn down. The walls were whitewashed and the ceilings were twelve or fourteen feet in height. But the chief charm of the rooms was the tall windows across the front of the buildings — wide sash windows with small window lights, windows looking down onto Front Street and from which you could catch glimpses of the brown Mississippi River at the foot of the bluff, and even of the Arkansas shoreline on the other side. I was sitting on a cotton trough beside one of those windows, eating my club sandwich, when I heard the telephone ring back in the inner office. I remember that when it rang my eyes were on a little stretch of the Arkansas shoreline roughly delineated by its scrubby trees, and my thoughts were on the Arkansas roadhouses where we often went with the demimonde girls on a Saturday night. At first I thought I wouldn't answer the phone. I let it ring for a minute or two. It went on ringing — persistently. Suddenly I realized that a normal business call would have stopped ringing before now. I jumped down from my perch by the window and ran back between the cotton troughs to the office. When I picked up the receiver, a girl's voice called my name before I spoke.

"Yes," I said. The voice had sounded familiar, but I knew it wasn't Caroline's. And it wasn't Lee Ann's. I couldn't identify it exactly, though I did say to myself right away that it was one of the city girls.

"Nat," the voice said, "Lee Ann wants you to stop trying to trail her."

"Who is this?" I said. "Where is Lee Ann?"

"Never mind," the girl on the other end of the line said. "We're not going to let you find her, and you're making her very uncomfortable with your going around with the police after her and all that."

"The police aren't 'after her,' " I said. "They just want to be sure she's all right."

"She'll be all right," the voice said, "if you'll lay off and stop chasing her. Don't you have any decency at all? Don't you have a brain in your head? Don't you know what this is like for Lee Ann? We all thought you were her friend."

"I am," I said. "Just let me speak to Lee Ann."

But there was a click in the telephone, and no one was there any longer.

I turned back into the room where the cotton troughs were. When I saw my milkshake carton and the sandwich paper up by the window, and remembered how the girl had called my name as soon as I picked up the telephone, I felt sure that someone had been watching me from down in the street or from a window across the way. Without going back to my lunch, I turned quickly and started down the stairs toward the street. But when I looked at my watch, I realized it was time for the policemen to pick me up again. And there they were, of course, waiting at the entrance to our building. When I got into the police car, I didn't tell them about my call. And we began our rounds again, going to the addresses where some of Lee Ann's friends worked.

Lee Ann Deehart and other girls like her that we went about with, as I have already indicated, were not literally ladies of any Memphis demimonde. Possibly they got called that first by the only member of our generation in Memphis who had read Marcel

Proust, a literary boy who later became a college professor and who wanted to make his own life in Memphis — and ours — seem more interesting than it was. Actually, they were girls who had gone to the public high schools, and more often than not to some school other than Central High, which during those depression years had a degree of acceptance in Memphis society. As anyone could have observed on that morning when I rode about town with the policemen, those girls came from a variety of backgrounds. We went to the houses of some of their parents, some of whom were day laborers who spoke in accents of the old Memphis Irish, descendants of the Irish who were imported to build the railroads to Texas. Today some of the girls would inevitably have been black. But they were the daughters also of bank clerks and salesmen and of professional men, too, because they made no distinction among themselves. The parents of some of them had moved to Memphis from cities in other sections of the country or even from southern small towns. The girls were not interested in such distinctions of origin, were not conscious of them, had not been made aware of them by their parents. They would have been highly approved of by the present generation of young people. Like the present generation in general, these girls — Lee Ann included — tended to be bookish and artistic in a middlebrow sort of way, and some of them had real intellectual aspirations. They did not care who each other's families were or where they had gone to school. They met and got to know each other in roadhouses, on double dates, and in the offices and stores where they worked. As I have said, they tended to be bookish and artistic. If they had found themselves in Proust's Paris, instead of in our Memphis of the nineteen-thirties, possibly they would have played some role in the intellectual life of the place. But of course this is only my ignorant speculation. It is always impossible to know what changes might have been wrought in people under circumstances of the greatest or slightest degree of difference from the actual.

The girls we saw that afternoon at their places of work were generally more responsive to the policemen's questions than to my own. And I became aware that the two policemen — youngish men in their late thirties, for whom this special assignment was somehow distasteful — were more interested in protecting these girls from any embarrassment than in obtaining information about Lee Ann. With all but one of the half-dozen girls we sought out, the policemen sent me in to see the girl first, to ask her if she would rather be questioned by them in her place of business or in the police car. In each case the girl treated my question concerning this as an affront, but always she finally sent word back to the policemen to come inside. And in each case I found myself admiring the girl not only for her boldness in dealing with the situation (they seemed fearless in their talk with the police and refused absolutely to acknowledge close friendship with Lee Ann, insisting — all of them — that they saw her only occasionally at nightspots, sometimes with me, sometimes with other young men, that they had no idea who her parents were or where she came to Memphis from) but also for a personal, feminine beauty that I had never before been fully aware of. Perhaps I saw or sensed it now for the first time because I had not before seen them threatened or in danger. It is true, I know, that the effect of all this questioning seemed somehow to put them in jeopardy. Perhaps I saw now how much more vulnerable they were than were the girls in the set my parents more or less intended me to travel in. There was a delicacy about them, a frailty even, that didn't seem to exist in other girls I knew and that contrasted strangely — and disturbingly — with the rough surroundings of the roadhouses they frequented at night and the harsh, businesslike atmosphere of the places where they worked. Within each of them, moreover, there seemed a contrast between the delicate beauty of their bodies, their prettily formed arms and legs, their breasts and hips, their small feet and hands, their soft natural hair — hair worn so becomingly, groomed, in each case, on their pretty little heads to direct one's eyes first of all to the fair or olive complexion and the nicely proportioned features of the face — a contrast, that is to say, between this physical beauty and a bookishness and a certain toughness of mind and a boldness of spirit that were unmistakable in all of them.

The last girl we paid a call on that afternoon was one Nancy Minnifee, who happened to be the girl who was always frankest and crudest in making jokes about families like my own and who had made the crack that the other girls had laughed at so irrepressibly in the beer garden: "I haven't lost anything at the M.C.C." Or it may not have been that she just happened to be the last we called on. Perhaps out of dread of her jokes I guided the police last of all to the farm-implement warehouse where Nancy was a secretary. Or perhaps it wasn't so much because of her personality as because

I knew she was Lee Ann's closest friend and I somehow dreaded facing her for that reason. Anyway, at the warehouse she was out on the loading platform with a clipboard and pencil in her hands when we drove up.

"That's Nancy Minnifee up there," I said to the two policemen in the front seat. I was sitting in the back seat alone. I saw them shake their heads. I knew that it was with a certain sadness and a personal admiration that they did so. Nancy was a very pretty girl, and they hated the thought of bothering this lovely creature with the kind of questions they were going to ask. They hated it without even knowing she was Lee Ann's closest friend. Suddenly I began seeing all those girls through the policemen's eyes, just as next day, when I would make a similar expedition in the company of my father and the newspaper editor, I'd see the girls through their eyes. The worst of it, somehow, for the policemen, was that the investigation wasn't really an official investigation but was something the newspapers had forced upon the police in case something had happened that they hadn't reported. The girl hadn't been missing long enough for anyone to declare her "officially" missing. Yet the police, along with the mayor's office and the newspaper editor, didn't want to risk something's having happened to a girl like Lee Ann. They — all of them — thought of such girls, in a sense, as their special wards. It would be hard to say why they did. At any rate, before the police car had fully stopped I saw Nancy Minnifee up there on the platform. She was wearing a fur-collared overcoat but no hat or gloves. Immediately she began moving along the loading platform toward us, holding the clipboard up to shield her eyes from the late-afternoon winter sun. She came down the steps to the graveled area where we were stopped, and when the policeman at the wheel of the car ran down his window she bent forward and put her arm on his door. The casual way she did it seemed almost familiar — indeed, almost provocative. I found myself resenting her manner, because I was afraid she would give the wrong impression. The way she leaned on the door reminded me of the prostitutes down on Pontotoc Street when we, as teen-age boys, used to stop in front of their houses and leave the motor running because we were afraid of them.

"I've been expecting you two gentlemen," Nancy said, smiling amiably at the two policemen and pointedly ignoring my presence in the back seat. The policemen broke into laughter.

"I suppose your friends have been calling ahead," the driver said. Then Nancy laughed as though he had said something very funny.

"I could draw you a map of the route you've taken this afternoon," she said. She was awfully polite in her tone, and the two policemen were awfully polite, too. But before they could really begin asking her their questions she began giving them her answers. She hadn't seen Lee Ann since several days before the accident. She didn't know anything about where she might be. She didn't know anything about her family. She had always understood that Lee Ann came from Texas.

"That's a big state," the policeman who wasn't driving said.

"Well, I've never been there," she said, "but I'm told it's a mighty big state."

The three of them burst into laughter again. Then the driver said quite seriously, "But we understand you're her best friend."

"I don't know her any better than most of the other girls do," she said. "I can't imagine who told you that." Now for the first time she looked at me in the back seat. "Hello, Nat," she said. I nodded to her. I couldn't imagine why she was lying to them. But I didn't tell her, as I hadn't told the other girls or the police, about the call I had had in the cotton office. I knew that she must know all about it, but I said nothing.

When we had pulled away, the policeman who was driving the car said, "This Lee Ann must be all right or these girls wouldn't be closing ranks so. They've got too much sense for that. They're smart girls."

Presently the other policeman turned his head halfway around, though not looking directly at me, and asked, "She wouldn't be pregnant by any chance, would she?"

"Uh-uh," I said. It was all the answer it seemed to me he deserved. But then I couldn't resist echoing what he had said. "They've got too much sense for that. They're smart girls." He looked all the way around at me now and gave me what I am sure he thought was a straight look.

"Damn right they are," said the driver, glancing at his colleague with a frown on his forehead and speaking with a curled lip. "Get your mind out of the gutter, Fred. After all, they're just kids, all of them."

We rode on in silence after that. For the first time in several hours, I thought of Caroline Braxley, and I wondered again whether or not she would break our engagement.

When the policemen let me off at my office at five o'clock, I went to my car and drove straight to the apartment house at Crosstown where Nancy Minnifee lived. I was waiting for Nancy in the parking lot when she got home. She invited me inside, but without a smile.

"I want to know where Lee Ann is," I said as soon as she had closed the door.

"Do you imagine I'd tell you if I knew?" she said.

I sat myself down in an upholstered chair as if I were going to stay there till she told me. "I want to know what the hell's going on," I said with what I thought was considerable force, "and why you told such lies to those policemen."

"If you don't know that now, Nat," she said, sitting down opposite me, "you probably won't ever know."

"She wouldn't be pregnant by any chance, would she?" I said, without really having known I was going to say it.

Nancy's mouth dropped open. Then she laughed aloud. Presently she said, "Well, one thing's certain, Nat. It wouldn't be any concern of yours if she were."

I pulled myself up out of the big chair and left without another word's passing between us.

Lee Ann Deehart and Nancy Minnifee and that whole band of girls that we liked to refer to as the girls of the Memphis demimonde were of course no more like the ladies of the demimonde as they appear in French literature than they were like some band of angels. And I hardly need say — though it does somehow occur to me to say — their manners and morals bore no resemblance whatsoever to those of the mercenary, filthy-mouthed whores on Pontotoc Street. I might even say that their manners were practically indistinguishable from those of the girls we knew who had attended Miss Hutchison's School and St. Mary's and Lausanne and were now members of the debutante set. The fact is that some of them — only a few perhaps — were from families who were related by blood, and rather closely related, to the families of the debutante set, but families who, for one reason or another, now found themselves economically in another class from their relatives. At any rate, they were all freed from old restraints put upon them by family and community, liberated in each case, so it seems to me, by sheer strength of character, liberated in many respects, but above all else — and I cannot say how it came about — liberated sexually. The most precise thing I can say about them is that they, in their little band, were like hordes of young girls today. It seems to me that in their attitude toward sex they were at least forty years ahead of their time. But I cannot say how it came about. Perhaps it was an individual thing with each of them — or partly so. Perhaps it was because they were the second or third generation of women in Memphis who were working in offices. They were not promiscuous — not most of them — but they slept with the men they were in love with and they did not conceal the fact. The men they were in love with were usually older than we were. Generally speaking, the girls merely amused themselves with us, just as we amused ourselves with them. There was a wonderful freedom in our relations that I have never known anything else quite like. And though I may not have had the most realistic sense of what their lives were, I came to know what I did know through my friendship with Lee Ann Deehart.

She and I first met, I think, at one of those dives where we all hung out. Or it may have been at some girl's apartment. I suspect we both would have been hard put to it to say where it was or exactly when. She was simply one of the good-looking girls we ran around with. I remember dancing with her on several occasions before I had any idea what her name was. We drifted into our special kind of friendship because, as a matter of fact, she was the good friend of Nancy Minnifee, whom my own close friend Bob Childress got very serious about for a time. Bob and Nancy may even have been living together for a while in Nancy's apartment. I think Bob, who was one of six or eight boys of approximately my background who used to go about with these girls, would have married Nancy if she'd consented to have him. Possibly it was at Nancy's apartment that I met Lee Ann. Anyway, we did a lot of double-dating, the four of us, and had some wonderful times going to the sort of rough nightspots that we all liked and found sufficiently exciting to return to again and again. We would be dancing and drinking at one of those places until about two in the morning, when most of them closed. At that hour most of us would take our girls home, because we nearly all of us had jobs — the girls and the boys, too — that we had to report to by eight or nine in the morning.

Between Lee Ann and me, as between most of the boys and their girls, I think, there was never a serious affair. That is, we never actually — as the young people today say — "had sex." But in the car on the way home or in the car parked outside her rooming-house or even outside the nightspot, as soon as we came out, we would regularly indulge in what used to be known as "heavy neck-ing." Our stopping at that I must attribute first of all to Lee Ann's resistance, though also, in part, to a hesitation I felt about insisting with such a girl. You see, she was in all respects like the girls we called "nice girls," by which I suppose we really meant society girls. And most of us accepted the restriction that we were not to "go to bed" with society girls. They were the girls we were going to marry. These girls were not what those society girls would have termed shopgirls. They had much better taste in their clothes and in their general demeanor. And, as I have said, in the particular group I speak of there was at least an intellectual strain. Some of them had been to college for as much as a year or two, whereas others seemed hardly to have finished high school. Nearly all of them read mag-azines and books that most of us had never heard of. And they found my odd addiction to Latin poetry the most interesting thing about me. Most of them belonged to a national book club, from which they received a new book each month, and they nearly all bought records and listened to classical music. You would see them sometimes in groups at the art gallery. Or whenever there was an opera or a good play at the city auditorium they were all likely to be there in a group — almost never with dates. If you hadn't known who they were, you might easily have mistaken them for some committee from the Junior League, or for an exceptionally pretty group of schoolteachers — from some fashionable girls' school probably.

But mostly, of course, one saw them with their dates at one of the roadhouses, over in Arkansas or down in Mississippi or out east on the Bristol Highway, or yet again at one of the places we called the "town joints." They preferred going to those roadhouses and town joints to going to the Peabody Hotel Roof or the Claridge — as I suppose nearly everyone else did, really, including society girls like Caroline. You would, as a matter of fact, frequently see girls like Caroline as such places. At her request, I had more than once taken Caroline to a town joint down on Adams Street called The Cellar and once to a roadhouse called The Jungle, over in Arkansas. She had met some of the city girls there and said she found them "dead attractive." And she once recognized them at a play I took her to see and afterward expressed interest in them and asked me to tell her what they were like.

The fact may be that neither the roadhouses nor the town joints were quite as tough as they seemed. Or they weren't as tough for the demimonde girls, anyway. Because the proprietors clearly had protective feelings about them. At The Jungle, for instance, the middle-aged couple who operated the place, an extremely obese couple who were forever grinning in our direction and who were usually barefoot (we called them Ma and Pa), would often come and stand by our table — one or the other of them — and sing the words to whatever was playing on the jukebox. Often as not, one of them would be standing there during the entire evening. Some-times Ma would talk to us about her two little daughters, whom she kept in a private school in Memphis, and Pa, who was a practicing taxidermist, would talk to us about the dogs whose mounted heads adorned the walls on every side of the dimly lit room. All this afforded us great privacy and safety. No drunk or roughneck would come near our table while either Ma or Pa was close by. We had similar protection at other places. At The Cellar, for instance, old Mrs. Power was the sole proprietor. She had a huge goiter on her neck and was never known to smile. Not even in our direction. But it was easy to see that she watched our table like a hawk, and if any other patron lingered near us even momentarily she would begin moving slowly toward us. And whoever it was would catch one glimpse of her and move on. We went to these places quite regularly, though some of the girls had their favorites and dislikes among them. Lee Ann would never be taken to The Cellar. She would say only that the place depressed her. And Caroline, when I took her there, felt an instant dislike for The Jungle. She would shake her head afterward and say she would never go back and have those dogs' eyes staring down through the darkness at her.

On the day after I made the rounds with the two policemen, I found myself following almost the same routine in the company of my father and the editor of the morning paper, and, as a matter of fact, the mayor of Memphis himself. The investigation or search was, you see, still entirely unofficial. And men like my father and the mayor and the editor wanted to keep it so. That's why after that routine and off-the-record series of questionings by the police, they preferred to do a bit of investigation themselves rather than entrust the matter to someone else. As I have said, that generation of men in Memphis evidenced feelings of responsibility for such girls — for "working girls of a superior kind," as they phrased it — which I find somewhat difficult to explain. For it wasn't just the men I drove about town with that day. Or the dozen or so men who gathered for conference in our driveway before we set out — that is, Caroline's father, his laywer, the driver of the other vehicle, his lawyer, my father's lawyer, ministers from three church denominations, the editor of the afternoon newspaper, and still others. That day, when I rode about town with my father and the two other men in our car, I came as near as I ever had or ever would to receiving a satisfactory explanation of the phenomenon. They were of a generation of American men who were perhaps the last to grow up in a world where women were absolutely subjected and under the absolute protection of men. While my father wheeled his big Cadillac through the side streets on which some of the girls lived and then along the wide boulevards of Memphis, they spoke of the changes they had seen. In referring to the character of the life girls like Lee Ann led — of which they showed a far greater awareness than I would have supposed they possessed — they agreed that this was the second or third generation there of women who had lived as independently, as freely as these girls did. I felt that what they said was in no sense as derogatory or critical as it would have been in the presence of their wives or daughters. They spoke almost affectionately and with a certain sadness of such girls. They spoke as if these were daughters of dead brothers of their own or of dead companions-in-arms during the First World War. And it seemed to me that they thought of these girls as the daughters of men who had abdicated their authority and responsibility as fathers, men who were not strangers or foreign to them, though they were perhaps of a different economic class. The family names of the girls were familiar to them. The fathers of these girls were Americans of the great hinterland like themselves, even southerners like themselves. I felt that they were actually cousins of ours who had failed as fathers somehow, had been destined to fail, even required to do so in a changing world. And so these men of position and power had to act as surrogate fathers during a transitional period. It was a sort of communal fatherhood they were acting out.

Eventually, they seemed to say, fathers might not be required. I actually heard my father saying, "That's what the whole world is going to be like someday." He meant like the life such girls as Lee Ann were making for themselves. I often think nowadays of Father's saying that, whenever I see his prediction being fulfilled by the students in the university where I have been teaching for twenty years now, and I wonder if Father did really believe his prediction would come true.

Yet while he and the other two men talked their rather sanguine talk that day, I was thinking of a call I had had the night before after I came back from seeing Nancy Minnifee. One of the servants answered the telephone downstairs in the back part of the house, and she must have guessed it was something special. Because instead of buzzing the buzzer three times, which was the signal when a call was for me, the maid came up the back stairs and tapped gently on my door. "It's for you, Nat," she said softly. "Do you want to take it downstairs?"

There was nothing peculiar about her doing this, really. Since I didn't have an extension phone in my room, I had a tacit understanding with the servants that I preferred to take what I considered my private calls down in that quarter of the house. And so I followed the maid down the back stairway and shut myself in the little servants' dining room that was behind the great white-tiled kitchen. I answered the call on the wall phone there.

A girl's voice, which wasn't the same voice I had heard on the office telephone at noon, said, "Lee Ann doesn't want another day like this one, Nat."

"Who is this?" I said, lowering my voice to be sure even the servants didn't hear me. "What the hell is going on?" I asked. "Where is Lee Ann?"

"She's been keeping just one apartment or one roominghouse ahead of you all day."

"But why? Why is she hiding this way?"

"All I want to say is she's had about enough. You let up on pursuing her so."

"It's not me," I protested. "There's nothing I can do to stop them."

Over the phone there came a contemptuous laugh. "No. And you can't get married till they find her, can you?" Momentarily I thought I heard Lee Ann's voice in the background. "Anyhow," the same voice continued, "Lee Ann's had about as much as she can take of all this. She was depressed as it was, when she called you in the first place. Why else do you think she would call you, Nat? She was desperate for some comic relief."

"Relief from what?"

"Relief from her depression, you idiot."

"But what's she depressed about?" I was listening carefully to the voice, thinking it was that of first one girl and then another.

"Nat, we don't always have to have something to be depressed about. But Lee Ann will be all right, if you'll let her alone."

"But what is she depressed about?" I persisted. I had begun to think maybe it was Lee Ann herself on the phone, disguising her voice.

"About life in general, you bastard! Isn't that enough?" Then I knew it wasn't Lee Ann, after all.

"Listen," I said, "let me speak to Lee Ann. I want to speak to Lee Ann."

And then I heard whoever it was I was talking with break off the connection. I quietly replaced the receiver and went upstairs again.

In those days I didn't know what it was to be depressed — not, anyway, about "life in general." Later on, you see, I did know. Later on, after years of being married and having three children and going to grown-up Memphis dinner parties three or four times a week and working in the cotton office six days a week, I got so depressed about life in general that I sold my interest in the cotton firm to a cousin of mine (my father and uncles were dead by then) and managed to make Caroline understand that what I needed was to go back to school for a while so that we could start our life all over. I took degrees at three universities, which made it possible for me to become a college professor. That may be an awful revelation about myself — I mean to say, awful that what decided me to become a teacher was that I was so depressed about life in general. But I reasoned that being an English professor — even if I was relegated to teaching composition and simple-minded survey courses — would be something useful and would throw us in with a different kind of people. (Caroline tried to persuade me to go into the sciences, but I told her she was just lucky that I didn't take up classics again.) Anyway, teaching has made me see a lot of young people over the years, in addition to my own children, and I think it is why, in retrospect, those Memphis girls I'm writing about still seem interesting to me after all these many years.

But the fact is, I was still so uneasy about the significance of both those calls from Lee Ann's friends that I was unwilling to mention them to Caroline that night. At first I thought I would tell her, but as soon as I saw her tall and graceful figure in her white, pleated evening dress and wearing the white corsage I had sent, I began worrying again about whether or not she might still break off the engagement. Besides, we had plenty of other matters to discuss, including the rounds I had made with the two policemen that day and her various activities in preparation for the wedding. We went to a dinner that one of my aunts gave for us at the Memphis Country Club that night. We came home early and spent twenty minutes or so in her living room, telling each other how much we loved each other and how we would let nothing on earth interfere with our getting married. I felt reassured, or I tried to feel so. It seemed to me, though, that Caroline still had not really made up her mind. It worried me that she didn't have more to say about Lee Ann. After I got home, I kept waking all night and wondering what if that had not been Lee Ann's voice I had heard in the background and what if she never surfaced again. The circumstances of her disappearance would have to be made public, and that would certainly be too embarrassing for Caroline and her parents to ignore.

Next day, I didn't tell my father and his two friends, the editor and the mayor, about either of the two telephone calls. I don't know why I didn't, unless it was because I feared they might begin monitoring all my calls. I could not tolerate the thought of having them hear the things that girl said to me.

In preference to interviewing the girls whose addresses I could give them, those three middle-aged men seemed much more interested in talking to the girls' roominghouse landladies, or their apartment landlords, or their mothers. They did talk to some of the girls themselves, though, and I observed that the girls were so impressed by having these older men want to talk to them they could hardly look at them directly. What I think is that the girls were *afraid* they would tell them the truth. They would reply to their questions respectfully, if evasively, but they were apt to keep their eyes on me. This was not the case, however, with the mothers and the landlords and the landladies. There was an immediate rapport between these persons and the three men. There hardly needed to be any explanation required of the unofficial nature of the investigation or of the concern of these particular men about such a girl as Lee Ann. One woman who told them that Lee Ann had roomed with her for a time described her as being always a moody sort of girl. "But lots of these girls living on their own are moody," she said.

"Where did Miss Deehart come from?" my father asked. "Who were her people?"

"She always claimed she came from Texas," the woman said. "But she could never make it clear to me where it was in Texas."

Later the mayor asked Lee Ann's current landlady, Mrs. Troxler, where she supposed Lee Ann might have gone. "Well," Mrs. Troxler said, "a girl, a decent girl, even among these modern girls, generally goes to her mother when there's trouble. Women turn to women," she said, "when there's real trouble."

The three men found no trace of Lee Ann, got no real clue to where she might have gone. When finally we were leaving the editor at his newspaper office on Union Avenue, he hesitated a moment before opening the car door. "Well," he began, but he sat for a moment beating his leg thoughtfully with a newspaper he had rolled up in his hand. "I don't know," he said. "It's going to be a matter for the police, after all, if we can't do any better than this." I still didn't say anything about my telephone calls. But the calls were worrying me a good deal, and that night I told Caroline.

And when I had told her about the calls and told her how the police and my father and his friends had failed to get any information from the girls, Caroline, who was then sitting beside me on the couch in her living room, suddenly took my hand in hers and, putting her face close to mine and looking me directly in the eye, said, "Nat, I don't want you to go to work at all tomorrow. Don't make any explanation to your father or to anybody. Just get up early and come over here and get me. I want you to take me to meet some of those girls." Then she asked me which of the girls she might possibly have met on the rare occasions when I had taken her dancing at The Jungle or at The Cellar. And before I left that night she got me to tell her all I knew about "that whole tribe of city girls." I told her everything, including an account of my innocent friendship with Lee Ann Deehart, as well as an account of my earlier relations, which were not innocent, with a girl named Fern Morris. When, next morning, I came to fetch Caroline for our expedition, there were only three girls that she wanted to be taken to see. One of the three was of course Fern Morris.

There was something that had happened to me the day before, when I was going about Memphis with my father and his two friends, that I could not tell Caroline about. You see, I had been imagining, each place we went, how as we came in the front door Lee Ann was hurriedly, quietly going out the back. This mental picture of her in flight I found not merely appealing but strangely exciting. And it seemed to me I was discovering what my true feelings toward Lee Ann had been during the past two years. I had never dared insist upon the occasional advances I had naturally made to her, because she had always seemed too delicate, too vulnerable, for me to think of suggesting a casual sexual relationship with her. She had seemed too clever and too intelligent for me to deceive her about my intentions or my worth as a person. And I imagined I relished the kind of restraint there was between us because it was so altogether personal and not one placed upon us by any element or segment of society, or by any outside circumstances whatever. It kept coming to my mind as we stood waiting for an answer to the pressure on each doorbell that she was the girl I ought and wanted to be marrying. I realized the absolute folly of such thoughts and the utter impossibility of any such conclusion to present events. But still such feelings and thoughts had kept swimming in and out of my head all that day. I kept seeing Lee Ann in my mind's eye and hearing her soft, somewhat husky voice. I kept imagining how her figure would appear in the doorway before us. I saw her slender ankles, her small breasts, her head of ash-blonde hair, which had a way of seeming to fall about her face when she talked but which with one shake of her head she could throw back into perfect place. But of course when the door opened there was the inevitable landlady or mother or friend. And when the next day came and I saw Caroline rolling up her sleeves, so to speak, to pitch in and settle this matter once and for all, then my thoughts and fantasies of the day before seemed literally like something out of a dream that I might have had.

The first two girls Caroline had wanted to see were the two that she very definitely remembered having met when I had taken her — "on a lark" — to my favorite nightspots. She caught them both before they went to work that morning, and I was asked to wait in the car. I felt like an idiot waiting out there in the car, because I knew I'd been seen from some window as I gingerly hopped out and opened the door for Caroline when she got out — and opened it again when she returned. But there was no way around it. I waited out there, playing the car radio even at the risk of running down the battery.

When she came back from seeing the first girl, whose name was Lucy Phelan, Caroline was very angry. She reported that Lucy Phelan had pretended not to remember ever having met her. Moreover, Lucy had pretended that she knew Lee Ann Deehart only slightly and had no idea where she could be or what her disappearance meant. As Caroline fumed and I started up the car, I was picturing Lee Ann quietly tiptoeing out the back door of Lucy's roominghouse just as Lucy was telling Caroline she scarcely knew the girl or while she was insisting that she didn't remember Caroline. As Caroline came back down the walk from the big Victorian house to the car, Lucy, who had stepped out onto the narrow porch that ran across the front of the house and around one corner of it, squatted down on her haunches at the top of the wooden porch steps and waved to me from behind Caroline's back. Though I knew it was no good, I pretended not to see her there. As I put the car into second gear and we sped away down the block, I took a quick glance back at the house. Lucy was still standing on the porch and waving to me the way one waves to a little child. She knew I had seen her stooping and waving moments before. And knew I would be stealing a glance now.

For a short time Caroline seemed undecided about calling on the second girl. But she decided finally to press on. Lucy Phelan she remembered meeting at The Cellar. The next girl, Betsy Morehouse, she had met at The Jungle and at a considerably more recent time. Caroline was a dog fancier in those days and she recalled a conversation with Betsy about the mounted dogs' heads that adorned the walls of The Jungle. They both had been outraged. When she mentioned this to me there in the car, I realized for the first time that by trying to make these girls acknowledge an acquaintance with her she had hoped to make them feel she was almost one of them and that they would thus be more likely to confide in her. But she failed with Betsy Morehouse, too. Betsy lived in an apartment house — an old residence, that is, converted into apartments — and when Caroline got inside the entrance hall door she met Betsy, who was just then coming down the stairs. Betsy carried a purse and was wearing a fur coat and overshoes. When Caroline got back to the car and told me about it, I could not help feeling that Betsy had had a call from Lucy Phelan and even perhaps that Lee Ann was hiding in her apartment, having just arrived there from Lucy's. Because Betsy didn't offer to take Caroline back upstairs to her apartment for a talk. Instead, they sat down on two straightbacked chairs in the entrance hall and exchanged their few words there. Betsy at once denied the possibility of Caroline's ever having met her before. She denied that she had, herself, ever been to The Jungle. I knew this to be a lie, of course, but I didn't insist upon it to Caroline. I said that perhaps both she and I were mistaken about Betsy's being there on the night I had taken Caroline. As soon as Caroline saw she would learn nothing from Betsy, she got up and began to make motions of leaving. Betsy followed her to the door. But upon seeing my car out at the curb — so Caroline believed — she turned back, saying that she had remembered a telephone call she had to make. Caroline suspected that the girl didn't want to have to face me with her lie. That possibly was true. But my thought was that Betsy just might, also, have a telephone call she wanted to make.

There was now no question about Caroline's wanting to proceed to the third girl's house. This was the girl I had told her about having had a real affair with — the one I had gone with before Lee Ann and I had become friends. Caroline knew that she and Fern Morris had never met, but she counted on a different psychology with Fern. Most probably she had hoped it wouldn't be necessary for her to go to see Fern. She had been sure that one of those two other girls would give her the lead she needed. But as a last resort she was fully prepared to call on Fern Morris and to take me into the house with her.

Fern was a girl who still lived at home with her mother. She was in no sense a mama's girl or even a home-loving girl, since she was unhappy unless she went out on a date every night of her life. Perhaps she was not so clever and not so intellectual as most of her friends — if reading books, that is, on psychology and on China and every new volume of André Maurois indicated intellectuality. And though she was not home-loving, I suppose you would have to say she was more domestic than the other girls were. She had never "held down" a job. Rather, she stayed at home in the daytime and kept house for her mother, who was said to "hold down" a high-powered job under Boss Crump down at City Hall. Mrs. Morris was a very sensible woman, who put no restrictions on her grown-up daughter and was glad to have her as a housekeeper. She used to tell me what a good cook and housekeeper Fern was and how well fixed she would leave her when she died. I really believe Mrs. Morris hoped our romance might end in matrimony, and, as a matter of fact, it was when I began to suspect that Fern, too, was entertaining such notions that I stopped seeing her and turned my attentions to Lee Ann Deehart.

Mrs. Morris still seemed glad to see me when I arrived at their bungalow that morning with Caroline and when I proceeded to introduce Caroline to her as my fiancée. Fern herself greeted me warmly. In fact, when I told her that Caroline and I were going to be married (though she must certainly have already read about it in the newspaper) she threw her arms about my neck and kissed me. "Oh, Natty," she said, "I'm so happy for you. Really I am. But poor Lee Ann." And in later life, especially in recent years, whenever Caroline has thought I was being silly about some other woman, usually a woman she considers her mental and social inferior, she has delighted in addressing me as "Natty." On more than one such occasion I have even had her say to me, "I am so happy for you, Natty. Really I am."

The fact is, Mrs. Morris was just leaving the house for work when we arrived. And so there was no delay in Caroline's interview with Fern. "I assume you know about Lee Ann's disappearance?" Caroline began as soon as we had seated ourselves in the little front parlor, with which I was very familiar.

"Of course I do," said Fern, looking at me and laughing gleefully.

"You think it's a laughing matter, then?" Caroline asked.

"I do indeed. It's all a big joke," Fern said at once. It was as though she had her answers all prepared. "And a very successful joke it is."

"Successful?" both Caroline and I asked. We looked at each other in dismay.

"It's only my opinion, of course. But I think she only wants to make you two suffer."

"Suffer?" I said. This time Caroline was silent.

Fern was now addressing me directly. "Everybody knows Caroline is not going to marry you until Lee Ann turns up safe."

"Everybody?" Both of us again.

"Everybody in the world practically," said Fern.

Caroline's face showed no expression. Neither, I believe, did mine.

"Fern, do you know where Lee Ann is?" Caroline asked gently.

Fern Morris, her eyes on me, shook her head, smiling.

"Do you know where her people are?" Caroline asked. "And whether she's with them or hiding with her friends?"

Fern shook her head again, but now she gazed directly at Caroline. "I'm not going to tell you anything!" she asserted. But after a moment she took a deep breath and said, still looking at Caroline, "You're a smart girl. I think you'll likely be going to Lee Ann's room in that place where she lives. If you do go there, and if you are a smart girl, you'll look in the left-hand drawer of Lee Ann's dressing table." Fern had an uneasy smile on her face after she had spoken, as if Caroline had got her to say something she hadn't really meant to say, as if she felt guilty for what she had just done.

Caroline had us out of there in only a minute or so and on our way to Lee Ann's roominghouse.

It was a red brick bungalow up in north Memphis. It looked very much like the one that Fern lived in but was used as a roominghouse. When Mrs. Troxler opened the front door to us, Caroline said, "We're friends of Lee Ann's, and she wants us to pack a suitcase and bring it to her."

"You know where she is, then?" Mrs. Troxler asked. "Hello, Nat," she said, looking at me over Caroline's shoulder.

"Hello, Mrs. Troxler," I said. I was so stunned by what I had just heard Caroline say that I spoke in a whisper.

"She's with her mother — or with her family, at least," Caroline said. By now she had slipped into the hallway, and I had followed without Mrs. Troxler's really inviting us in.

"Where are her family?" Mrs. Troxler asked, giving way to Caroline's forward thrust. "She never volunteered to tell me anything about them. And I never think it's my business to ask."

Caroline nodded her head at me, indicating that I should lead the way to Lee Ann's room. I knew that her room was toward the back of the house and I headed in that direction.

"I'll have to unlock the room for you," said Mrs. Troxler. "There have been a number of people coming here and wanting to look about her room. And so I keep it locked."

"A number of people?" asked Caroline casually.

"Yes. Nat knows. There were the police. And then there were

some other gentlemen. Nat knows about it, though he didn't come in. And there were two other girls. The girls just seemed idly curious, and so I've taken to locking the door. Where do her people live?"

"I don't know," said Caroline. "She's going to meet us downtown at the bus station and take a bus."

When Mrs. Troxler had unlocked the door she asked, "Is Lee Ann all right? Do you think she will be coming back here?"

"She's fine," Caroline said, "and I'm sure she'll be coming back. She just wants a few things."

"Yes, I've wondered how she's been getting along without a change of clothes. I'll fetch her suitcase. I keep my roomers' luggage in my storage closet down the hall." We waited till she came back with a piece of plaid luggage and then we went into the room and closed the door. Caroline went to the oak dresser and began pulling things out and stuffing them in the bag. I stood by, watching, hardly able to believe what I saw Caroline doing. When she had closed the bag, she looked up at me as if to say, "What are you waiting for?" She had not gone near the little mahogany dressing table, and I had not realized that was going to be my part. I went over and opened the left-hand drawer. The only thing in the drawer was a small snapshot. I took it up and examined it carefully. I said nothing to Caroline, just handed her the picture. Finally I said, "Do you know who that is? And where the picture was taken?" She recognized the woman in the picture at once. It was the old woman with the goiter who ran The Cellar. The picture had been taken with Mrs. Power standing in one of the flower beds against the side of the house. The big cut stones of the house were unmistakable. After bringing the snapshot up close to her face and peering into it for ten seconds or so, Caroline looked at me and said, "That's her family."

By the time we had stopped the car in front of The Cellar, I had told Caroline all that I knew about Lee Ann's schooling and about how it was that, though she had a "family" in Memphis, no one had known her when she was growing up. She had been to one boarding school in Shreveport, Louisiana, to one in east Texas, and to still another in St. Charles, Missouri. I had heard her make references to all of those schools. "They kept her away from home," Caroline speculated. "And so when she had finished school she wasn't prepared for the kind of 'family' she had. That's why she moved out on them and lived in a roominghouse."

She reached that conclusion while I was parking the car at the curb, near the front entrance to the house. Meanwhile, I was preparing myself mentally to accompany Caroline to the door of the old woman's living quarters, which were on the main floor and above The Cellar. But Caroline rested her hand on the steering wheel beside mine and said, "This is something I have to do without you."

"But I'd like to see Lee Ann if she's here," I said.

"I know you would," said Caroline. "Of course you would."

"But, Caroline," I said, "I've made it clear that ours was an innocent —"

"I know," she said. "That's why I don't want you to see her again." Then she took Lee Ann's bag and went up to the front entrance of the house.

The main entrance to The Cellar was to the side of and underneath the high front stoop of the old house. Caroline had to climb a flight of ten or twelve stone steps to reach the door to the residence. From the car I saw a vague figure appear at one of the long first-floor windows. I was relatively certain that it was Lee Ann I saw. I could barely restrain myself from jumping from the car and running up that flight of steps and forcing myself past Caroline and into the house. During the hundred hours or so since she had fled into the woods of Overton Park, Lee Ann Deehart had come to represent feelings of mine that I didn't try to comprehend. The notion I had had yesterday that I was in love with her and wanted to marry her didn't really adequately express the emotions that her disappearance had stirred in me. I felt that I had never looked at her really or had any conception of what sort of person she was or what her experience in life was like. Now it seemed I would never know. I suddenly realized — at that early age — that there was experience to be had in life that I might never know anything about except through hearsay and through books. I felt that this was my last moment to reach out and understand something of the world that was other than my own narrow circumstances and my own narrow nature. When, nearly fifteen years later, I came into a comfortable amount of money — after my father's death — I made my extraordinary decision to go back to the university and prepare myself to become a teacher. But I knew then, at thirty-seven, that I was only going to try to comprehend intellectually the world about me and beyond me and that I had failed somehow at some time to reach out and grasp direct experience of a larger life that no amount of intellectualizing could compensate for. It may be that the moment of my great failure was when I continued to sit there in the car and did not force my way into the house where the old woman with the goiter lived and where it now seemed Lee Ann had been hiding for four days.

I was scarcely aware of the moment when the big front door opened and Caroline was admitted to the house. She was in there for nearly an hour. During that time I don't know what thoughts I had. It was as though I ceased to exist for the time that Lee Ann Deehart and Caroline Braxley were closeted together. When Caroline reappeared on the high stone stoop of the house, I was surprised to see she was still carrying Lee Ann's suitcase. But she would soon make it all clear. It *was* Lee Ann who received her at the door. No doubt she had seen that Caroline was carrying her own piece of luggage. And no doubt Caroline had counted on just that mystification and its efficacy, because Caroline is an extremely clever psychologist when she sets her mind to it. At any rate, in that relatively brief interview between them Caroline learned that all she had surmised about Lee Ann was true. Moreover, she learned that Lee Ann had fled the scene of the accident because she feared that the publicity would reveal to everyone who her grandmother was.

Lee Ann had crossed the little strip of snow-covered golf course and had entered the part of the woods where the old-forest trees were. And something had made her want to remain there for a while. She didn't know what it was. She had leaned against one of the trees, feeling quite content. It had seemed to her that she was not alone in the woods. And whatever the other presences were, instead of interfering with her reflections they seemed to wish to help her clear her thoughts. She stood there for a long time — perhaps for an hour or more. At any rate, she remained there until all at once she realized how cold she had grown and realized that she had no choice but to go back to the real world. Yet she wasn't going back to her room or to her pretty possessions there. That wasn't the kind of freedom she wanted any longer. She was going back to her grandmother. But still she hoped to avoid the publicity that the accident might bring. She decided to go, first of all, and stay with some of her friends, so that her grandmother would not suppose she was only turning to her because she was in trouble. And while making this important change in her life she felt she must be protected by her friends. She wanted to have an interval of time to herself and she wanted, above all, not to be bothered during that time by the silly society boy in whose car she had been riding.

During the first days she had gone from one girl's house to another. Finally she went to her grandmother. In the beginning she had, it was true, been mightily depressed. That was why she had telephoned me to start with, and had wanted someone to cheer her up. But during these four days she had much time for thinking and had overcome all her depression and had no other thought but to follow through with the decision to go and live openly with her old grandmother in her quarters above The Cellar.

Caroline also, in that single interview, learned other things about Lee Ann that had been unknown to me. She learned that Lee Ann's own mother had abandoned her in infancy to her grand-mother but had always through the years sent money back for her education. She had had — the mother — an extremely successful career as a buyer for a women's clothing store in Lincoln, Ne-braska. But she had never tried to see her daughter and had never expressed a wish to see her. The only word she ever sent was that children were not her dish, but that she didn't want it on her conscience that, because of her, some little girl in Memphis, Ten-nessee, had got no education and was therefore the domestic slave of some man. When Caroline told me all of this about the mother's not caring to see the daughter, it brought from her her first emo-tional outburst with regard to the whole business. But that was at a later time. The first thing she had told me when she returned to the car was that once Lee Ann realized that her place of hiding could no longer be concealed, she was quickly and easily persuaded to speak to the newspaper editor on the telephone and to tell him that she was safe and well. But she did this only after Caroline had first spoken to the editor herself, and obtained a promise from him that there would be no embarrassing publicity for Lee Ann's grandmother.

The reason Caroline had returned with Lee Ann's suitcase was that Lee Ann had emptied it there in her grandmother's front parlor and had asked that we return to her roominghouse and bring all of her possessions to her at her grandmother's. We obliged her in this, making appropriate, truthless explanations to her landlady, whom Lee Ann had meanwhile telephoned and given whatever little authority Mrs. Troxler required in order to let us remove her things. It seemed to me that that poor woman scarcely listened to the explanations we gave. Another girl was already moving into the room before we had well got Lee Ann's things out. When we returned to the grandmother's house with these possessions in the car, Caroline insisted upon making an endless number of trips into the house, carrying everything herself. She was firm in her stipulation that Lee Ann and I not see each other again.

The incident was closed then. I could be certain that there would be no broken engagement — not on Caroline's initiative. But from that point — from that afternoon — my real effort and my real concern would be to try to understand why Caroline had not been so terribly enraged or so sorely wounded upon first discovering that there had been another girl with me in the car at the time of the accident, and by the realization that I had not immediately disclosed her presence, that she had not at least once threatened to end the engagement. What her mental processes had been during the past four days, knowing now as I did that she was the person with whom I was going to spend the rest of my life, became of paramount interest to me.

But at that age I was so unquestioning of human behavior in general and so accepting of events as they came, and so without perception or reflection regarding the binding and molding effect upon people of the circumstances in which they are born, that I actually might not have found Caroline's thoughts of such profound interest and so vitally important to be understood had not Caroline, as soon as we were riding down Adams Street and were out of sight of The Cellar and of Mrs. Power's great stone house above it, suddenly requested that I drive her out to the Bristol Highway, and once we were on the Bristol Highway asked me to drive as fast and as far out of town as I could or would, to drive and drive until she should beg me to turn around and take her home; and had she not, as soon as we were out of town and beyond city speed limits, where I could press down on the accelerator and send us flying along the three-lane strip of concrete that cut through the endless expanse of cotton fields and swamps on either side, had she not then at last, after talking quietly about Lee Ann's mother's sending back the money for her education, burst into weeping that began with a kind of wailing and grinding of teeth that one ordinarily associates more with a very old person in very great physical pain, a wailing that became mixed almost immediately with a sort of hollow laughter in which there was no mirth. I commenced slowing the car at once. I was searching for a place where I could pull off to the side of the road. But through her tears and her harsh, dry laughter she hissed at me, "Don't stop! Don't stop! Go on. Go on. Go as far and as fast as you can, so that I can forget this day and put it forever behind me!" I obeyed her and sped on, reaching out my right hand to hold her two hands that were resting in her lap and were making no effort to wipe away her tears. I was not looking at her — only thinking thoughts of a kind I had never before had. It was the first time I had ever witnessed a victim of genuine hysteria. Indeed, I wasn't to hear such noises again until six or seven years later, during the Second World War. I heard them from men during days after a battle, men who had stood with great bravery against the enemy — particularly, as I remember now, men who had been brought back from the first onslaught of the Normandy invasion, physically whole but shaken in their souls. I think that during the stress of the four previous days Caroline Braxley had shed not a tear of self-pity or of shame and had not allowed herself a moment of genuine grief for my possible faithlessness to her. She had been far too busy with thinking — with thinking her thoughts of how to cope with Lee Ann's unexplained disappearance, with, that is, its possible effect upon her own life. But now the time had come when her checked emotions could be checked no longer.

The Bristol Highway, along which we were speeding as she wept hysterically, was a very straight and a very wide roadway for those days. It went northeast from Memphis. As its name implied, it was the old road that shot more or less diagonally across the long hinterland that is the state of Tennessee. It was the road along which many of our ancestors had first made their way from Virginia and the Carolinas to Memphis, to settle in the forest wilderness along the bluffs above the Mississippi River. And it occurred to me now that when Caroline said go as fast and as far as you can she really meant to take us all the way back into our past and begin the journey all over again, not merely from a point of four days ago or from the days of our childhood but from a point in our identity that would require a much deeper delving and a more radical return.

When we had got scarcely beyond the outskirts of Memphis, the most obvious signs of her hysteria had abated. Instead, however, she began to speak with a rapidity and in tones I was not accustomed to in her speech. This began after I had seen her give one long look over her shoulder and out the rear window of the car. Sensing some significance in that look and sensing some connection between it and the monologue she had now launched upon, I myself gave one glance into the rearview mirror. What met my eye was the skyline of modern Memphis beyond the snow-covered suburban rooftops — the modern Memphis of 1937, with its two or three high-rise office buildings. It was not clear to me immediately what there was in that skyline to inspire all that followed. She was speaking to me openly about Lee Ann and about her own feelings of jealousy and resentment of the girl — of *that* girl and of all those other girls, too, whose names and personalities and way of life had occupied our thoughts and had seemed to threaten our future during the four-day crisis that had followed my accident in the park.

"It isn't only Lee Ann that disturbs me," she said. "It began with her, of course. It began not with what she might be to you but with her freedom to jump out of your car, her freedom *from* you, her freedom to run off into the woods — with her capacity, which her special way of living provided her, simply to vanish, to remove herself from the eyes of the world, literally to disappear from the glaring light of day while the whole world, so to speak, looked on."

"*You* would like to be able to do that?" I interrupted. It seemed so unlike her role as I understood it.

"*Any*body would, wouldn't they?" she said, not looking at me but at the endless stretch of concrete that lay straight ahead. "*Men* have always been able to do it," she said. "In my own family, for as many generations back as our family stories go, there have been men who seemed to disappear from the face of the earth just because they wanted to. They used to write 'Gone to Texas' on the front door and leave the house and the farm to be sold for taxes. They walked out on dependent old parents and on sweethearts or even on wives and little children. And though they were considered black sheep for doing so, they were something of heroes, too. It seemed romantic to the rest of us that they had gone Out West somewhere and got a new start or had begun life over. But there was never a woman in our family who did that! There was no way it could happen. Or perhaps in some rare instance it did happen and the story hasn't come down to us. Her name simply isn't recorded in our family annals or reported in stories told around the fire. The assumption of course is that she is a streetwalker in Chicago or she resides in a red-plush whorehouse in Cheyenne. But with girls like Lee Ann and Lucy and Betsy it's all different. They have made their break with the past. Each of them has had the strength and intelligence to make the break for herself. But now they have formed a sort of league for their own protection. How I do admire and envy them! And how little you understand them, Nat. How little you understand Lee Ann's loneliness and depression and bravery. She and all the others are wonderful — even Fern. They occupy the real city of Memphis as none of the rest of us do. They treat men just as they please. And not the way men are treated in *our* circles. And men like them better for it. Those girls have learned to enjoy life together and to be mutually protective, but they enjoy a protection also, I hope you have observed, a kind of communal protection, from men who admire their very independence, from a league of men, mind you, not from individual men, from the police and from men like my father and your father, from men who would never say openly how much they admire them. Naturally we fear them. Those of us who are not like them in temperament — or in intelligence, because there is no use in denying it — we must fear them and find a means to give delaying action. And of course the only way we know is the age-old way!"

She became silent for a time now. But I knew I was going to hear what I had been waiting to hear. If I had been the least bit impatient with her explanation of Lee Ann and her friends, it was due in part to my impatience to see if she would explain *herself* to me. We were now speeding along the Bristol Highway at the very top speed the car would go. Except when we were passing through some crossroad or village I consciously kept the speed above ninety. In those days there was no speed limit in Tennessee. There were merely signs placed every so often along the roadside saying "Speed Limit: Please Drive Carefully." I felt somehow that, considering Caroline's emotional state and my own tension, it would be altogether unreasonable, it would constitute careless and unsafe driving, for me to reduce our speed to anything below the maximum capability of the car. And when we did of necessity slow down for some village or small town it was precisely as though we had arrived at some at once familiar and strange point in the past. And on each occasion I think we both experienced a sense of danger and disappointment. It was as though we expected to experience a satisfaction in having gone so far. But the satisfaction was not to be had. When we had passed that point, I felt only the need to press on at an even greater speed. And so we drove on and on, at first north and east through the wintry cotton land and corn land, past the old Orgill Plantation, the mansion house in plain view, its round brick columns on which the plaster was mostly gone, and now and then another white man's antebellum house, and always at the roadside or on the horizon, atop some distant ridge, a variety of black men's shacks and cabins, each with a little streamer of smoke rising from an improvised tin stovepipe or from an ill-made brick chimney bent away from the cabin at a precarious angle.

We went through the old villages of Arlington and Mason and the town of Brownsville — down streets of houses with columned porticoes and double galleries — and then we turned south to Bolivar, whose very name told you when it was built, and headed back to Memphis through Grand Junction and La Grange. (Mississippi towns really, though north of the Tennessee line.) I had slowed our speed after Bolivar, because that was where Caroline began her second monologue. The tone and pace of her speech were very different now. Her speech was slow and deliberate, her emotions more under control than usual, as she described what she had felt and thought in the time since the accident and explained how she came to reach the decision to take the action she had — that is, action toward searching out and finding Lee Ann Deehart. Though I had said nothing on the subject of what she had done about Lee Ann and not done about our engagement, expressed no request or demand for any explanation unless it was by my silence, when she spoke now it was almost as though Caroline were making a courtroom defense of accusations hurled at her by me. "I finally saw there was only one thing for me to do and saw why I had to do it. I saw that the only power in the world I had for saving myself lay in my saving you. And I saw that I could only save you by 'saving' Lee Ann Deehart. At first, of course, I thought I would have to break our engagement, or at least postpone the wedding for a year. That's what *every*body thought, of course — everybody in the family."

"Even your father and mother?" I could not help interjecting. It had seemed to me that Caroline's parents had — of all people — been most sympathetic to me.

"Yes, even my mother and father," she went on, rather serenely now. "They could not have been more sympathetic to you personally. Mother said that, after all, you were a mere man. Father said that, after all, you were only human. But circumstances were circumstances, and if some disaster had befallen Lee Ann, if she was murdered or if she was pregnant or if she was a suicide or whatever other horror you can conjure up, and it all came out, say, on our wedding day or came out afterward, for that matter — well, what then? *They* and *I* had to think of that. On the other hand, as I kept thinking, what if the wedding *was* called off? What then for me? The only power I had to save myself was to save you, and to save you by rescuing Lee Ann Deehart. It always came to that, and comes to that still. Don't you see, it was a question of how very much I had to lose and how little power I had to save myself. Because *I* had not set *my*self free the way those other girls have. One makes that choice at a much earlier age than this, I'm afraid. And so I knew already, Nat, and I know now what the only kind of power I can ever have must be."

She hesitated then. She was capable of phrasing what she said much more precisely. But it would have been indelicate, somehow, for her to have done so. And so I said it for her in my crude way: "You mean the power of a woman in a man's world."

She nodded and continued. "I had to protect *that*. Even if it had been *I* that broke our engagement, Nat, or even if you and I had been married before some second scandal broke, still I would have been a jilted, a rejected girl. And some part of my power to protect myself would be gone forever. Power, or strength, is what everybody must have some of if he — if she — is to survive in any kind of world. I have to protect and use whatever strength I have."

Caroline went on in that voice until we were back in Memphis and at her father's house on East Parkway. She kissed me before we got out of the car there, kissed me for my silence, I believe. I had said almost nothing during the whole of the long ride. And I think she has ever since been grateful to me for the silence I kept. Perhaps she mistook it for more understanding than I was capable of at the time. At any rate, I cannot help believing that it has much to do with the support and understanding — rather silent though it was — that she gave me when I made the great break in my life in my late thirties. Though it clearly meant that we must live on a somewhat more modest scale and live among people of a sort she was not used to, and even meant leaving Memphis forever behind us, the firmness with which she supported my decision, and the look in her eyes whenever I spoke of feeling I must make the change, seemed to say to me that she would dedicate her pride of power to the power of freedom I sought.

JOHN UPDIKE

Gesturing

(FROM PLAYBOY)

SHE TOLD HIM with a little gesture he had never seen her use before. Joan had called from the station, having lunched, Richard knew, with her lover. It was a Saturday, and his older son had taken his convertible; Joan's Volvo was new and for several minutes refused to go into first gear for him. By the time he had reached the center of town, she had walked down the main street and up the hill to the green. It was September, leafy and warm, yet with a crystal chill on things, an uncanny clarity. Even from a distance they smiled to see each other. She opened the door and seated herself, fastening the safety belt to silence its chastening buzz. Her face was rosy from her walk, her city clothes looked like a costume, she carried a small package or two, token of her "shopping." Richard tried to pull a U-turn on the narrow street, and in the long moment of his halting and groping for reverse gear, she told him. "Darley," she said and, oddly, tentatively, soundlessly, tapped the fingers of one hand into the palm of the other, a gesture between a child's clap of glee and an adult's signal for attention, "I've decided to kick you out. I'm going to ask you to leave town."

Abruptly full, his heart thumped; it was what he wanted. "O.K.," he said carefully. "If you think you can manage." He glanced at her rosy, alert face to see if she meant it; he could not believe she did. A red, white, and blue mail truck that had braked to a stop behind them tapped its horn, more reminder than rebuke; the Maples were known in the town. They had lived here most of their married life.

Richard found reverse, backed up, completed the turn, and they headed home, skimming. The car, so new and stiff, in motion felt high and light, as if it, too, had just been vaporized in her little playful clap. "Things are stagnant," she explained, "stuck; we're not going anywhere."

"I will not give her up," he interposed.

"Don't tell me, you've told me."

"Nor do I see you giving him up."

"I would if you asked. Are you asking?"

"No. Horrors. He's all I've got."

"Well, then. Go where you want, I think Boston would be most fun for the kids to visit. And the least boring for you."

"I agree. When do you see this happening?" Her profile, in the side of his vision, felt brittle, about to break if he said a wrong word, too rough a word. He was holding his breath, trying to stay up, high and light, like the car. They went over the bump this side of the bridge; cigarette smoke jarred loose from Joan's face.

"As soon as you can find a place," she said. "Next week. Is that too soon?"

"Probably."

"Is this too sad? Do I seem brutal to you?"

"No, you seem wonderful, very gentle and just, as always. It's right. It's just something I couldn't do myself. How can you possibly live without me?"

In the edge of his vision her face turned; he turned to see, and her expression was mischievous, brave, flushed. They must have had wine at lunch. "Easy," Joan said. He knew it was a bluff, a brave gesture; she was begging for reprieve. But he held silent, he refused to argue. This way, he had her pride on his side.

The curves of the road poured by, mailboxes, trees, some of which were already scorched by the turn of the year. He asked, "Is this your idea, or his?"

"Mine. It came to me on the train. All Andy said was, I seemed to be feeding you all the time."

Richard had been sleeping, most nights, in the weeks since their summer of separated vacations, in a borrowed seaside shack two miles from their home; he tried to sleep there, but each evening, as the nights grew longer, it seemed easier, and kinder to the children, to eat the dinner Joan had cooked. He was used to her cooking; indeed, his body, every cell, was composed of her cooking. Dinner would lead to a postdinner drink, while the children (two were off at school, two were still homebound) plodded through their homework or stared at television, and drinking would lead to talking, confidences, harsh words, maudlin tears, and an occasional uxorious collapse upward, into bed. She was right; it was not healthy, nor progressive. The twenty years were by when it would have been convenient to love each other.

He found the apartment in Boston on the second day of hunting. The real-estate agent had red hair, a round bottom, and a mask of make-up worn as if to conceal her youth. Richard felt happy and scared, going up and down stairs behind her. Wearier of him than he was of her, she fidgeted the key into the lock, bucked the door open with her shoulder, and made her little openhanded gesture of helpless display.

The floor was neither wall-to-wall shag nor splintered wood, but black-and-white tile, like the floor in a Vermeer; he glanced to the window, saw the skyscraper, and knew this would do. The skyscraper, for years suspended in a famous state of incompletion, was a beautiful disaster, famous because it was a disaster (glass kept falling from it) and disastrous because it was beautiful: The architect had had a vision. He had dreamed of an invisible building, though immense; the glass was meant to reflect the sky and the old low brick skyline of Boston, and to melt into the sky. Instead, the windows of mirroring glass kept falling to the street and were replaced by ugly opacities of black plywood. Yet enough reflecting surface remained to give an impression, through the wavery old window of this sudden apartment, of huge blueness, a vertical cousin to the horizontal huge blueness of the sea that Richard awoke to each morning, in the now bone-deep morning chill of his unheated shack. He said to the redhead, "Fine," and her charcoal eyebrows lifted. His hands trembled as he signed the lease, having written "Sep" in the space for marital status. From a drugstore he phoned the news, not to his wife, whom it would sadden, but to his mistress, equally far away. "Well," he told her in an accusing voice, "I found one. I signed the lease. Incredible. In the middle of all this fine print, there was the one simple sentence, 'There shall be no water beds.'"

"You sound so shaky."

"I feel I've given birth to a black hole."

"Don't do it, if you don't want to." From the way Ruth's voice paused and faded, he imagined she was reaching for a cigarette, or an ashtray, settling herself to a session of lover babying.

"I do want to. She wants me to. We all want me to. Even the children are turned on. Or pretend to be."

She ignored the "pretend." "Describe it to me."

All he could remember was the floor, and the view of the blue disaster with reflected clouds drifting across its face. And the redhead. She had told him where to shop for food, where to do his laundry. He would have laundry?

"It sounds nice," was Ruth's remote response, when he had finished saying what he could. Two people, one of them a sweating black mailman, were waiting to use the phone booth. He hated the city already, its crowding, its hunger.

"What sounds nice about it?" he snapped.

"Are you so upset? Don't do it if you don't want to."

"Stop *saying* that." It was a tedious formality both observed, the pretense that they were free, within each of their marriages, to do as they pleased; guilt avoidance was the game, and Ruth had grown expert at it. Her words often seemed not real words but blank counters, phrases of an etiquette, partitions in a maze. Whereas his wife's words always opened in, transparent with meaning.

"What else can I say," Ruth asked, "except that I love you?" And at its far end, the phone sharply sighed. He could picture the gesture: She had turned her face away from the mouthpiece and forcefully exhaled, in that way she had, expressive of exasperation even when she felt none, of exhaling and simultaneously stubbing out a cigarette smoked not halfway down its length, so it crumpled under her impatient fingers like an insect fighting to live. Her conspicuous unthriftiness pained him. All waste pained him. He wanted abruptly to hang up but saw that, too, as a wasteful, empty gesture, and hung on.

Alone in his apartment, he discovered himself a neat and thrifty housekeeper. When a woman left, he would promptly set about restoring his bachelor order, emptying the ashtrays that, if the visitor had been Ruth, brimmed with long pale bodies prematurely extinguished and, if Joan, with butts so short as to be scarcely more than filters. Neither woman, it somehow pleased him to observe, ever made more than a gesture toward cleaning up — the bed a wreck, the dishes dirty, each of his three ashtrays (one glass, one pottery, and one a tin cookie-jar lid) systematically touched, like the bases in baseball. Emptying them, he would smile, depending, at Ruth's messy morgue or at Joan's nest of filters, discreet as white pebbles in a bowl of narcissi. When he chastised Ruth for stubbing out cigarettes still so long, she pointed out, of course, with her beautiful unblinking assumption of her own primary worth, how much better it was for *her*, for her lungs, to kill the cigarette early; and, of course, she was right, better other-destructive than self-destructive. Ruth was love, she was life, that was why he loved her. Yet Joan's compulsive economy, her discreet death wish, was as dearly familiar to him as her tiny repressed handwriting and the tight curls of her pubic hair, so Richard smiled emptying her ashtrays also. His smile was a gesture without an audience. He, who had originated his act among parents and grandparents, siblings and pets, and who had developed it for a public of schoolmates and teachers, and who had carried it to new refinements before an initially rapt audience of his own children, could not in solitude stop performing. He had engendered a companion of sorts, a single grand spectator — the blue skyscraper. He felt it with him all the time.

Blue, it showed greener than the sky. For a time Richard was puzzled, why the clouds reflected in it drifted in the same direction as the clouds behind it. With an effort of spatial imagination he perceived that a mirror does not reverse our motion, though it does transpose our ears, and gives our mouths a tweak, so that the face even of a loved one looks unfamiliar and ugly when seen in a mirror, the way she — queer thought! — always sees it. He saw that a mirror posed in its midst would not affect the motion of an army; and often half a reflected cloud matched the half of another beyond the building's edge, moving as one, pierced by a jet trail as though by Cupid's arrow. The disaster sat light on the city's heart. At night, it showed as a dim row of little lights, as if a slender ship were sailing the sky, and during a rain or fog, it vanished entirely, while the brick chimney pots and ironstone steeples in Richard's foreground swarthily intensified their substance. He tried to analyze the logic of window replacement, as revealed in the patterns of gap and glass. He detected no logic, just the slow-motion labor of invisible workers, emptying and filling cells of glass with the brainlessness of bees. If he watched for many minutes, he might see, like the condensation of a dewdrop, a blank space go glassy, and reflective, and greenish-blue. Days passed before he realized that, on the old glass near his nose, the wavery panes of his own

window, ghostly previous tenants armed with diamonds had
scratched initials, names, dates, and, cut deepest and whitest of all,
the touching, comical vow, incised in two trisyllabic lines:

> *With this ring*
> *I thee wed*

What a transparent wealth of previous lives overlay a city's present joy! As he walked the streets, his own happiness surprised him.
He had expected to be sad, guilty, bored. Instead, his days were
snugly filled with his lists, his quests for food and hardware, his
encounters with such problematical wife substitutes as the laundro-
mat, where students pored over Hesse and picked at their chins
while their clothes tumbled in eternal circular fall, where young
black housewives hummed as they folded white linen. What an
unexpected pleasure, walking home in the dark hugging to himself
clean clothes hot as fresh bread, past the bow windows of Back Bay
glowing like display cases. He felt sober and exhilarated and
justified at the hour when, in the suburbs, rumpled from the
commute, he would be into his hurried second predinner drink.
He liked the bringing home of food, the tautological satisfaction of
cooking a meal and then eating it all, as the radio fed Bach or
Bechet into his ears and a book gazed open-faced from the reading
stand he had bought; he liked the odd orderly game of consuming
before food spoiled and drinking before milk soured. He liked the
way airplanes roamed the brown night sky, a second, thinner city
laid upon this one, and the way police sirens sang, scooping up
some disaster not his. It could not last, such happiness. It was an
interim, a holiday. But an oddly clean and just one, rectilinear,
dignified, though marred by gaps of sudden fear and disorienta-
tion. Each hour had to be scheduled, lest he fall through. He
moved like a water bug, like a skipping stone, upon the glassy tense
surface of his new life. He walked everywhere. Once he walked to
the base of the blue skyscraper, his companion and witness. It was
hideous. Heavily planked and chicken-wired tunnels, guarded by
barking policemen, protected pedestrians from falling glass and
the owners of the building, already millions in the hole, from more
lawsuits. Trestles and trucks jammed the cacophonous area. The
lower floors were solid plywood, of a Stygian black; the building,
so lovely in air, had tangled mucky roots. Richard avoided walking
that way again.

When Ruth visited, they played a game, of washing — scouring, with a Brillo pad — one white square of the Vermeer floor, so eventually it would all appear clean. The black squares they ignored. Naked, scrubbing, Ruth seemed on her knees a plump little steed, long hair swinging, soft breasts swaying in rhythm to her energetic circular strokes. Behind, her pubic hair, uncurly, made a kind of nether mane. So lovably strange, she rarely was allowed to clean more than one square. Time, so careful and regular for him, sped for them, and vanished. There seemed time even to talk only at the end, her hand on the door. She asked, "Isn't that building amazing, with the sunset in it?"

"I love that building. And it loves me."

"No. It's me who loves you."

"Can't you share?"

"No."

She felt possessive about the apartment; when he told her Joan had been there, too, and, just for "fun," had slept with him, her husband, Ruth wailed into the telephone, "In *our* bed?"

"In *my* bed," he said, with uncharacteristic firmness.

"In your bed," she conceded, her voice husky as a sleepy child's.

When the conversation finally ended, his mistress sufficiently soothed, he had to go lean his vision against his inanimate, giant friend, dimming to mauve on one side, still cerulean on the other, faintly streaked with reflections of high cirrus. It spoke to him, as the gaze of a dumb beast speaks, of beauty and suffering, of a simplicity that must perish, of loss. Evening would soften its shade to slate; night would envelop its sides. Richard's focus shortened and he read, with irritation, for the hundredth time, that impudent, pious marring, that bit of litany, etched bright by the sun's fading fire.

With this ring
I thee wed

Ruth, months ago, had removed her wedding ring. Coming here to embark with him upon an overnight trip, she wore on that naked finger, as a reluctant concession to imposture, an inherited diamond ring. In the hotel, Ruth had been distressed to lose her name in the false assumption of his, though he explained it to her as a mere convenience. "But I *like* who I am now," she protested.

That was, indeed, her central jewel, infrangible and bright: She liked who she was. They had gone separate ways and, returning before him, she had asked at the hotel desk for the room key by number.

The clerk asked her her name. It was a policy. He would not give the key to a number.

"And what did you tell him your name was?" Richard asked, in this pause of her story.

In her pause and dark-blue stare, he saw re-created her hesitation when challenged by the clerk. Also, she had been, before her marriage, a second-grade teacher, and Richard saw now the manner — prim, fearful, and commanding — with which she must have confronted those roomfuls of children. "I told him Maple."

Richard had smiled. "That sounds right."

Taking Joan out to dinner felt illicit. She suggested it, for "fun," at the end of one of the children's Sundays. He had been two months in Boston, new habits had replaced old, and it was tempting to leave their children, who were bored and found it easier to be bored by television than by their father, this bossy visitor. "Stop telling me you're bored," he had scolded John, the most docile of his children and the one he felt guiltiest about. "Fifteen is *supposed* to be a boring age. When I was fifteen, I lay around reading science fiction. You lie around looking at *Kung Fu*. At least I was learning to read."

"It's good," the child protested, his adolescent voice cracking in fear of being distracted from an especially vivid piece of slow-motion *tai chi*. Richard, when living here, had watched the program with him often enough to know that it was, in a sense, good, that the hero's Oriental passivity, relieved by spurts of mystical violence, was insinuating into the child a system of ethics, just as Richard had taken ideals of behavior from dime movies and comic books — coolness from Bogart, debonair recklessness from Errol Flynn, duality and deceit from Superman.

He dropped to one knee beside the sofa where John, his upper lip fuzzy and his eyebrows manly dark, stoically gazed into the transcendent flickering; Richard's own voice nearly cracked, asking, "Would it be less boring if Dad still lived here?"

"No-*oh*": The answer was instantaneous and impatient, as if the question had been anticipated. Did the boy mean it? His eyes did not for an instant glance sideways, perhaps out of fear of betraying himself, perhaps out of genuine boredom with grownups and their gestures. On television, satisfyingly, gestures killed. Richard rose from his supplicant position, relieved to hear Joan coming down the stairs. She was dressed to go out, in the timeless black dress with the scalloped neckline, and a collar of Mexican silver. At least — a mark, perhaps, of their fascinating maladjustment — he had never bored *her,* nor she, he dreaded to admit, him. He was wary. He must be wary. They had had it. They must have had it.

Yet the cocktails, and the seafood, and the wine, displaced his wariness; he heard himself saying, to the so familiar and so strange face across the table, "She's lovely, and loves me, you know" (he felt embarrassed, like a son suddenly aware that his mother, though politely attentive, is indifferent to the urgency of an athletic contest being described), "but she does spell everything out, and wants everything spelled out to her. It's like being back in the second grade. And the worst thing is, for all this explaining, for all this glorious fucking, she's still not real to me, the way — you are." His voice did break, he had gone too far.

Joan put her left hand, still bearing their wedding ring, flat on the tablecloth in a sensible, level gesture. "She will be," she said. "It's a matter of time."

The old pattern was still the one visible to the world. The waitress, who had taught their children in Sunday school, greeted them as if their marriage were unbroken; they ate in this restaurant three or four times a year, and were on schedule. They had known the contractor who had built it, this mock-antique wing, a dozen years ago, and then left town, bankrupt, disgraced, and oddly cheerful. His memory hovered between the beams. Another couple, older than the Maples — the husband had once worked with Richard on a town committee — came up to their booth beaming, jollying, loving, in that obligatory American way. Did they know? It didn't matter, in this country of temporary arrangements. The Maples jollied back as one, and tumbled loose only when the older couple moved away. Joan gazed after their backs. "I wonder what they have," she asked, "that we didn't?"

"Maybe they had less," Richard said, "so they didn't expect more."

"That's too easy." She was a shade resistant to his veiled compliments; he was grateful. Please resist.

He asked, "How do you think the kids are doing? John seemed withdrawn."

"That's how he is. Stop picking at him."

"I just don't want him to think he has to be your little husband. That house feels huge now."

"You're telling me."

"I'm sorry." He was; he put his hands palms up on the table.

"Isn't it amazing," Joan said, "how a full bottle of wine isn't enough for two people anymore?"

"Should I order another bottle?" He was dismayed, secretly: the waste.

She saw this and said, "No. Just give me half of what's in your glass."

"You can have it all." He poured.

She said, "So your fucking is really glorious?"

He was embarrassed by the remark now and feared it set a distasteful trend. As with Ruth there was an etiquette of adultery, so with Joan some code of separation must be maintained. "It usually is," he told her, "between people who aren't married."

"Is dat right, white man?" A swallow of his wine inside her, Joan began to swell with impending hilarity. She leaned as close as the table would permit. "You must *promise*" — a gesture went with "promise," a protesting little splaying of her hands — "never to tell this to anybody, not even Ruth."

"Maybe you shouldn't tell me. In fact, don't." He understood why she had been laconic up to now; she had been wanting to talk about her lover, holding him warm within her like a baby. She was going to betray him. "Please don't," Richard said.

"Don't be such a prig. You're the only person I can talk to; it doesn't mean a thing."

"That's what you said about our going to bed in my apartment."

"Did she mind?"

"Incredibly."

Joan laughed, and Richard was struck, for the thousandth time, by the perfection of her teeth, even and rounded and white, bared by her lips as if in proof of a perfect skull, an immaculate soul. Her glee whirled her to a kind of heaven as she confided stories about herself and Andy — how he and a motel manageress had quarreled over the lack of towels in a room taken for the afternoon, how he fell asleep for exactly seven minutes each time after making love. Richard had known Andy for years, a slender, swarthy specialist in corporation law, himself divorced, though professionally engaged in the finicking arrangement of giant mergers. A fussy dresser, a churchman, he brought to many occasions an undue dignity and perhaps had been more attracted to Joan's surface glaze, her smooth New England ice, than to the mischievous demons underneath. "My psychiatrist thinks Andy was symbiotic with you, and now that you're gone, I can see him as absurd."

"He's not absurd. He's good, loyal, handsome, prosperous. He tithes. He has a twelve handicap. He loves you."

"He protects you from me, you mean. His buttons! — we have to allow a half hour afterward for him to do up all his buttons. If they made four-piece suits, he'd wear them. And he washes — he washes *everything,* every time."

"Stop," Richard begged. "Stop telling me all this."

But she was giddy amid the spinning mirrors of her betrayals, her face so flushed and tremulous the waitress sympathetically giggled, pouring the Maples their coffee. Joan's face was pink as a peony, her eyes a blue pale as ice, almost transparent. He saw through her words to what she was saying — that these lovers, however we love them, are not us, are not sacred as reality is sacred. We are reality. We have made children. We gave each other our young bodies. We promised to grow old together.

Joan described an incident in her house, once theirs, when the plumber unexpectedly arrived. Richard had to laugh with her; that house's plumbing problems were an old joke, an ongoing saga. "The back-door bell rang, Mr. Kelly stomped right in, you know how the kitchen echoes in the bedroom, we had *had* it." She looked, to see if her meaning was clear. He nodded. Her eyes sparkled. She emphasized, of the knock, "Just at the *very* moment," and, with a gesture akin to the gentle clap in the car a world ago, drew with one fingertip a V in the air, as if beginning to write "very." The motion was eager, shy, exquisite, diffident, trusting: He saw all its meanings and knew that she would never stop gesturing within him, never; though a decree come between them, even death, her gestures would endure, cut into glass.

NORMAN WAKSLER

Markowitz and the Gypsies

(FROM ASCENT)

THERE'S THIS FELLOW Al Markowitz, a man in his fifties, who runs a little kosher deli and luncheonette in Brookline, on Harvard Street. He has a brother Reuben, otherwise known as Ruby, who also runs a delicatessen, not so kosher, across the city in Boston, near South Station. The brother's place is ten, fifteen times the size of Al Markowitz's and includes a huge restaurant with a reputation and an enormous following, and every time Al Markowitz visits his brother's place he feels jealousy like indigestion bubbling around in his upper GI tract. He sees RUBY'S — the long tables and booths with the red tablecloths, waitresses running around in red nylon uniforms, red-jacketed bus boys, the whole wall length of glass cases with the herrings, the sturgeon, the roast beefs (hams too, however), the kishkehs and flanken and potato pancakes, the breads and pastries and pies, and the long service counter with the men in their white pants and jackets and hats — and he thinks of MARKOWITZ's with the double case, the dozen shelves behind it, the green Formica lunch counter with the curve, the four little tables against the opposite wall where the old men from the neighborhood eat their brisket and drink their coffee black, and without invitation jealousy rises in his gullet.

At the same time, Al Markowitz knows how inappropriate this jealousy is. If it's connected to anything constant in him it isn't a desire to be in his brother's shoes. He doesn't wish his brother's deli, wouldn't want to be responsible for such a large operation, couldn't command the number of people who work there, knows it would be out of character for him to behave in the gregarious, mein-host manner of his broad-chested, boom-voiced brother.

Naturally. Al Markowitz is a different type entirely. Balding, paunchy, disarrayed, with droopy eyelids, sharp nose, a little, skeptic's smile. Behind the two counters of MARKOWITZ'S, where he's as comfortable as in his kitchen at home and the customers are as familiar as the faces he sees in temple every Friday night (sometimes are), he's a mild, even-toned, ironic confabulator, whose strongest charge to one of the high-school girls working the counter might be, "Darling, do you think you could spare a minute to get Mrs. Leiben a tuna on toast and a cup of tea?" And his favorite occupation, besides being in the deli business and schmoozing with friends, relatives, or his redheaded wife Bella, is to make up jokes and rework them until they're ready for telling, which is rarely, Al Markowitz having maybe two dozen jokes he's thought up over the years that he'll tell, and even those he's always taking out of circulation for revision. He never laughs at his own jokes, by the way, though he doesn't mind being asked to tell one.

So how could a man like this run a place like RUBY'S? And how could he not know that would be the last thing in the world he would need? And how could he want it? Being Al Markowitz, he couldn't. But the sensuous splendor of the red tablecloths and red nylon of the hurrying waitresses and lights gleaming off the white porcelain of the wall-length row of cases, and the excitement his powerhouse brother derives from manipulating his enterprise and being a personage (mentioned in the paper as having greeted the mayor, the governor, a visiting movie star) — these stir him up, shake loose his otherwise occupied urges, make his own satisfactions lose flavor, fire his potential jealousy, which, rising as a powerful, acidulous pang, embarrasses his feelings for Ruby, whom he loves like a brother, and seems shameful and petty on general moral grounds, so that after he leaves he tries to escape it by almost any means — visiting someone he likes, turning his mind to another subject, going back to MARKOWITZ'S and working hard.

O.K.

So one day Al Markowitz goes to RUBY'S, talks to his brother, tastes jealousy, stays awhile, leaves. He decides: it's a beautiful spring day, bright and delighting. Instead of getting on the subway right away and riding in gloom to his change, he'll walk through the city and by the green of the Common to where he catches the

train that returns him to his neighborhood. The route he plans
makes a leisurely jaunt for someone his age who doesn't get any
exercise.

He sets off, paunchy man, bald except for a graying fringe,
pouchy face, sharp little nose, black-and-white-check overcoat,
spring weight, slightly askew. Hands in his coat pockets, he goes
slow, through a business district, across the expressway, past
Chinese restaurants and gift shops, along the edge of the Combat
Zone, toward the shopping area. Well before that, maybe by the
time he's halfway across the footbridge over the expressway, he's
stopped paying attention to his surroundings. Balding head bent,
pouchy face contemplative, focus inward, he's thinking of his new-
est joke.

First line appears to him the previous morning while he's putting
a roast beef through the slicer. He hears himself think, in the more
dramatic still even-toned voice he uses for telling jokes, "A lion, a
giraffe, a baboon, and a goat are walking through the forest one
day." That's all. A natural first line for a joke, variation on old
themes, which comes to him for no reason except he's always
ready. At odd moments of semihypnotized suspensions of attention the rest of that day, this morning, on the subway to his
brother's place, Markowitz works the joke, nudges it, plays with it,
hears it come forth in pieces, chunks, lines, wriggling and turning,
scintillating with energy, stirring the moist jangle of nervous
pleasure that is one of the reasons he does this, leaving in its wake
the calm orderly satisfaction that is another.

Up to this point — Markowitz walking through the city slowly,
hands in pockets, head bent — the joke goes like this:

*A lion, a giraffe, a baboon, and a goat are walking through the forest
one day, when the lion suddenly emits a roar and says, "I'm bored, I want
some entertainment," and he turns to the baboon and says, "You. I'm the
king of the beasts! Get me some entertainment, or else." And the baboon,
who's no dope, immediately says, "Yessir, yessir, your majesty," and runs
off, finds some monkeys he knows, and says, "Look, the lion's bored and
he needs some entertainment, and if he doesn't get it, he's going to take it
out on me. So you better arrange something entertaining and present it
to the king, and he better like it, or I'll take it out on you." Well, the
monkeys are no dopes either. They know the baboon can beat them up, so
they get together an act, and when it's ready the baboon brings them to*

the lion. Singing, dancing, crazy antics — more fun than a barrel of monkeys. The lion's delighted, he roars with laughter, tears roll down his cheeks. The monkeys finish. He claps his paws till they ache. The baboon is very relieved. The four animals resume their walk. A little while later, the lion lets out another huge roar. The other two animals gulp — baboon's not worried. The lion says, "I'm the king of the beasts and I'm horny, so to speak. I want a female. You," turning to the goat. "Get me a female, or else!" And the goat says, "Yessir, yessir," and runs off. Well, as everyone knows, there's nothing randier than a rutting goat, so he knows everything there is to know about sex, including where to look for a female for the king of beasts, which is just as well since he's aware of the consequences if he fails. He goes to a local pride, and from a very great distance he yells out to a certain lioness he's heard about, "Hey, the king of beasts, the lion, is horny, so to speak. Are you willing?" "Hey," says the lioness, who is not only willing but able, "sure." The two beasts get together, go into a grove of trees where the other three animals can't see them, though they can hear all kinds of grunting and growling, roaring and giggling, etc. Eventually everything falls quiet, and the two lions walk out of the grove. The female goes her way, and the king looks at the goat and the goat sees that his eyelids are drooping and he's got a little smile on his face and the goat feels relief. The lion says, "I'm going to take a little nap. But you all wait here, and when I wake up we can continue our walk." So the lion takes his nap and the other three animals sit around waiting for him, dozing every now and again, talking quietly, sometimes pacing in circles, happy to be going no place, content. Eventually, though, the lion wakes up and they start their walk again. Sure enough, they've hardly gone half a block when the lion lets out another huge roar and says, "I'm hungry. You," to the giraffe. "Get me something to eat, and it better be good, or I'll make a meal out of all of you." Well, the giraffe's heart sinks, not to mention the hearts of the baboon and the goat. After all, it's well known that what the lion likes is meat, and how is the giraffe supposed to get meat for the hungry king of beasts when he's not even a carnivore, never mind a hunter? But the giraffe says, "Yessir, yessir, your majesty, anything you say," and goes off. His heart is pounding with fear, he's in a daze, doesn't know what he's going to do —

From RUBY'S to the outskirts of the Combat Zone, Markowitz retells himself this and tries to proceed. Nothing happens. No jangles, no forthcoming lines or chunks or pieces, no turning and wriggling. The joke rests in his mind like a bright whitefish in an otherwise empty and dark display case. Markowitz feels frustrated, stale, dyspeptic. Other emotions simmer thickly. He pushes at the joke. Nothing happens. Hears a loud, irrelevant snapping, tapping noise. Looks up, like anyone deep in the geography of his own mind, needs a moment to adjust to being where he's been seeing but not registering.

Finds he's gotten onto a quiet, dirty side street, cars parked both sides, dark atmosphere, though there's light sky further on. The road looks particularly black, squat granite buildings especially begrimed. Ahead of him two men stroll. One turns into a bar that looks like a shanty. Across the street a derelict lolls in a doorway. *A lovely neighborhood,* Markowitz thinks, and definitely it's not his element, though there's less difference in city streets than he's aware of. Anyway there's the tapping, snapping noise again. Markowitz, paunchy, white-and-black-checked overcoat, droopy eyelids, vestigially preoccupied, bemused, looks left. There's a small storefront — one narrow glass door with a red curtain, one display window, glass above a couple of feet of blackened brick, also with red curtains, pulled back. The noise is being made by a woman rapping backhand against the window with a ring. All Markowitz can make out, since the woman's half behind the curtain and the window's not so clean, she has dark hair, wears a pink dress. He sees she sees she has his attention, and she gestures with a hand and slender bare arm signaling him to come inside.

His first reaction is a reflex step toward the store, as natural as his first inquiring movement toward the counter when a customer sits down, though here, because the gesture seems urgent, Markowitz is gently alarmed, thinks the woman's in trouble, needs help. He takes his step, understands the neighborhood, realizes the woman's a prostitute. A little jangle of distaste. He raises his eyebrows, droops his eyelids even more, starts to turn away. Realizes, just because it's in him somewhere and he knows it, the woman's a gypsy (which releases through him his accumulated sense of a whole historyful of dark, fiery people being wanderers, gonifs, and fortunetellers), wants to tell his fortune, a notion that feels to him like a joke. Markowitz walks to the store, opens the door, goes in.

Something jingles. He smells warm sweet air. Coming toward him the gypsy woman from the window. The door slams. Around him an unexpected incongruous little sitting room. Under his feet a maroon Oriental with peacocks. On the walls textured maroon-and-white wallpaper. The woman is wearing a pink and white flowered dress with ruffled white shoulder straps. To his left a little walnut table, two small armchairs. In one chair, a fat olive-skinned woman in blue velvet. She's sweating. Despite the balmy weather outside, the heat's on, Markowitz can't imagine why. The gypsy woman coming toward him has dark thick hair down around a tan, long, oval face, dark eyes, a wry mouth, delicate pinched nose, a dissatisfied expression. On the right-hand wall, a picture, gypsy caravan in the woods. Straight ahead a doorway with a red velveteen curtain. Her bare tan arms are slender and unusually long. Inside the white ruffled shoulder straps tan flesh lies bare from collarbones all the way down the inner curves of loaf-length tan breasts — for Markowitz a particularly telling detail, which takes him unprepared and makes him hawk phlegm as his throat constricts. Pink and white flowered skirt sways. The woman's feet are bare and unusually long. She makes a peculiar flat-edged curling motion with one hand and says in a suede voice with an exceptional number of lightly touched D's and trilled R's, "You want your fortune told? You want love spell? You want curse for your enemy? I can do this. Come. Follow me." Turns bare scapulas, also tanned, to Markowitz and glides toward the red velvet curtain. Markowitz, who neither curses his enemy nor is in the market for love, and knows it, nonetheless feels blank necessitude marbled with nervous obligation and prickles of confusion, follows anyway.

Woman steps to the curtain, pulls it aside for Markowitz. He brushes through, finds himself in a little chamber not much bigger than a supply closet. The room's made up of one solid wall, the wall with the doorway through which he's just entered, and two walls that are red velveteen curtaining hung from the ceiling. Same kind of rug underfoot. Same wallpaper where possible. Curtain falls, room darkens, the only light's from a hanging fixture with a red shade. The woman approaches Markowitz. Markowitz backs up, touches the side wall with his right hip. Woman keeps coming. The little closet is airless, hot. A strong sweet perfume rises from the woman. She toes toward him, hips swaying, looks purposeful as a lioness stalking some animal innocently nibbling a branch at the edge of a clearing. Markowitz's stomach turns over. Layers of gaseous agitation rise into his chest. Her hair sways one way, skirt another, hips a third, bare tan arms a fourth and fifth. She stops half an inch from him. Those tan breasts, half out of the white and pink flowered fabric, almost brush the mustard-colored spring-weight sports jacket he wears under his now-unbuttoned white-and-black-check spring-weight overcoat. Her dark thick hair is inches away from his mouth and nose. Her perfume fills his nasal cavity like sweet mucous from a hay-fever attack. By pulling in his stomach and looking down at her, he can both avoid her alarming touch and see her thin, plucked eyebrows, intent dark eyes, wry mouth as she stares into his face, says, "Now I will tell you about yourself." Suede voice is smooth, hardened only by the edges of her multiple D's, trilled R's. "You want to know about yourself, don't you? Everybody's interested in themselves, no?"

What can Markowitz do, the gypsy lady so close he can smell sweet coffee, cigarettes on her breath? "Yeh, sure, of course," he agrees in a constricted voice reminiscent of his normal one, feels like he's conceding a lot more than her point.

"Give me a personal object," the gypsy woman says, holds out a long-palmed, long-fingered tan hand that tickles his jacket. Embarrassed, vacant panic. Markowitz tries to pull his ventral portions into contact with his dorsal, croaks, "You want a personal object?" Then, "Which? What do you want?" as the woman responds by patting, left hand, right hand, his side pockets under the coat, under the sports jacket, over his thighs. Think's he'll either throw up from excitement or have a heart attack, no matter the doctor says his heart's in wonderful condition. Pouchy face, sharp nose, droopy lids, no little smile, Markowitz is sweating, looks as uncomfortable as a turtle with two shells. Naturally. Ninety-five percent of him is out of his element, wishes this weren't happening.

The gypsy lady says, "What's in here?" Her hand has slid around and is patting his rear pocket, pressing his wallet.

Markowitz shrugs and tries to look like he doesn't know. The suede voice sways closer, dark eyes widen, sweet smell overpowers. Those bosoms seem independently to emerge inches more. Gypsy woman says, "Give me this object. From it I can tell everything about yourself. Your whole life lives in an object like this." D's and R's soft and hard like little fingers poking Markowitz in his paunchy stomach and flabby chest. His body chemistry wafts its confusing effluents through his system. Even so he doesn't intend to give the gypsy lady his wallet. He's no fool, Markowitz. Gypsy lady slides the wallet from his pocket, holds it flat on her palm between the two of them.

This is a terrible shock, completely unexpected, beyond what Markowitz imagines anyone would do. His hand twitches toward the wallet. The gypsy woman lays her other hand on it. "What's the matter?" she says, tosses her head back, arches her long tan throat. "Is a big man like you afraid a little woman like me will steal his money while he stands so close to her?" In a moment of normal self-control, Markowitz wouldn't hesitate to admit this is just his fear, but now he's shamed into silence by the woman's flouncing contempt, resigns himself to her holding the wallet.

"So, now I tell you about yourself," the gypsy woman says. Tightens her hands against the leather, half closes her eyes, assumes a trancelike expression, says, "I feel emanations from this object. It belongs to a man of business, a man with a family, a good man, a kind man, a generous man —" midst all his other feelings Markowitz's pride nonetheless preens — "but wait, I feel something, something hidden, some secret passion, some deep, deep, unfulfilled —" From beyond the velveteen curtain of the doorway, a somewhat high male voice calls, "Darka!"

Gypsy eyes open. The woman looks confused, upset. Male voice repeats, more urgently, "Darka!" Voice has the same light accents as the woman's but is hoarse, pale, strained.

Woman looks a little angry, says to Markowitz, "You must wait." Sways off in a hurry, exits by the curtain.

This leaves Markowitz in the little chamber wrought up, confused, out of his element, sweating down his pouchy face, not sure if he's coming or going. Still, it says nothing about his character that he ignores her command and starts to follow her and his wallet. A normal instinct for self-preservation explains that. But he's barely at the curtain when the pale hoarse voice says, "Who's that with you, Darka?" and the woman's suede voice replies with utter indifference, "Eh. Nobody. Just a mark."

Gentle indignation! Mild outrage! Hurt pride! Markowitz is about to lunge through the curtain, ask them what they think this is! — he hears the high, hoarse, pale, male voice say, "Well, you get rid of him! The police are on the way!"

"Police!?" The woman's voice, surprised.

"Police!?" Markowitz thinking from undifferentiated tumult.

The male voice says, "They think this is a whorehouse!"

A whorehouse! Ho ho! What a picture Markowitz suddenly sees
— police, paddy wagons, handcuffs, TV reports. Oh boy. Without
further ado he pushes aside the curtain, pops into the antechamber.

After the hot, airless confinement of the inner room, the front
parlor with its maroon rug and wallpaper, bright picture, and
afternoon light coming past the storefront window is like release
into the cool, rational, and cheery. There's the gypsy woman holding his wallet. A man in a black turtleneck jersey stands over her.
The other woman's gone, armchair's empty. The two look up as
Markowitz bubbles, "Look, trouble I don't want, so if you don't
mind, just give me my wallet and I'll go." The man, mid-twenties,
thick droopy black mustache, tan face with a confiding, melancholy
quality, says, "Darka, give him his wallet so he can get out," hoarse,
high, lightly accented. The woman presses the wallet to her chest,
says, "He must pay!" "You must pay," the fellow says to Markowitz
— he's tall, wide-shouldered, narrow-chested, has unusually long
arms — "Give her the ten dollars and go, quickly." This is incomprehensible to Markowitz, makes no sense at all. He asks reason-
ingly, "Ten dollars? Ten dollars for what? She didn't even tell my
fortune." The woman clutches the wallet. "He must pay!" "All
right, all right," the fellow says. "Five dollars, but get out of here
before we're all arrested." Markowitz's stomach plummets, panic
rises. The risk's not worth the argument. The woman opens the
wallet, takes a five-dollar bill, shoves the wallet at Markowitz. Upset,
panic, sense of rush, he opens the wallet, glances over the rest of
his money, sees it's all there, says, "Okay, five dollars." Finds himself moving, the man and the woman on either side of him, toward
the door, the man saying, "Okay, five dollars, now go, for God's
sake, go." The door opens, something jingles, he finds himself on
the street, the door closes. A shade on the door is pulled down.
The curtains on the storefront are pulled across. The last thing he
sees between them, a slender hand.

What happens next is this. A week goes by in which Markowitz is
miserable, suffers like he's never suffered before. Everywhere he
goes he's accompanied by a writhing pang in his stomach, which is
the knowledge he's been made a complete fool of. Whatever he
does he's tormented by hot-flushed memories of gypsy bravo,
swaying woman, swamps of warmth, his childish inability to think,

his fear of the woman's touch. In every semihypnotized suspended moment he hears — hoarse, strained — "Who's that with you?" — suede, indifferent — "Eh. Nobody. Just a mark," and feels indignation, outrage, offended amour-propre — paring knife, carving knife, meat cleaver in the heart. And not only that. Bella, loving wife of twenty-seven years' happy marriage, always solicitous, understanding, perceptive, she sees there's a problem, asks what's wrong, and he can't bring himself to tell her. He feels so foolish about what's happened, he can't imagine her knowing and not thinking less of him.

Naturally he tries to change his feelings or escape them. Even in his present state he knows it's laughable that a fifty-two-year-old man, thirty years amatory experience, should suffer the sexual confusion of a fifteen-year-old confronted by his first naked woman. Knows he must have looked pretty funny, bald and sweating, pulling in his stomach to avoid the woman's hand and breast, as if something dreadful would happen should she touch him. But it's as though the side chamber has disappeared from which he used to view his behavior and judge it neither better nor worse than that of the rest of the world, and he can't find his way to the irony that would let him feel the humor he knows is there. He tries to distract himself by working on his lion-giraffe, etc., joke, finds it dry, dusty, juiceless, hard and uninteresting as an antique piece of salt fish from a buried corner of the storeroom. Tries to talk himself out of his feelings. "Al, what's the matter with you? What are you doing? Getting worked up like this doesn't make any sense. You've made a fool of yourself before. You'll do it again. Don't worry. So O.K., when it comes to half-naked gypsy women, you're Peter Pan, that's all. So everybody's got their soft spots. Come on. Be reasonable. Don't act this way." Useless. He might as well be talking to the roast beef. After a while he decides he'll just have to ignore them, his feelings. Eventually they'll go away. They don't. Every morning there they are, just as strong as the day before: embarrassment, indignation, sense of being a fool, offended self-respect, the writhing pang, the hot flashes, the cutlery in the heart, and always, swaying through his imagination, the gypsy woman with her sweet-smelling warmth, her dissatisfied wry mouth, big black eyes. Sure, Markowitz knows he was harried and squeezed, his fear of the police played upon by the gypsy man, and this has its part in making him feel foolish, but much more it makes him wonder what would have happened if the police hadn't been on their way, what further brands of embarrassment the gypsy woman had been working toward for her money, how much deeper into helplessness her warm sweet smells and baring bosoms would have driven him, what she would have said then to discount him altogether.

Finally this is too much for Al Markowitz. He can't stand it any more. It's ruining his life. He's got to do something. So one afternoon he leaves the deli early, goes downtown, finds the same street — squat grimy buildings, dirty pavement, lolling drunk, overcast sky — and walks until he sees the storefront. It's a week later, warmer. He's not wearing the black-and-white-check, spring-weight overcoat, is also not wearing the same sports jacket, is wearing a reddish-brown, white-flecked double-knit jacket that would be a little tight over his paunch if it were buttoned, and a fat, dark maroon tie, knot askew. His face — pouchy, sharp-nosed, droopy eyelids, thin lips — is purposeful, but unhappy and out of sorts.

No sooner does he reach the little storefront than there's the same snapping tapping noise, there's the slender arm motioning through the white curtains, the half-glimpse of dark hair. Markowitz goes to the door, opens it, steps inside. Jingles, warm sweet air, the door closes. Everything's just the same. The blue Oriental with the pale yellow lions, the blue wallpaper, gold flowered, the picture of the dancing gypsy lovers, the olive-skinned lady sweating in her red velvet dress sitting next to the table with the coffeepot and cups on it. And here comes the gypsy woman, swaying toward him, shorter than he remembered her, but otherwise an exact replica of his memory — long black hair, tan oval face, wry dissatisfied mouth, pinched nose, dark eyes. Dressed differently though. In a long-skirted, gold-and-green-and-white cotton affair that slides mildly over her chestal area right up to her neck. Leaves bare her tan shoulders, which rotate as she glides toward him saying, with all those D's and R's, "You want fortune told? You want love spell, curse for your enemy? I can do this."

By which point she's looking Markowitz full in the face and he's looking back at her, catching her eyes, trying to make an impression on them. What he wants is she should acknowledge him, say, "I know you. You were here last week when the police came. You want fortune told now? Okay, you come, follow me. We tell your fortune, no charge."

Nothing. No change in her expression — eyes don't flicker, wry mouth doesn't tighten, fall open, purse. "Come," she says, "follow me." Turns, and it's the old trick. You expect boiled hamburg, but it's chili. The gypsy woman's lithe tan back is bare from shoulders to waist, and what covered her front is so loose at the sides that Markowitz can see the rounding out of bare perfect globes, bright as two-hundred-fifty-watt bulbs in his eyes. Internal organs all drop to the floor of his stomach, lie there scrambled, but this time surprise, excitement, and confusion do not incapacitate him. They fire his determination instead. He strides to where the gypsy woman waits with the blue velveteen curtain pulled back, pauses — Al Markowitz grim faced — then with his left hand pats her right cheek, which is smooth and soft as boiled chicken breast, says, "Thank you, darling," rough, uneven, insinuating. Proceeds across the little chamber — same blue-curtain walls, blue wallpaper, blue-shaded bulb — and turns to wait as the woman drops the curtain, dims the room, sways toward him, hips, arms, shoulders, hair, skirt of gold and green and white all going in their own directions. His chest feels like he's swallowed a large, rank, alien lump that won't digest if it goes down, but that he's determined not to throw up. He eyes the tan oval face for some sign of reaction, sees none. Gypsy woman reaches him, stops with her chest almost touching his reddish-brown, double-knit, spring-weight sports jacket. Sweat breaks on his brow, but he holds his ground, even leans forward a little. She says, "I give you gypsy blessing." Sweet coffee, pungent cigarette breath warms his face. He speaks directly into it, rough, suggestive. "You're a very attractive young lady, you know?"

"You want gypsy blessing?" she asks from inches away, tan oval bland.

"Sure," growls Markowitz. "Give me your gypsy blessing."

"Give me what you have in your pockets." Suede-voiced.

"Take them." Gruff-voiced.

Gypsy lady doesn't hesitate, assumes a trancelike air, scours Markowitz's pockets, speaks in sleepy tones. "Bless these keys, may all the doors they open lead to happiness. Bless these coins, may they multiply. Bless this hanky, may it never be needed. Bless this notebook — bless it."

Naturally, extracting these goods she touches him, and he sweats, stomach stews, but between hanky and notebook, he raises his hand lightly to her waist for an instant, then drops it from her waist to her tender rump, which he pats twice. It springs softly under his pats with a pliant self-mobilized resiliancy he hadn't expected. This makes the lump in his chest feel independently alive and kicking. He says, hoarse, strained, "You know you've got a wonderful physique, young lady." Gypsy woman doesn't even blink. The wry dissatisfied mouth just goes on blessing in sleepy, suede tones. Markowitz can't imagine what to do next. Meanwhile, she gets to his wallet, holds it in her unusually long, tan hands, says, "Bless the money in this wallet, may it increase a thousand-fold."

From beyond the blue-velvet curtains a high, hoarse, pale, male voice with gypsy accents calls, "Darka!"

Gypsy eyes widen. The woman looks confused, upset. Markowitz looks confused himself. This he'd expected even less than he'd expected it the first time. The male voice repeats, "Darka!" more urgently. The woman looks a little angry, says to Markowitz, "You must wait," and sways off in a hurry, exits by the curtain.

This leaves Markowitz in the little chamber, sweating, wrought up, his fat maroon tie further askew, his ideas of how he'd been made a fool of before considerably stirred around, especially when he hears — hoarse, strained — "Who's that with you, Darka?" and — utterly indifferent, suede — "Eh. Nobody. Just a mark." Then, pale, male voice, hoarse, high, lightly accented, "Well, get rid of him! The police are on their way!" "Police!" The gypsy woman sounding surprised. And Markowitz from very specific greater outrage, immense indignation, "*Ich ob dir in bod!*" ("I have you in the bath." It's really true that Yiddish can't be literally translated and make much sense, so, roughly, "The hell you say!") Even so, it still indicates nothing about his character that he pushes through the curtain into the lighter, airier, cooler, blue-Orientaled, blue-and-gold papered front chamber. The unusual force of his outrage and indignation explains that.

So, there's the gypsy woman holding his wallet, the gypsy man, dark mustache, black turtleneck, standing over her. The other woman is gone. The two look up, gypsy man's eyes widening, woman's expression unchanged, as Markowitz comes into the antechamber, voice hoarse, rough-edged with his emotions, saying, "Mark, schmark, don't give me that. I'm no mark. I'm Al Markowitz, and I'll thank you to give me my wallet back and no five dollars this time."

Gypsy woman's expression is like boloney. No matter which way you slice, it doesn't change, but the gypsy man tilts his head to one side, looks thoughtful on his tan, melancholy, confiding face, says, "Al Markowitz?" — high, hoarse, strained. "Are you the Al Markowitz runs a little kosher deli on Harvard Street, Brookline?"

Markowitz is completely taken aback. What kind of question is that? It's his brother Ruby has the deli people know about. Then he notices the gypsy man's question was without gypsy accent. This is getting serious. He's beginning to lose the sense of what's going on. "Yeah, that's right," he says, uncomprehending, suspicious. "So?"

"No kidding," says the gypsy man sounding excited, happy. "No kidding." Holds out one long tanned hand. "Mr. Markowitz! I'm Rick Goldstein, Lew Goldstein's kid! I went to school with your son Harold!" Turns his hand toward the gypsy woman. "This is my second cousin Susan Gersh — Manny Gersh's daughter? Susie, I used to go to school with Mr. Markowitz's son Harold. Isn't that something?"

Gypsy lady — Susan Gersh — finally changes expression. She stretches her lips, shows her teeth, imitates a smile with no attempt to suggest amusement, says, "That's very nice." Suede voice without accent, also without conviction.

Markowitz is astonished, dizzy. He's never heard of such a thing. Stares at the two in front of him, his pouchy face, sharp nose, droopy lids, thin mouth, all flaccid with a much greater confusion. If boiled hamburg had been chili, this is the unexpected figure in the house at 2:00 A.M. turning out to be his own image in the floor-length mirror, which then boffs him with a rubber salami. It's not male and female gypsies? It's the grown son and daughter of people he knows from temple Friday nights, from Brotherhood meetings, weddings, bar mitzvahs, funerals? "What kind of business is this?" Markowitz exclaims in the face of such a phenomenon.

"What do you mean?" asks the Goldstein kid, excitement suddenly cooled.

"What do you mean, what do I mean?" says Markowitz. "I mean I DON'T UNDERSTAND WHAT'S GOING ON HERE. That's what I mean. What else should I mean?"

"Ah, Mr. Markowitz" — hoarse, unconcerned, lighthearted — "what's to understand? Susie, give Mr. Markowitz his wallet back." Markowitz receives the wallet from Susan Gersh's long, slender, tan hand, Rick Goldstein continuing the while, "We aren't doing research for a Ph.D. thesis, and we aren't collecting for UJA." The melancholy, confiding face smooshes together, suggests common interest, mutual understanding. The young man puts his unusually long, heavy arm over Markowitz's shoulder, gives an affectionate little hug. "This is how we make our living, Susie and me."

Wonderful. Here Markowitz is asking a basic question about the constancy of facts in the universe, and the Goldstein kid's giving him a report on their employment situation. On the other hand, in the midst of this temporary confusion about the persistence of things, still stirred-up from the time before, still with the disturbing lump in his chest and the floating sense of being out of his element, for Markowitz to hear the kid say that is like seeing *biftek* on a menu featuring *cervelle, civet de lapin,* and *ris de veau:* this he's pretty sure of what it is and how he feels about it. "You call this 'making a living'?" he says to the mustachioed, tan face much too close to his. Of course he's not happy with the long arm draped over his shoulder, the little hug, or the patronizing fatherly explanation of the facts of life, but that's just a little carrot in the bubbling stew of his distress.

"Mr. Markowitz," says the Goldstein kid, high, hoarse, pale, expansive in his ear, "you'd be surprised how many people come through here in a day, like yourself. Besides, this isn't all we do."

Just as Markowitz begins to wonder what that *all* might encompass (before the kid's last statement this would have read: just as Markowitz is beginning to wonder why the Goldstein kid never answers what he is actually asking), Susan Gersh interrupts. "Ricky," she says, suede voice sweet as sucrose, "aren't you getting carried away? Maybe Mr. Markowitz isn't interested in what else we do." Same stretch of lips to suggest she knows a smile fits here and one would take place were she being pleasant.

"Oh, come on, Susie. Why wouldn't Mr. Markowitz be interested? He's been here twice already." Another affectionate little hug. "Right, Mr. Markowitz?"

If there's such a thing as a statement being so ironical it's irrelevant, the Goldstein kid's is it, and this renders Markowitz speechless as a clubbed calf. Fortunately he doesn't have to respond. The wry dissatisfied oval, up to this point still mistakable for gypsy face, now assumes the out-of-patience, eye-wide, lip-bitten look of a mother about to scream at her child if he does one more thing against her wishes. Rick Goldstein says, "Well, anyway, Mr. Markowitz" — hoarse, pale, subdued — "it's been a pleasure meeting you." Markowitz is moved toward the door by the pressure of the young man's arm, the young woman on the other side of him, not too close. "Give my regards to Harold, if you see him," hoarse, low. Door opens, something jingles. "Good-bye now." Markowitz finds himself on the sidewalk in the bright of the spring afternoon. Door closes, shade on the door is pulled down, curtains on the window pulled across. Last thing Markowitz sees before he moves off, the same slender hand.

Well, if things were bad for Markowitz before, now they're terrible. Not right away, first he has to calm down, stop being confused, adjust. But once he accepts that dark-eyed gypsies had been dark-eyed Jews, once it really settles in him that Darka and Shmarka there were parts played by Susan Gersh, daugher of Manny Gersh, and Rick, son of Lew, Goldstein — once in short he is unambiguously clear that the new situation is the *situation*, then he's in for it. Why? Because once these things become accepted facts, what's also a fact is that he, Al — twenty-seven years married, moral man, templegoer, part of the Jewish community — has within the past so many hours been sexually suggestive to, and, in fact, played with the soft behind of, the daughter of a man who prays near him in temple Friday nights, and that with the collusion of her cousin, the young son of someone whom he sees at Brotherhood breakfasts in the vestry every third Sunday. This possibility is so alien to him, so strange and outside the pale, that he now feels like a visitor to his life. There's no Al Markowitz he personally knows or has ever known who could have done such a perverse, almost incestuous thing.

This is no joke. For the next twenty-four hours Al Markowitz lives in a state of near vacancy, feels only guilt and shame drawn together with this distance into a feverish metallic column in his mind, like the mercury of a cooking thermometer plunged into the heart of a roasting beef. Whatever he does, whoever he talks to, wherever he goes, it all seems to be taking place elsewhere and without his participation. Even Bella, beloved wife of, seems just a friendly native of another land, and when she, with obvious concern, wonders at his looking blank as a cake cover, Markowitz hears himself tell her he's caught up by a new joke, and wonders himself how he could say that, since he no longer has any idea where the waters lie in which those jokes once wriggled and swam. And if all this isn't bad enough, what comes next is worse. That second visit to the gypsy takes place on Wednesday. Until Friday he has this fevered, dissociated, perverse-feeling blank. Friday morning he wakes up, realizes he's supposed to go to temple that night, knows he can't possibly do so. Suppose he should see Manny Gersh or Lew Goldstein? How could he possibly face either, knowing he'd been playing with the former's daughter Susan's rear end and looming over her like some vulgar baboon telling her she had a "wonderful physique"? Then wouldn't his guilt and shame spill over from that distance and scald his whole interior? And worse than that, he sees — thought following thought, as thoughts do — what if Manny Gersh or Lew Goldstein should find out from their children what Al Markowitz has done?

This thought is so terrible to Al Markowitz there in the soupy light of the bedroom that he feels he'd give anything to escape the poisonous, gaping dread that is its essence, not to mention the picture that comes after, of himself passing the remainder of his existence eating strangely cooked meals of repellent, high-tasting ground meats in dirt-floored little restaurants somewhere foreign he's never been nor ever wanted to be.

So later that day, there's Markowitz — subway, downtown, same street, storefront window. Lukewarm day, overcast, looks like rain. He's wearing a gray rain hat on his balding head, an old tan raincoat over the usual sports jacket and tie. Otherwise it's the same story — the snapping, tapping noise, slender backhand against the window, half-glimpse of dark thick hair. Opens doors, enters, something jingles, warm sweet smell, door closes. Inside, also everything is just the same. There's the jungle-green wallpaper with the orange flowers, pale green pseudo-Oriental, picture of a knife fight in a moonlit encampment, the fat, olive-skinned woman in the rust-colored velvet dress sweating in the chair next to the table with the coffeepot and cups on it. And swaying toward him the woman — long black hair, dissatisfied mouth, pinched delicate nose, the big dark eyes. Her tanned oval face looks a little pale though, and she's dressed differently, in a long-skirted white dress with tiny lemon-and-lime flowers, a wraparound dress that X's loosely over her chest, gapes, promises more from some other angle. Her D's and R's are delicate bites in the suede sentence as she reaches him, looks in his face with an expression blank as a slice of salami. "You want fortune told? You want love spell? Curse for your enemy? Gypsy blessing?"

Markowitz, in his pickle, tastes nervous agitation like brine, strains hoarsely for his natural tone. "Well, young lady, I think I'm not right for that kind of love, and my religion takes care of the blessings. Maybe you could tell my fortune." Tries an ironic smile.

Expression doesn't change. Woman says, "You want this? I can tell you. Come, follow me." Turns, glides off, waits at the green velveteen curtain for Markowitz, who strides past into the little chamber with two green-curtain walls, jungle-green and orange-flowered wallpaper, orange hanging lamp. Curtain drops. Chamber dims. It's hot, stuffy, especially for Markowitz in his raincoat, rain hat, jacket, and tie. He's already sweating as he watches the woman sway toward him, arms, hips, hair, and skirt all twisting in their different directions. Half a foot from him, she stops, tan oval bland as white bread, D's and R's pointy little tines. "Give me your hand. I read your palm."

Markowitz renders his hand, strives for a mild even tone. "I'd rather not hear anything bad, if you don't mind. I haven't been feeling so great lately as it is."

"I can only tell the truth I see in your palm," says the woman. She holds his hand as casually as a diner holds a roll while talking to a friend. "I cannot tamper with what the universe reveals."

Al Markowitz feels his eyelids droop, lips of their own accord quirk skeptically at this tale. Woman, index-fingering lines on his palm, proceeds with his fortune. "— bachelor — long alone — unhappy affair — broken heart — creative individual, music, painting — happiness in future — love affair — success — riches — fame — strong heart line, long life line — fruitful old age, much beloved — must be careful of having too little sense of humor, being too serious — be happier — peace will be yours — three dollars, please."

This story is fine by Al Markowitz. He's very pleased, says in almost his own normal, ironic, mild-humored tones, "Young lady, I hope your living never depends on how well you tell fortunes." Reaches for his wallet. From beyond the green velveteen curtains, a pale, male, hoarse, high voice, "Darka!" Woman's eyes widen, she looks weary. Markowitz is not surprised by the summons, is concerned. Male voice repeats more urgently, "Darka!" Woman shrugs, says, "You must wait." Sways off slowly, exits by the curtain, leaving Markowitz in the little chamber sweating, wallet in hand, feeling drained, cleaned, but not properly plugged in quite yet. He hears the pale male voice ask — high — hoarse — "Darka, who's that with you?" And suede, unconcerned, dismissive, "Eh. Nobody. Just Markowitz."

— *wanders around thinking desperately, until finally, suddenly, he gets a wonderful idea. Rushes off through the jungle until he comes to a delicatessen, goes inside, says to the man behind the counter, "For heaven's sake, quick, give me half a pound of roast beef, rare!" Man behind the counter looks at him, says, "This is incredible! Who ever heard of a giraffe coming into a delicatessen and asking for half a pound of roast beef?" "Is that right?" says the giraffe. "Well, in that case, make it two pounds of cole slaw."*

GORDON WEAVER

Hog's Heart

(FROM THE ANTIOCH REVIEW)

> *Nor mouth had, no nor mind, expressed*
> *What heart heard of, ghost guessed*

IT IS EVERYTHING and it is nothing. Hog says, "Different times, it's different feeling. Sometimes I feel like that it might could just be a feeling."

"Goddammit, Hog," says Dr. Odie Anderson. Hog, perched on the edge of the examination table, feels ridiculous, feet suspended above the floor like a child's, wearing a paper hospital gown that, like a dress, barely covers his scarred knees. Though the air conditioning sighs incessantly, he exudes a light sweat, pasting the gown to his skin, thighs and buttocks cemented to the table's chill metal surface. "Is it chest pain?" the doctor says. "Is it pains in your arm or shoulder? Is it pain you feel in your neck or your jaw?"

Says Hog, "It might could be I just imagine it sometimes." Dr. Odie Anderson, team physician, sits in his swivel chair, shabby coat thrown open, crumpled collar unbuttoned, necktie askew, feet up and crossed on his littered desk. Hog sees the holes in the soles of the doctor's shoes. Odie Anderson's head lolls slightly. His eyes, bulging and glossy, like those of a man with arrested goiter, roll. His tongue probes his cheeks and teeth as if he seeks a particle of his breakfast. He licks his lips, moistens the rim of scraggly beard around his open mouth.

"Damn," says Dr. Anderson, "is it choking? Your breath hard to get? Sick to your stomach a lot?" Hog closes his eyes, wipes sweat from the lids with thumb and forefinger.

"All like that. Sometimes." Hog turns his head to the window before opening his eyes. The rectangle of searing morning light dizzies him. He grips the edge of the table with both hands, feels the trickle of sweat droplets course downward from the tonsure above his jug ears, from the folds of flesh at his throat, from the sausage rolls of fat at the back of his neck, from his armpits. He represses malarial shudders as the air conditioning blows on his bare back where the paper gown gaps.

"You-all want me to send you to Jackson to the hospital? You want all kind of tests, swallowing radioactivity so's they can take movies of your veins?" Almost touching the windowpane, the leaves of a magnolia tree shine in the brilliant light as if filmed with clear grease. One visible blossom appears molded of dull white wax, which will surely melt and run if the sun's rays reach it. A swath of campus lawn shimmers in the heat like green fire. The length of sidewalk Hog can see is empty. The cobbled street beyond is empty, stones buckled.

"Not now," Hog says. "I might could maybe go come spring if I can get off recruiting awhile."

"Well now," Dr. Anderson is saying, "you *are* fat as a damn house, Hog, and your blood pressure *is* high. You might could be a classic case, except you don't smoke and last I heard your old daddy's still kicking up there to Soso."

"Daddy's fine. He's a little bitty man, though. I come by my size favoring Mama's people." A pulpcutter's truck, stacked high as a hayrick with pine logs, passes on the street, headed north toward the Laurel Masonite plant.

"You just as leave get dressed, Hog," the doctor says. "I can't find nothing wrong in there. Hell, damn it to hell, you strong as stump whiskey and mean as a yard dog!" Hog focuses on buttoning his shirt, zipping his fly to evade Dr. Anderson's leering cackle.

Sometimes it is everything. It is the sticky, brittle feel of sweat drying on his skin, the drafty breath of the air conditioning that makes him shudder in spasms, raises goose bumps on his forearms. It is the late August morning's heat and humidity hovering like a cloud outside, waiting to drop on him, clutch him. It is baked streets and sidewalks, the withering campus and lawns, everyone in Hattiesburg driven indoors until dusk brings relief from the glaring sun of south Mississippi.

"Say hey for me to Marice and them big chaps," says Odie

Anderson. It is his wife and four sons, the steaming campus of Mississippi Southern University, the athletic dormitory and stadium, the office where his senior assistants wait to review game films, the approach of the season opener at home against Alabama, this fourth year of his five-year contract, two-a-day workouts, and recruiting trips across the Deep South, and a pending NCAA investigation. It is all things now and up to now — his people up at Soso, paying his dues coaching high school and junior college, his professional career cut short by injury in Canada — all things seeming to have come together to shape his conviction of his imminent demise from heart failure.

"We going to whip up on 'Bama, Hog?"

"We die trying," says Hog. They laugh. It is nothing. Hog decides he is not dying, not about to, not subject to be dying. It is something that is probably nothing, and because he cannot define or express it, it is a terror there is no point in fearing.

Fraternity and sorority pep-club banners limply drape the stadium walls. *Beat Bama. Roll Back the Tide. Go Southern. We Back Hog's Boys.* The stadium throws heat into Hog's face like the coils of a kiln. The painted letters swim before his eyes, air pressing him like leaden mist. He consciously begins to reach, pull for each breath, fetid on his tongue. Awash with sweat, he lurches, into the shade of the stadium entrance to his office.

Inside, the dimness of the hall leaves him lightblind, air conditioning a clammy shock, his heaving echoing off the glossy tiles and paneling. Hog finds himself, eyes adjusting, before the Gallery of Greats, a wall-length display of photos and newspaper clippings, trophies and pennants, locked behind glass. This pantheon of Mississippi Southern's finest athletes, record setters, and semi-All Americans is a vanity he cannot resist.

His breathing slows and softens, sweat drying in his clothes as he steps closer. There he is, the great Hog Hammond in the prime of his prowess and renown.

Three pictures of Hog: a senior, nineteen years ago, posed in half-crouch, helmet off to show his bullet head, arms raised shoulder high, fingers curled like talons, vicious animal snarl on his glistening face; Hog, nineteen years ago, down in his three-point stance, right arm lifting to whip the shiver-pad into the throat of an imaginary offensive guard; Hog, snapped in action in the leg-

endary Alabama game nineteen years ago, charging full-tilt, only
steps away from brutally dumping the confused Alabama quarterback for a loss. The Alabama quarterback is static, doomed; Hog is
motion, power, purpose.

The yellowed newspaper clippings are curled at the edges. *Southern Shocks Ole Miss. Southern Stalemates Mighty Tide. The Hog Signs for
Canada Pros.*

Athletic Director Tub Moorman is upon him like an assassin
with a garrote, the only warning the quick stink of the dead cigar
he chews, laced with the candy odor of his talc and hair oil. Hog
feels a catch in his throat, a twinge in his sternum, salivates.

"Best not live on old-timey laurels, Hog," says Athletic Director
Tub Moorman. A column of nausea rises from the pit of Hog's
belly to his chest, tip swaying into his gullet like a cottonmouth's
head. He tenses to hold his windpipe open. "Best look to *this*
season," Tub Moorman says. Hog, pinned against the cool glass of
the Gallery of Greats, gags, covers it with a cough.

"I'm directly this minute subject to review game films," he is able
to say. Tub Moorman is a butterball, head round as a cookpot,
dirty-gray hair slicked with reeking tonic, florid face gleaming with
aftershave. He dresses like a New Orleans pimp, white shoes,
chartreuse slacks, loud blazer, gaudy jewel in his wide tie, gold
digital watch, oversize diamond on his fat pinky, glossy manicured
nails. His sour, ashy breath cuts through the carnival of his lotions.
He limps slightly from chronic gout.

"This year four," Tub Moorman says. "Year one we don't care
much do you win, play what you find when you come on board.
Year two, three, your business to scout the ridges and hollows for
talent. Year four, we looking to see do you *pro*duce, see do we want
to keep you-all in the family after year five. This year four. Root
hog or die, hear?" The athletic director laughs without removing
his unlit cigar from his mouth. Hog can see the slimy, chewed butt
of the cigar, Tub Moorman's wet tongue and stained teeth.

Hog is able to say, "I'm feeling a touch puny today," before he
must clamp his lips.

"You *know* we-all mighty high on you, Hog," Tub Moorman says,
"you one of us and all." He flicks his lizard's eyes at the gallery's
pictures and clippings. "You a great one. Withouten you got injured so soon in Canada, you might could of been *truly* famous as
a professional."

"I'm subject to give it all I got," Hog gasps, bile in his mouth.

"It's subject to take it," says the athletic director, "and maybe then some. Fact, you got to beat Alabama or Ole Miss or Georgia Tech or Florida, somebody famous, or we got to be finding us the man will."

"I might could," Hog is able to say without opening his jaws, and, "I got me a nigger place kicker can be the difference."

Tub Moorman's laugh is a gurgling, like the flush of a sewer. "We-all ain't particular," says Tub Moorman, "but the NCAA is. Best not let no *in*vestigators find out your Cuba nigger got a forged transcript, son." Hog hurried to the nearest toilet, the athletic director's stench clinging to him, chest thick with sickness, throat charged with acid, head swimming. Wretching into the closet commode, Hog blows and bellows like a teased bull, purges his nostrils of the residue of Tub Moorman's smell.

On the portable screen, Alabama routs Ole Miss before a record homecoming crowd at Oxford. Slivers of the sun penetrate the room at the edges of the blackout curtains, casting an eerie illumination on the ceiling. The projector chatters, the air conditioning chugs. Only Sonny McCartney, Hog's coordinator, takes notes, writing a crabbed hand into manila folders, calling for freeze-frames and reruns. Sonny McCartney reminds Hog frequently that national ranking is only a matter of planning, implementation of strategy, time.

Wally Everett, offensive assistant, mans the projector. Once a fleet wide receiver for the Tarheels of North Carolina, he wears a prim and superior expression on his patrician face. Because he wears a jacket and necktie in even the warmest weather, he is sometimes mistaken by students for a professor. Believing there is no excuse for vulgar or obscene language, on or off the playing field, he is a frequent speaker at Fellowship of Christian Athletes banquets. He sits up straight in his chair, one leg crossed over the other at the knee, like a woman, hands, when not operating the projector's levers and buttons, folded in his lap.

The defensive assistant, Gary Lee Stringer, slouches in a chair at the back of the room. He played a rugged noseguard for a small Baptist college in Oklahoma, looks like an aging ex-athlete should, unkempt, moody, unintellectual. He shifts his weight in his chair, stamps his feet often as Alabama's three-deep-at-every-position squad shreds the Rebels on the screen. He snorts, says, "I seen two county fairs and a train, but I ain't never seen nothing like them! Them sumbitches *good,* Hog!"

"The problem," says Sonny McCartney, "is to decide what we can do best against them."

"They execute to perfection," says Wally Everett.

Wally rewinds the film for one more showing. Sonny rereads his notes. Gary Lee Stringer spits a stream of juice from his Red Man cud into the nearby wastebasket. The room is darker with the projector bulb off, the air conditioning louder in the greater silence. Hog holds tightly to the arms of his chair, sensing the formation of an awful formlessness in his chest.

It feels to him as if, at the very center of his heart, a hole, a spot of nothingness, appears. He braces himself. The hole at the center of his heart doubles in size, doubles again; his vital, central substance is disappearing, vanishing without a trace left to rattle against his ribs. He tries to hear the movement of his blood, but there is only the perpetual churning of the air conditioning, the click and snap of the projector being readied.

"Hog," says Gary Lee Stringer, pausing to rise an inch off his chair, break wind with a hard vibrato, "Hog, they going to eat our lunch come opening day."

"Every offense has a defense," Sonny McCartney says.

"There is little argument with basic execution," Wally says.

It will grow, Hog believes, this void in his chest, until he remains, sitting, a hollow shell with useless arms, legs, head. At which point he will be dead. He waits in his chair to die.

"Alabama don't know we have Carabajal," Sonny says.

"Neither does the NC double-A. Yet," Wally says. "But they will if we permit just one person close enough to speak to him."

"Is that tutoring done learned him some English yet?" Gary Lee asks.

"Again?" says Wally, finger on the projector's start button.

"Ain't this a shame?" says Gary Lee. "Our best offense a nigger from Cuba don't talk hardly no English."

"*I* did not forge his transcript," Wally says.

"He *can* kick," says Sonny, and, "Hog?"

Hog, dying, rises from his chair. "You-all discuss this without me," he says and finds he can take a step toward the door. "I got to get me some fresh air, I am feeling puny, boys," says Hog, reaches the door, opens it, leaves, walking slowly, carefully, afraid to bump anything, afraid that he will break like a man made of blown glass, no core left to him at all, no heart.

There is no reason Hog should wake in the still-dark hours of early morning, no stomach upset or troubling dream. At first, he is merely awake, Marice beside him; then his eyes focus, show him the lighter darkness, false dawn at the bedroom windows; and then he sees the ceiling, walls, furniture, the glow of the nightlight from the master bedroom's full bath, the light blanket covering him and his wife, Marice in silhouette, the back of her head studded with curlers. He hears the gentle growl of her snoring. He hears the cooled air cycling through the house on which the mortgage runs past the year 2000.

He lies very still, in the king-size bed, shuts out what he can see and hear and the rich smell of Marice's Shalimar perfume, closes himself away, then knows what has awakened him, so totally, from a deep sleep. Now Hog listens, measures the rhythms, recognizes the subtle reduction in pace, tempo, intensity of his heartbeat. His heart is slowing, and this has awakened him, so that he can die knowing he is dying. There comes a minuscule hesitation, a near-catch, a stutter before the muffled thump of each beat. He lies very still, holds his breath, then inches his left hand free of the cover, moves it into position to press the declining pulse in his right wrist with his forefinger.

His heart will run down like a flywheel yielding up its motion to the darkness of the master bedroom. He is dying here and now, at the moment of false dawn that shows him the shafts of pine trunks in his yard, the wrinkled texture of his new lawn of Bermuda grass. He will die and be discovered by Marice when she wakes to the electric buzz of the alarm on her bedside table.

"Marice," Hog croaks. "Marice." His voice surprises him; how long can a man speak, live, on the momentum of his last heart-beats? "Marice." She groans, turns to him, eyes shut, groping. Her arm comes across his chest, takes hold of his shoulder. She nuzzles his jaw, kisses him clumsily in her half-sleep, presses her head into his throat, her curlers stabbing the soft flesh.

Hog says, "Marice, I do love you and thank you for marrying me, when my people is just redneck pulpcutters and you are from fine high-type people in Biloxi. It is always a wonder to me why you married me when I was just a football player, and now coach, and you was runnerup Miss Gulf Coast and all. They is mortgage life insurance on the house, Marice, so's you will have the house all paid for."

"Big sweet thing," his wife mumbles into his collarbone.

"No, Marice," he says. "I love you and thank you for giving me our boys. I am dying, Marice, and it is just as good I do now, because we will not beat Alabama or Ole Miss nor nobody big-timey, and the NCAA will likely soon get me for giving a scholar-ship to a Cuba nigger has to have a interpreter to play football, and we would lose this house and all except I am dying and you will get it because of insurance."

"Lovey, you want me to be sweet for you?" Marice says, kisses his hairy chest, strokes his face, the slick bald crown of his head.

"No," Hog says. "Listen, Marice. Tell me can you hear my heart going." She mutters as he turns her head gently, places her ear against his breast, then resumes her light growling snore.

Dying, Hog lifts her to her side of the bed, throws back the cover, rises, pads out of the master bedroom. Dying, he walks down the hall to the bedrooms where his four sons sleep the perfect sleep of children.

He can stand at the end of the hall, look into both bedrooms, see them sleeping, two to each room, and he stands, looking upon the future of his name and line, stands thinking of his wife and sons, how he loves them, in his wonderful new home with a mortgage that runs beyond the year 2000. Hog thinks it cruel to die when he can see the future sleeping in the two bedrooms.

It is the coming of true dawn, flaring in the windows of his sons' bedrooms, that grants him a reprieve. True dawn comes, lights the trees and grass and shrubbery outside, stirs a mockingbird to its first notes high in some pine tree, primes his flickering heart to fresh rhythm. He feels it kick into vigor like a refueled engine, then goes to the hall bathroom and sits, grateful and weeping, on the edge of the bathtub, staring at his blank-white toes and toenails and his lavender-tinged white feet, his heart resuming speed and strength for another day.

Marice and his sons are somewhere outside with Daddy and Brother-boy, seeing the new machinery shed or feeding Brother-boy's catfish. Hog's mama serves him a big square of cornbread with a glass of cold buttermilk.

The golden cornbread, straight from the oven, radiates heat like a small sun. Hog bites, chews, swallows, breaks into a film of sweat as he chills his mouth with buttermilk. Not hungry, he gives himself over to the duty of eating for her — bite, chew, swallow, drink — his mama's presence. He sweats more freely with the effort, feels a liquid warmth emerge in his belly, grow. Hog feigns gusto, moans, smacks his lips, slurps for her. A viscous heat squirts into his chest, warming it.

"No more," he says as she reaches toward the pan with a knife to cut him another helping. "Oh, please, Mama, no," says Hog. He tries to smile.

"I want to know what is the matter with my biggest boy," she says. "You say you are feeling some puny, but I know my boy, Euliss. I think you are troubled in your spirit, son."

"I have worries, Mama," he tells her. "We got to play Alabama."

"Is it you and Marice? Is it your family, Euliss, my grandbabies?"

"We all fine, Mama. Truly." He averts his eyes. She does not look right, not his old mama, in this modern kitchen, chrome and Formica and plastic-covered chairs, double oven set in the polished brick wall, blender built into the countertop, bronze-tone refrigerator large as two football lockers, automatic ice-cube maker, frostless, Masonite veneer on the cupboards. Hog remembers her cooking at an iron woodstove, chopping wood for it as skillfully as she took the head off a chicken, while he clung to her long skirts, sucking a sugar-tit. He remembers her buying fifty-pound blocks of ice from the nigger wagon driver from Laurel, taking his tongs and carrying it into the house herself (she wouldn't allow a nigger in her kitchen) until Hog was old enough to fetch and carry for her, his daddy out in the woods cutting pulp timber dawn to dusk.

Hog covers his eyes with his hand to hide the start of tears, hurt and joy mixing in him like a gumbo in a cauldron, that his mama has this fine kitchen in this fine new brick home built by his daddy and Brother-boy on a loan secured by Hog's signature and Hog's life insurance, that his mama is old and will not ever again be like he remembers her, that she will not live forever.

"I do believe my boy is troubled in his soul," Mama says.

"Not my soul, Mama." Hog favors his mama's people, comes by his size from her daddy, a pulpcutter who died before he was born. Hog remembers her telling how her daddy lacked four and one-half fingers from his two hands, cutting pulpwood for Masonite in

Laurel all his life until a falling tree killed him. Hog looks at her fingers, at his own.

"Are you right with Jesus, Euliss?" she says. She leans across the table, hands clenched in prayer now. "I pray to Jesus," says his mama, "for my boy Euliss. I pray for him each day and at meeting particular." It is as if a dam bursts somewhere on the margins of Hog's interior, a deluge of tepidness rushing to drown his heart.

"We go to church regular in Hattiesburg, Mama," he is able to say before this spill deprives him of words and will, his heart now a remoteness, like the sound of children swimming in a far pond.

"Pray with me, Euliss," she says. "Oh, pray Jesus ease your trouble, drive doubt and Satan out! Oh, I am praying to You, Jesus, praying up my biggest boy to You!" Her locked hands shake as if she tries to lift a weight too great for her wiry arms, her eyes squeezed shut to see only Blessed Jesus, lips puckered as though she drew the Holy Spirit into her lungs. Hog cannot look.

It is his old mama, old now, who attends the Primitive Baptist Church of Soso, where she wrestles Satan until she falls, frothing, to the floor before the tiny congregation, where she washes the feet of elders, weeping. "Jesus, Jesus, speak to my boy Euliss," she prays in the fine, modern kitchen of the modern brick ranch built on land won by two generations' driving scrub cattle and cutting pulpwood.

Nose clogged with sobbing, Hog's heart moves like a wellhouse pump lifting a thick, hot sweetness into his mouth. This death is filling, filled with Mama's love, all he feels of his memories of her, Daddy, Brother-boy. "JesuspleaseJesusplease," she chants.

"Mama," says Hog, standing up, voice breaking on his lips like a bubble of honey, "I got to go find Daddy and Marice and Brother-boy and those chaps. Time flying, Mama." He flees, the waters of her love receding in his wake, her prayer echoing damply in his ears.

Hog and his daddy pause at the electrified strand of fencing to admire the glossy Angus at the salt lick, clustered in the narrow shade of the old mule-driven mill where Hog helped his daddy crush cane for syrup. Hog sees the Angus melded with the scrubby mavericks he ran in the woods with razorbacks for his daddy, hears the squeak and crunch of the mill turning, crackle of cane stalks. "Now see this, Euliss," says his daddy, a small man who has aged by shriveling, drying, hardening. "Don't it beat all for raising a shoat in a nigger-rigged crib?" his hardness glowing redly in the terrible sunshine, burnished with pride over the new cement floor of his pigpen. Hog, gasping, clucks appreciation for him. "Wait and see Brother-boy feed them fish!" his daddy says.

"Daddy," Hog says, "how is it Mama so much for churching and you never setting foot in it, even for revivals?" Hog's daddy expertly blows his nose between thumb and forefinger, flicks snot into the grass as they pass the row of humming beehives, their stark whiteness conjuring the weathered stumps and gums Hog helped rob in his youth, wreathed in smoke, veiled.

"I never held to it," his daddy says, and would go on toward the pond, stopped by Hog's heavy hand on his shoulder.

"You didn't never believe in God? Ain't you never been so scared of dying or even of living so's you wanted to pray like Mama?" His voice sounds muffled, as if cushioned by water.

"I never faulted her for it, Euliss," says his daddy. And, "And no man dast fault me for not. Son, a man don't get hardly no show in life, most of us. Now, not you, but me and Brother-boy and your mama. Life wearies a man. Them as needs Jesus-ing to die quiet in bed or wherever, I say fine, like for Mama. Me nor mine never got no show, excepting you, naturally, Euliss, a famous player and coach and all. I guess I can die withouten I screech to Jesus to please let me not have to."

"Daddy," says Hog. Blood fills his chest, a steady seeping, a rich lake about his heart, pooling in the pit of his belly, pressing his lungs. "Daddy, was I a good boy?"

"Now, Euliss!" His daddy embraces him there near the line of beehives, the spread fingers of his horny hands clasping Hog's heaving sides. "Euliss, don't you know I have bragged on you since you was a chap?"

"Are you proud of me still now I'm growed a man?" His daddy laughs, releases him.

"Oh, I recollect you then, son! You was a pistol for that football. I recollect you not ten years old going out to lift the new calf day by day to build muscles for football playing!"

"Daddy." He feels a pleasant cleft in his breast widen, a tide of blood.

"Recollect the time I *told* you not to be blocking yourself into the gallery post for football practice? I had to frail you with a stick to

teach you not. Oh, son, you was a pure pistol for that footballing!
Your daddy been bragging on you since, Euliss!"

"Find Brother-boy, see them fish," Hog chokes with his last
breath, heart and lungs and belly a sweet sea of blood, this death
almost desirable to him. He staggers away, suffocating in the fluids
of his emotions.

"Brother," says Hog, "Brother-boy, are you resentful you stayed
and lived your life here? Ain't you never wanted a wife and chaps
of your own? Do you resent I went away to school for football and
to Canada for my own life whiles you just stay working for Daddy?"
Brother-boy looks like Hog remembers himself half-a-dozen years
ago, less bald, less overweight. From a large cardboard drum, he
scoops meal, sows it over the dark green surface of the artificial
pond. The catfish swim to the top, thrash, feeding, rile the pond
into bubbles and spray. "Was I a good brother to you? Is it enough
I signed a note so's you can start a fish farm and all this cattle and
stock of Daddy's?"

Brother-boy, sowing the meal in wide arcs over the pond, says,
"I never grudged you all the fine things you got, Euliss. You was a
special person, famous playing football in college and Canada, now
a coach." His brother's voice dims, lost in the liquid whip of the
pond's surface, the frenzied feeding of the catfish. "I am a happy
enough man, Euliss," says Brother-boy. "Mama and Daddy need
me. They getting old, Euliss. I don't need me no wife nor chaps,
and I got a big brother was a famous player once and now a coach,
and your sons is my nephews." Hog remembers Brother-boy, a
baby wearing a shift, a chap following after him at chores, coming
to see him play for Jones Agricultural Institute & Junior College in
Laurel, for Mississippi Southern, once coming by train and bus all
the way up to Calgary, there to see Hog's career end. Says his
brother, "It is my way to accept what is."

Hog lurches away, seeking an anchor for his heart, tossed in a
wave of sweet blood. He wishes he could wish to die here and now
if he must die. But this wish is like a dry wind that evaporates the
splash of love and memory within him, turning this nectar stale,
then sour.

Seeking an overview of the last full drill in pads, Hog takes to a
stubby knoll, shaded by a massive live oak tree. From here, the
practice field falls into neat divisions of labor.

At the far end of the field, parallel to the highway running toward Laurel and Soso, chimeric behind the rising heat waves, Fulgencio Carabajal placekicks ball after ball through jerrybuilt wooden goalposts, the first-string center snapping, third-team quarterback holding, two redshirts to shag balls for the Cuban, who takes a break every dozen or two dozen balls to talk with his interpreter. Hog watches Fulgencio's soccer-style approach, hears the hollow strike of the side of his shoe on the ball, the pock of this sound like a counterpoint to the beating of Hog's heart. He tries to follow the ball up between the uprights, loses it in the face of the sun that washes out the green of the grass.

Closest to Hog's shady knoll, the first- and second-team quarterbacks alternate short spot passes with long, lazy bombs to a selfrenewing line of receivers who wait their turns casually, hands on hips. Catching balls in long fly patterns, receivers trot up to the base of Hog's knoll, showboating for him. The slap of ball in hands comes as if deliberately timed to the throb of his heart, adding its emphasis to the twist of its constrictions.

At the field's center, Sonny McCartney coordinates, wears a gambler's green eyeshade, clipboard and ballpoint in hand. Sonny moves from offense to defense in the shimmer of the heat like a man wading against a current. Hog squints to find Gary Lee Stringer, on his knees to demonstrate firing off the snap to his noseguard, his jersey as sweated as any player's. Wally Everett, as immobile as Hog, stands among his offensive players, stopping the drill frequently with his whistle, calling them close for short lectures, as unperturbed by the temperature and humidity as if he chalked on a blackboard in an air-conditioned classroom.

Hog's heart picks up its pace, the intensity of each convulsion increasing to a thud, a bang. Now he cannot distinguish the echo of his accelerating heartbeat from the smack of pads down on the practice field, the slap of balls on sweaty palms, thumping of the tackling dummy, crash of shoulders against the blocking sled, squealing springs, hollow pock of Fulgencio Carabajal's kicking.

Hog closes his eyes to die, digs with his cleats for a firmer stance on the knoll, prepared to topple into the dusty grass. He tenses his flesh, wonders why this raucous slamming of his heart does not shake him, why he does not explode into shards of flesh and bone. And wonders why he is not yet dead, still holding against his chest's

vibrations, when he hears Sonny McCartney blow the final whistle
to end the drill. The blood's song in his ears fades like Sonny's
whistle in the superheated air of late afternoon.

It is light. Light, falling upon Hog, his wife still sleeping as he rises.
Special, harder and brighter light, Hog fixing himself a quick
breakfast in the kitchen, chrome trim catching and displaying early
morning's show of light to him while Marice is dressing, his sons
stirring in their bedrooms. Light, the morning sky clear as creek
water, climbing sun electric-white, overwhelming Hog's sense of
trees, houses, streets, driving slowly through Hattiesburg to the
stadium. And lighting his consciousness, pinning his attention in
the gloom of the squad's locker room, his talk to his players before
they emerge into the light of the stadium.

Hog tells them, "It is not just football. It is like life. It is mental
toughness. I do not know if you are as good as Alabama. Newspapers and TV is saying not, saying they will whip our butts. If it
is, they is nothing any of us or you-all can do. We-all have to face
that. It is Alabama we are playing today. Maybe it is like that you-
all have to go out and play them knowing you will not have any
show. It might could be I am saying mental toughness is just having
it in you to face up knowing they will whip your butt. I don't know
no more to say." He leads them out into the light.

He sees, hears, registers it all, but all is a dependency of this
light. The game flows like impure motes in perfect light. The game
is exact, concrete, but still only a function of this light. The opening
game against Alabama is a play of small shadows within the mounting intensity of light.

At the edge of the chalked boundary, Hog notes the legendary
figure of the opposing coach across the field, tall, chain-smoking
cigarettes, houndstooth-checked hat, coatless in the dense heat
Hog does not feel. This light has no temperature for Hog, a light
beyond heat or cold.

"They eating our damn lunch, Hog!" Gary Lee Stringer screams
in his ear when Alabama, starting on their twenty after Fulgencio
Carabajal sends the kickoff into the end-zone bleachers, drives in
classic ground-game fashion for the first touchdown. The kick for
extra point is wide, the snap mishandled.

"I do declare we can run wide on them, Hog," says Wally Everett
as Southern moves the ball in uneven spurts to the Crimson Tide
thirty-seven, where, stalled by a broken play, Fulgencio Carabajal

effortlessly kicks the three-pointer. "I have seen teams field-goaled to death," Wally says.

Late in the second quarter, Southern trails only 13–9 after Fulgencio splits the uprights from fifty-six yards out. "We *got* the momentum, Hog," says Sonny McCartney, earphones clamped on to maintain contact with the press-box spotters. "We can run wide and pray Fulgencio don't break his leg."

Gary Lee Stringer, dancing, hugging the necks of his tackles, spits, screams, "I seen a train and a fair, but I ain't never see *this* day before!"

"Notice the Bear's acting nervous over there?" Wally says, points to the excited assistants clustering in quick conference around the houndstooth hat across the field.

Says Hog, "You can't never tell a thing about nothing how it's going to be."

His death comes as light, as clarity, comprehensive and pervasive. There is nothing Hog does not see, hear, know. Everything is here, in this light, and not here. It is a moment obliterating moments, time, place.

He knows a possible great legend is unfolding on the playing field, an astounding upset of Alabama's Crimson Tide. Hog knows he has come to this possible wonder by clear chronology, sequence of accident and design, peopled since the beginning with his many selves and those who have marked and made him who and what he is in this instant of his death. Light draws him in, draws everything together in him, Hog, the context of his death.

Dr. Odie Anderson sits on a campstool behind the players' bench, feet up on the bench, scratching his beard with both hands, rolling his bulged eyes at the scoreboard. Athletic Director Tub Moorman's face is wine-red with excitement, unlit cigar chewed to pulpy rags. Gary Lee Stringer drools tobacco juice when he shouts out encouragement to his stiffening defense. Wally Everett smirks as he counsels his quarterback. Sonny McCartney relays information from up in the press box, where Marice and the four sons of Hog watch the game through binoculars, drinking complimentary Coca-Colas. On the bench next to his chattering interpreter, Fulgencio Carabajal waits indifferently for his next field-goal attempt.

In the new modern kitchen in Soso, Mississippi, Hog's people, Mama, Daddy, Brother-boy, listen to the radio broadcast, proud and praying. Folded into Hog's memory like pecans in pralines are the many Hogs that make him Hog: a boy in Soso lifting new calves to build muscle, football find at Jones Agricultural Institute & Junior College, bona fide gridiron legendary Little All American on this field, sure-fire prospect with Calgary's Stampeders in the Canadian Football League, career cut short by knee and ankle injuries, high-school coach, defensive assistant, coordinator, Hog here and now, head coach at Mississippi Southern University—all these in the marvel of his death's light.

Dying, Hog looks into the glare of the sun, finds his death is not pain or sweetness but totality and transcendence, dies as they rush to where he lies on the turf, dying, accepting this light that is the heart of him joining all light, Hog and not-Hog, past knowing and feeling or need and desire to say it is only light. He dies hearing Fulgencio Carabajal say, *"Es muerte?"* gone into such light as makes light and darkness one.

Biographical Notes

Biographical Notes

DONALD BARTHELME was born in Philadelphia and raised in Houston. His stories have appeared in *The New Yorker, New American Review, Paris Review,* and other publications. Some of these stories were collected in *Come Back, Dr. Caligari,* published in 1964, and in two later collections, *Unspeakable Practices, Unnatural Acts* (1968) and *City Life,* which the *New York Times Book Review* called one of the twelve outstanding books of 1970. Mr. Barthelme's other books include a novel, *Snow White* (1967), *Sadness* (1972), *The Slightly Irregular Fire Engine,* a book for children that was awarded the 1972 National Book Award, and *Guilty Pleasures,* nominated for a National Book Award in the category of fiction in 1974. His most recent novel, *The Dead Father,* was published in 1975. *Amateurs,* a collection of short stories, was published in 1976, and *Great Days,* Mr. Barthelme's most recent collection of stories, was published in 1979.

FREDERICK BUSCH lives in Poolville, New York, with his wife and their two sons. "Long Calls" is included in his 1979 collection, *Hardwater Country.* His seventh book of fiction, *Rounds,* a novel, was published in 1980.

DAVID EVANIER has published fiction in many literary journals, among them *The Paris Review, Commentary, Pequod, Transatlantic Review, Midstream, Moment,* and *Confrontation.* He was the recipient of the Aga Khan Fiction Prize in 1975. He has received three writing fellowships from the MacDowell Colony and one from the Wurlitzer Foundation. Mr. Evanier taught creative writing at Douglas College in British Columbia, and was founder and editor of the literary magazine *Event*. His first novel, *The Swinging Headhunter*, was published in 1973. Currently he is at work on two novels and a play.

MAVIS GALLANT is the author of five collections of short stories and two novels. Nearly all her short fiction has appeared in *The New Yorker*, to which she has been a contributor since 1950. Her most recent book, *From the Fifteenth District*, a collection of short fiction, was published in 1979. Mrs. Gallant is at present completing a long study of the Dreyfus Affair. She lives and writes in Paris.

WILLIAM H. GASS has written a novel, *Omensetter's Luck*, a collection of short stories, *In the Heart of the Heart of the Country*, and three volumes of essays. His most recent book, written in collaboration with the architect Peter Eisenman, is called *The House VI Book*. He teaches philosophy at Washington University in St. Louis.

T. GERTLER lives in New York City.

ELIZABETH HARDWICK's most recent books are *Seduction and Betrayal*, essays on women in literature, and *Sleepless Nights*, a novel. Miss Hardwick was born and educated in Kentucky. She has lived in New York City for many years and is a contributor of essays and fiction to many magazines, most notably *The New York Review of Books*, of which she was one of the founders. One of Miss Hardwick's first published stories appeared in *The Best American Short Stories 1947*.

LARRY HEINEMANN was born and raised in Chicago, Illinois. In 1967–1968 he served a tour of duty in Vietnam as a combat infantryman with the 25th Division. His Vietnam War novel, *Close Quarters*, won the Society of Midland Authors Best Novel of 1977 award. His shorter fiction has appeared in *Harper's*, *The Hyde Parker*, *Penthouse*, *The Story Workshop Reader*, *TriQuarterly*, and elsewhere. In 1979 he was named the Fletcher Pratt Fellow at the Breadloaf Writers' Conference in Vermont. Mr. Heinemann lives in Chicago with his family. He is senior Story Workshop director in the Advanced Fiction Writing Program of Columbia College, Chicago.

ROBERT HENDERSON was born in Chicago. He attended the University of Illinois and taught English there. He joined the staff of *The New Yorker* in 1937 and, after four war years in the U.S. Air

Force, returned to the magazine, where he was a fiction editor for 25 years. He has published a number of stories and essays in *The New Yorker* and has also appeared occasionally in *Esquire, The Saturday Evening Post,* and others. A book of essays (*The Enameled Wishbone*) was published by Macmillan in 1963, and a story ("Immortality") was included in *The O. Henry Prize Stories, 1960,* and in *Stories from The New Yorker, 1960.*

CURT JOHNSON is an editor and writer living in Chicago. He has had stories anthologized in *The O. Henry Prize Stories, 1973,* and *The Vagabond Anthology* (1978), and has had three novels, a novella, and a collection of essays published. He has edited four collections of short stories, including *Writers in Revolt,* with Jack Conroy, and has received a National Endowment for the Arts fellowship. Since 1962 he has been editor of the little magazine *December.*

GRACE PALEY was born in New York City in 1922. She has published two books — *The Little Disturbances of Man* and *Enormous Changes at the Last Minute.* She teaches at Sarah Lawrence College and lives mostly in New York, although every couple of years she lives in Vermont. She is married to Robert Nichols.

JAMES ROBISON was born in 1946 in Worthington, Ohio. He has worked as a commercial artist and has lived in Buffalo, New York City, Los Angeles, Baltimore, and Providence, Rhode Island, where he received an M.A. degree from Brown University. He is presently in the Midwest, teaching fiction and working on a novel.

LEON ROOKE has published nearly 100 short stories in Canadian and U.S. literary magazines. Collections include *Last One Home Sleeps in the Yellow Bed* (Louisiana State University Press), *Vault* (Lillabulero Press), *The Love Parlour* (Oberon Press, Canada), and *The Broad Back of the Angel* (Fiction Collective). A new collection, *Cry Evil,* appeared earlier this year (Oberon Press), and a novel, *Fat Woman,* is forthcoming in the U.S. from Alfred A. Knopf and in Canada from Oberon. A special Leon Rooke issue of *The Canadian Fiction Magazine* (No. 33) is being published this year. Born in North Carolina, Mr. Rooke has lived the past several years in Victoria, British Columbia.

JOHN SAYLES is author of the novels *Pride of the Bimbos* and *Union Dues* and of the story collection *The Anarchists' Convention.* He has written several screenplays and recently completed writing, directing, and editing his first feature film, *Return of the Secaucus Seven.* He currently lives in Hoboken, New Jersey.

ISAAC BASHEVIS SINGER, the son and grandson of rabbis, was born in Radzymin, Poland, in 1904. He came to the United States in 1935 and his writing has appeared in the *Jewish Daily Forward* for many years. Although he originally wrote in Hebrew, Mr. Singer long ago adopted Yiddish as his medium of expression. Dozens of Mr. Singer's novels and story collections are available in English — as many for children as for adults — from his publishers, Farrar, Straus & Giroux. Mr. Singer has been the recipient of many literary awards, including two National Book Awards, the Louis Lamed Prize, and a grant from the Academy and National Institute of Arts and Letters, of which he is a member. In 1978 the Swedish Academy of Letters awarded him the Nobel Prize for literature. Mr. Singer lives in New York with his wife, Alma.

RICHARD STERN's third collection of stories, *Packages,* was published in the fall of 1980 by Coward McCann. He is presently working on his seventh novel. Others include *Golk, Stitch, In Any Case, Other Men's Daughters,* and *Natural Shocks.* He has been Professor of English at the University of Chicago since 1955.

BARRY TARGAN was born in Atlantic City, New Jersey. His fiction, poetry, and essays have appeared in many magazines and journals, among them *Esquire, Sewanee Review, Southwest Review, Salmagundi, New Republic,* and *Saturday Review.* He received the University of Iowa School of Letters Award for Short Fiction in 1975 for his collection *Harry Belten and the Mendelssohn Violin Concerto.* Another collection of stories, *Surviving Adverse Seasons,* has been published by the University of Illinois Press. His stories have previously appeared in *The Best American Short Stories* for 1974, 1975, and 1976. He teaches at the State University of New York at Binghamton, where he is associate director of the creative writing program.

PETER TAYLOR was born in Tennessee in 1917. He was educated in schools in Nashville, Memphis, and St. Louis. He later attended Kenyon College and Vanderbilt University. He now lives in

Charlottesville, Virginia, and teaches at the University of Virginia, where he holds the Henry Hoynes Chair of Creative Writing. He is married to the poet Eleanor Ross Taylor. They have two children. His most recent collection of short stories, published by Alfred A. Knopf, is entitled *In the Miro District and Other Stories.*

JOHN UPDIKE was born in Shillington, Pennsylvania, in 1932. After attending the public schools of that town, he attended Harvard College and the Ruskin School of Drawing and Fine Art in Oxford, England. After two years on the staff of *The New Yorker* magazine, he moved to Massachusetts, where he has resided ever since. He is the author of some 22 books, including nine novels and six collections of short stories. This is his fifth appearance in *The Best American Short Stories.*

NORMAN WAKSLER was born and raised in Providence, Rhode Island. In 1959 he went to Boston University, to which he later returned for a graduate degree. He has held a small variety of jobs and done a fair amount of writing. "Markowitz and the Gypsies" is his second published story. Mr. Waksler is married to the sociologist Frances Chaput Waksler; they presently live on the Cambridge-Somerville line.

GORDON WEAVER is married and the father of three daughters. Professor of English at Oklahoma State University, he is the author of three novels and three collections of stories, the most recent of which are *Circling Byzantium* and *Getting Serious,* both published by Louisiana State University Press in 1980. One of his stories won first prize in the 1979 *O. Henry Prize Stories.* His work has also been recognized by the St. Lawrence Award for Fiction (1973) and a National Endowment for the Arts fellowship in creative writing (1974). Editor of Cedar Creek Press, and consulting editor for fiction at *Cimarron Review,* he founded and edited *Mississippi Review* from 1972 to 1975.

The Yearbook of the American Short Story

January 1 to December 31, 1979

100 Other Distinguished
Short Stories of the Year 1979

Editorial Addresses of American
and Canadian Magazines
Publishing Short Stories

Agni Review, P.O. Box 349, Cambridge, Massachusetts 02138

American Poetry Review, Temple University City Center, 1616 Walnut Street, Room 405, Philadelphia, Pennsylvania 19103

Ann Arbor Review, Washtenaw Community College, Ann Arbor, Michigan 48106

Antaeus, 1 West 30th Street, New York, New York 10001

Antioch Review, P.O. Box 148, Yellow Springs, Ohio 45387

Apalachee Quarterly, P.O. Box 20106, Tallahassee, Florida 32304

Ararat, 628 Second Avenue, New York, New York 10016

Arizona Quarterly, University of Arizona, Tuscon, Arizona 85721

Ark River Review, English Department, Wichita State University, Wichita, Kansas 67208

Ascent, English Department, University of Illinois, Urbana, Illinois 61801

Aspen Anthology, The Aspen Leaves Literary Foundation, Box 3185, Aspen, Colorado 81611

Atlantic Monthly, 8 Arlington Street, Boston, Massachusetts 02116

Bachy, 11317 Santa Monica Boulevard, Los Angeles, California 90025

Back Bay View, 52 East Border Road, Malden, Massachusetts 02148

Bennington Review, Bennington College, Bennington, Vermont 05201

Blood Root, P.O. Box 891, Grand Forks, North Dakota 58201

Blueboy, Blueboy Incorporated, 6969 N.W. 69th Street, Miami, Florida 33166

California Quarterly, 100 Sproul Hall, University of California, Davis, California 95616

Canadian Fiction, Box 46422, Station G, Vancouver, British Columbia V6R 4G7, Canada

Canto, Canto, Inc., 9 Bartlet Street, Andover, Massachusetts 01810

Capilano Review, Capilano College, 2055 Purcell Way, North Vancouver, British Columbia, Canada

Carleton Miscellany, Carleton College, Northfield, Minnesota 55057

Carolina Quarterly, P.O. Box 1117, Chapel Hill, North Carolina 27514

Chariton Review, Division of Language & Literature, Northeast Missouri State University, Kirksville, Missouri 63501

Chelsea, P.O. Box 5880, Grand Central Station, New York, New York 10017

Chicago Review, Faculty Exchange, Box C, University of Chicago, Chicago, Illinois 60637

Cimarron Review, 208 Life Sciences East, Oklahoma State University, Stillwater, Oklahoma 74074

Colorado Quarterly, Hellems 134, University of Colorado, Boulder, Colorado 80309

Commentary, 165 East 56th Street, New York, New York 10022

Confrontation, English Department, Brooklyn Center for Long Island University, Brooklyn, New York 11201

Cosmopolitan, 224 West 57th Street, New York, New York 10019

Cumberlands (formerly Twigs), Pikeville College Press, Pikeville College, Pikeville, New York 41501

Cutbank, Department of English, University of Montana, Bainville, Montana 59812

Dark Horse, c/o Barnes, 47A Dana Street, Cambridge, Massachusetts 02138

Denver Quarterly, University of Denver, Denver, Colorado 80210

Descant, P.O. Box 314, Station P, Toronto, Ontario M5S 2S5, Canada

descant, Department of English, Texas Christian University Station, Fort Worth, Texas 76129

Ellery Queen's Mystery Magazine, 229 Park Avenue South, New York, New York 10022

Esquire, 2 Park Avenue, New York, New York 10016

Event, Douglas College, P.O. Box 2503, New Westminster, British Columbia V3L 5B2, Canada

Fiction, c/o Department of English, The City College of New York, New York, New York 10031

Fiction International, Department of English, Saint Lawrence University, Canton, New York 13617

Fiction-Texas, College of the Mainland, Texas City, Texas 77590

Fiddlehead, The Observatory, University of New Brunswick, Fredericton, New Brunswick E3B 5A3, Canada

Forum, Ball State University, Muncie, Indiana 47306

Four Quarters, La Salle College, 20th and Olney Avenues, Philadelphia, Pennsylvania 19141

Gallimaufry, Gallimaufry Press, P.O. Box 32364, Calver St. Station, Washington, D.C. 20007

Georgia Review, University of Georgia, Athens, Georgia 30602

Good Housekeeping, 959 Eighth Avenue, New York, New York 10019

GPU News, c/o The Farwell Center, 1568 North Farwell, Milwaukee, Wisconsin 53202

Graffiti, Box 418, Lenoir Rhyne College, Hickory, North Carolina 28601

Grain, Box 1885, Saskatoon, Saskatchewan S7K 3S2, Canada

Great River Review, 59 Seymour Avenue, S.E., Minneapolis, Minnesota 55987

Greensboro Review, Department of English, University of North Carolina at Greensboro, Greensboro, North Carolina 27412

Harper's Magazine, 2 Park Avenue, New York, New York 10016

Helicon Nine, 6 Petticoat Lane, Kansas City, Missouri 64106

Hudson Review, 65 East 55th Street, New York, New York 10022

Indiana Writes, 110 Morgan Hall, Indiana University, Bloomington, Indiana 47401

Iowa Review, EPB 321, University of Iowa, Iowa City, Iowa 52242

Kansas Quarterly, Department of English, Denison Hall, Kansas State University, Manhattan, Kansas 66506

Kenyon Review, Kenyon College, Gambier, Ohio 43022

Ladies' Home Journal, 641 Lexington Avenue, New York, New York 10022

Lilith, The Jewish Women's Magazine, 250 West 57th Street, New York, New York 10019

Literary Review, Fairleigh Dickinson University, Madison, New Jersey 07940

Louisville Review, University of Louisville, Louisville, Kentucky 40208

Mademoiselle, 350 Madison Avenue, New York, New York 10017

Malahat Review, University of Victoria, Box 1700, Victoria, British Columbia, Canada

Massachusetts Review, Memorial Hall, University of Massachusetts, Amherst, Massachusetts 01002

McCall's, 230 Park Avenue, New York, New York 10017

MD, MD Publications, 30 East 60th Street, New York, New York 10022

Michigan Quarterly Review, 3032 Roakham Building, University of Michigan, Ann Arbor, Michigan 48109

Midstream, 515 Park Avenue, New York, New York 10022

Mississippi Review, Department of English, Box 37, Southern Station, University of Southern Mississippi, Hattiesburg, Mississippi 39401

Missouri Review, Department of English 231 A & S, University of Missouri, Columbia, Missouri 65211

Mother Jones, 607 Market Street, San Francisco, California 94105

Ms., 370 Lexington Avenue, New York, New York 10017

National Jewish Monthly, 1640 Rhode Island Avenue, N.W., Washington, D.C. 20036

New Directions, 333 Sixth Avenue, New York, New York 10014

New England Review, Box 170, Hanover, New Hampshire 03755

New Letters, University of Missouri at Kansas City, 5346 Charlotte, Kansas City, Missouri 64110

New Mexico Humanities Review, Box A, New Mexico Tech, Socorro, New Mexico 87801

New Orleans Review, Loyola University, New Orleans, Louisiana 70118

New Renaissance, 9 Heath Road, Arlington, Massachusetts 02174

New River Review, Radford College Station, Radford, Virginia 24142

New Yorker, 25 West 43rd Street, New York, New York 10036

North American Review, University of Northern Iowa, Cedar Falls, Iowa 50613

Northwest Review, University of Oregon, Eugene, Oregon 97403

Ohio Journal, Department of English, Ohio State University, 164 West 17th Avenue, Columbus, Ohio 43210

Ohio Review, Ellis Hall, Ohio University, Athens, Ohio 45701

Old Hickory Review, P.O. Box 1178, Jackson, Tennessee 38301

Only Prose, 54 East 7th Street, New York, New York 10003

Ontario Review, 9 Honey Brook, Princeton, New Jersey 08540

Paris Review, 45–39 171 Place, Flushing, New York 11358

Partisan Review, 128 Bay State Road, Boston, Massachusetts 02215

Penthouse, 909 Third Avenue, New York, New York 10022

Pequod, P.O. Box 491, Forest Knolls, California 94933

Phantasm, Heidelberg Graphic, P.O. Box 3606, Chico, California 95927

Playboy, 919 North Michigan Avenue, Chicago, Illinois 60611

Ploughshares, P.O. Box 529, Cambridge, Massachusetts 02139

Prairie Schooner, 201 Andrews Hall, University of Nebraska, Lincoln, Nebraska 68588

Present Tense, 165 East 56th Street, New York, New York 10022

Primavera, 1212 East 59th Street, University of Chicago, Chicago, Illinois 60637

Prism International, University of British Columbia, Vancouver, British Columbia, Canada

Quarry West, College V, University of California, Santa Cruz, California 95060

Quarterly West, 312 Olpin Union, University of Utah, Salt Lake City, Utah 84112

Queen's Quarterly, Queens University, Kingston, Ontario, Canada

RE:AL, Stephen F. Austin State University, Nacogdoches, Texas 75962

Redbook, 230 Park Avenue, New York, New York 10017

Richmond Literature & History Quarterly, P.O. Box 12263, Richmond, Virginia 23241

Rocky Mountain Review, Box 1848, Durango, Colorado 81301

St. Andrews Review, St. Andrews Presbyterian College, Laurinburg, North Carolina 28352

Salmagundi Magazine, Skidmore College, Saratoga Springs, New York 12866

Sam Houston Review, English Department, Sam Houston State University, Huntsville, Texas 77341

San Jose Studies, San Jose State University, San Jose, California 95192

Sands, 7170 Briar Cove, Dallas, Texas 75240

Sandscript, Box 333, Cummaquid, Massachusetts 02637

Saturday Night, 69 Front Street East, Toronto M5E 1R3, Canada

Seattle Review, Padelford Hall GN–30, University of Washington, Seattle, Washington 98195

Seneca Review, Box 115, Hobart and William Smith College, Geneva, New York 14456

Seventeen, 850 Third Avenue, New York, New York 10022

Sewanee Review, University of the South, Sewanee, Tennessee 37375

Shadows, Creighton University, 2500 California Street, Omaha, Nebraska 68178

Shenandoah, Box 722, Lexington, Virginia 24450

Shout in the Street, Queen's College of the City University of New York, 63–30 Kissena Boulevard, Flushing, New York 11367

South Carolina Review, Department of English, Clemson University, Clemson, South Carolina 29631

South Dakota Review, University of South Dakota, Vermillion, South Dakota 57069

Southern Review, Drawer D, University Station, Baton Rouge, Louisiana 70893

Southwest Review, Southern Methodist University, Dallas, Texas 75275

Sou'wester, Department of English, Southern Illinois University, Edwardsville, Illinois 62026

Spectrum, Box 14800, Santa Barbara, California 93107

Steelhead, Knife River Press, 2501 Branch Street, Duluth, Minnesota 55812

Story Quarterly, 820 Ridge Road, Highland Park, Illinois 60035

Sun and Moon, 433 Hartwick Road, College Park, Maryland 20740

Swift River, Box 264, Leverett, Massachusetts 01054

Tamarack Review, Box 159, Station K, Toronto M4P 2G5, Canada

Texas Quarterly, Box 7517, University Station, Austin, Texas 78712

TriQuarterly, Northwestern University, 1735 Benson Avenue, Evanston, Illinois 60201

U.S. Catholic, 221 West Madison Street, Chicago, Illinois 60606

University of Windsor Review, Department of English, University of Windsor, Windsor, Ontario N9B 3P4, Canada

Virginia Quarterly Review, 1 West Range, Charlottesville, Virginia 22903

Vision, 3000 Harry Hines Boulevard, Dallas, Texas 75201

Wascana Review, Wascana Parkway, Regina, Saskatchewan, Canada

Webster Review, Webster College, Webster Groves, Missouri 63119

Weekend Magazine, Suite 504, 390 Bay Street, Toronto, Ontario M5H 2Y2, Canada

Western Humanities Review, University of Utah, Salt Lake City, Utah 84112

Wind/Literary Review, RFD Route #1, Box 809K, Pikeville, Kentucky 41501

Yale Review, 250 Church Street, 1902A Yale Station, New Haven, Connecticut 06520

Yankee, Yankee, Inc., Dublin, New Hampshire 03444